SUBPRIME NATION

A volume in the series

CORNELL STUDIES IN MONEY
edited by Eric Helleiner and Jonathan Kirshner

A list of titles in the series is available at www.cornellpress.cornell.edu

SUBPRIME NATION

American Power, Global Capital, and the Housing Bubble

HERMAN M. SCHWARTZ

Cornell University Press
Ithaca and London

First published 2009 by Cornell University Press
First printing, Cornell Paperbacks, 2009

Printed in the United States of America

Library of Congress Cataloging-in-Publication Data

Schwartz, Herman M., 1958–
  Subprime nation : American power, global capital, and the housing
bubble / Herman M. Schwartz.
     p. cm. — (Cornell studies in money)
  Includes bibliographical references and index.
  ISBN 978-0-8014-4812-6 (cloth : alk. paper)—
  ISBN 978-0-8014-7567-2 (pbk. : alk. paper)
  1. Financial crises—United States.   2. Subprime mortgage loans—
United States.   3. Housing—United States—Finance.   4. Credit—
United States.   5. United States—Economic conditions—1981–2001.
6. United States—Economic conditions–2001–   7. United States—
Foreign economic relations.   8. International finance.   9. Capital
market.   I. Title.   II. Series: Cornell studies in money.

  HB3722.S36 2009
  332'.0420973   2009007315

Cornell University Press strives to use environmentally responsible
suppliers and materials to the fullest extent possible in the publishing
of its books. Such materials include vegetable-based, low-VOC inks
and acid-free papers that are recycled, totally chlorine-free, or partly
composed of nonwood fibers. For further information, visit our
website at www.cornellpress.cornell.edu.

Cloth printing   10 9 8 7 6 5 4 3 2 1
Paperback printing   10 9 8 7 6 5 4 3 2 1

For ELS

Contents

Selected Figures and Tables

Tables

Preface

A sound banker, alas, is not one who foresees danger and avoids it, but one who, when he is ruined, is ruined in a conventional way along with his fellows, so that no one can really blame him.

John Maynard Keynes, *Consequences to the Banks of a Collapse in Money Values*, 1931

Given these widely held expectations of rising interest rates, it is difficult to avoid the judgment that these ARM [adjustable rate mortgage] loans were poorly underwritten at the outset. It was imprudent for mortgage brokers and lenders to approve borrowers who likely could not service the loans when rates rose, and it is surprising to me that sophisticated capital-market investors willingly purchased securities backed by such poorly underwritten mortgages.

William Poole, Federal Reserve Bank of St. Louis, July 2007

Mountains of Mortgage Debt

In July 2007, a relatively modest German Bank, IKB Deutsche Industriebank, suddenly found itself in trouble. IKB was a typical German bank, specializing in loans to the German *mittelstand* (small and medium industrial firms). Yet IKB faced €700 million in losses on a €17.5 billion offshore investment in derivatives based on U.S. subprime mortgage securities. Fearing panic, German authorities used the giant state development bank KfW to construct a consortium that provided €3.5 billion in emergency loans and €8 billion in guarantees to IKB—to no avail. IKB later defaulted on $7 billion of the debt that financed those investments and ended up sold off to a U.S. private equity firm.

Fifteen months later, this small crisis had metastasized into a global financial crisis with unprecedented levels of state intervention. By September 2008, $1.3 trillion of equity in U.S. financial firms had evaporated, banks worldwide had written down $0.5 trillion just in subprime mortgage losses, and legendary and lucrative Wall Street firms such as Lehman Brothers, Bear Stearns, and Merrill Lynch had disappeared as independent entities. Global stock markets were in free fall. In the supposed bastion of neoliberal orthodoxy and free markets, U.S. taxpayers suddenly found themselves renationalizing the housing finance giants Fannie Mae and

Freddie Mac, as well as owning substantial holdings in the giant AIG insurance company, the largest commercial banks in the United States, and the one remaining independent investment bank. The Federal Reserve meanwhile was providing liquidity to all parts of the financial system against any kind of collateral, in a sharp departure from normal practices limiting lending to depository institutions and against U.S. Treasury and agency bonds. By October 2008, the Fed and the U.S. Treasury had committed in excess of $2.25 trillion in bailouts and liquidity, more than 16 percent of U.S. GDP at that time. The European central banks followed suit, guaranteeing depositors' funds, injecting capital into troubled banks, and pledging up to €1.3 trillion in various forms of aid. Next to this, the sums deployed in prior global financial crises looked like rounding errors.

How did a global financial crisis emerge from housing finance, which had long been one of the most boring parts of the financial system and thus long ignored by academics? International financial flows and housing have been inextricably bound together during the growth cycle of the past twenty years.[1] Houses and mortgages brought the current cycle of global growth to an abrupt halt because houses and mortgages—and especially U.S. houses and mortgages—were one of the main engines transmitting growth to the United States and thence to the world economy during what I call the long 1990s (1991–2005).

Previous bank failures and global financial crises were all connected in some obvious way to the international circulation of goods and money. Back in the mists of time, when the Bretton Woods agreements first started to unravel at the beginning of the 1970s, a series of bank failures temporarily locked up the international payments system. But the difficulties of Franklin National Bank, the Swiss Union Bank, and the Westdeutsche Landesbank Girozentrale and the iconic collapse of Bank Herstatt all derived from failed foreign exchange speculation. Similarly, the 1982 Latin American debt crisis was the ultimate cause of the collapse of Continental Illinois in 1984. And the international origins of the 1997–98 Asian financial crisis and the associated collapse of long-term credit management are obvious.

During the long 1990s, the United States borrowed abroad, grew vigorously, and consumed lavish quantities of imports. On the other side, developing Asia loaned to the United States, grew vigorously, and produced staggering quantities of exports. As the U.S. current account deficit and net debt grew through the long 1990s, more and more Cassandras stepped forward to predict the hollowing of the U.S. economy. And why not? By the end of 2007, net U.S. external debt equaled nearly 25 percent of U.S. GDP and one euro bought $1.47, in contrast to the near-parity prevailing at the 1999 launch of the euro.

I am not Pollyannaish about the U.S. economy, but I think predictions of the demise of U.S. global economic power and the reserve position of the dollar rest on three misunderstandings about the dynamics of the long 1990s. The first misunderstanding arises from the use of aggregated or net debt figures in people's assessments of the U.S. balance sheet. Disaggregating the U.S. balance sheet shows not only that the United States makes money despite its large net debt but why it makes money. The second misunderstanding concerns the role that housing, or more precisely housing finance systems, in the rich countries played in generating growth during the past fifteen years. Differences in housing systems created above-average employment and GDP growth in the U.S. and similar economies, which in turn solidified U.S. economic centrality and U.S. global economic power. It also bolstered the economic attractiveness of the U.S. dollar. The third misunderstanding is a habitual tendency to think about these issues in terms of "national interests" or "public goods" rather than in terms of the private and particular interests of the people, firms, and parties that control the allocation of capital globally. By examining the private goods that lie behind every public good, we can better parse the motivations of actors with respect to their willingness to lend to the United States and thus, in turn, to their support for the position of the dollar as *the* international reserve currency.

This book thus explains why the U.S. housing finance system gave the U.S. economy above-average employment and GDP growth in 1991–2005, how international financial flows connected to that housing system, and what this means both for the past and future of the U.S. global economic power and for growth in the U.S. economy. Among other things—although you must plunge into the chapters for the analysis—significant differences between two different kinds of European economies help make the euro less plausible as a replacement reserve currency and hinder growth in parts of the euroland economy. These factors bolster the central position of the U.S. economy in global markets. This is not to say that all is right, although parts of the book will undoubtedly be read as being altogether too cheerful and optimistic. Still, I ask the reader to remember, first, that this is the medical history of patient in apparent good health over a twenty-year period, not just an autopsy of the 2008 financial crisis, and, second, that power is about differential gains, not absolute gains.

My Own Net Debt Position

Just like the United States, I ended up with tremendous intellectual and personal debts at the end of this venture into differential accumulation. At home, Eve Schwartz patiently tolerated an elevated level of distraction from summer 2007 to summer 2008. Three people deserve special thanks with respect to the genesis of this project: Uwe Becker, who first got me thinking about housing and its connection to domestic political economy during a project on employment miracles; Shelley Hurt, who organized the American Political Science Association (APSA) panel that compelled me to write my first paper on this topic; and Leonard Seabrooke, who helped put together a parallel project on the new politics of housing in Europe and Australia. R. H. Mazal similarly helped at an early stage with insights into the writing process. The University of Virginia book scrub team—Gerard Alexander, John Echeverri-Gent, Jeffrey Legro, John Owen, James Savage, and Len Schoppa— as well as Mark Blyth, Randall Germain, and Hubert Zimmermann criticized the entire manuscript, helping me to clean up the underbrush while leaving the trees standing. Anne-Marie Durocher patiently generated the many figures and also read significant portions of the manuscript. Eric Helleiner and Jonathan Kirshner, who invited me into a project on the U.S. dollar, provided many useful comments on material incorporated into chapters 4 and 7, as did other conference participants.

Finally, Peter Breiner, Benjamin Cohen, Peter Hall, Erik Hoffman, Aida Hozic, Sjur Kasa, Mark Kesselman, Carol Mershon, Lars Mjøset, Jens Mortensen, Stephen Nelson, Jonathan Nitzan, Greg Nowell, Ronen Palan (who was especially helpful with the "offshore"), Neil Richardson, Bent Sofus Tranøy, Gunnar Trumbull, and Jane Zavisca all commented on various parts of the manuscript. The staff at the European Mortgage Foundation and Value New Zealand were extremely helpful in providing privately held data on house prices and other issues. Len Kenworthy and my colleague Brantly Womack shared data sets on corporatism and China, respectively. Roger Haydon and the Cornell University Press staff were their usual helpful selves.

The University of Virginia funded the writing of this manuscript through the Bankard Fund and a Sesquicentennial fellowship. Material based on this project was presented at the 2004 and 2008 APSA annual meetings, the 2006 Rethinking Marxism conference, the 2007 and 2008 International Studies Association (ISA) annual meetings, the University of California–Santa Cruz, the University of Florida, the University of Oslo, SUNY Albany, Syracuse University, Temple University, and a workshop in Sørmarka funded by Res Publica of Norway. I thank any participant at each venue who has not already been named. Portions of chapters 4 and 7 were published in *The Political Consequences of Property Bubbles* (special issue of *Comparative European Politics* 6, no. 3 [September 2008]) and are used with permission. All errors of omission and commission remain mine, until I can securitize them and sell them offshore.

SUBPRIME NATION

1. Our Borrowing, Your Problem

To those critics who are so pessimistic about our economy I say, "Don't be economic girlie-men. The U.S. economy is the envy of the world."

Arnold Schwarzenegger, September 2004

International financial flows and speculation appear to be irredeemably universal, abstract, and delocalized. By contrast, housing appears to be irredeemably local, impacted, and granular. Yet the two became inextricably bound together and formed the basis for the revival of U.S. global economic power during the long 1990s (1991–2005). It is no accident that falling house prices and mortgage defaults have halted the current cycle of global growth because houses and mortgages—and especially U.S. houses and mortgages—were one of the main gears transmitting growth to the U.S. and, thence, the world economy. Given a disinflationary environment and what I will term the U.S. global financial arbitrage, the U.S. housing finance system enabled the United States to grow relatively faster than most of its rich country competitors, even after adjusting for faster population growth. Differential growth, and not just absolute growth, is the basis for economic power.[1]

How did this U.S. global economic power operate from 1991 to 2005? Why did housing and mortgage finance prove central to the economic downturn and financial crisis that erupted after 2006? How did the growing U.S. foreign debt—usually seen as a signal of economic decline—become one key fuel for the global growth engine? What will happen now that the current cycle of global disinflation bordering on deflation has ended? Answering these questions exposes the operation and durability of U.S. economic power as well as the sources of stability and instability in the global economy. Yet most studies of U.S. economic power are ill suited to answering these questions. They look at incidents where deliberate U.S. policy choices constrained the behaviors of other countries or forced them into policies they would not have otherwise accepted. By contrast, this book employs a structural understanding of power in which actors' deliberate choices are less important than the interaction of institutionally generated aggregate behaviors with the larger environment. U.S. global economic power during the long 1990s emerged more from the unexpected and differential interaction of global capital flows with housing finance systems in the Organisation for Economic Cooperation and Development (OECD) economies and less from specific, targeted policy decisions.

Put far too briefly—indeed this book is an iterated unpacking of this paragraph—global disinflation combined with U.S. arbitrage in global financial markets to activate a normal process of Keynesian demand stimulus. Abstractly, U.S. arbitrage involved borrowing short term at low interest rates from foreigners while lending back to them long term at higher returns. Concretely, U.S. arbitrage operated via the housing finance system, with the sale of U.S. mortgage-backed securities (MBSs) to foreigners both stimulating the U.S. economy and, in a mechanical sense, offsetting U.S. investment into foreign factories and firms. Foreign purchases of U.S. MBSs depressed U.S. interest rates and allowed homeowners to cash out their growing home equity cheaply, stimulating the U.S. economy. U.S. investment offshore produced a disinflationary backwash of cheap imports, which also depressed interest rates. Disinflation and arbitrage flowed through the U.S. housing finance system to create a powerful Keynesian demand stimulus that, in turn, accounts for the *difference* in growth rates among rich countries, although not their absolute level. Countries with housing finance markets similar to the U.S. market also experienced this Keynesian stimulus, generating above-OECD-average growth for them in the long 1990s. In turn, above-OECD-average economic growth in the United States passively attracted more foreign capital into the United States, reinforcing its differential growth. Above-average growth created the relative gains underlying U.S. international economic power.

Dear reader, I know this argument is complicated. The argument here has four distinct steps and two feedback loops, and it privileges structures over actors. Each of these four steps presents a somewhat novel interpretation of the information relevant to that step, so the reader deserves both a road map and an explanation of how I approach each issue. The following sections provide both. To help you follow, figure 1.1 provides a schematic of the argument, and each chapter will reprise this figure with that chapter's issues highlighted to indicate roughly what is at stake in that chapter. In chapters 6–8, the reprised figure 1.1 changes to signal how the dynamics driving differential growth reversed. Please also note an important feature of figure 1.1 and thus of the argument here—it loops; outcomes on the right-hand side reinforce the processes on the left-hand side in a classic feedback model.[2] Readers looking for a linear, monocausal explanation of the long 1990s should probably buy a different book.

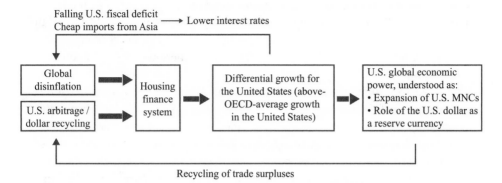

Fig. 1.1. Schematic of the argument.

Argument and Findings

This book is about politics, and politics is ultimately about power. But power is invisible and difficult to measure. Ideally, I should discuss how I think about power before turning to how I operationalize it for the purposes of this book. But presenting how the book operationalizes power will help make the dry and abstract discussion of power per se more palatable. U.S. economic power in the long 1990s was generated by and reflected in three different self-reinforcing ways, partially captured in figure 1.1: the absence of constraint, differential growth, and increased control over global production. Although I order them this way for purposes of exposition, differential growth is closer to being a cause for power, followed by increased control and then the absence of constraint. Differential growth both generated large volumes of profit that could be used to take control of critical nodes in production chains and encouraged and validated investment in new production processes related to those critical nodes. Control assured continued profitability. Differential growth attracted foreign capital, removing constraints on the U.S. economy. Yet these processes were not fully independent because capital inflows helped activate U.S. differential growth.

Thus, for purposes of exposition, I begin by noting first that in the long 1990s the U.S. economy enjoyed a new version of what Charles de Gaulle, president of France in the 1960s, called the "exorbitant privilege" and what Benjamin Cohen, U.S. economist, sees as the essence of monetary power: it was able to operate without constraint and to delay any adjustment to its rising current account deficit.[3] In figure 1.1, the absence of constraint partially appears as U.S. (financial) arbitrage—an unparalleled inflow of capital—on the left side. During the long 1990s, the U.S. economy avoided the normal trade-offs across domestic consumption, domestic investment, and overseas investment. Massive foreign lending relieved the normal constraints, providing between 10 and 20 percent of total lending in U.S. credit markets annually after 1994; by 2005 it accounted for 25 percent.[4] Wily foreigners lent against collateral, or so they thought, buying huge volumes of MBSs. With the nominal market value of U.S. houses rising by about $14 trillion and mortgage debt rising by nearly $7 trillion from 1991 to 2006, there was plenty of collateral to go around.

Second, this foreign capital enabled the United States to enjoy differential domestic growth. That is, the United States grew so much faster than its rich-country competitors that its "market share" in the global economy grew relative to other rich countries. The U.S. share of the total GDP of the rich OECD countries rose by an astonishing 4.2 percentage points to 42.7 percent in 1991–2005.[5] Put aside quibbles about outsized U.S. consumption; GDP measures output excluding imports. U.S. differential growth in the long 1990s reversed the trends of the 1980s, when both Germany and, particularly, Japan grew faster than the United States. After 1990 and 1992, respectively, each of these countries lost ground relative to the United States on an aggregate and per capita basis.

Real U.S. per capita GDP increased 60 percent faster than in the euroland economies, enabling a slightly faster increase of 64 percent in personal consumption. U.S. private *nonresidential* fixed-capital formation also increased at three times the rate in the anemic euroland and more than ten times the rate in ailing Japan—and, surprisingly, at more than double the rate of U.S. consumption. Ironically, although housing accounts for the difference in average-growth rates, private housing fixed-capital formation in some euroland economies actually exceeded nonresidential fixed investment, unlike in the United States. This says more about their overall investment underperformance than it does about any local housing mania. Consistent with Verdoorn's law, which argues that rapid aggregate growth facilitates rapid productivity growth, U.S. manufacturing productivity and value-added increased at roughly double the pace of continental Europe and Japan in 1991–2005, indicating that the U.S. expansion was deep as well as broad. Finally, the United States also generated nearly one-half the net new jobs in the OECD.[6]

Third, foreign lending and differential growth funded U.S. passive and active acquisitions abroad, expanding the U.S.-controlled share of global production relative to its rich-country competitors. From 1994 to 2006, the U.S.-owned share of the Morgan-Stanley MSCI All Country World ex-U.S. market index rose from 10 to 24 percent of total market capitalization.[7] By contrast, foreign holdings of U.S. equities rose more slowly, from 5.1 to 9.7 percent of market capitalization. U.S. firms also grew faster overseas than foreign firms grew in the U.S. market in 1995–2004. Despite a 10 percent increase in the exchange rate for the dollar (which diminishes measures of overseas activity), their overseas value-added increased by 40 percent while turnover nearly doubled to 7.8 percent of gross world product.[8] Moreover, despite slower growth in other rich countries, the ratio of overseas sales of U.S. multinational corporations (MNCs) to sales in the United

States by firms engaged in foreign direct investment (FDI) into the United States also rose from 1.3 to 1.5 in 1995–2004.

The absence of constraint also appears as the revival of the role of the U.S. dollar as the international reserve currency, on the right-hand side of figure 1.1. This revival both reinforced and facilitated foreigners' willingness to recycle their trade surpluses into U.S. MBSs (the arrow back to the left-hand side in the figure). For the purposes of this book, *international reserve currency* indicates both public and private foreign use of dollar-denominated securities as the major store of value for export surpluses. More expansive understandings that encompass the use of the dollar as a unit of account, as an invoice currency, and as a reference currency are largely secondary to escaping constraint because they do not imply public or private willingness to offer finance on the scale needed to escape the usual trade-offs. This is not to deny that the dollar surely also has been attractive because of the uniquely deep, liquid, and sophisticated U.S. financial markets. Yet fully one-third of the debt securities in those markets are MBSs, and the reserve role of the dollar historically has waxed and waned as the United States grew relatively faster or slower than its peer rivals.

Differential growth and increased control were mirrored in complementary weaknesses outside the United States. The United States was not the sole beneficiary of differential growth. A set of countries I call here the Americanized Rich[9] also enjoyed differential growth, for reasons similar to the United States. They lifted their share of rich-country GDP by 1.2 percentage points, a significant increase on their 16.6 percent 1991 share; their employment gains were equally impressive. Gains for the United States and the Americanized Rich came at the expense of a different group, the Repressed Rich,[10] whose growth was decidedly below the OECD average. Later sections in the chapter define the differences among the non-U.S.-rich countries. For now, what matters is that the growth dynamics of the long 1990s split up any potential rich-country coalition that might have imposed constraints on the United States, particularly by promoting the euro as an alternative reserve currency.

The Americanized Rich actively benefited from drafting behind the U.S. juggernaut. But the Repressed Rich, as well as several rapidly growing developing Asian economies, also benefited from U.S. growth. Elites in all these countries benefited from a politics that depressed local consumption and that thus made their economies reliant on external demand for growth. In this limited sense, they internalized U.S. interests. This internalization secured the position of the dollar as a global reserve currency and, thus, also secured the capital inflows—U.S. global financial arbitrage—powering U.S. differential growth. Foreigners opted to recycle their trade surpluses with the United States by purchasing various flavors of U.S. debt securities rather than increasing domestic consumption or, in the Repressed Rich, investment. By strengthening the exchange rate of the U.S. dollar, these purchases also cheapened U.S. import costs, reinforcing disinflation and again powering U.S. differential growth.

From a post-2008 perspective, it is tempting to dismiss these expressions of U.S. economic power in the long 1990s as mirages generated by financial hot air floating over the bleaching bones of U.S. manufacturing. Among other things, the 13 percent fall in the trade-weighted price-adjusted exchange rate of the dollar in February 2002 through January 2004, and a subsequent 14 percent fall from November 2005 through July 2008, is taken as evidence of the end of U.S. economic centrality.[11] Equally so, the large and growing U.S. foreign debt, the product of huge current account deficits, is often taken as evidence of economic fragility. But these views mischaracterize the data about U.S. foreign debt, elevate what are at best proxy measures into causal drivers, and incorrectly periodize this era.

The United States undeniably became a substantial net international debtor during the long 1990s, despite above-OECD-average growth. By 2007, net U.S. international debt approximated the combined GDP of Latin America and Africa at $2.5 trillion. Contrary to conventional economic theory, which predicts that capital flows from rich countries to poor countries, over one-half of this debt was held by developing countries. In broad terms, as of 2006, Japan held one-quarter of U.S. foreign debt; oil exporters held a second and rapidly growing quarter; Europeans held the third quarter; and the rest of Asia, primarily China, held the final quarter. The more imprecise data for 2008 somewhat diminish the European share in favor of China and the oil exporters.

This rich-poor connection was not accidental because one driver of global growth over the past two decades has been a symbiotic relationship between the United States and East Asia, particularly China. The Chinese energy-intensive growth also ultimately drove growth in the oil exporters. Asian states pegged their currencies against the dollar and recycled their trade surpluses with the United States as purchases of U.S. securities. Indeed, on a net basis this recycling ultimately was the crucial fuel for the U.S. housing growth machine and constitutes the U.S. net foreign debt. Yet not all debt is created equal. The structure, currency, and dispersion of foreign obligations all affect the degree to which debt hobbles or benefits the debtor and the creditor. The vast majority of U.S. foreign debt is dollar denominated, passively held, public and quasi-public debt yielding low rates of interest. This was the basis for U.S. financial arbitrage. Asian holdings hold the Asian U.S. creditors hostage as much as the United States because they simply hold too much to liquidate them in a panic. If foreigners cash out their passive holdings of U.S. bonds by buying more U.S. exports, this will renew growth in the United States. And if they do not cash out their holdings, then the United States will continue to enjoy an absence of constraints and a degree of financial arbitrage.

The plummeting exchange rate of the dollar versus the euro after 2002 looks equally problematic to some Cassandras, although movement against the euro through 2004 simply restored both currencies to their initial starting positions in

December 1998. The temptation to focus on the exchange rate of the dollar is obvious. A central problem that any argument about U.S. power must confront is that power is invisible and essentially impossible to measure directly. Exchange rates are an easily viewed, but misleading, proxy measure for power. They tell us little directly about control or growth. A rising exchange rate certainly makes buying control easier, but it might just as easily choke off growth, as Japan discovered. The real issue is whether the U.S. dollar retains its central role as a—or the—international reserve currency.

If power is inherently invisible and unmeasurable, how can we assess it? Our focus on global and domestic capital flows through housing finance systems, on the connection of those flows to differential growth, and on the distribution of foreign holdings of U.S. assets provide a better, although not ideal, grasp on U.S. power. These flows provide us with a cloud chamber that reveals the contours of U.S. global economic power. Like power, subatomic particles cannot be seen directly. Physicists use cloud chambers to reveal the motion of these otherwise undetectable particles and thus develop inferences about their composition. The structure of capital flows in and out of specific U.S. economic sectors similarly reveals the contours of the otherwise invisible structure of U.S. power.

In practical terms, the actual holdings of U.S. dollar-denominated assets give us one proxy measure of the scale and qualitative aspects of U.S. power. I build on Susan Strange's concepts top and negotiated currencies to reveal a finer-grained understanding of the reserve currency role of the dollar. More on this later, but for now the distinction between the two is whether a currency and assets denominated in that currency are widely and privately held for economic reasons or are held by a narrow group of public authorities for political reasons. The position of the dollar ultimately reflects whether the U.S. real economy is growing above or below the OECD average, and thus the status of the dollar proxies for the real issue, which is *relative growth*—differential growth—not absolute growth. In this respect my analysis departs from Benjamin Cohen's "power to delay" adjustment, which he casts at a purely financial level.[12]

Our cloud chamber also reveals the positive aspects of U.S. foreign debt (however counterintuitive this may seem) that a simple consideration net debt obscures. Disaggregating and analyzing the actual structure of inward and outward claims reveals considerable differences in the type of control that actors might exert. Foreign claims on the United States are largely passive, concentrated in U.S. Treasury bonds and MBSs. By contrast, the bulk of U.S. claims on foreigners are ownership of equities and the overseas assets of U.S. MNCs. This large net source of control provides a second proxy measure for U.S. power.

Finally, our cloud chamber shows the central role that foreign capital flowing through housing finance systems played in creating disparities in GDP and employment growth between the United States and other rich countries. It also shows that the U.S. housing finance growth machine was neither a permanent nor timeless engine for above-average economic growth, allowing us to periodize the 1990s correctly. The literal and figurative cheap raw materials fueling the housing machine at the beginning of the long 1990s—disinflation, low interest rates, and new homebuyers at the bottom of the housing ladder—had disappeared by 2005, causing the housing growth machine to seize up. Indeed, as inflation and interest rates rose, the machine began running in reverse, bulldozing paper financial houses built on MBSs and collateralized debt obligations. But this says nothing about whether a new machine will emerge. The rubble from the subprime crisis might fertilize another round of above-average growth, just as the various financial crises of the 1980s set the stage for growth in the 1990s. Moreover, although the U.S. growth rate dropped during the 2007–2008 crises, growth in the Repressed Rich dropped even more, maintaining the pattern of U.S. differential growth characterizing the long 1990s.

Why the emphasis on differential growth and control? Because politics is ultimately about power, the analysis of economic processes obliges us to pay attention to *differential rates of growth* and not just absolute growth. In political economy, power flows from differential accumulation, that is, above-average growth rates for output, profitability, and capitalization. All other things being equal, relatively faster growth enables an economy or firm to command more resources of all kinds from a market economy. And we must attend to control, and in particular control over production chains, because control affects the distribution of profits and value across actors and, thus, their ability to consolidate or expand their control. Academic readers will therefore understand immediately that the book blends what are usually seen as realist and Marxist perspectives on power in what I hope are commensurate ways.[13] And although figure 1.1 indicates the impossibility of fully disentangling causal priority, this orientation also indicates a relative hierarchy among our three proxies, with priority running from differential growth to control and thence to an absence of constraint, even though temporally capital inflows necessarily preceded differential growth.

Markets are systems of power because the constitution and regulation of property rights determine the profitability of enterprises. In turn, differing degrees of profitability mean that firms will have different abilities to buy up other firms and thus take control of production chains. Most goods today are complex bundles of intermediate goods. At each step in the process of designing, producing, shipping, and selling the good, a firm faces make or buy decisions. Each step thus represents a potential site of conflict as firms struggle to secure the best possible price. Nearly a century ago, Max Weber pointed out that "the price system [is] an expression of the struggle of man against man [or firms against firms]," and not simply a neutral consequence of the impersonal forces of supply and demand. In this struggle,

> capitalist interests are interested in the continuous extension of the free market up and until some of them succeed, either through the purchase of privileges from the

political authority [*politischen Gewalt*] or exclusively through the power exerted by their capital [*kraft ihrer Kapitalmacht*], in obtaining a monopoly for the sale of their products or the acquisition of their means of production, and in this way close the market for themselves alone.[14]

In the struggle over price, firms that can use their ability to withhold production from the market (as in Oliver Williamson's "hold-up" power, or Thorstein Veblen's "restriction") are able to push prices upward and extract more profit from a given chain of exchanges.[15] Controlling the architecture of a commodity or value chain conveys the ability to determine the distribution of profit within that chain. Weber's *kraft ihrer Kapitalmacht* encompasses the vulnerability of publicly traded firms to buy-out by firms with larger capitalizations. As Jonathan Nitzan has brilliantly argued, vulnerability to buy-out explains why firms always seek to do better than the average rate of profit in their economy rather than simply seeking profitability. Profitability per se does not assure continued control; rather, control assures above-average profitability and thus continued control. Nitzan argues that

> The value of capital represents a *distributional* claim. This claim is manifested partly through ownership, but more broadly through the *whole spectrum of social power*. Moreover, power is not only a means of accumulation, but also its most fundamental end. For the absentee owner, the purpose is not to "maximize" profits but to "beat the average". The ultimate goal of business is not hedonic pleasure, but *differential* gain [because the] capitalist seeks higher profit, not in order to buy *more goods and services*, but in order to assert his or her *differential power* [in the market].[16]

Markets as systems of power thus are about differential rates of growth and not absolute rates of growth. It should now be clear why this book gives causal priority to differential growth and control rather than to financial arbitrage and the related reserve currency role of the dollar. Above-average domestic growth in the United States gave many U.S. firms greater profitability than their overseas competitors because it valorized their investment in their home market. This enabled U.S. firms to expand overseas in ways that allowed them to capture and control critical nodes in their commodity chains overseas. At the same time, greater profitability and faster growth stimulated the U.S. housing market, creating a self-reinforcing process of faster growth in the United States than in most of its rich-country competitors. Differential growth anchored the status of the U.S. dollar as a top currency. In the 1970s and 1980s, the United States possessed deeper and more liquid capital markets compared to its major rich-country competitors. Yet the reserve currency position of the dollar waned relative to the deutschemark and the yen because real U.S. growth lagged behind German and, especially, Japanese growth in the 1970s and 1980s.

These analyses also help interpret the U.S. net foreign debt. Debt and production per se do not convey power in markets. This insight matters because it runs directly counter to the central point of those arguing that the rise of East Asian production is a certain sign of declining U.S. hegemony.[17] Such analyses fetishize manufacturing, but, as Nitzan's update of Veblen shows, markets are about control not output, about business not industry. Chinese firms are—perhaps—profitable,[18] but U.S. firms that control their domestic and foreign commodity chains are even more profitable and able to deploy greater masses of value in equity markets to capture potential threats to that control. On the other hand, this perspective implies that, if Asian countries and oil exporters shift out of U.S. Treasury debt into equities via sovereign wealth funds (SWFs), they pose an immediate threat to U.S. power as they accumulate controlling stakes in firms.

Defining power as an absence of constraint, differential growth, and control creates ambiguity about which are the relevant actors in this analysis. This ambiguity arises because much of what happened in the long 1990s does not stem from the conscious or deliberate policy choices of actors. No one planned housing market–driven U.S. differential growth. Here the analysis aligns with Benjamin Cohen's in diminishing the analytic significance of power understood as influence over others. Although I ultimately argue that the housing growth machine was truly a machine with little real human agency, it is worth ventilating arguments that actors both had choices and acted on them strategically.

Certainly we can credit the deliberate choices of actors for producing much of the disinflationary impulse that is featured in the box at the upper left-hand side of figure 1.1. This disinflation created an environment in which individual U.S. debtors might seek to refinance their mortgages, thus freeing up billions of dollars in purchasing power. Disinflation had three powerful engines. First, central banks launched a *jihad* against inflation in 1979, initially creating high real interest rates but eventually bringing inflation and thus nominal interest rates down by the 1990s. Second, U.S. and other MNCs and retail firms did go to Asia and then China, creating a flood of ever-cheaper goods, even in nominal terms. Third, the George Bush (1988–1992) and, even more so, Bill Clinton (1992–2000) administrations deliberately sought fiscal balance, which lowered interest rates by easing public-sector demands on capital markets.

Yet the degree of agency here is easy to overstate, and not just because actors could not foresee the consequences of their actions. Central bankers represent creditor interests, which inflation harms. The disinflationary goals of central banks required cooling off the economy, not pumping it up. Production of labor-intensive goods had already begun moving to Asia in the 1960s, and once Wal-Mart reached China, everyone else had to follow to stay competitive. With respect to one of the key policy decisions of the Clinton administration to balance the federal budget, James Carville, Clinton's political advisor, famously noted that he wished to be reincarnated as the bond market because it "could intimidate anybody." Similarly, on the eve of the financial crisis, Charles Prince, chairman and CEO of Citigroup, noted his inability to buck the markets, saying that "As long as the [liquidity] music is playing, you've got to get up and dance. When the music stops, in terms of liquidity, things will be complicated."[19]

Grant these actors full agency—a real variety of choices, an accurate assessment of the consequences of their choices, and the will to act. Still, the core impulse for differential growth came from institutional structures first planted in the Depression and that had matured by the 1960s and 1970s—housing market finance institutions. Actors (and academics) largely ignored these until quite late. Before explaining why, I must preempt one potential confusion: housing-based growth does not account for *all* GDP or employment growth in the rich countries. Rather, differences in housing finance systems plausibly explain the *difference* in growth rates (adjusted for population growth) among the United States, the Americanized Rich, and the Repressed Rich. These shared broadly similar growth impulses in the 1990s: the mobile telecoms/deregulated telecoms revolution, the Internet boom, the supply chain revolution, cheaper manufactures from Asia, and stock market booms. All experienced roughly similar real interest rates (and real interest rates matter for business investment if we take the standard *nonhousing* view of the world). So, arguably all three sets of economies should have grown at roughly the same rates. Yet they did not. This book singles out housing finance systems as the source of the *difference* among the rich, not the *absolute level* of growth (see also chapter 4).

The salience of housing emerged as the outcome of action behind the backs of actors, which is why this book downplays agents and their overt efforts to dominate other actors. This obviously departs somewhat from Max Weber's classic definition that *power* is "the probability that one actor in a social relationship will be in a position to carry out his will despite resistance, regardless of the basis on which this probability rests."[20] Analyses using this definition tend to focus on actors' deliberate choices and conflicts over outcomes from crises.[21] Instead, I emphasize Weber's concept of *auslese* (or selection and action behind the backs of actors) rather than deliberate actor choice. Institutionally structured behavior and the uncoordinated behavior of many dispersed actors constituted most of the forces activating differential growth in the United States, but few actors consciously sought to activate the housing market for this purpose. Indeed, the George W. Bush administration (2000–2008) consciously tried to harness the housing market for economic and political purposes through deregulation and the promotion of homeownership, with quite deleterious consequences.

Again, this does not imply that U.S. policy was totally irrelevant and that the United States was purely a beneficiary of good luck. Rather, it suggests that actors in markets and other competitive arenas often overestimate the effects of deliberate strategic action in producing both good and bad outcomes.[22] Actors face severe information problems when they deliberately seek to create and enforce new large-scale economic behaviors. As Friedrich Hayek argues, actors find it impossible to generate the information they need to take action large enough to change the environment in ways that allow them to avoid unintended consequences.[23] Even when less powerful actors can only respond to the initiatives of the powerful, they often do so in unexpected ways. Large-scale action thus inevitably creates surprises; although actors make moves based on their assessment of the current environment and the plausible responses of other actors, it is impossible to anticipate fully the shape of the new environment. As actors make misjudgments and partial judgments about the consequences of their actions, and as they compete over scarce resources, they create and are confronted with a new and unanticipated environment.

Max Weber highlights this when he notes that competition among individuals and larger social units as they meet in economic, social, or political markets produce a specific form of selection (*auslese*). By *selection* he means a process "where one form of social action is selected (*auslese* again) as better adapted (*angepasst*) to the interests of those involved through a collective response to changed environmental conditions."[24] For Weber, selection is a collective and thus system-level process, not a unit-level process, in the sense that, just as any given producer has no control over prices in a competitive market, any given actor cannot necessarily affect outcomes in social and political competition. Although Weber does not intend selection in a normative Social Darwinian sense, he is clear that selection operates through efforts to seek power over others, to impose one's will on them, because this is for him the essence of competition. Thus, selection is not an early parsing of the superficially benign process we now label institutional isomorphism, although Weber stresses the role of ideational factors rather than material ones with respect to selection of (new) institutions and behaviors. In this sense, although selection is like economics it is not *only* about economics and does not always operate on marginalist principles even when the struggle is about economics.[25]

A central conceptual feature of *auslese* is the notion that selection often occurs without actors' cognizance of the actual factors determining the outcome of that competition. Selection occurs behind the backs of the actors. The process of selection (*auslese*) suggests that we should not credit actors' deliberate actions for producing what those actors consider a successful outcome. As Weber cautions, "When this [the explanation of the processes of selection] is done, there is always the danger of introducing uncritical value-judgments into empirical investigation. There is, above all, a danger of being primarily concerned with justifying the success of an individual case. Since individual cases are often dependent on highly exceptional circumstances, they may be in a certain sense 'fortuitous.'"[26]

The analysis here corrects for the privileging of intentional action in its explanation. It explicitly considers two additional routes to successful outcomes. First, success might arise from good luck. The external environment might change in ways that make formerly dysfunctional institutional structures suddenly functional. Second, success might arise when actors make policy choices that are essentially endogenous outcomes of specific existing institutional structures and routines rather than truly strategic responses to changing environmental conditions. Although actors might consider their actions to be intentional responses to policy problems, the institutional constraints on policy choice might be such that no other choice is possible. In this situation, should actors get credit for success when their policies do not represent a substantial change of direction?

Thus, any analysis of events has to account for the possibility that actors did not intend the actual outcome and were (un-)lucky rather than smart. The U.S. housing-based differential growth in the long 1990s emerged in unforeseen ways from the way that U.S. policy choices made in pursuit of growth in general interacted with rich-country housing market financial structures and developing-country developmental goals. The same dysfunctional housing finance institutions in the inflationary environment of the 1970s and early 1980s (and after 2005) became functional, or at least pro-growth, in the disinflationary environment of the long 1990s. U.S. growth had substantial positive consequences for the United States and the Americanized Rich, including, for the United States, the restoration of the top currency status of the dollar. The reverse is also true—the mechanisms producing above-average U.S. growth also generated the current financial crisis.

Mechanisms and Plan of the Book

Now we can turn to the actual dynamics operating in the long 1990s that restored U.S. economic power after declines in the 1970s and 1980s. Because the chapters of the book move systematically through the boxes and flows in figure 1.1, this section also provides a somewhat detailed guide to the chapters. Recall the core argument: U.S. global financial arbitrage and global disinflation combined to power above-average U.S. economic growth in the long 1990s, that growth premium originated from the different capacities of housing finance systems to translate disinflation and foreign capital into increased aggregate demand and economic growth, above-average U.S. growth and differential accumulation are the primary bases for U.S. economic power, and secondary and visible manifestations of that power are the reserve currency status of the U.S. dollar and the above-average expansion of U.S. MNCs abroad.

Two feedback loops operated in this process. Above-average U.S. growth initially had self-sustaining aspects by validating disinflationary investment in China and elsewhere and by helping to balance the federal budget. Faster growth led to higher tax receipts, and the narrowing deficit allowed the Federal Reserve to ease interest rates after 1995. Meanwhile, disinflationary imports from low-wage China and Hong Kong rose from 5.7 to 15 percent of total U.S. imports from 1991 to 2005. By contrast, the share of U.S. imports from high-wage Japan shrank by almost the same 10 percentage points.[27] Much the same was true for the European economies.[28] Successful production in China led to yet more investment and yet more of the cheap imports that powered disinflation. Ultimately, however, Chinese growth led to greater and greater calls on global raw materials and thus generated inflationary rather than deflationary pressures, undoing one source of U.S. growth. At the same time, U.S. adventurism in Iraq combined with reckless tax cuts to return the federal budget to deficit. What had been a positive reinforcement for growth eventually turned negative.

Above-average growth also induced foreigners to recycle their trade surpluses with the United States into an increasing volume of dollar-denominated securities. This recycling was the second major fuel for the U.S. growth machine, permitting the United States to operate free of the normal economic constraints. Recycling strengthened the dollar, encouraging even more foreign accumulation of dollar-denominated securities. Ultimately, this asset accumulation had to be validated by U.S. economic growth, and foreign capital flowing into the U.S. housing finance system did generate growth. But continued U.S. growth generated such large trade deficits that only states could stomach a continued accumulation of U.S. debt. This curtailed opportunities for U.S. financial arbitrage because those states moved to establish SWFs in order to shift out of low-yielding bonds. Once more, a positive reinforcement for growth eventually turned negative. All this occurred before the 2008 financial crisis upset the global financial system.

Disinflation and dollar recycling drove U.S. global economic power in a huge parabolic arc over the long 1990s, generating a recovery from the difficult 1970s and 1980s and a return to a new set of difficulties at the end of the first decade of the twenty-first century. Thus, chapters 2 and 3 stint imports, which are both the accounting and real counterparts to these capital flows. Put simply, it is enough to note the downward pressure on both wages and prices that sourced goods from the Association of South East Asian Nations (ASEAN) and later China exerted on U.S. markets. Instead, chapters 2 and 3 address global capital flows into and out of the United States to establish the connections among U.S. financial arbitrage, the absence of constraint on the United States, and the disinflationary inputs into the housing growth machine.

Chapter 2 starts on the left-hand side of figure 1.1 to take a first cut at U.S. financial arbitrage. The central point: not all debt is created equal. Foreign investment in the United States is passive and low yielding, whereas U.S. investment overseas is active, controlling, and high yielding. Thus U.S. overseas investments historically have yielded more income than did foreign investments in the United States. Although a savvy *individual* investor might be able to borrow money, invest only part of it, and still net a positive return, it is implausible that, on average, every U.S. investor is smarter than every foreign investor and has been smarter every year since the United States became a net debtor in the late 1980s.[29]

Instead, the United States benefits from a global system of financial arbitrage with other nations, borrowing low and lending high. This allows U.S. investors to garner net positive returns. The bulk of U.S. investment overseas occurs as higher-yielding investments in equities and as FDI. The bulk of foreign investment into the United States occurs as passive holdings of low-yielding bonds; most of these bonds are U.S. government and agency (i.e., mortgage) bonds. The foreign money flow into Treasury bonds and agencies is significant because, as chapter 4 shows, these flows generated additional housing-based aggregate demand in the U.S. economy and thus U.S. differential growth. Chapter 2 also considers alternative explanations for capital flows into the United States, particularly Michael Dooley, David Folkerts-Landau, and Peter Garber's "Bretton Woods 2" argument that links Chinese exports and U.S. borrowing, and William Cline's and Ricardo Hausmann and Federico Sturzenegger's accounting exercises.[30] Ultimately, all these explanations miss the political and economic significance of these mismatched capital flows. Politically, disparities in these flows segment any potential opposition to U.S. policies. Economically, these flows power differential growth in the United States and a few other countries.

Chapter 3 continues to follow the money, using finer-grained data to clarify the political implications of these mismatched capital flows; chapter 4 considers the economic implications. Chapter 3 demonstrates the political significance of different foreign capital flows into the United States to elaborate the divisions among any potential opposing coalition seeking to elevate the euro as a replacement reserve currency. Investors into the United States fall into four groups based on distinctly different investment portfolios; these I call the Corporate Shells, the Americanized Rich, the Repressed Rich, and the Lockboxes. The first group, the Corporate Shells, comprises sunny offshore banking centers that largely hold corporate bonds and is simply a tool for corporations.

The second group, the Americanized Rich, is made up of Britain, the Netherlands, Scandinavia, Australia, and Canada. They are Americanized in three senses. First, they invest globally like the United States, taking largely long-term active positions concentrating on FDI, equities, and, to a lesser extent, corporate bonds. Second, their investment into the United States and U.S. investment into these nations occurs at levels disproportionate to their share of global GDP or ability for FDI. Finally, they also tend to have housing finance systems—and thus growth rates—similar to that in the United States.

The third group, the Repressed Rich, is made up of Japan, Germany, Italy, Austria, Belgium, Portugal, and Spain. These countries, for the most part, have housing finance systems that repress demand by requiring high down payments and offering short maturities.[31] Their investment in the United States takes a mix of active and passive positions weighted toward the latter, which is to say more corporate bonds and fewer equities. This group underinvests in the United States and receives less U.S. investment of all types than their level of GDP or FDI capability would suggest.

The fourth group, the Lockboxes, is developing Asia and the oil exporters and holds almost exclusively passive instruments such as Treasury bonds, with relatively few corporate bonds and equities. Because these economies are poor, we would expect a low level of capacity for FDI, and in fact few make any FDI into the

United States. Putting aside the Corporate Shells, U.S. investment overseas mirrors the remaining three-way division; not only does U.S. investment disproportionately go to the Americanized Rich, but, as we will see, the highest-yielding U.S. investment goes to that group.

Chapter 3 thus shows that U.S. global power in part rests on a passive divide-and-conquer strategy that manifests itself in durable investments in specific (in both senses) assets. These investments flow in both directions, tying the economic fortunes of elites together but often in very different ways. The investment patterns create different mixes of incentives for elites by locking those elites into different long-term patterns of economic activity and, thus, political preferences.

What about the economic consequences of global capital flows? How did disinflation and arbitrage matter for U.S. growth? Chapter 4 shows how housing finance systems translated disinflation and recycled dollars into growth. It examines housing markets as a source of economic power via differential accumulation favoring the United States, explaining the different rates of employment and GDP growth in the United States and the two rich-country groups identified in chapter 3. Most analyses of growth in the 1990s, particularly those on the left, focus on real interest rates or on the effects of corporatist intermediation. Real interest rates were high in the 1990s, arguably posing an impediment to the *level* of growth in the rich OECD economies. But these analyses ignore the *differential* effects of falling nominal interest rates. Foreign capital inflows abetted this fall, with decisive effects on housing, given that foreign holdings of agency MBSs (i.e., those issued by the Federal National Mortgage Agency, Fannie Mae; and the Federal Home Loan Mortgage Corporation, Freddie Mac) amounted to approximately $250 billion (or 10 percent of the outstanding amount) by 2000 and approximately $1.5 trillion (or 23 percent) by 2008.

Chapter 4, instead, shows that different housing market institutional configurations translated the global disinflation of the 1990s into differing volumes of increased aggregate demand. Countries that, like the United States, possessed high rates of homeownership, high levels of mortgage debt in relation to GDP, and relatively easy refinancing options for mortgages outperformed other economies from the early 1990s on. As *nominal* interest rates fell, these systems allowed mortgagers to call their loans, retiring expensive old debt in favor of cheap new debt. This freed up purchasing power. Lower interest rates also induced more people into the housing market, driving prices up. Both phenomena created the usual kind of Keynesian stimulus and the usual multiplier effects. The United States built 17.7 million units of housing in 1990–2000 and an additional 10 million units through mid-2006, which helped the United States create half of the new OECD jobs in 1991–2005.

By contrast, Japan and Germany, the two largest developed economies in the Repressed Rich category, in effect ran the U.S. cycle backward. High transaction costs for refinancing mortgages, relatively low levels of mortgage debt, no cash out of home equity, and little or no securitization of mortgages marked the housing finance markets in these countries. Consequently the transmission belt linking the 1990s global disinflation to their domestic markets had weaker effects. Housing prices fell, employment markets were weak, and physical investment faltered. Sluggish growth confronted German and Japanese banks with low domestic returns. Sluggish growth confronted German and Japanese households with increased insecurity about their employment and the ability of their state to make good on its pension and health liabilities. Both groups responded by saving more and exporting those savings in search of better yields abroad. In turn, this slowed their economies further while reinforcing U.S. economic growth. Thus, by 2005 virtually the same number—note: number, not percentage—of people were employed in Germany and Japan as had been employed in 1991, and the 2005 level of gross fixed-capital formation was absolutely lower in Japan and barely higher in Germany than it had been in 1991. The Americanized Rich countries (which resembled the United States) were double winners, primarily from growth at home and secondarily from their investments in the United States. Indeed, Britain, like the United States, maintained positive international investment income in the 1990s.

The tight connections among international investment positions, domestic financial structures, and economic outcomes show that our division of countries into Americanized Rich and Repressed Rich is not arbitrary. Chapter 4 thus dismisses the conventional wisdom on European employment outcomes, which argues that corporatist social pacts were decisively important for employment growth. The faster growing Americanized Rich countries straddle the liberal versus coordinated market economy divide, suggesting that corporatism itself explains little about differential growth. Instead, the analysis suggests that action did indeed occur behind the backs of the actors. Housing finance systems are, thus, the crucial variable for explaining the *difference* in growth rates among the rich countries, although not their absolute level.

Chapter 5 turns from domestic differential accumulation to considering differential growth and control at a global level, the rightmost box in figure 1.1. Whereas chapters 2 and 3 largely look at U.S. liabilities, chapter 5 looks at the asset side of the U.S. international balance sheet and at the international role of the U.S. dollar. The key point is that the absence of constraints—capital inflows—facilitated capital outflows that produced profitable control over global commodity chains. For Giovanni Arrighi, a Marxist, the rising foreign debt—the accumulation of years of trade deficits—is simply a proxy indicator for declining U.S. manufacturing competitiveness and, thus, for declining U.S. hegemony.[32] Realist Robert Gilpin similarly argues that the massive shift of production offshore by U.S. MNCs undermined U.S. power.[33] Chapter 5 dismisses these misplaced analogies with nineteenth-century British hegemonic decline and addresses the real economy foundations of U.S. economic power. British trade deficits in the nineteenth century reflected continued British specialization in declining industrial sectors and the failure to generate both the investment and organizational structures needed to be successful in new leading sectors. The United States currently runs a trade deficit far in excess of the nineteenth-century British deficit. This deficit, however, does not reflect a lack of U.S. competitiveness in advanced manufacturing but the massive shift of low-technology production offshore to Asia and U.S. investment in and control over high-technology production in a broad mix of developed economies. U.S. firms substituted offshore production for exports while upgrading production processes.

Far from supporting either Arrighi's or Gilpin's analyses of U.S. financialization and decline, the disaggregated data on profitability show that U.S. financial firms overseas not only underperform the average U.S. overseas firm with respect to return on assets but also underperform the average U.S. manufacturing firm overseas. Indeed, U.S. overseas manufacturing value-added increased relative to foreign manufacturing production in the United States. Despite this, the highest performing U.S. firms are in sectors in which U.S. service-sector deregulation and technological innovation in the 1970s–1980 gave U.S. firms an early lead at home and abroad. The service sector, particularly wholesale and retail trade, grew the fastest, with services value-added increasing from 25 to 40 percent of total value-added for U.S. firms abroad. Differential growth in the U.S. domestic economy, where U.S. MNCs still do the bulk of their business, helped those same MNCs experience differential growth overseas despite slower overall foreign growth. And differential growth enabled the emergence of new sectors by reducing the risks involved in starting new businesses or lines of production.

What about the position of the dollar as the international reserve currency, which is critical to the recycling that sustained low U.S. interest rates? As already noted, mere changes in exchange rates provide little analytic traction, and simple measures of "market share" are also somewhat blunt. Instead, chapter 5 builds on Susan Strange's distinction among top, negotiated, and master currencies.[34] For Strange, *top currencies* are attractive on their own economic merits, much like the U.S. dollar for most of the 1990s; *negotiated currencies* are those whose international role rests on implicit or explicit political deals between the countries involved. *Master currencies* are imposed by force.

I operationalize Strange's concepts by mapping them on to competitive, oligopolistic, and monopoly markets and using the Herfindahl-Hirschman index to measure the degree of oligopoly. Master currencies, like monopolies, deny consumers choice. Top currencies are like competitive markets in that no consumer has any ability to influence the output (volume of currency in circulation) or price (exchange rate) of that currency. Politically, this implies that holders of those assets can exert little pressure on the emitter of the top currency. Negotiated currencies are those in which some consumers, generally political actors, have concentrated holdings large enough to affect the price and output of the international reserve currency. Thus, the emitter of that currency has to take these consumers' preferences into account when it sets price and volumes. But chapter 5 notes the shift of the dollar from negotiated to top and back to negotiated currency during the long 1990s. This discussion helps set up the issues discussed in chapter 6, which looks at political motivations for holding U.S. dollar-denominated securities.

Chapter 6 closes the loop back to U.S. financial arbitrage to understand the domestic motivations of countries funding the United States. If U.S. arbitrage and the dollar operated to the macroeconomic benefit of the United States and a few other countries, and to the microeconomic benefit of U.S. MNCs, why have other countries and actors tolerated this outcome? Put simply, nearly all potential opponents of the central role of the dollar are engaging in their own internal arbitrage. Shifting from export-led growth to domestic growth would involve not just economically painful choices but politically painful choices. If the Repressed Rich reduced their reliance on the U.S. market for growth, they would have to create robust private pension markets, which is politically unacceptable, and force firms to rely more on equity finance rather than loans, which recent research suggests might be economically deleterious for those firms.

A different domestic politics binds developing Asia. To be sure, as Dooley, Folkerts-Landau, and Garber have argued, Asian central banks hold dollars to support job-generating exports and thus political stability.[35] But, in addition, just as the U.S. economy arbitrages globally, these states arbitrage locally, borrowing at essentially a zero real rate of interest in order to invest in U.S. instruments yielding a positive real return. And in China an economic elite largely composed of relatives of party members arbitrages against the subjects of the party, socializing the risks of the Bretton Woods 2 system through the exposure of the Chinese state to capital losses on U.S. dollar-denominated securities while privatizing the profits from trade. Although chapter 6 suggests strong pressure to continue dollar recycling, it is essentially retrospective. The current crisis unquestionably will upset many existing political and economic relationships. Chapter 6 thus closes the circle on the processes characterizing the long 1990s, allowing us to move forward and consider what went wrong.

Chapter 7 starts the discussion of how the housing machine identified in chapter 4 exhausted its raw materials and ground to a halt. The 2007–2008 financial crisis was endogenous to the workings of the housing machine. The U.S. boom required a continuous supply of new entrants at the bottom of the housing ladder. But the very sources of disinflation—increasing volumes of Asian imports—undercut income at the bottom of the U.S. income pyramid by depressing wages and driving up Chinese demand for oil and other raw materials. At the same time, the low interest rates caused by foreign capital inflows drove house prices up. The dubious subprime mortgages that triggered the current financial crisis bridged the gap between new entrants' weak incomes and rising home prices. The chapter elaborates the specific mechanisms that turned relatively small defaults among subprime borrowers into a self-sustaining and widening financial crisis. Chapter 7 thus runs the housing machine argument backward: put inflation and rising interest rates into the U.S. housing machine, and it produces a sharp reversal of growth, just as it did in the 1970s and early 1980s.

Chapter 7 also considers current conflicts over politically acceptable levels of inflation and taxation. Many U.S. families with mortgages currently face a structural situation that should incline them to favor lower taxes and inflation. Although they are not a majority of households, elections are won at the margin. By contrast, the finance industry needs huge injections of liquidity to bail them out of the mess they created by bundling subprime mortgages into collateralized debt obligations. Just as in the Repressed Rich, efforts to stabilize the housing market will require large painful changes. These changes can already be seen in the renationalization and deleveraging of much of the financial sector. A real recovery, however, requires an end to the system of internal arbitrage that U.S. firms have been operating. After all, most of the U.S. foreign debt is public debt—Treasury bonds—or MBSs aggregating the mortgages on people's houses. Both represent a claim on individual incomes through taxes and interest payments. But U.S. investment overseas is largely done by corporations, so U.S. claims on foreigners largely accrue to those corporations, 65 percent of whose stock is held by the top 5 percent of the population by income. This is one reason why that top 5 percent also commands 25 percent of disposable income in the United States. U.S. firms thus have socialized the risks of U.S. global arbitrage while privatizing the benefits thereof. But any sustained recovery for housing prices and the MBSs based on them requires that incomes at the bottom rise enough to make housing affordable at current prices. Finally, the chapter discusses political responses to the 2007–2008 financial crisis.

Chapter 8 returns to the global level to consider a second reversal of fortune and its implications for U.S. financial arbitrage and thus global power. U.S. foreign economic policy had the aim of prying open foreign financial markets so that U.S. financial firms could position themselves in control of foreign commodity chains. But the exaggeration of the housing cycle after 2004 and the resulting financial crisis gave foreign central banks the wherewithal to establish SWFs. Major U.S. broker dealers and investment banks turned to SWFs to recapitalize. This reverses U.S. policy; states are once more reestablished at the heart of the global financial system. These states now have an enormous pile of cash—approximately $2.5 trillion in 2007 on the way to an estimated $12 trillion by 2015—to deploy in the global equity and securities markets. Nothing better illustrates what Weber calls "political capitalism" than the fusion of some of those SWFs with the largest private-equity firms and investment banks in the United States. (And if anyone thinks these funds will be administered on a purely fiduciary basis for the benefit of the citizens of those states, without regard to elite interests and state security, I have some MBSs I would like to sell you.[36]) But at the same time, SWFs represent a continuation of the kind of financial repression that sustains U.S. arbitrage in world financial markets and U.S. differential growth. Most SWFs divert current income away from current consumption by the masses and, instead, favor the political elites that control those SWFs.

The second part of chapter 8 considers the future of U.S. economic power beyond the current crisis. It suggests that differential growth and a dominant dollar are likely to continue for some time. The absence of economic decoupling in 2007–2008 continues a long pattern of global economic expansion centered on the United States. Because it is *relative* economic performance that matters, the rich-country competitors of the United States have to find some formula for faster domestically driven growth. Both the current pattern of arbitrage and U.S. centrality can persist for considerably longer than the raw numbers might suggest. Put simply, politically powerful overseas actors that have more at stake than just the value of their dollars have considerable incentives both to continue to hold those dollar-denominated securities and to control the market actors who might disrupt the current position of the U.S. dollar. Although this political support suggests that the current pattern of arbitrage has long legs, this book ends by suggesting a range of policy prescriptions to help unwind the current extreme imbalance. As SWFs come to hold more and more of U.S. overseas debt, their expectations about a higher return will force an end to the pattern of arbitrage that I describe in chapter 2, forcing the United States to find other sources of growth. One such source should be greater volumes of exports.

This book thus has four novel aspects. First, it focuses on differential growth rather than absolute growth. Second, unlike the vast majority of books on global finance, it looks at disaggregated capital flows to trace the real economy effects of those flows. Third, it does not assume that trends continue in a linear fashion but, instead, offers a reflexive model for the long 1990s. And, finally (although this matters only to academics), it suggests that the usual division between liberal and coordinated market economies and the usual analytic focus on coordinated wage bargaining as an explanation for growth outcomes should be reconsidered.

This also raises an issue of methodology. I make no claim that I am delivering anything approaching scientific law–like statements about the international political economy. In that sense, this book is not like much recent international political economic writing about narrower issues such as trade politics or banking regulation.

Lawlike statements can be made only about regularities that resist conscious transformation. The great macroeconomic imbalance at the heart of this analysis is not this kind of regularity. Indeed, the 2007–2008 financial crisis flowed directly from the fact that high-powered financial models based on regularities came undone when actors suddenly deviated from those past regularities. The events analyzed here constitute a singularity—a historically particular and ultimately evanescent structure of power that a relatively small number of actors forged contingently from a specific set of antecedent conditions, tools, and opportunities but that also reflects choices that the populations of the rich OECD countries made given the structural constraints they faced with respect to housing choices. As Barry Eichen-green notes in his perceptive set of lectures on some of this same terrain, "there is a sense then, in which we really have only one [comparable] data point, the transition from sterling to the dollar, from which to draw clear inferences."[37] This situation makes systematic econometric analysis impossible. The analysis, thus, does not present a formal model for behavior, nor does it test all its claims statistically. This is not to say that models and statistical tests are useless, and indeed I use some simple statistical tests to confirm that the relationships elucidated in the book probably did not occur by chance.[38]

Nevertheless, methods that are appropriate and useful for analyzing regularities are inappropriate and useless for analyzing one-of-a-kind or few-of-a-kind phenomena and, particularly, turning points in the economy. Otherwise, more hedge funds and investment banks would have anticipated the collapse of the subprime mortgage market in mid-2007, avoiding the financial catastrophe of 2008. Instead, this book lays bare what I consider to be the most important global financial dynamics of the past two decades—the ways those global flows meshed with local housing finance systems and how each reflected and supported U.S. global economic power, understood as the absence of constraint, differential growth, and increased control over global production. Let us begin by following the money to understand the absence of constraint.

2. Global Capital Flows and the Absence of Constraint

> I come now to the heart of the problem, as a Nation we are con-
> suming and investing, that is spending, about 6% more than we are
> producing. What holds it all together?—High consumption—high
> leverage—government deficits—What holds it all together is a re-
> ally massive and growing flow of capital from abroad. A flow of
> capital that today runs to more than $2 Billion per day.
>
> Paul Volcker, Stanford University, February 11, 2005

An Unbalanced U.S. Balance Sheet?

How can a superpower have continuously rising net foreign debt? Why is that debt
not a constraint? As we see in this chapter, the United States benefited from a huge
system of financial arbitrage that transformed short-term, low-return foreign investment into the United States into long-term, high-return U.S. investment overseas and above-OECD-average U.S. domestic growth. U.S. economic power is not
reducible to this transformation of short-term borrowing into long-term investment. But foreign debt was one of two key factors that allowed the United States
to generate differential growth relative to what I call here the Repressed Rich, a
group of slower-growing developed countries characterized by financial repression
and wage restraint. U.S. foreign debt also allowed U.S. firms to expand overseas
faster than their foreign competitors. At the end of the day, U.S. differential growth
and long-term investment helped maintain the reserve status of the U.S. dollar.
The reverse is also true, although to a lesser extent—the central position of the
U.S. dollar in international exchange and reserves enabled U.S. global financial
arbitrage and thus above-average U.S. growth. U.S. financial arbitrage helped free
the United States from the normal constraints linking domestic consumption and
domestic and overseas investment. This chapter, thus, begins establishing the lack
of constraint that facilitated U.S. differential growth.

Conceptually, the issues around U.S. foreign debt seem deceptively easy to ap-
prehend through a balance sheet approach. Indeed, most conventional (neoclas-
sically oriented) analyses treat the United States as if it were a unified economic
entity and tot up assets on the left side of the ledger and liabilities on the right.

This provides a snapshot picture of the net stock of debt or liabilities. The net liability and its corresponding flow of interest payments can then be compared to the U.S. GDP (a flow of income) to assess the long-term wisdom and afford-ability of this debt, just as a bank might compare an individual's current debts to her income before deciding whether to extend fresh credit. In the case of the United States, the issue of income is a bit more complicated because potential foreign income—production of exports or tradables—is the most relevant flow, not income from goods and services that cannot be sold overseas. But the essence is the same. If U.S. consumption consistently exceeds its production, it will have to borrow to cover the shortfall. If the nominal interest rate on those borrowings exceeds the rate of growth of nominal income and, in particular, the growth of production of tradables, then debt will rise continuously as a percentage of GDP (income). At some point, a prudent banker will stop lending when it becomes clear that the debt is unsustainable. Yet this has not happened, largely because the U.S. economy grew faster than most of the competing rich-country economies in the long 1990s.

The deceptively simple aggregate approach obscures important aspects about the long 1990s. First, it tells us nothing about the specific flows that compose the stock of debt on both sides of the ledger. Understanding these flows helps explain why we see the pattern of assets and liabilities on the balance sheet and the sources of U.S. global financial arbitrage (see figure 2.1). Second, because the balance sheet approach is rooted in accounting identities, it tells us nothing about the sources of U.S. growth (see chapter 4) or the evolution of productive capacity (see chapter 5). In this chapter, I disaggregate international investment flows into and out of the United States to show how the structure of U.S. foreign liabilities and assets became a source of U.S. strength in the long 1990s. Disaggregated debt data allow us to connect large-scale global capital flows to the more intermediate-level institutional structures for housing finance that drove U.S. differential growth. From a policy standpoint, this also helps us understand the current basis for and durability of the U.S. dollar as a reserve currency by illuminating the reasons for the acquiescence by other countries to U.S. global arbitrage and the barriers to their cooperation in a project to displace the dollar. Disaggregation also reveals the limits to above-average employment and GDP growth in the United States. Both illuminate the long-term sustainability of U.S. global economic power (see chapters 6–8). This chapter thus starts our examina-tion of the sources of U.S. differential growth in the long 1990s at the beginning, with U.S. arbitrage.

Why disaggregate? At the end of 2007, the United States had a net foreign debt of roughly $2.5 trillion. This amount, a bit less than one-fifth of the U.S. GDP, is roughly similar to the level in debt-crisis Mexico and Brazil in 1982 and equals the 2006 GDP of China (at market prices). The United States accumulated this debt

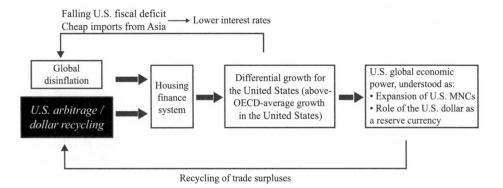

Fig. 2.1. Chapter 2: analytic concerns.

by consuming more than it produced in nearly every one of the past twenty-five years, but particularly so in 2004–2007. Meanwhile, the rest of the world produced more than it consumed annually and took claims on future U.S. production (i.e., debt) in exchange. Flows in 2008 suggested a moderation of imbalance, with U.S. exports rising modestly and non-oil imports falling sharply. Most analysts, whether sanguine or alarmist in their predictions, neoclassical or Marxist in their analytic framework, or celebratory or condemnatory in their tone, use aggregate data on trade, investment, and debt to assess the structure and probable consequences of this global macroeconomic imbalance.

But these aggregate data conceal more than they reveal. For example, aggregate data create an apparent paradox that is central to the analysis in this chapter: even though the United States has a considerable net debt to the rest of the world, the world continues to pay its U.S. creditors more money than U.S. debtors pay their global creditors. U.S. overseas investments consistently yielded more income than did foreign investments in the United States. In 2007, if we remove six zeros, this is rather like a private investor who owed $20,082 while holding investments worth only $17,640 somehow managing to pay out only $726 on her debts while earning $818 from her own investments, thus receiving a net income of $92. It is perfectly plausible that a savvy individual investor might be able to borrow money, invest only part of it, and still net a positive return. But it is implausible that, on average, every U.S. investor is smarter than every foreign investor. It is even less plausible that every U.S. investor has gotten even smarter after the United States became an apparent net debtor, as the data from Pierre-Olivier Gourinchas and Hélène Rey suggest. Gourinchas and Rey calculate that from 1960 to 2001 U.S. overseas assets earned an annualized rate of return 2 percentage points higher than U.S. liabilities to foreigners—5.6 versus 3.6 percent.[1] Furthermore, the gap expanded after 1973, as U.S. assets yielded 6.8 percent while liabilities cost only 3.5 percent. This is one reason why, despite five more years of cumulating trade deficits, U.S. net foreign debt was the same 20 percent of GDP in 2007 as it was in 2002.

Disaggregating the investment data explains this paradox by showing that the world is not composed of generic investors holding generic assets for generic reasons. Not all debt is created equal. Some forms of debt generate greater returns than other forms, different forms of debt create different possibilities for long-term economic growth, and different institutional structures transmit growth impulses with varying degrees of strength. Disaggregating the data allows us to understand how U.S. financial arbitrage operates as a system of power relations rather than a narrow set of economic flows. Disaggregation thus makes it possible to explain the fundamentally political basis for global macroeconomic imbalances and to have a better handle on the policy question "How long can this go on?" Understanding the political basis shows us that U.S. power neither is unidimensional nor imbricates all parts of the rest of the world in the same way. Instead, U.S. power resembles a ring of ramparts around the United States, with each ring built from differing stones of allegiance. Those stones are the bilateral investment and trade flows connecting different areas to the United States. U.S. creditors can be divided into four groups. Table 2.1 provides a breakdown of portfolio investment by type of security and holder. First, we must survey the conventional analyses of the sources of net U.S. foreign debt.

TABLE 2.1.
Major foreign portfolio holders of U.S. securities by country and type, June 2007 (US$)

	Total	Equities	LT Treasury Debt	Agency LT Debt		Corporate LT Debt		ST Debt
				ABS	Other	ABS	Other	
Japan	1,197	220	553	103	126	30	89	76
China[a]	922	29	467	206	170	11	17	23
Britain	921	421	43	18	10	142	263	24
Cayman Islands	740	279	23	46	6	190	157	38
Luxembourg	703	235	45	23	16	81	259	44
Canada	475	347	18	1	3	22	62	22
Belgium	396	25	14	2	31	54	267	3
Ireland	342	81	14	20	6	56	80	85
Switzerland	329	174	34	6	10	34	55	15
Netherlands	321	185	16	20	3	44	40	13
Middle East oil exporters[b]	308	139	79	12	18	7	10	44
Rest of world	2,904	995	659	113	336	230	325	246
Total	9,772	3,130	1,965	570	735	902	1,835	635
Total held by official institutions	2,823	266	1,452	570	735	44	55	256

Source: U.S. Treasury, Foreign Portfolio Holdings of US Securities, June 2007 (Washington, D.C. U.S. Treasury Department, 2007), 10.
Notes: ABS, asset-backed securities; LT, long term; ST, short term.
[a]Excludes Hong Kong.
[b]Bahrain, Iran, Iraq, Kuwait, Oman, Qatar, Saudi Arabia, and the United Arab Emirates.

Terms of the Debate on U.S. Debt and Tentative Answers

Five explanations for and elaborations of the significance of rising U.S. foreign debt pit those who are sanguine against those who are worried and pit three flavors of economists against one another. Each explanation yields valuable information that I deploy in later chapters because none is totally wrong. But all these arguments share two common flaws. First, they back up their central claims either with aggregate data on international financial flows and stocks or with data disaggregated only one level down. This blinded almost all of them to the subprime mortgage financial crisis. Sanguine analysts expected no crisis; anxious analysts expected a currency crisis.

Second, these arguments also display a more specific blindness peculiar to their methodological biases. Neoclassical economists, such as Ben Bernanke, are wedded to the view that markets are the aggregation of individual choices. Their arguments tend to assume that individuals make decisions about savings and investment without substantial state direction, and that markets allocate these savings. These arguments failed to understand that global financial flows were shaped by deeper power relationships.[2] Marxists, for their part, are commendably concerned with power. But their attachment to a labor theory of value makes them unduly obsessed with manufacturing. This blinded them to the fundamentally Keynesian process of demand stimulation at the heart of the U.S. boom. Finally, Dooley, Folkerts-Landau, and Garber benefit from their association with the International Monetary Fund (IMF) and an investment bank, which orients them toward political rather than economic exchange as an explanation for behavior. For this reason, I code them as "realists," and indeed their analysis is fairly accurate about the U.S.–China relationship. Methodologically, however, they remain neoclassical economists, which makes them far too sanguine.

These biases blind each flavor of argument to the dynamics that drove U.S. differential accumulation in the long 1990s. Disaggregating the data allows us to show how different domestic housing finance systems translated capital flows into growth. This permits a more accurate assessment of the import and sustainability of global macroeconomic imbalances in relation to U.S. power.

Sanguine Neoclassicals: Ben Bernanke and the Global Savings Glut

Ben Bernanke provides a simple and optimistic explanation for the rising U.S. debt, and as chairman of the Federal Reserve Open Market Committee his views matter. He argues that the rising net U.S. foreign debt is simply U.S. consumers' individually rational response to a global overabundance of savings available at low interest rates. This argument puts the causal burden for the current macroeconomic imbalance on the shoulders of Asian savers, who save too much, rather than U.S. consumers, who save too little. Although by accounting definitions the U.S.

current account deficit reflects shortfalls in U.S. saving (or excesses in U.S. consumption), Bernanke rightly points out that the real issue is why these shortfalls or excesses occur, not their mere existence.

Bernanke considers four possible causes for the imbalance and dismisses the influence of all but the level of Asian saving.[3] Bernanke dismisses any connection between the U.S. fiscal deficit and the current account deficit. On the one hand, the U.S. combined fiscal surpluses with current account deficits in the late 1990s, as did Australia for most of the past decade. By contrast, Germany and Japan have simultaneously run fiscal deficits and current account surpluses for most of that same decade. If there is a fiscal-trade deficit connection, it certainly is not a direct connection.

What about different patterns of saving caused by different age distributions? The rapidly aging populations of Europe and Japan confront the already high levels of public debt that compromise their retirement systems. The prospect of public shortfalls could plausibly motivate them to save more now in anticipation of having to fund a bigger portion of their own retirement.[4] This would generate current account surpluses. But here, too, troubling facts vitiate the argument. Although Japan has one of the largest current account surpluses absolutely and as a percentage of GDP, the Japanese have been saving less and less of their income over the past decade even as the pension system got less and less financially robust. In Europe, the correlation of population growth and aging with aggregate national savings is weak, despite the obvious anecdotal example of gray, trade-surplus Germany. As an aggregate, Europe does not run a large current account surplus. The EU-27, the EU-25, and the euroland-13[5] each runs a slight deficit. So although intra-European flows do matter, Europe's net contribution to global savings became minimal after 2000 and alone cannot be responsible for the U.S. borrowing or trade deficits. When Europe did matter, back in the mid-1990s, European public debt levels and deficits were improving, even in Italy and Belgium.

From Bernanke's point of view, this leaves Asia as the key causal driver of global savings. He identifies two mainsprings for excess Asian saving. Both in some sense spring from the 1997–1998 Asian financial crises. Most obviously, developing Asia was hammered by a crisis in which the central banks quickly exhausted their foreign currency reserves while defending pegged currencies. Consequently, Bernanke notes, it is perfectly reasonable for these countries to build up a higher level of reserves in the form of easily liquidated U.S. dollar-denominated securities and specifically U.S. public debt. These reserves provide a shield against a rerun of the 1997 crises.

Less obviously, Bernanke argues that the 1997 financial crisis and the subsequent implosion of the dot-com boom diminished local investment opportunities in Asia without simultaneously diminishing the desired level for local savings. Existing industrial capacity in Asia is apparently perfectly adequate for servicing U.S. and Chinese demand. (Marxists, of course, see this as a problem or crisis of overproduction.) These two processes produced a glut of savings in Asia that found its counterpart in U.S. borrowing. High Asian savings produced low global interest rates, and U.S. consumers rationally responded by borrowing this cheap money. Although Bernanke does not think this situation can persist indefinitely, he is sanguine about policymakers' ability to unwind the situation through better financial supervision in Asia, which makes it more attractive to invest there, and more fiscal restraint in the United States, which will slow consumption growth.

For Bernanke, everyone is acting rationally and any imbalances are short-term ones. But Bernanke's analysis misreads history. In the past few years, Japan, China, and the oil exporters largely account for the U.S. deficit, and by extension, foreign financing of that deficit. The oil exporters plausibly lack domestic investment opportunities, although Dubai is going out of its way to invest in real estate the hard way—by literally manufacturing more out of sand. Japan also plausibly lacks investment opportunities at home given its continued overcapacity in major export industries. The same cannot be said of China, which suffers from a huge infra-structure deficit relative to its income level, let alone developed-country levels. At the same time, the smaller ASEAN economies, which did suffer large relative drops in investment subsequent to the Asian financial crisis, account for a very small portion of the U.S. deficit. This suggests that Bernanke's causal argument is weak because China sailed through the Asian crisis with unaffected investment levels. Finally, does western Europe, which arguably has much catch-up to do in informa-tion technology, really lack investment opportunities?

Bernanke also cannot explain why the huge Asian trade surpluses with the United States do not translate into increased domestic demand, given the relative importance of those exports in the total GDP. China, after all, currently invests between 40 and 50 percent of its GDP, which hardly indicates a dearth of invest-ment. Even in Malaysia, which should be suffering somewhat from competition in final markets with China, invests roughly 25 percent more of its GDP than does the United States. Meanwhile, Malaysian exports to the United States in 2005 equaled 27 percent of Malaysian GDP, suggesting that exports should have had a strong multiplier effect in the economy and thus have led to even more domestic investment or consumption. Yet this investment does not seem to generate the usual multiplier effects. (Figure 3.2 in the next chapter shows the relative growth of the reserve holdings in several countries.)

Moreover, rapid growth in East Asia means productivity is also growing more rapidly than in the United States. Why would local investors not want to capture those gains and, in doing so, bid up local prices to the point where savings were ab-sorbed? Alternately, why do they save so much, given the relatively low standard of living they enjoy and their easy ability to compare their own situation with that in the developed world? Given the historically high rates of growth, and thus ex-pectations of higher future income, why do Asian individuals not consume more of their current incomes? After all, precisely this "life-cycle" theoretical argument is supposed to explain why Americans borrow for consumption today rather than saving more for the future.

The blindness of neoclassical economics to the issue of power obscures the barriers that Asian states have erected in front of Asian individuals' consumption. These barriers range from compulsory savings (the Singapore National Provident Fund automatically captures approximately 30 percent of wage income) to state oversight of capital goods purchases (the Chinese state must approve every purchase of imported civilian aircraft). As Dooley, Folkerts-Landau, and Garber argue, Asian states manipulate a key price—their exchange rates—to maintain export shares. Finally, Bernanke can explain neither the forms that foreign investment into the United States takes nor why the crisis he did not foresee erupted in the housing sector rather than somewhere else. Bernanke's purely economic argument is thus unsatisfactory, although it does point strongly to the central role of Asia in financing U.S. consumption after 2000. What about less sanguine explanations?

Anxious Neoclassicals: Cline and Hausmann and Sturzenegger

Two other neoclassical analyses, by William Cline and by Ricardo Hausmann and Federico Sturzenegger, provide less sanguine assessments.[6] Each links an explanation of the U.S. net international income paradox to a prediction about continued stability for the U.S. foreign debt. Both move somewhat beyond fully aggregated data to assess long-term stability. Both arbitrarily create U.S. assets to balance the accounts, turning the United States into a net creditor again. But both note that this accounting exercise does not leave very many years before the United States truly becomes a net debtor. Thus, they both argued that action was needed sooner rather than later, yet, as with Bernanke, they failed to see the origins of the crisis in the housing sector.

Cline begins with the paradox about positive U.S. net international investment income and the equally problematic puzzle that, even though the United States ran a cumulative $2.55 trillion current account deficit from 2001 through 2005, net U.S. foreign debt rose by only $207 billion.[7] How could either be so? Cline considers whether temporary causes might have depressed the value of U.S. assets overseas while enhancing the value of foreign-held U.S. liabilities, but he finds that these temporary phenomena account for very little of the difference in asset values.

Instead, Cline accounts for the still substantial remainder by arguing that the positive flow of international investment income must imply—*by accounting logic*—a parallel set of assets because theoretically speaking any predictable flow of income can be capitalized. Excess net international income logically implies excess international assets that somehow are not captured in official statistics. To determine the size of these excess net assets, Cline simply calculates how much additional capital is implied by the net income flow to the United States and then assigns the label "capitalized net capital income" to those assets. *Et voila!* This creates a balancing entry that transforms the United States from a net international debtor into a net creditor by approximately 7 percent of U.S. GDP. Cline cautions, however, that this cushion is rapidly eroding given current account deficits on the order of 4–5 percent per year, and thus he calls for budget balancing, further weakening of the exchange rate of the U.S. dollar, and demand stimulation abroad.[8]

Hausmann and Sturzenegger similarly argue from aggregated data, but go a bit beyond simple accounting. Like Cline, they argue that official statistics, particularly those concerning FDI, probably "grossly mismeasure the real evolution of…net foreign assets" because the presence of net income indicates that some unmeasured asset must exist.[9] Like Cline, they eliminate U.S. net debt by capitalizing the net income flow to come up with roughly $3 trillion in U.S. assets that are not captured by official data. They diverge from Cline in two ways. First, they creatively label these notional assets "dark matter" rather than the less exciting "capitalized net capital income." Second, they ground dark matter in processes that go beyond a simple bookkeeping exercise.

Hausmann and Sturzenegger claim dark matter has two major components that balance the U.S. books. They allot part of dark matter to a failure by the official trade statistics to adequately measure trade in services and insurance, which exaggerates the U.S. trade deficit and thus apparent borrowing. They, in effect, argue that the United States operates as a trusted financial intermediary that sells both insurance and financial services to the rest of the world. Just as a bank sells liquid assets (savings account deposits) to its customers, the United States sells liquid assets (Treasury debt and its ilk) to the rest of the world. Like a bank, the United States then turns around and lends long term to other customers and profits from the spread between its liquid liabilities and (relatively) illiquid assets. The insurance and security aspects of this deal exist because few countries would want to default on debt owed to U.S. banks or the United States, whereas many might hesitate less before defaulting on debt owed, say, to Paraguayan banks. Similarly, foreign depositors trust U.S. banks (and government securities) more than they trust their own banks and governments. Thus, they park their assets in the United States for insurance against inflation and expropriation.

This part of Hausmann and Sturzenegger's argument thus revives the 1966 Emile Despres, Charles Kindleberger, and Walter Salant argument that the United States is simply acting like a giant bank.[10] The disparity in the rates of return between foreign investment into the United States and outward U.S. investment reflects the normal working of the market for intermediation services—no institution or country would act as an intermediary if it did not make money doing so. There is undoubtedly some truth to this argument. But there are two major problems. First, other rich and presumably stable countries account for roughly 50 percent of U.S. foreign debt. As Barry Eichengreen has pointed out, Germany and Japan do not need intermediation.[11] While their markets are not as deep or liquid as that in the United States, the general trend has been increasing sophistication and depth in Europe. Yet this positive shift correlates with increasing flows into the United States and larger dollar-denominated reserve holdings rather than the expected diminution. Second, the bank analogy conceals as much as it reveals. The ability of banks to make money on the spread between deposits and loans depends heavily on political management of the maturity mismatch between short-term deposits and long-term investments. Without the political infrastructure of central banks and deposit insurance, intermediation usually results in bank runs and failures. And, as we know, banks often ration credit and allocate credit on nonmarket criteria. It is precisely these political factors that need explanation.

Hausmann and Sturzenegger's second major source of dark matter is the unmeasured market value of the better management of U.S. firms. This intangible technical knowledge and know-how is hard for the market to evaluate even though it does generate excess profits. Instead, it is captured in the reputation of firms and brands such as Disney and Coca Cola. Consequently, the market systematically undervalues U.S. firms. A lower stock market capitalization produces more, albeit imaginary, net foreign debt for the United States. Adding these notional amounts back in balances the U.S. books with the rest of the world on both a flow and stock basis. There is some truth to this argument (see chapter 5), but it is hardly reason to create notional assets to balance the books.

Cline's and Hausmann/Sturzenegger's claims are logically true. But accounting exercises do not move us to any complete understanding of either the political or economic dynamics of the situation. Hausmann and Sturzenegger do point us in the right direction by asking whether U.S. firms have some competitive advantage that the market does not capitalize. But as Eichengreen points out, arguing that official data on the current account and stock of debt are wrong based on the assumption that official data about net international investment income are right involves a little bit of hand waving.[12] The data, disaggregated to a lower level, provide a more robust way of supporting their arguments—and without having to invent assets. First, however, we must discover what the Marxists have to say about all this.

Anxious Marxists

What about the left? Surprisingly enough, not all economists on the left are anxious, despite their predilection for announcing crises. But it is true that sanguine Marxist arguments have to be teased out of the anxious ones and that, in general, most Marxists are anxious, in the sense of predicting a catastrophic drop in the value of the U.S. dollar and a corresponding drop in U.S. power. Like the neoclassicals, the Marxists have a blind spot. The labor theory of value causes many of them to focus too much on manufacturing and the physical location of manufacturing, and not enough on control over the stream of profit in the economy.

In addition, anxious Marxist or left analysts, such as Giovanni Arrighi and Peter Gowan, pay even less attention to the details behind the aggregated data they use, including the paradoxical net income flow, than do the sanguine neoclassicals. Anxious Marxists focus on the trade deficit and its associated accumulation as foreign debt. For them, trade deficits and foreign debt are simply a proxy indicator for "substantially diminished [U.S. manufacturing] competitiveness in the world economy" and thus for declining U.S. hegemony, which they see as flowing more or less directly from the material base of manufacturing supremacy.[13] Arrighi presents the clearest version of the anxious Marxist analysis, which turns out to be the mirror image of Ben Bernanke's sanguine neoclassical analysis. Whereas Bernanke's analysis rests on excess saving in Asia, Arrighi's rests on insufficient investment in manufacturing in the United States.

Arrighi's analysis rests on a suspect analogy between British and U.S. decline that nonetheless points to an important issue. Arrighi argues that British hegemony in the nineteenth century unraveled when Britain ceased to be a competitive manufacturer, missed the boat for new (twentieth-century) technologies, and instead shifted into unproductive financial activities. Capital that could not find productive manufacturing outlets at home spilled over into international markets. Arrighi states flatly that:

As in Britain's case at a comparable stage of relative decline, escalating US current-account deficits reflect a deterioration in the competitive position of American business at home and abroad. And as in Britain's case, though less successfully, US capital has partially countered this deterioration by specializing in global financial intermediation. Unlike Britain, however, the US has no territorial empire from which to extract the resources needed to retain its politico-military pre-eminence in an increasingly competitive world.[14]

Arrighi thus predicts an even quicker collapse of U.S. hegemony because the financialization of the U.S. economy is occurring without any apparent territorial cushion and because seignorage now yields not just diminishing but radically diminished returns. Indeed, from Arrighi's point of view, U.S. efforts to find a territorial cushion through adventurism in Iraq actually accelerate the erosion of the U.S. financial position through larger fiscal deficits and, thence, through larger interest payments to overseas creditors.[15] Unlike Britain, which could finance its deficits on the backs of colonial Indian taxpayers, Arrighi argues that the United States must compete in international capital markets for funds. The huge U.S. debt thus makes a financial and/or dollar crisis inevitable. Arrighi and Beverly Silver paint a quite dark picture of the consequences of financialization:

The global financial expansion of the last twenty years or so [1979–1999] is neither a new stage of world capitalism nor the harbinger of a "coming hegemony of global markets." Rather, it is the clearest sign that we are in the midst of a hegemonic crisis. As such, the expansion can be expected to be a temporary phenomenon that will end more or less catastrophically, depending on how the crisis is handled by the declining hegemon.[16]

But are this analogy and its conclusions correct? Arrighi's concern with manufacturing is important. The United States does ultimately need some way to validate at least part of the claims represented by U.S. net foreign debt. But Arrighi overstates U.S. decline (see chapter 5). Arrighi's argument rests on three points that are sensitive to the empirics: the U.S. economy is capital short; U.S. firms are not competitive; and, contrary to Veblen and Nitzan, industry trumps business. Each point is contestable (see chapter 5). U.S. investment rose throughout the long 1990s. U.S. firms remain competitive and have expanded their control over world output. Arrighi's counterfactual rests on the assumption that in the Veblenian duality of industry and business, industry matters more. But suppose that business—that is, control—matters more, as Veblen and Nitzan, the neo-Veblenian, assert? This would call into question the first half of the analysis. If British manufacturers had been able to transform their existing cash flow into control over nascent U.S. and German industry through FDI or passive equity stakes, the history of British decline would have been written differently.

For now, let me just point out the specific divergences from the British decline story. Not only has fixed-capital formation trended upward, but aggregate investment levels conceal increased investment in durable goods manufacturing (see chapter 4). At the same time, U.S. firms have expanded their control over production overseas, as well as creating new manufacturing capacity overseas. The huge U.S. foreign debt has financed this U.S. investment at home and abroad.

Because I pick up each theme later in later chapters, I briefly address here only the question of financialization because it leads directly to our last sort of analysis, the sanguine Marxist. Arrighi's analysis on its face seems somewhat contradictory with respect to its treatment of financialization. Britain retreated into financialization because it was capital rich and had no other domestic outlet for its funds; the United States has retreated into financialization because it is capital short and needs financing from overseas. And, in the end, it rests on the classical Marxist interpretation of finance as something that is epiphenomenal to the "real" world of manufacturing. But what if financialization is, instead, an indicator of state strength and U.S. hegemony? This is the thrust of the final set of arguments about the macroeconomic imbalance.

Sanguine Marxists

Leo Panitch and Sam Gindin provide the clearest version of the argument that financialization is an indicator of state strength and U.S. hegemony, although they too lack a detailed analysis and are sanguine and anxious in equal measures.[17] Panitch and Gindin are alarmist only because they think the political basis for U.S. hegemony is fragile. Like Bernanke, they argue that the United States is able to draw on a global pool of savings to cover its deficits. Unlike Arrighi, they do not think finance is an epiphenomenon.

Instead, Panitch and Gindin argue that U.S. hegemony has been rooted in control over finance, not manufacturing, for the past half century. Two assertions precisely capture their argument. First, they say that "the globalization of finance has included the *Americanization* of finance, and the deepening and extension of financial markets [have] become more than ever fundamental to both the reproduction and universalization of American power. It is with an American empire that has been materially strengthened rather than weakened by its financialization that we need to contend." Second, they directly contradict Arrighi, claiming that "to suggest, as Arrighi does, that because the holders of American Treasury bills are now primarily in Asia we are therefore witnessing a shift in the regional balance of power, is to confuse the distribution of assets with the distribution of power."[18] In the main, I agree with both points (however, as I show in chapter 5, there is a continued U.S. strength in manufacturing).

Panitch and Gindin thus connect financialization to U.S. power rather than U.S. decay. They argue that four features characterize U.S. hegemony.[19] First, unified global finance allows for the unfettered global operation of the law of value. Second, the U.S. state acts for all capital not just U.S. capital, superintending global accumulation. Third, the activities of the U.S. state (re-)structure the options available to other countries by aligning their interests with U.S. interests. And fourth, both the Keynesian welfare state and neoliberalism are part of the same process.

Panitch and Gindin are correct that financialization has strengthened U.S. hegemony, and they correctly link hegemony to an alignment of interests rather than abstract forms of power or arbitrary shares of manufacturing output. But their arguments have two weaknesses. First, they are too general; the devil really is in the details. Although it is easy enough to argue that the U.S. structures other countries' interests so that they are aligned with U.S. interests, what matters analytically and politically is precisely how those interests are aligned.[20] Because the specific connections between U.S. and overseas economies have changed over the past fifty years, the continuity that Panitch and Gindin assert between the Bretton Woods period and the current period is at best superficial. Although both are periods in which the world economy was capitalist, different specific logics of accumulation operate in each period. In the first Bretton Woods period, the link between productivity gains and wage gains generated new aggregate demand and growth; in the long 1990s, the combination of wage restraint and de-unionization opened a space for mortgage equity withdrawal to generate new aggregate demand. And although finance and financialization matter in both, it is how they matter that is important. In the first period, the United States was a net capital exporter; in the second period it was a net capital importer. The global operation of the law of value is nothing particularly new.

Second, as with other York University–style analyses, is it not clear why the global capitalist class should be united behind the U.S. state. The argument for a Karl Kautsky-esque ultra-imperialism needs to be proven rather than asserted. Global capitalist elites are just as likely to hold a range of interests that are sometimes conflicting and sometimes complementary to those of U.S. elites. What precisely binds at least some, if not all, economic and political elites to a U.S.-centered project of global accumulation?

Next, I analyze partially disaggregated foreign investment flows to show that U.S. global financial arbitrage works and to show more precisely where Panitch and Gindin are right and wrong. Later, in chapter 3, I expand this analysis to show the different forms of economic attachment to the United States by breaking the rich countries up into two broad camps with differing degrees of attachment to the United States. And in chapter 4, I show the real-economy benefits of financialization.

A More Political Argument: Dooley, Folkerts-Landau, and Garber and Bretton Woods 2

What about more explicitly political arguments? And what about developing countries? Dooley, Folkerts-Landau, and Garber (DFG) have articulated a political version of the "Asia is responsible" argument in a series of papers.[21] They argue that the current imbalance reflects a new political deal akin to that which underpinned the first Bretton Woods arrangement of 1944–1971. They argue that the current Bretton Woods system largely links the United States and developing Asia rather than the United States and developed Europe. But the basic structure of political exchange resembles the original one. On the one side, a set of developing countries willingly undervalues its currencies and ties them to the dollar to enjoy development-generating export surpluses that provide the current account surpluses needed to credibly back up their peg against the dollar. On the other side, the United States enjoys an overvalued dollar and the additional consumption that this makes possible but at the cost of some hollowing out of the manufacturing sector and a buildup of future claims on the U.S. economy as U.S. current account deficits cumulate as foreign debt.

The Asian accumulation of claims on the United States is risky. If Asian currencies rise against the dollar, their holdings of U.S. assets create capital losses for them. China now holds about $1.7 trillion in U.S. dollar assets, so these losses are not negligible. DFG argue that Asian access to U.S. markets makes the long-term risk of dollar devaluation worthwhile because it is the only way for Asia to absorb the billion or so people that need to leave agriculture for industry and it is the only way to create the physical plant corresponding to that new manufacturing population. A modern economy, capable of delivering continued income growth, is a reasonable prize to exchange for once-only capital losses incurred from currency manipulation. Thus, DFG are sanguine about Bretton Woods 2. China is the single largest exporter and holder of U.S. debt in developing Asia and the bulk of the poor agricultural population of Asia lives in China. DFG predict that the current Chinese-driven accumulation of U.S. dollar assets can continue for a decade as China absorbs its overhang of rural labor. Moreover, they argue that China has bought political insurance against a closure of the U.S. market both through its holdings of U.S. government securities and its relative openness to FDI, which in effect promises U.S. firms a share of future Chinese growth.

The DFG argument suffers from three problems. First, despite being political, it employs a typical economist "as if" argument. As Barry Eichengreen and, separately, Nouriel Roubini and Brad Setser have noted, the original Bretton Woods agreement and later political deals in support of that accord (e.g., the 1961 Gold Pool and 1967 Two Tier Market) involved an explicit political deal between the United States and Europe. There is no explicit deal between the United States and China about exchanging market access, dollar stability, and FDI.[22] Roubini and Setser also argue that Bretton Woods 2 only really makes sense as a stylization of the international economy in 2000–2007, suggesting limits to its durability.

Second, DFG's argument necessarily involves a consideration of the motives of the primary and secondary players who hold the other 75 percent of U.S. foreign debt, but DFG do not provide such an analysis. Japan, for example, does not have an overhang of rural labor that needs to be absorbed, and the key oil exporters are short of labor. Finally, the end game in DFG is unclear. The overhang of Chinese-held U.S. securities has future value only to the extent that China or East Asia uses it to import U.S. dollar-denominated goods in the future. Inevitably, that means much greater imports of U.S.-produced goods. Yet these imports—except perhaps for cultural goods—are likely to be in high-value, high-technology sectors targeted by the Chinese and some East Asian states for growth and thus are likely to be protected from international competition. One of the most important U.S. exports is civilian aircraft. China imports about $6 billion worth of aircraft annually from Europe and the United States and is estimated to need around 1,500–1,800 new aircraft in the next fifteen years. Yet the Chinese government is determined to create its own civil airframe manufacturing capacity and has bludgeoned Airbus into building a factory to assemble A320s in Tianjin.[23]

The DFG model thus implicitly aggregates too much in its political departure from vanilla neoclassical economics. Rather than assuming that individual behavior explains everything, DFG have pushed market actors aside in favor of unitary states. Although it is true that states and central banks wield considerable power in global capital markets, elite behavior strongly conditions what states do. This suggests that we look at the specific forms that U.S. foreign debt takes and at who owns what.

First, however, it is worth recapping what we have learned from the arguments so far in order to better understand the disaggregation below. Bernanke's analysis suggests a natural transfer of savings from an overly thrifty Asia to the United States. But it cannot explain why Asians consume so little nor why the United States grows enough to absorb those exports. DFG make a compelling political argument about the deliberate recycling of Asian trade surpluses into U.S. Treasury bonds and other forms of debt but likewise without any explanation of U.S. growth. Arrighi shows the need to really track down what U.S. firms are doing and whether those firms are indeed increasing productivity and output while retaining Veblenian control. And Panitch and Gindin suggest that we look closely at the connections between investment flows, the alignment of U.S. and non-U.S. interests, and the political bases for and against U.S. hegemony. Despite their flaws, each argument will help us make sense of the data we uncover next and in chapter 3.

U.S. Global Financial Arbitrage—a First Cut

Recall that we started with the same paradox as Cline and Hausmann/Sturzenegger: the United States has enjoyed a continued net positive flow of international investment income despite being a net international debtor. Understanding why fills in the missing elements in Bernanke's analysis and the unexplained assumptions in DFG's analysis. Huge differences in the choice of investment vehicles explain the continued flow of income into the United States. Put simply, disaggregating gross investment shows that U.S. investors behave as if they were from Mars, insouciantly choosing longer-term, higher-risk, higher-return investment vehicles; meanwhile, foreign investors behave as if they were from Venus, choosing shorter-term, low-risk, low-return investment vehicles. This is the essence of U.S. financial arbitrage in global markets.

Natural psychological differences between Americans and others do not cause this behavioral difference. The political structuring of financial markets makes insouciance possible. U.S. arbitrage is a *mechanism* for producing differential growth rather than simply a complicated form of seignorage. Seignorage simply takes advantage of the omnipresence of the U.S. dollar in global transactions and of people's willingness to hold U.S. currency, despite a lack of return on physical currency. U.S. financial arbitrage is at the heart of processes that produce a durable alignment of the interests of *some* foreign elites with the interests of some U.S. elites and the U.S. mass public largely to the benefit of those U.S. elites. The details of U.S. arbitrage show that U.S. power does not operate uniformly, as Panitch and Gindin seem to assert.

In the remaining part of this chapter, I partially disaggregate the international investment data to establish U.S. arbitrage in international financial markets. The disaggregation is partial because I treat the rest of the world as one homogenous unit. In chapter 3, I then disaggregate the rest of the world to show that there are four distinct groups of countries holding four different kinds of stakes in the U.S. economy as well as in the U.S. system of arbitrage. The partial disaggregation here shows that U.S. investments are generally in longer-term, higher-return venues. Second, even within specific types of investment venue, U.S. investments tend to be longer term and higher return. Overall, U.S. holdings are disproportionately invested in FDI, whereas foreign holdings are disproportionately passive instruments such as bonds. But even within passive instruments, U.S. holdings are disproportionately long-term corporate bonds, whereas foreign holdings are disproportionately short-term government securities. This creates superior aggregate returns for U.S. international investment, despite the huge U.S. net international debt. The concentration of foreign holdings in passive portfolio debt, and particularly U.S. Treasury and agency bonds, helps power U.S. differential growth at home and expansion by U.S. MNCs abroad.

U.S. Martians, Foreign Venusians

Table 2.2 breaks foreign investment into and out of the United States into four broad categories: FDI, portfolio equity holdings, bonds (portfolio debt), and loans.[24] I do not consider derivatives here because they are simply too opaque, because they essentially net out, and because there is no rate-of-return information on them. The reader should recall that FDI involves the establishment of an overseas subsidiary by a parent company that retains operational control over that subsidiary. Operational control means that not only does the parent retain control over profits but also that it is able to influence the level of profitability by changing production practices and markets. Portfolio holdings of corporate stock, or equity, do not convey control, where control is arbitrarily defined by a 10 or 20 percent threshold;

TABLE 2.2.
Relative share of FDI, portfolio equities, portfolio debt, and loans in international holdings, year end 2007

	FDI[a]	Portfolio Equities	Portfolio Debt[b]	Loans	Total
A. In billions of dollars					
United States	5,148	5,171	1,478	5,002	18,615
Rest of world	3,524	2,833	6,965	5,387	19,810
Central banks			2,931	406	3,307
B. In percentage of shares					
United States	27.7	27.8	7.9	26.9	100.0
Rest of world	17.8	14.3	35.2	27.2	100.0
Central banks			88.6	12.3	16.7

Source: Bureau of Economic Analysis, *International Investment Position,* available at: http://www.bea.gov/international/index.htm#iip.
  Notes: FDI, foreign direct investment.
  [a] Market valuation.
  [b] Omits trivial U.S. holdings of currency and foreign holdings of U.S. currency totaling $279 billion.

I use the U.S. Department of Commerce 10 percent threshold here. Portfolio equity holdings return dividends and capital gains to owners. These shares are often, but not always, held by individuals through unit trusts or mutual funds. Bonds are best thought of as loans that do not involve a bank—the owners of bonds loan money to firms or governments in exchange for interest payments and the return of their cash when the bond matures. Bonds do not convey control, although bonds are often contracted with covenants that bind the borrower's future behavior. Finally, loans are made by banks in return for interest and the ultimate return of principal. Loans also do not convey control, aside from covenants set forth in the loan document. The reasons for stressing operational or active control should be evident from the previous chapter.

Aside from the obvious net U.S. debt position, what emerges from this first cut is the active versus passive distinction previously noted. Americans investing overseas take riskier positions than foreigners investing into the United States, given that equities in general are more risky than bonds. Approximately three-fifths of U.S. overseas assets take the form of FDI and holdings of equities (stocks in U.S. parlance). These holdings have the potential for capital appreciation and for the capture of profits if firms are well managed. By contrast, over three-fifths of foreign investment in U.S. assets is in the form of passive holdings of bonds and loans. Neither has the potential to capture the benefits of growth in the form of increased profits or the capitalization of that growth in profits. But this broad aggregation conceals similar disparities in the appetite for risk and reward that exist at every level in every instrument.

Why do U.S. and foreign investors hold substantially different passive investment portfolios? Perhaps these different general and, especially, passive investment patterns reflect the assets available to investors seeking to diversify overseas. Perhaps foreigners largely invest in bonds and especially in government bonds because that is all that is for sale in U.S. securities markets. And perhaps U.S. investors' equity-heavy foreign portfolios reflect shallow bond markets and deep equity pools overseas. In fact, the reverse is true. Investors on both sides of the equation buy the *scarcer* overseas asset when they enter foreign markets. Table 2.3 compares the distribution of foreign investment in the United States to a neutral basket from the U.S. market, and table 2.4 compares U.S. investment overseas to the pool of globally available securities, using data from 2004 and 2006 (there is a lack of comparable data for 2007). Table 2.3 shows that foreign investment is grossly overweight in U.S. bonds relative to a neutral basket of U.S. securities. Foreigners hold 16.6 percent of all U.S. securities by market value, but they hold over one-half of all marketable Treasuries, more than three times foreign investors' overall share of U.S. securities. By contrast, they only hold 10.2 percent of U.S. equities, which is one-third lower than their overall share of marketable U.S. securities. These imbalances show why overseas investment is not a purely natural market phenomenon or simple intermediation.

TABLE 2.3.
U.S. market available to foreigners: Asset composition of U.S. securities markets, 2006

	Total Market	Equities	Marketable Treasury Debt	Agency Debt[a]	Corporate Debt
Market value at June 2006 (billions of dollars)	43,074	23,760	3,321	5,709	10,284
Neutral weight (%)	(100)	55.2	7.7	13.3	23.9
Foreign weight (%)	(100)	33.9	24.1	13.7	28.2
Memo 1: Foreign share of outstanding U.S. securities (%)	16.6	10.2	52.0	17.2	19.7
Memo 2: Foreign official (central bank) share of foreign holdings of U.S. securities (%)	27.9	8.8	70.2	48.1	4.8
Memo 3: Foreign official share of outstanding U.S. securities (%) (Memo 1 × Memo 2)	4.3	1.1	19.5	2.3	0.4

Source: Data from U.S. Treasury, *Report on Foreign Portfolio Holdings of US Securities, June 2007* (Washington, D.C.: U.S. Treasury Department, June 2008), 8, 13.
Notes: Excludes assets of commercial banks.
[a]Fannie Mae and Freddie Mac the issuers of mortgage-backed securities.

Table 2.4 presents a similar table for foreign markets for 2004 and 2006, although with less detail; 2004 is the last year for which there are data breaking out U.S. overseas holdings of public versus private debt. Table 2.4 shows that U.S. investors behave abroad just as they behave at home. U.S. investors' foreign equity holdings occupy a disproportionate share of their investment overseas, just as U.S. public debt looms large in foreign investors' holdings. U.S. investors overseas appear to hold approximately 13.8 percent of the shares available in the rest of the world, nearly double their 8.2 percent share of all vehicles. U.S. equity holdings overseas thus represent a disproportionate stake in real productive activity by U.S. investors compared to a neutral pool of assets. Meanwhile, relatively speaking, and at least until 2004, U.S. investors exhibited a greater willingness to hold higher-yielding—and riskier—private debt rather than public debt compared to foreign investors in the United States. Indeed, U.S. investors appear to have a positive distaste for public debt that mirrors foreigners' distaste for U.S. equities.

So, the disparity in U.S. and foreign appetites for investment risk overseas does not reflect differences in what is for sale in various markets. In fact, the reverse is true—although both U.S. and foreign investors obtain *geographical* diversification through overseas investment, they do not pursue diversification with respect to the kind of investment vehicles they hold. U.S. investors come from an equity-rich market, yet buy even more equities when abroad; foreign investors come from a debt-rich environment, yet buy more debt when they go to the United States. In the aggregate, foreign investors in U.S. debt securities thus subsidize U.S. purchases of their equities, trading capital gains and possibly corporate control for income.

TABLE 2.4.
Market available to Americans: Asset composition of the world securities market, net of U.S. securities, 2004 and 2006

	Total Market	Equities	Public Debt	Private Debt
Value in 2004 (billions of dollars)	56,267	20,845	17,536	17,886
Neutral weights (%)	(100)	37.0	31.2	31.8
U.S. investors' weights (%)	(100)	67.6	9.6	22.8
Memo: U.S. share of outstanding foreign securities (%)	6.7	12.3	2.1	4.8
	Total Market	Equities	All Debt, Public and Private	
Value in 2006 (billions of dollars)	73,256	31,258	41,998	
Neutral weights (%)	(100)	42.7	57.3	
U.S. investors' weights (%)	(100)	72.3	27.7	
Memo: U.S. share of outstanding foreign securities (%)	8.2	13.8	4.0	

Source: Data from International Monetary Fund (IMF), Global Financial Stability Report (Washington, D.C.: IMF, September 2005), 117; IMF, Global Financial Stability Report (Washington, D.C.: IMF, September 2007), 138; U.S. Treasury, Report on US Holdings of Foreign Securities December 2006 (Washington, D.C.: U.S. Treasury Department, 2007), 3, 13.
   Notes: Excluding all U.S. securities and assets of commercial banks.

The same is true for FDI into the United States. Let us examine each category of investment in turn to see why.

Portfolio Investment in Equities and Bonds

The Mars–Venus dichotomy that produces stable but low returns for foreign investors and larger returns for U.S. investors repeats itself even when we look inside each of our four major vehicles for investment. Table 2.5 displays the different patterns of U.S. and foreign passive portfolio investment in 2006. As already noted, U.S. passive investors overseas have over three-quarters of their money in equities, which yield both dividends and capital appreciation. Foreign investors have almost three-quarters of their passive bets in U.S. bonds, which yield low fixed rates of interest. Consequently, a much larger volume of foreign passive investment into the United States does not generate a proportionally larger volume of income compared to the much smaller volume of U.S. passive holdings overseas. U.S. portfolio holdings generated $235 billion in earnings in 2005 and, as interest rates rose, $444 billion by 2007.[25] By contrast, foreign portfolio holdings generated $332 billion in 2005 and $591.5 billion by 2007. The ratio of U.S. to foreign holdings is thus approximately 0.68, whereas the ratio of U.S. income to foreigners' income is 0.74, showing that U.S. passive investments overseas outperform foreign investment in the United States. These ratios understate the degree of underperformance by foreign portfolio holdings because U.S. portfolio equity holdings generate not only the dividend income captured in these ratios but also typically larger capital gains than do bonds over the

TABLE 2.5.
Relative share of equities and debt in portfolio holdings, December 2006

	Equities (%)	Debt[a] (%)	Value (billions of dollars)	Ratio of U.S. to Foreign Holdings
United States to rest of world	78.3	21.7	5,432	
Rest of world into United States	31.9	68.1	7,946	0.683
U.S. government obligations			2,699	
U.S. portfolio income	n/a	n/a	351.3	
Rest-of-world portfolio income	n/a	n/a	474.1	0.741
From U.S. government obligations			135	

Source: Bureau of Economic Aanalysis, "International Investment Position; International Transactions," http://www.bea.gov.
Note: n/a, not available.
[a]Includes corporate and government bonds, not loans.

long run, and these gains are not captured in these figures. The asymmetry in the *form* that portfolio investment takes (equities vs. debt) accounts for only part of the difference in returns. The share of long-term securities in U.S. overseas holdings tends to be slightly higher than for foreign holdings of U.S. bonds.[26]

Finally, an asymmetry in the specific vehicles used for investment in bonds also reduces foreigners' returns. Sixty percent of foreign investment in U.S. bonds as of December 2005 occurred as purchases of U.S. government and government-sponsored agency (e.g., Fannie Mae and Freddie Mac) debt.[27] Because government debt is theoretically the least risky form of investment with respect to default and because investors believe this to be true of agency debt as well, these investments of course yield the lowest possible interest rate. By contrast, only 30 percent of U.S. investors' bond holdings in December 2004 were the public debt of foreign countries. Instead, U.S. investors primarily held foreign corporate bonds, whose higher risks yield higher returns.[28]

Nonetheless, the United States ends up with a net negative outflow on portfolio holdings because of the enormous net difference in holdings. Indeed, the net difference in income flows is almost entirely attributable to interest on U.S. Treasury and agency bonds. And these bonds are largely in the hands of foreign central banks. This is why we could say even more pointedly that, in the aggregate, it is not just foreign investors in U.S. debt securities that subsidize U.S. purchases of their equities, trading capital gains and possibly corporate control for income, but also foreign states that do so, much as DFG argue. What offsets this outflow? The net U.S. international investment income comes almost entirely from the huge difference in the scale of and returns on FDI.

Direct Investment

Foreign portfolio investors use vehicles that generate low fixed-interest returns, degrading their returns relative to similar U.S. investment overseas. But what about foreign firms that invest directly in the United States and thus control their own operations? For the sake of clarity, I follow here the U.S. government convention, calling U.S. (foreign) direct investment abroad USDIA and calling inward foreign direct investment into the United States FDIUS. USDIA is absolutely and relatively larger than FDI into the United States, so it would not be surprising if the United States earned a bit more from USDIA than foreigners did from FDIUS. In fact, however, USDIA earns disproportionately more than FDIUS. In 2005, USDIA generated $151 billion in net income; in 2007, that jumped up to $234 billion, despite the phasing out of a tax credit encouraging profit repatriation. Despite any incomparability introduced by U.S. tax policy, over the past four years payments to foreign investors typically equaled approximately 40 percent of inward income, even though FDIUS was 75 percent of USDIA at current cost valuation and 70 percent at market valuation.

This disparity in rates of return is central to the net income paradox. Although U.S. passive investment is slightly more lucrative than foreigners' passive investment, the huge disparity in the absolute volumes of passive foreign investment overwhelms superior U.S. returns per dollar invested. The United States still runs a deficit on passive income of $101 billion and $165 billion in 2005 and 2007, respectively, because of the net $2.5 trillion debt. But, as the previous paragraph shows, this is not true for FDI. Earnings from USDIA more than offset the passive deficit. A U.S. Bureau of Economic Analysis (BEA) analysis of the data for the 1990s shows that the 11 percent return on assets (ROA) obtained by U.S. firms from foreign operations was on average 6 percentage points higher than the average rate of ROA for foreign FDI into the United States.[29] Aside from a steep fall associated with the first few years of the Latin American debt crisis of the 1980s, this proportion has been fairly consistent from 1960 to the present. Moreover, as Gerard Dumenil and Dominique Levy have pointed out, the superior performance of U.S. firms overseas is central both to the U.S. balance of payments and to the profitability of U.S. firms. The overseas profits of U.S. firms account for roughly 25 percent of all profits for U.S. nonfinancial firms.[30]

By contrast, foreign firms doing FDIUS (as opposed to simply exporting to the U.S. market) earned an average 5.1 percent ROA in 1988–1997. This ROA was 2 percentage points lower than the corresponding average ROA for U.S.-owned firms operating in the U.S. economy during that decade, although the gap narrowed to only 1 percentage point by 1997. This weaker foreign ROA was not a statistical artifact caused by weak performance in a few sectors; a few sectors, such as transportation equipment (primarily cars) overperformed. But foreign firms are invested in almost all sectors of the U.S. economy and generated below-average ROAs in two-thirds of all sectors in which they had investments. What explains this startling disparity?

Daniel Gros makes a case that is exactly opposite to that advanced by Hausmann and Sturzenegger and by Cline.[31] He argues that, rather than U.S. liabilities being much smaller than the data suggest, they are larger by $2.7 trillion. This suggests a net U.S. foreign debt on the order of 35 percent of GDP. Gros argues that it is implausible that foreigners would systematically invest via FDI at a rate of return of approximately 2.5 percent in 1999–2005 when portfolio investment in the United States could yield them 5 or 5.15 percent per year.[32] Yet this is what the data on reported and repatriated profits on FDIUS suggest. Gros argues that the efforts of foreign MNCs to dodge taxes by shifting profits through transfer pricing does not create this anomaly. This concurs with the official U.S. government position, as represented by BEA studies, that the weak foreign ROA is apparently not a function of transfer pricing shifting profits out of the United States.[33]

Gros, instead, argues that foreign firms in the United States systematically underreport reinvested earnings for straightforward tax purposes because corporate taxes in the United States are higher than those in Europe. Conversely, U.S. firms are not taxed by the United States on their overseas profits until they repatriate those profits (and sometimes not even then). This leads U.S. firms to overreport their reinvested earnings overseas. Because the BEA calculates reinvestment using the behavior of U.S. firms, it biases its calculation of reinvestment in favor of those U.S. firms. The underreporting of foreign firms lowers the estimates of U.S. liabilities because reinvestment appears to be lower and because the U.S. current account, which includes reinvested earnings, appears to be approximately $100 billion, or 1 percent of GDP, lower than it actually is. Gros also argues that foreign holdings of real estate are not captured in the U.S. official data because there is no reporting requirement for most of these holdings.[34] Similarly, foreign holders of U.S. bonds might prefer non-U.S. custodians to avoid U.S. withholding taxes. In effect, Gros is saying that it is the rest of the world that has dark matter, not the United States, and that things are considerably worse than the U.S. statistics suggest.

Still, it is equally implausible that in the aggregate U.S. firms overseas have lower returns than foreign firms in the United States. The average ROA for all U.S. firms includes domestic U.S. firms as well as those with USDIA. Mathematically, reducing the contribution of USDIA to that average ROA implies increasing the ROA of the domestic firms. This still leaves FDIUS at a disadvantage in terms of return—they underperform U.S. firms in the U.S. market. And even Gros admits that U.S. firms abroad have higher rates of return than FDIUS.[35] So why does USDIA abroad generate disproportionately high returns compared to FDIUS?

Clues to the origins of the disparity in ROAs can be found in the different performances turned in by firms with different market shares. Most foreign firms control less than 20 percent of the U.S. market in their respective sector, and these account for the bulk of the subpar ROAs. By contrast, the handful of foreign firms with market shares above 30 percent had ROAs that matched the average for U.S. nonfinancial firms. Put simply, foreign firms operating in the United States were able to generate reasonable returns only when they had enough of a competitive advantage to establish a securely oligopolistic position in the U.S. market. Looking at foreign firms by industrial sector reinforces this conclusion. By 1997, foreign firms in the motor vehicle and equipment sector—which includes stellar, best-in-class manufacturers such as Toyota and Honda—had ROAs above their U.S. competitors. But foreign firms generated below-average ROAs in a broad array of other industrial sectors and particularly in service sectors, where the gap was over 4 percentage points.[36]

Standard economic theory argues that firms establish foreign subsidiaries only when they possess some production or technological advantage strong enough to overcome the additional costs of coordination at a distance and of operating in a foreign environment, compared with simply exporting from their home market.[37] The below-average ROA of foreign firms indicates that on average these firms do not possess any overwhelming competitive advantage; instead, it suggests the operation of one or all of four possible motivations for investment in the United States.

1. Foreign firms may accept returns from FDI that are below average because they feel they cannot be a globally competitive firm unless they are operating in the U.S. market, which accounts for approximately one-quarter of global GDP and a larger share of global growth in the long 1990s. Giving up on the U.S. market means surrendering a huge market of fairly sophisticated consumers to U.S.-based competitors and other non-U.S. firms that are willing to accept below-average ROAs.

2. Firms may invest in the United States to hedge against the risks of exchange rate shifts that make exporting unprofitable, although it is not clear why this risk could not be hedged through financial instruments rather than direct investment. Although both involve costs, surely the cost of establishing a full-fledged manufacturing subsidiary exceeds the cost of hedging, given how liquid foreign exchange futures markets are.

3. Foreign firms may hedge against a protectionist Congress by locating production in the United States.[38]

4. Foreign firms may find that their low ROAs in the United States may still be higher than the ROAs on their home market operations.

A lack of broader comparable ROA data makes it difficult to assess the importance of the fourth motivation, although many commentators allege that capital productivity is somewhat lower in Europe than in the United States. But the first two motivations imply that foreign firms are willing to pay a "tax" to get into the U.S. market, where the "tax" is their inferior ROAs compared to those of U.S. firms.

By the same token, the disparity in income from FDI suggests that U.S. firms in foreign markets are disproportionately profitable because their ROA is 6 percentage points higher than the average ROA for U.S. firms in the U.S. market. How can this be? It could only be if U.S. firms were exploiting new sectors of the economy in which competition was limited or in which they controlled new proprietary technology or (patentable/copyrightable/manageable) information that yielded superior returns, somewhat as Hausmann and Sturzenegger argue. It is mathematically *not* the case that higher profitability for USDIA rests on the exploitation of seriously low-wage labor (e.g., in China) because the bulk of USDIA goes to high-wage countries. Although USDIA in China returned almost double the income per dollar invested globally (18 vs. 9 percent in 2001–2005), USDIA in China amounted to less than 1 percent of USDIA in 2005.[39]

Although U.S. firms account for a huge share of Chinese exports, little of this is FDI. Most, instead, is simply sourcing from China à la Wal-Mart. Although foreign firms produce roughly two-thirds of Chinese exports, most of these foreign firms are not U.S. based. Rather, they are Taiwanese, Hong Kong, and other overseas Chinese firms (indeed, many may be Chinese firms dodging local taxes). Wal-Mart, which accounts for approximately 10 percent of all Chinese exports to the United States, subcontracts production to Chinese and foreign firms.

The contrast in ROA generated by foreign firms operating in the United States and by U.S. firms operating overseas suggests that, as with portfolio investment, the United States arbitrages between low-cost borrowing from overseas and high-return investment overseas. Foreign inflows into the United States break the normal constraints governing domestic investment, consumption, and overseas investment and make it possible for the United States to export capital that earns returns superior to those available in the U.S. market. Foreign firms invest in low-profitability niches in the U.S. economy, whereas U.S. firms occupy higher-yielding ones both at home and abroad. We return to both issues in chapters 4 and 5. For now, however, we must consider our fourth and last category of investment flows, loans.

The Pure Carry Trade

What about bank lending, our last category? Although loans do not add too much to U.S. foreign debt on a net basis, the flow of lending into and out of the United States is extremely profitable for U.S. banks and hedge funds. These banks and hedge funds engage in a carry trade. The carry trade adds slightly to net income flows for the U.S. economy. More important, it helps assure that the U.S. economy remains one of the most economically dynamic, rich economies (see chapter 4).

In a carry trade, a bank or other financial intermediary borrows short term at low interest rates in one market and then relends the money long term at higher interest rates in a second market. This can occur in one currency or in two. Typically in the 1990s and 2000s, U.S. banks borrowed yen at trivial interest rates in Japan, converted those yen into dollars, and then relent the money in the U.S. mortgage market or, somewhat less frequently, to third-world borrowers. The yen carry trade was profitable—assuming stable exchange rates—because yen-based interest rates in the 2000s were around 0.25 percent. In the major destinations for the carry trade, interest rates were much higher, between 3 and 5.25 percent for U.S. dollar mortgage debt, around 6.35 percent for Australian dollar debt, and 8 percent for New Zealand dollar debt. In some cases, traders were apparently borrowing in yen to buy Brazilian *real*-denominated debt yielding 12.5 percent.[40] Banks could arbitrage between these different interest rates, coining money on the difference between their cost of borrowing and their price for lending money. Estimates of the scale of the yen carry trade vary enormously, from an annual low of $150 billion to a high of $1 trillion.[41]

The carry trade, combined with the more general absorption of dollars by Asian central banks, helped drive down interest rates on U.S. mortgages during the 1990s, enabling U.S. homeowners to refinance almost $1 trillion of mortgage debt annually. In turn, this allowed U.S. consumers to substitute low-interest and tax-favored mortgage payments for higher-interest credit card debt even as they considerably increased their consumption. The best estimates suggest that Asian central bank purchases of dollar-denominated securities (one counterpart of the borrowing of yen by U.S. banks for carry purposes) depressed yields on the benchmark ten-year U.S. Treasury note by about 100 basis points, or 1 percentage point.[42]

The carry trade may look like getting money for nothing, but the kicks are not for free. The carry trade involves two huge risks in addition to the usual credit and interest rate risks. The first is a maturity mismatch, and the second is exchange rate risk. The maturity mismatch in the carry trade occurs because banks are borrowing on a short-term basis and then lending out money on a long-term basis. If the short-term Japanese lender to the U.S. bank suddenly needs its money back and declines to roll the loan over to the U.S. financial intermediary, then that intermediary will have to find cash to liquidate its liability to the short-term Japanese lender. But banks that have transformed the borrowed yen into dollar-denominated mortgages or commercial loans in the United States cannot suddenly liquidate those loans in order to return capital to their own creditors. Calling in long-term loans is often legally and practically difficult, if not impossible, because long-term debt is typically used to purchase fixed or specific assets. The final borrower, a homeowner or industrial firm perhaps, would not contract for a mortgage that could be called in arbitrarily and without cause. Moreover, an intermediary bank that calls in a long-term loan to meet short-term obligations risks forcing the long-term borrower to liquidate at fire-sale prices, which reduces the ability of the bank to recover its principal anyway. The carry trade also exposes the intermediary U.S. bank to the risk of unfavorable exchange rate shifts. If the yen were to rise against the dollar in our example, the intermediary would find itself having to use many more dollars to pay interest on its yen-denominated loan, as well as many more dollars to repay the principal.

Readers who know something about the 1997–1998 Asian financial crises have already noticed that Southeast Asian banks engaged in precisely the kind of dual-risk carry trade just described; alert readers will recognize the germ of the current financial crisis. Southeast Asian banks borrowed dollars short term at low interest rates from Japanese and European banks. They then turned around and made long-term domestic currency loans to local borrowers investing mostly in property and, somewhat less so, in manufacturing. These banks found themselves bankrupt when both the maturity and currency bets went against them. Foreign banks refused to roll over short-term loans, and local currencies were devalued against the dollar. Southeast Asian banks found it nearly impossible to liquidate their long-term loans to local clients, and even when they did, the local currency they realized was often worth only half the dollars they needed to pay their own creditors. Southeast Asian economies paid an enormous price for the willingness of their banks to speculate on a carry trade. How then can U.S. banks and nonbank financial intermediaries take on these risks with such insouciance? What, if anything, makes them different from the banks in Southeast Asia?

Political realities, in the form of the U.S. Federal Reserve (the Fed), Bank of Japan, and People's Bank of China protect U.S. banks from their risks. On the one side, the Fed is the ultimate guarantor that maturity mismatch will not bring down U.S. banks. Under Alan Greenspan, the Fed consistently showed that it would flood the banking system with liquidity to bail U.S. banks out from their errors. After the early 1990s saving-and-loans debacle, the Fed drove short-term interest rates down 500 basis points (5 percentage points) in 1990–1993; after the 1997–1998 Asian financial crisis, the Fed drove short-term interest rates down another 340 basis points in 1998–2002. Under Bernanke, the Fed has gone to extreme lengths to save U.S. banks from their bad bets.

On the other side, the Bank of Japan and more recently the People's Bank of China have defended U.S. banks against their currency risks, although not out of any love for U.S. banks. Since 1990, the Japanese economy has largely depended on exports either to the United States or to China (and, even then, capital goods exports to China often create factories that sell product in the United States) to create economic growth. A rising yen would have put many Japanese firms out of business at a time when the Japanese economy was already suffering from deflation and slow growth. Consequently, the Bank of Japan has heavily intervened every time the yen has started to rise against the dollar. An exchange rate of ¥105 per dollar has been a traditional trigger point because the break-even point for Japanese exporters was ¥110 per dollar in the late 1990s. In 2003 and early 2004, the Bank of Japan sold around $200 billion worth of yen to buy dollars, helping to drive Japanese holdings of dollar-denominated securities to over $700 billion and keeping the yen at ¥105 per dollar. Until 2008 the yen traded in the ¥120 per dollar range.

By the same token, the carry trade itself helps keep the yen weak. U.S. borrowers of yen must sell those borrowed yen for the dollars that they will relend in the U.S. economy. So, U.S. banks have asymmetric risks. If the yen weakens against the dollar, they reap extra profits by using strong dollars to buy cheap yen to repay their creditors; if the dollar weakens against the yen, threatening U.S. banks with foreign exchange losses, intervention by the Bank of Japan shields banks from those losses. Although China is not a source of cheap money for U.S. banks, Chinese efforts to hold the renminbi at a favorable exchange rate with the dollar also prevent the dollar from falling against the yen.[43]

This chapter starts by noting both a problem and a paradox at the heart of our investigation of U.S. global economic power. On the one hand, net U.S. foreign debt has grown more or less continuously since the late 1980s. On the other hand, the United States has equally consistently had net international investment income and in the long 1990s consistently outgrew most of the other developed countries. What does this tension between net debt and net positive investment income mean? How have massive capital inflows permitted the United States to escape the normal constraints on consumption, investment at home, and investment abroad?

In the first half of this chapter, I have looked at different analyses of this problem and paradox. Analyses of the large net U.S. foreign debt, whether Marxist or neo-classical in their analytic orientation, are divided about the long-term implications of that debt. Some are immediately alarmed, but others are more sanguine. At the same time, the different methodological orientations naturally establish different analytic foci. Some Marxists want to find a crisis of U.S. hegemony looming in the alleged decline of U.S. manufacturing, whereas others appreciate the political and economic importance of huge capital flows into the United States. The neoclassicals, meanwhile, can only parse the paradox using accounting identities, which then produce vague policy recommendations. If by definition current account deficits are the result of low levels of domestic savings, then by definition savings must increase to eliminate the deficit. Alternately, if by definition capital income must derive from a capital asset, then by definition net positive U.S. investment income implies a net positive asset position, not net debt. But all these analyses rely on aggregate data, which hinders their appreciation of the actual dynamics of the situation. None connects the data to U.S. differential growth because all the analyses focus too much on the apparent use of borrowed money for consumption and assume that consumption has no secondary effects.

Thus in the second half of the chapter, I have partially disaggregated the stock of debt and corresponding flows of income to better understand those dynamics. This disaggregation showed that the United States benefited from a massive system of financial arbitrage in which the United States borrowed short term and with low returns from the rest of the world and then invested funds back into the rest of the world long term and with high returns. Each class of asset shows this pattern, although it is most extreme for FDI. This initial disaggregation raises two obvious questions, both central to the issue of U.S. power, that suggest a need for further disaggregation. First, why does the rest of the world tolerate this situation, which after all promotes U.S. differential accumulation to their detriment? And, second, what explains the huge difference in rate of return on FDI?

The next chapter presents a partial answer to the first question by continuing the disaggregation of the U.S. balance sheet. This disaggregation shows that U.S. creditors have different forms of exposure to the U.S. market, which leads them into different political stances with respect to U.S. financial arbitrage and U.S. policy in general.

3. Investing in America

Three Creditors and a Brassplate

We are subsidizing the American economy.
These are scarce resources that can be put to better use.

Indian Finance Ministry Official, 2004

Who's Who

U.S. global financial arbitrage helped drive differential growth favoring the United States. But foreign investment into the United States was not uniformly distributed. Foreign investors differ in ways that bolster U.S. global economic power in the long run. In chapter 2, I disaggregated the U.S. balance sheet and argued that not all debt is created equal. The United States has been able to maintain a net positive investment income despite being a net debtor because the U.S. claims on the world return more money than the U.S. debts to the world. In turn, this helps free the United States from the normal constraints with respect to domestic consumption and domestic and overseas investment. Whereas in chapter 2 I in essence compared the United States to its foreign creditors, in this chapter, I compare creditors to show that not all creditors are created equal. Foreign investors into the United States (unlike Gaul) are divided into four parts, but (like Gaul) only three parts really matter: the Americanized Rich, the Repressed Rich, and the Lockboxes. The foreign sites for U.S. outward investment also sort into the same four camps, of which again only three matter politically. Disaggregating the creditors of the United States matters because doing so opens up a discussion of the political bases for U.S. power. The three types of investors that matter display different types of attachment to the U.S. project, based on their different investment profiles. Attachment to the U.S. project drops off as the investment portfolio of a group becomes more passive and a smaller part of their global portfolio—and as a group matters less to U.S. investors. The degree of direct state control over the economy also rises as the portfolio of a country becomes more passive. As in chapter 2, I remain

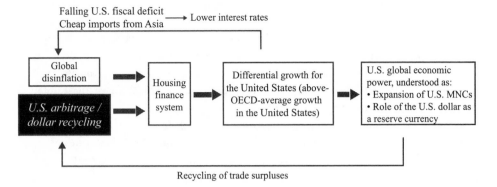

Fig. 3.1. Chapter 3: analytic concerns.

concerned with the lower left-hand box in figure 3.1, but whereas in chapter 2 I disaggregated flows by type of instrument, in this chapter, I disaggregate flows by type of creditor to get at the political side of financial arbitrage.

Two cautions for the reader. First, differences among the categories are relative, not absolute, and involve measurements on a continuum. Some of the categorizations necessarily involve an arbitrary decision. This is particularly true for Japan, which blends Repressed Rich and Lockbox characteristics. The discussion presented here is sensitive to this problem. I sometimes put forward alternate presentations of the data to see how this changes the conclusions. This matters because I employ these categories in chapter 4 to contrast the macroeconomic effects of housing finance markets in our two rich groups and in chapter 5, to analyze changes in manufacturing competitiveness over the long 1990s. Second, the natural tendency to focus on the immediate past means that oil exporters and China loom large. But over the long 1990s, rich countries provided the bulk of U.S. foreign financing, and looking forward, rich countries continue to account for the bulk of global GDP, even on a purchasing power parity (PPP) basis. The only plausible competition that the dollar faces as a reserve currency is the euro. Moreover, the moderation of oil prices in late 2008 suggests that oil exporters will not be accumulating wealth quite so quickly. So my analysis here devotes more attention to our two rich-country groups than to China or the petro-states; and it then picks up China in chapter 6 and the sovereign wealth funds of the oil exporters in chapter 8.

Which countries populate these four groups: the Americanized Rich, the Repressed Rich, the Lockboxes, and the corporate shells? To answer this, the analysis asks four questions about any given country: (1) To what extent do its portfolio investments into the United States replicate American investments abroad in their orientation toward equities; (2) to what extent does it overinvest in the United States relative to its share of developed OECD country GDP; (3) to what extent does the United States return this favor by overinvesting relative to the host country share of developed OECD GDP; and (4) to what extent is its housing finance system pro-cyclic, like that in the United States? The central political point, obviously, is that the more these conditions hold, the more tightly tied a country is to economic structures favoring continued U.S. economic power.

Using these criteria, the first group, the Americanized Rich, comprises developed countries that display overseas investment patterns like those of the United States and that both receive disproportionately large volumes of USDIA (U.S. outward FDI) and send out disproportionate amounts of FDIUS (inward FDI to the United States). The stakes of their citizens and firms in the U.S. economy are weighted toward direct investment, equity holdings, and, to a lesser extent, corporate bonds—that is, a more "Martian" or U.S. portfolio. Although the absolute level of investment from these countries into the United States is often is lower than that from the Repressed Rich, the Americanized Rich invest in the United States at levels that are roughly double what their aggregate share of non-U.S. global GDP or control over MNCs would lead us to expect. Similarly, U.S. investment into these countries also is overweight and displays a marked preference for equities and for USDIA. Finally, these countries have housing and corporate finance markets that are similar to the U.S. housing and corporate finance markets, which is to say they are financially unrepressed (see chapter 4). Britain, the Netherlands, Canada, Ireland and, to a lesser extent, Australia, New Zealand, and the Scandinavian countries populate this group. The case of Switzerland is murky because it has a repressed housing finance system plus corporatist wage restraint and, thus, could fall into the Repressed Rich. But I arbitrarily assign it to the Americanized Rich group because its own MNCs have large stakes in the U.S. economy independent of its role as an entrepôt for mobile capital and because U.S. investors have an extremely large stake in Swiss equities. This is a conservative assignment with respect to the arguments in the book, given the extremely slow growth of Switzerland in the long 1990s.

The second group, the Repressed Rich, comprises more "Venusian" developed countries. These countries often have quite sizable positions in the U.S. market via FDIUS and sometimes sizable holdings of U.S. securities. Indeed, for some of them FDIUS comprises a bigger share of their investment into the United States than for the first group. But, compared to their *ability* to invest overseas, this second group nonetheless displays *relatively* low levels of FDIUS. Although the Repressed Rich largely use FDI to invest into the United States, their direct investment into the United States is in aggregate approximately two-thirds the level we would expect based on their share of non-U.S. global GDP and their share of the Fortune Global 500 (a proxy for the ability to make direct investment). The United States returns this apparent diffidence. U.S. direct investment in Germany is approximately one-half what we would expect based on the size of the German economy, and U.S. investors hold almost as many Dutch securities in dollar terms as they do German securities, even though the German economy is four times as large. In the other direction, Germany has an economy almost half again as large as that of Britain during the 2000s and is home to a slightly larger share of the Fortune Global 500 than Britain. But Britain has a stake in U.S. equities that is almost double the German stake and has an FDIUS stake that is 60 percent larger.

The Repressed Rich countries also repress both their housing and corporate finance markets, with consequences we explore in later chapters. They also typically use corporatist intermediation to repress wage growth. Germany, France, Italy, Belgium, Austria, Spain, Portugal, and Japan populate this group. Like Switzerland, Japan presents us with a difficult case. It is underinvested in both directions with respect to direct investment. But its huge holdings of U.S. Treasury and agency bonds make it more like a Lockbox, as we will see. I therefore both include Japan and break it out in presentations of aggregate data comparing the Repressed Rich with the Americanized Rich to see if this matters. Similarly, whereas Spain has enjoyed a spectacular housing boom, on the basis of investment criteria it is more like the Repressed Rich than the Americanized Rich. Its assignment (like that of Switzerland) is an analytically conservative choice because it has clearly enjoyed a housing boom in the past decade.

The label *repressed* sounds somewhat negative, but is intended as a term of art. Our categories cut across the usual liberal market economy (LME) versus coordinated market economy (CME) categories because the coordinated Scandinavian economies are grouped with the usual liberal suspects.[1] This requires us to use a different descriptive label. *Repressed* refers not to the political systems of these countries or to a psychological state of mind but, rather, to their highly organized and regulated financial and collective bargaining institutions—it is used here in the technical sense that state actions hold prices below market-clearing levels.

The third group, the Lockboxes, comprises economies that were mostly passively invested in U.S. Treasury and agency debt during the long 1990s. These economies lack direct investment in the United States and the United States provides relatively little direct investment in return. Asian economies largely populate this group, as do the bulk of the rich oil exporters—at least on the basis of publicly available data. Some of them—think Kuwait—hold U.S. Treasuries and agency debt well out of proportion to their share of global GDP, but as a group they did not hold U.S. debt securities in excess of their share of global GDP until quite recently. For most of our period, they were thus underinvested the United States. Even when we shift Japan from the Repressed Rich category to this group, its investment position remains underweight on all counts. The Lockboxes thus blend classic Asian developmental states—the core of Dooley, Folkerts-Landau, and Garber's (DFG's) Bretton Woods 2 arrangement—with rentier economies that rely on the United States for external and internal security.

Like the other groups, this group contains some anomalies. Singapore hosts USDIA well out of proportion to its size. More troubling from a categorical perspective, many of these economies have recently formed SWFs, government investment agencies with a remit that extends well beyond passive investment in U.S.

Treasuries. Several of these funds recently took substantial equity positions in core developed-country financial firms. The rising share of assets held by SWFs might be politically problematic as well (see chapter 8), but for now let us put aside the SWF issue. During most of the period covered by this book, oil exporters were a minor source of funds for the United States, and most SWFs were of limited significance. The explosion of oil prices and thus oil exporter wealth seems very salient today, but during the long 1990s, oil prices were at historic lows and some Middle East oil exporters were net international debtors.

Finally, the fourth group, the Corporate Shells, largely comprises countries that serve as, well, corporate shells. Sunny spots such as the Cayman Islands, Bermuda, and the British West Indies populate this group, although Luxembourg provides a European variation for businessmen who favor gloomy forests over sparkling beaches. This group accounts for considerable holdings in both directions. In 2006, Luxembourgeois entities owned $680 billion of U.S. securities and FDIUS; the Cayman Islands held $485 billion of U.S. securities.[2] The United States, meanwhile, held smaller but still substantial positions in each country. Holdings on both sides of the ledger are improbably large for countries that, like Bermuda, have a physical footprint of barely 21 square miles (54 square kilometers). Instead of factories and office towers, these economies contain the "brassplates" of the chapter title—shiny announcements of the notional, legal presence of corporations whose real activities occur somewhere else. Measuring their holdings in relation to their GDP is not meaningful because their underlying economic activity is not what makes them attractive places to domicile securities. This group accounts for the bulk of the global investment into the United States not accounted for by the first three groups.

A First Analytic Cut

The criteria for classifying countries are intended to capture the degree and kind of integration with the U.S. economy. First, is the share of total portfolio investment of a country into the United States overweight or underweight based on its share of the GDP of the OECD countries net of the United States? Second, is the share of FDIUS of a country above or below its share of the Fortune Global 500—the largest five hundred firms by revenue, and thus a reasonable proxy for the ability of a country to make significant volumes of FDI? This metric differs from the more straightforward GDP metric because the distribution of MNCs is not directly related to the size of a given economy or to per capita GDP, but the distribution of cash for portfolio investment is. Most MNCs are large firms, and so the distribution of potential carriers of FDI is not necessarily the same as the distribution of GDP by country. Third, does equity or debt bulk larger in a country's purely portfolio holdings, again relative to its share of rich country GDP net of the United States? Fourth, is portfolio debt composed more of corporate bonds or U.S. Treasury or agency debt? Finally, I ask the same questions in reverse about U.S. investment into each country. In principle, these questions should yield a large number of discrete "types" of country, but in practice most countries fall into one of our four types.

Figure 3.2 charts the location of countries based on the share of FDIUS in their total average investment into the United States in 2000–2006, against the share of all U.S. Treasury and agency debt in their average total investment into the United States in 2000–2006. I use the multiyear average to eliminate distortions caused by the run up in oil prices after 2003 and to temper the sudden increase in Chinese passive holdings after 2004. Each would distort dynamics operating over the entire 1991–2005 period. Unfortunately, good comparable data for the whole 1990s are not available. Countries with high proportions of FDIUS in their total invest-ment are toward the right; countries holding high proportions of U.S. public debt are toward the top. The bubble sizes are proportional to total investment. Thus, Japan is a large bubble with roughly 75 percent of its investment in U.S. Treasury and agency bonds but only around 15 percent of its investment taking the form of FDIUS. (Corporate bonds and portfolio equity holdings account for the residual.) Three of our four groups can be seen clearly here; disentangling the two rich-country groups takes a bit more work.

Readers who are willing to take things or trust or who are easily bored should just look at tables 3.1 and 3.2, which summarize the main data points, and then move on to chapter 4. The central point is that the Asian Lockboxes during this period of time mostly held U.S. government debt and similar low-yielding assets. So, too, until recently, did the oil-exporting Lockboxes. Both were quite under-weight on U.S. equities, particularly if we subtract Singapore. The Repressed Rich had a more normal portfolio, but one that tilted away from U.S. equities and also was relatively smaller than we would expect on the basis of the size and sophistica-tion of their economies. And the Americanized Rich had an investment portfolio that mimicked that of the United States, tilting heavily toward equities and with a disproportionate stake in the United States overall. Moreover, their stake in the United States was roughly twice what we would expect. Some of this undoubtedly reflects the use of Britain by oil exporters as a channel for their investment into the United States, but the absolute size of the Americanized Rich stake in the United States suggests it is still overweight.

Table 3.2 presents the reverse flow of U.S. investment into our groups, mirror-ing the findings in table 3.1. The United States overinvests in the Americanized Rich relative to their salience in the world economy and significantly slights the Repressed Rich. The United States is also underinvested in the Asian Lockboxes, whether or not Japan is included. Oil exporters have been excluded because in many cases the data have been suppressed by BEA or involve trivial amounts. We consider the easier groups, Corporate Shells and the Lockboxes first, before disen-tangling the two rich groups.

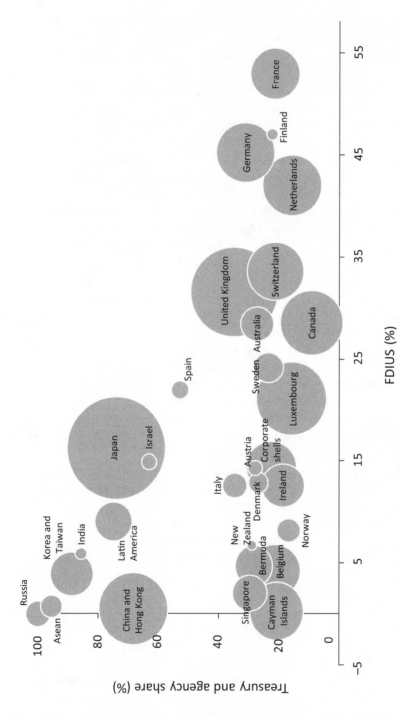

Fig. 3.2. Average percentage share of FDIUS versus U.S. Treasury and agency debt in the investments of countries into the United States, 2000–2006. FDIUS, foreign direct investment into the United States.

Source: Data from Bureau of Economic Analysis, http://www.bea.gov; U.S. Treasury Department, http://www.treas.gov/tic/shlhistdat.csv; International Monetary Fund, http://www.imf.org/external/ns/cs.aspx?id=28; Fortune Global 500.

TABLE 3.1.
Over- or underinvestment by foreign country groups in the United States, using average level of investment 2000–2007 and average GDP share 2000–2007

	[1] Global GDP^a (%)	[2] All Foreign Investment into United States (%)	[3] Ratio of Columns 2/1	[4] All Portfolio Investment into United States (%)	[5] Ratio of Columns 4/1	[6] All U.S. Equities Held (%)	[7] Ratio of Columns 6/1	[8] All FDIUS (%)	[9] Ratio of Columns 8/1
Americanized Rich	18.3	35.1	1.92	31.1	1.69	49.3	2.69	50.4	2.75
Repressed Rich	39.9	29.5	0.74	28.3	0.71	20.8	0.52	34.0	0.85
Asian Lockboxes	14.3	13.0	0.91	16.2	1.14	9.1	0.64	1.0	0.07
Oil-exporter Lockboxes	5.0	2.8	0.56	3.4	0.69	3.6	0.73	0.3	0.07
Alternative specifications									
Asian Lockboxes with Japan	29.3	28.1	0.96	32.2	1.10	17.9	0.61	12.6	0.43
Repressed Rich without Japan	24.0	14.4	0.58	12.3	0.49	12.0	0.48	22.3	0.90
Sum of four original groups^b	77.5	80.4	1.02	70	1.04	82.8	1.07	85.7	1.11

Sources: US Treasury Department TIC website: http://www.ustreas.gov/tic/, *Foreign Portfolio Holdings of US Securities 1974–2006*, June 2007; BEA website: http://www.bea.gov/international/di1fdibal. htm, *FDIUS by Country*; International Monetary Fund website: http://www.imf.org/external/pubs/ft/weo/2008/02/weodata/index.aspx, *World Economic Outlook Database, all countries*.

Notes: Percentages and ratios based on weighted averages. Americanized Rich, Australia, Britain, Canada, Finland, Ireland, Netherlands, New Zealand, Norway, Sweden, and Switzerland; Asian Lockboxes, China, Hong Kong, India, Indonesia, Korea, Malaysia, Singapore, Taiwan, and Thailand; FDIUS, foreign direct investment into the United States; oil-exporter Lockboxes, Algeria, Bahrain, Gabon, Iran, Kuwait, Libya, Nigeria, Oman, Qatar, Russia, Saudi Arabia, United Arab Emirates, and Venezuela; Repressed Rich, Austria, Belgium, France, Germany, Japan, and Italy.

^a Excluding the United States.

^b Residue is mostly Corporate Shell economies.

TABLE 3.2.
Over- or underinvestment by the United States in foreign country groups using average level of investment 2000–2005 and average GDP share 2000–2005

	[1] Global GDP^a (%)	[2] All investment from United States (%)	[3] Ratio of columns 2/1	[4] All portfolio investment from United States (%)	[5] Ratio of columns 4/1	[6] All foreign equities held by United States (%)	[7] Ratio of columns 6/1	[8] All USDIA (%)	[9] Ratio of columns 8/1
Americanized Rich	19	48	2.58	48	2.54	45	2.39	50	2.58
Repressed Rich	39	23	0.58	26	0.66	29	0.74	16	0.58
Asian Lockboxes	14	8	0.48	7	0.61	9	0.61	9	0.51
Alternative specifications									
Asian Lockboxes with Japan	29	15	0.53	17	0.58	22	0.74	13	0.43
Sum of original three groups	72	78	1.08	80	1.11	83	1.14	75	1.03

Sources: U.S. Treasury Department TIC website: http://www.ustreas.gov/tic/, *US Portfolio Holdings of Foreign Securities, 1974–2005*; BEA website: http://www.bea.gov/international/di1usdop.htm, *USDIA by Country*; International Monetary Fund website: http://www.imf.org/external/pubs/ft/weo/2008/02/weodata/index.aspx, *World Economic Outlook Database, all countries.*

Notes: Percentages and ratios based on weighted averages. Americanized Rich, Australia, Britain, Canada, Finland, Ireland, Netherlands, New Zealand, Norway, Sweden, and Switzerland; Asian Lockboxes, China, Hong Kong, India, Indonesia, Korea, Malaysia, Singapore, Taiwan, and Thailand; Repressed Rich, Austria, Belgium, France, Germany, Japan, and Italy; USDIA, U.S. (foreign) direct investment abroad.

^a Excluding the United States.

Corporate Shells

Let us start in the southwest quadrant of figure 3.2, where our residual Corporate Shell group, plus Belgium, reside. Bermuda, the Cayman Islands, the British Caribbean Islands, the British Channel Islands, and Luxembourg are aggregated here into the Corporate Shells bubble. These countries in the aggregate accounted for an average of almost $1 trillion of U.S. foreign debt in 2000–2006. Indeed, Luxembourg and the Cayman Islands each hold more U.S. securities by value than Canada.

But these holdings do not represent some sort of solar-powered economic might. The locations of these countries close to the origin in figure 3.2 reflect the overwhelming predominance of corporate securities, rather than U.S. Treasuries or FDI, in their holdings and, thus, the overwhelming use of these locales for corporate bookkeeping purposes. What FDIUS and USDIA occurs from and to these nations is tightly related to the existence of favorable legal regimes for specific sectors. Thus, for example, the global reinsurance industry is concentrated in Bermuda. Corporations use these nations as convenient places to convey ownership of their assets through bespoke corporate vehicles such as the special purpose entities made infamous by Enron or the structured investment vehicles at the core of today's subprime meltdown. Similarly, when the collapse of the MBS market in 2007 forced the liquidation of two Bear Stearns hedge funds, Bear Stearns opted to have litigation by the fund shareholders moved away from the United States to the more favorable legal terrain of the Cayman Islands.[3] So the political significance of these holdings is minimal for our purposes, although they are highly salient if we care about tax equity or justice.

The United States owed these nations approximately $106 billion net with respect to long-term debt and equity holdings in 2005. What does this mean? Given the opacity of corporate structures, this could represent a real liability or it could represent debts literally owed by one U.S. corporate subsidiary to another subsidiary via special purpose entities. Alternately, this could represent capital flight from developing countries by elites who will eventually denationalize their holdings by acquiring U.S. green cards and apartments in Miami. Only Luxembourg (and, to a much lesser extent, the British Virgin Islands) is a substantial source of FDIUS—the Luxembourgeois share of FDIUS is over seventy times as large as its share of OECD GDP. Thus, Luxembourg, with a population smaller than Wyoming and a physical footprint the same as Albemarle County, Virginia, or Rhode Island, accounts for an improbable 10 percent of European FDI into the United States; the United States returns this favor to a smaller but equally improbable degree, locating approximately 6 percent of its USDIA into Europe there, mostly as holding companies.[4] Most Luxembourgeois FDIUS is thus probably also simply a carrier for investment from other countries. The same is true for Bermuda and the British Caribbean Islands, which receive USDIA on the same scale as Luxembourg and then presumably reinvest elsewhere.

The spirit of this book suggests that we should reallocate the holdings of this group to the actual beneficiary to discern the political and economic import of those holdings.[5] Alas, it is impossible to get detailed information on who owns what in and owes what to these islands, and so I make here the simplifying assumption that Europeans using Luxembourg as a conduit to the United States do so in the same rough proportions as they invest from their own countries. Meanwhile, I can only offer up table 3.3, which presents a detailed breakdown of the net position for United States, Europe, and Japan with respect to these islands in 2005. The United States appears to have a net $200 billion deficit globally against a surplus for Europe and Japan twice that size. But it would be foolish to assume that the whole of the deficit is accounted for by the European or Japanese surplus. Luxembourg alone has nearly a net $608 billion asset surplus with the world. At the same time, the Cayman Islands appear to have a $964 billion liability to the world. The absence of reliable information about FDI from Japan and Europe into these countries also makes drawing up a real balance sheet impossible. Data about USDIA and FDIUS, however, would reduce the U.S. deficit by $100 billion if they were included.

Although Belgium clusters with this group, it reflects both a peculiarity about the Belgian economy and the role of Belgium as a corporate shell. The position of Belgium—low on FDIUS and low on U.S. Treasuries—reflects its large holdings of corporate debt, of which roughly one-sixth is mortgage and other asset-backed securities, not including agency MBSs issued by Fannie Mae and Freddie

TABLE 3.3.
Net position of Corporate Shells with respect to the United States, Europe, and Japan, 2005 (billions of US$)

	From United States to	Into United States	Net[a]	From Europe to	Into Europe	Net[a]	From Japan to	Into Japan	Net[a]
Bahamas	3.3	9.4	−6.2	3.7	1.9	1.8	2.6	0.08	2.6
Barbados	0.3	10.8	−10.6	445	2.7	−2.3	0.08	0.09	0.01
Bermuda	186.7	253.6	−66.9	35.8	68.1	−32.4	14.7	12.6	2.1
Cayman Islands	248.8	46.8[b]	202.0	302.7	5.6	297.1	297.7	0.03	297.7
Guernsey	6.4	18.6	−12.2	26.9	54.0	−27.2	3.6	?	?
Isle of Man	0.06	1.6	−1.6	1.4	21.3	−20.0	?	?	?
Jersey	19.1	39.3	−20.3	127.9	162.7	−34.9	233.0	180.0	53
Luxembourg	46.3	303.8	−257.5	1,035.3	1,104.2	−68.8	76.0	104.7	−28.8
Netherlands Antilles	47.2	7.5	39.8	61.9	1.8	60.1	9.2	0.4	8.8
British Virgin Islands	8.4	79.1	−70.7	11.3	?	?	1,003	?	?
Total:[c]	566.4	770.6	−204.2	1,595.9	1,422.5	173.4	404.1	118.0	286.0

Sources: Data from Treasury International Capital (TIC), http://www.ustreas.gov/tic/; International Monetary Fund, Co-ordinated Portfolio Investment Survey (IMF CPIS), table 8 for 2005, http://www.imf.org/external/np/sta/pi/datarsl.htm.
Notes: ? indicates data unavailable.
[a] From point of view of the United States and Europe.
[b] Value reflects the IMF CPIS data, which are inconsistent with parallel TIC data.
[c] Data may not sum because of rounding and totals do not include Virgin Islands for Europe or Japan.

Mac. Many of these are undoubtedly held on a custodial basis, although the 2008 collapses of the Franco-Belgian bank Dexia and the Belgo-Dutch bank Fortis indicate large holdings on their own account. At the same time, Belgium has unusually low levels of outward FDI, reflecting the smothering of Belgian nonfinancial enterprise by firms from the Netherlands, France, and the United States. Unlike most of developed western Europe, Belgium is a substantial net recipient of FDI. Its biggest nonfinancial MNC, Inbev (beer and beverages) was largely active outside the United States until a 2008 acquisition of Anheuser-Busch; its multinational financial firms, Dexia aside, are small beer compared to neighboring Dutch banks.[6] There are only five purely Belgian firms in the Fortune Global 500, roughly the same number as Brazil and fewer than India, Spain, and Taiwan. On the other side, although still underweight overall, Belgium appears to be only about half again more attractive to U.S. investment than the rest of the Repressed Rich. This reflects an outsized level of USDIA, which in turn appears to be somewhat idiosyncratic in that it reflects the presence of firms locating coordination centers near Brussels and thus the de facto EU capital, as well as the long-term consequences of the second-best choice by Ford of Belgium over France for its first major post–World War II investment in Europe. So we consider Belgium to be in the Repressed Rich group rather than the Corporate Shells, on the theory that its high level of ownership of corporate debt reflects as much a relative inability to make FDI as it does its utility as a corporate shell.

Asian and Oil-Exporter Lockboxes

Giovanni Arrighi labels Asian U.S. creditors with the evocative phrase Asian Lockboxes. This does accurately sum up the situation because Asian exporters and oil exporters largely held U.S. Treasury and agency debt and not much of anything else until the explosion of investment by their SWFs in late 2007. For our purposes, we consider the Asian Lockboxes to be China, Hong Kong, Taiwan, Korea, Indonesia, Singapore, Malaysia, Thailand, and India. The related oil-exporter Lockboxes comprise an even dozen countries: Russia, Saudi Arabia, Kuwait, the Emirates, Bahrain, Qatar, Iran, Oman, Libya, Algeria, Gabon, and Nigeria. Data on Iraq are not available, but it is doubtful there is substantial investment in either direction; Norway, although a substantial oil exporter, is considered here with the rich countries because it had and has a more diversified economy than the Lockbox countries. For the most part, we consider the SWFs of the oil exporters in chapter 8. Japan, as already noted, sits uneasily between the Asian Lockboxes and the Repressed Rich. The Japanese economy is fundamentally a developed economy and not akin to the Lockboxes. But I will occasionally throw it into the Lockbox group to show that doing so does not change the analysis substantially.

On average, from 2000 through 2006, the Asian Lockboxes accounted for 14.2 percent of U.S. portfolio debt of all kinds versus a 14.3 percent share of global

GDP net of the United States. But this apparent aggregate parity conceals several interesting divergences from parity in addition to unfaithfully representing the trend. The ownership of holdings is unevenly distributed, with China and Hong Kong holding a bit more than one-half, Taiwan and Korea together one-quarter, and Singapore much of the remaining one-fifth. The share held by India is only one-tenth what might be expected from its GDP. Singapore and China/Hong Kong each holds portfolio debt approximately one-fifth larger than would be expected, and Singapore accounts for virtually all ASEAN holdings of U.S. equities and for 90 percent of FDIUS, mostly via its SWF, Temasek.

The Chinese holdings, even including Hong Kong, are not radically out of line with its GDP share if we take the average level over the past six years. But the rate of growth of Chinese holdings makes this average a bit misleading, and unlike the share of the oil exporters, the Chinese share is likely to continue growing. Figure 3.3 presents growth indices for holdings by the Lockbox countries. This shows that China is one of three Asian Lockboxes with very rapid accumulation in U.S. portfolio holdings in the past six years. The other two, India and Malaysia, have relatively small holdings, both absolutely and relatively. China, as previously noted, accounted for over 16 percent of all foreign holdings of U.S. portfolio debt by 2007 and probably closer to 18 percent in 2008. Virtually all of this was U.S. Treasury and agency debt, where China and Hong Kong accounted for 28 percent of this sort of U.S. foreign debt. By contrast, in 2000, China/Hong Kong accounted only for 8 and 13 percent, respectively, of total U.S. foreign debt and Treasury/agency debt. The same sort of sudden shift in relative shares characterizes the oil exporters, to the extent that data are available; those data suggest an improbably low 4 percent share of all U.S. portfolio debt.[7]

Thus, two central facts characterize the Lockboxes: (1) the Asian Lockboxes are the primary source of low return, passive investment into the United States, and (2) even the more developed of them exhibit this pattern, with Korea and Taiwan actually holding relatively and absolutely fewer equities than China/Hong Kong. The only exception to the rule is Singapore, for which equities accounted for one-half of holdings in 2006. The Asian Lockboxes thus account for much—although not all—of the arbitrage benefiting the United States over the past two decades. The picture with the oil exporters is murkier, given the lack of clear data. But it is important not to overstate their role; the Asian and oil-exporter Lockboxes assumed this role only recently. Until 2000, rich countries, including Japan, supplied the bulk of passive investment into the United States. Without Japan, all rich countries accounted for 38 percent of the portfolio investment in the United States in 2007; with Japan, it was 52 percent.

What about the oil-exporter Lockboxes? The oil exporters—at least according to official data—account for 4.6 percent of global GDP but only 3.3 percent of U.S. overseas debt on average in 2000–2006. There is, however, substantial reason to believe this is an understatement of the true scale of their holdings for two reasons.[8]

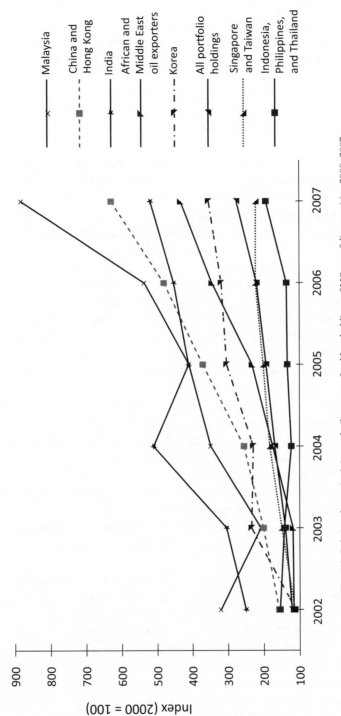

Fig. 3.3. Relative change in Asian and oil-exporter Lockbox holdings of U.S. portfolio securities, 2000–2007 (index: 2000 = 100).

Source: Data from U.S. Treasury Department, http://www.treas.gov/tic/shhistdat.csv.

First, to be consistent with the analyses of the other groups, I have used averages for the 2000–2006 period. This has the benefit of smoothing out fluctuations in value from exchange rates and once-only events. But it tends to diminish the scale of oil exporters' holdings because the price of oil rose dramatically after 2003. Indeed, if we just use the 2006 officially recorded holdings, oil exporters appear to account for 4.6 percent of all U.S. portfolio debt to foreigners. Ramin Toloui cautions that only approximately one-half of all oil-exporter overseas holdings are really accounted for.[9] The second reason to believe that these are underestimates is that all oil exporters (including Norway) ran a cumulative current account surplus of almost $1 trillion since 2001. Not all of this represents transactions with the United States, and not all of this was recycled into U.S. securities. Still, the United States had a cumulative $250 billion deficit with the oil exporters, less Russia, in 2001–2005, suggesting that there should have been accumulations of U.S. debt on roughly the same magnitude.[10] Russian holdings of U.S. securities were approximately $110 billion by mid-2006. Together these numbers approximate the official U.S. debt to oil exporters. Using this figure implies that oil exporters held approximately 5.8 percent of U.S. foreign portfolio debt in 2007, which is not substantially higher than the official figures.

Despite this probable jump, it is important not to exaggerate the importance of the oil exporters from both a flow and stock perspective. On a stock basis, as previously noted, our amendment to the official level of oil-exporter holdings amounts to only 5.8 percent of total U.S. debt. Even doubling that leaves the oil exporters with aggregate holdings smaller than those of China. The same is true on a flow basis. In 2005, the oil exporters accounted for only 13.4 percent of the U.S. trade deficit, whereas the bilateral deficit with Japan was approximately the same size and that with China alone was nearly twice that. The same is true for the long term. From 1990 to 2005, the Organization of Oil Exporting Countries (OPEC) accounted for only 10 percent of the cumulative U.S. trade deficit in goods, versus double that for China and somewhat more for Japan and Canada.[11] This was a period of relatively low oil prices, and if oil prices continue to equilibrate downward from the speculative peaks of mid-2008, it is likely the oil-exporter share will remain the same.

Each of the two types of security that the Lockboxes have accumulated carries particular risks and connects differently to the U.S. economy. U.S. Treasuries are easy to liquidate and directly influence U.S. interest rates. Asian central banks, and to a lesser extent the SWFs of the oil countries, are responsible for buying the overhang of U.S. Treasury debt that represents the net inflow of capital to the United States over the past six or so years. They have effectively replaced private (mostly European) buyers in that role. Second, when Asian and oil-exporter Lockboxes stayed away from agency bond auctions, yields on bonds from troubled-mortgage giants Fannie Mae and Freddie Mac jumped, helping to trigger their bankruptcies. (Chapter 4 has more on why Fannie and Freddie are important.) Asian Lockboxes hold the lion's share of the $400 billion in agency MBSs that foreign central banks openly bought from June 2005 on. China/Hong Kong alone accounts for $270 billion of total agency debt, whereas Japan accounts for an additional $180 billion (recall the ambiguous position of Japan between the Lockboxes and the Repressed Rich). Third, much of the post-2005 export of MBSs took the form of privately issued asset-backed securities built on the subprime and Alt-A (above-subprime, below-prime) mortgages that defaulted in droves from mid-2007 on. So even in the absence of a catastrophic U.S. dollar meltdown, the Asian Lockboxes took substantial losses on their U.S. debt. Finally, note that the fortunes of the Asian and oil-exporter Lockboxes are tied together. Continued growth by the Asian Lockboxes—most important, China—is central to continued high prices for oil, even though high oil prices curtail Asian growth.

Now, let us differentiate the rich-country categories.

The Americanized Rich versus the Repressed Rich

The rich countries have a distinctly different investment profile with respect to the United States than the Lockboxes, as their location in the southern and southeastern portions of figure 3.2 shows. Our first task is to separate them into two groups: the Americanized Rich and the Repressed Rich. The Americanized Rich, in general, invest more like the United States, favoring FDI over portfolio investment, favoring portfolio equity over portfolio debt, and favoring corporate bonds over U.S. Treasury bonds. The Repressed Rich, by contrast, exhibit the reverse pattern, favoring U.S. Treasuries over corporate debt, debt over equities, and, with the proper adjustments, portfolio investment over FDIUS. Finally, these groups of countries have very divergent domestic housing market financial structures and, as a consequence, received differential growth impulses from global financial flows in the 1990s and early 2000s (see chapter 4). The Americanized Rich encompass Britain, the Netherlands, Canada, Australia, the Scandinavian countries (perhaps less Finland), and to a lesser extent Ireland and New Zealand. As previously discussed, I also assign Switzerland to the Americanized Rich category. The Repressed Rich encompass Germany, Austria, Italy, France, Belgium, Spain, Portugal, and, to a lesser extent, Japan. Although the Japanese accumulation of U.S. Treasury debt puts it into something of a hybrid position between the Asian Lockboxes and the Repressed Rich, as a developed country it has more in common with Germany than with China. As previously noted, these are conservative choices.

On the surface, countries such as France and Germany appear to be more oriented toward FDIUS than are countries such as Britain and the Netherlands and, thus, much more "Martian," or American, in their investment patterns. The former have a greater proportion of FDIUS in their portfolio and thus appear to the right of the latter in figure 3.2. But this first-glance reading of the data is misleading. It reflects not an overinvestment in the United States by the Repressed Rich but, rather, their overall underinvestment, particularly with respect to U.S. equities and corporate debt. This comes out clearly when we consider the country groups on the basis of their investment stake relative to their *potential* for investing. Whereas Germany and France appear to have a more U.S.-like (Martian) investment profile, they are underinvestors into the United States relative to their ability to generate multinational enterprise and relative to their own GDP. By contrast, Britain, the Netherlands, and the other Americanized Rich have disproportionately large absolute and relative stakes through all sorts of investment vehicles into the U.S. economy (see table 3.1). And the United States reciprocates these attachments (see table 3.2). The Americanized Rich are mostly overweight in terms of their investment into the United States and are all overweight in terms of U.S. investment into them. The Repressed Rich, by contrast, are mostly underweight in both directions, Germany more so than France.

Figure 3.4 displays the rich countries ranked by the degree to which their holdings of FDIUS, U.S. portfolio equities, and U.S. portfolio debt are over- or underweight. I have determined whether a country is over- or underweight with respect to FDI by dividing its share of FDIUS by its average share of the Fortune Global 500 companies for revenues for 2005–2007, and its share of the stock of all global FDI assets for 2006, based on data from the United Nations Conference on Trade and Development (UNCTAD) *World Investment Report, 2006.* I determine the neutral weight for portfolio investment based on the share of OECD GDP net of the United States of each country.

Why use two different measures for these three sets of data? As previously noted, it seems counterintuitive to argue that France, with 56 percent of its investment into the United States as FDIUS, or Germany, with 47 percent of its investment into the United States as FDIUS, has a smaller stake than Britain at 34 percent or the Netherlands at 44 percent, using average levels for 2000–2006.[12] But this simple comparison is misleading in two ways. First, the level of outward FDI of a country is very sensitive to the presence of locally headquartered large firms. Even though falling transportation and telecommunication costs have allowed smaller and smaller firms to go overseas in recent decades, FDI fundamentally remains a large-firm game. Historically, most small firms overseas were suppliers that followed large firms to new production locations. Much as the original theories about FDI argue, the fixed costs of being foreign when locating production overseas are quite high, particularly compared to simply subcontracting production overseas. This is why overseas subcontracting, rather than FDI, predominates in sectors with large proportions of small firms, such as the garment-assembly industry.

So the fact that many of the smaller OECD economies have low absolute and proportional levels of FDIUS does not permit a straightforward interpretation of disinterest in the U.S. economy. An economy such as Denmark, in which small and medium enterprises predominate, will perforce probably have less FDIUS than an economy such as Sweden, in which large firms predominate. In GDP terms, the

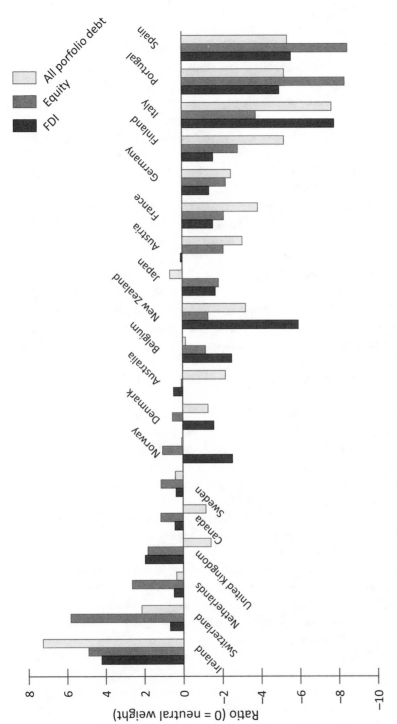

Fig. 3.4. Ratio of investment of Americanized Rich and Repressed Rich countries in the United States relative to their capacity to invest. FDI, foreign direct investment.

Source: Data from Bureau of Economic Analysis, http://www.bea.gov; U.S. Treasury Department, http://www.treas.gov/tic/shlhistdat.csv; International Monetary Fund, http://www.imf.org/external/ns/cs.aspx?id=28; Fortune Global 500.

Danish economy is about two-thirds the size of the Swedish economy. But Denmark has only two firms in the 2007 Fortune Global 500 list, whereas Sweden has six; the proportion of outward FDI stocks is similar. Moreover, both of the Danish MNCs are in the service sector, where multinationalization came late, whereas all of the Swedish MNCs are large manufacturing firms. On this basis, to take the countries with large stakes that matter, we would expect to see much more FDIUS by France and Germany and much less by Britain and the Netherlands because France and Germany each have more large world-class firms than Britain or the Netherlands.

Indeed, Germany does have substantial FDIUS. But, although it accounts for 12 percent of the OECD GDP net of the United States, it accounts for a slightly smaller share of FDIUS. The gap between the German share of global MNCs and the German FDIUS is even larger. Removing the 169 U.S. firms and the 55 firms from the least-developed countries (LDCs) that, on average in 2005–2007, populated the Fortune Global 500 list shrinks the 500 down to 276 firms. These firms originate from the comparison set in figure 3.4. Using them as the reference point makes the disproportion more obvious. Germany accounts for 13.2 percent of the Fortune Global 276 firms by head count and 16.1 percent of the Global 276 revenues. So we would expect this level of FDIUS, all other things being equal, rather than the 11.8 percent that we observe. Similarly, France accounts for 9.0 percent of non-U.S. OECD GDP, 13.9 percent of Global 276 firms, and 15.8 percent of Global 276 revenues, but only 10.3 percent of FDIUS. Relative to its GDP, France overinvests in FDIUS, but relative to its potential for FDI, it underinvests.

By contrast, Britain accounts for only 8.6 percent of OECD GDP net of the United States, 12.8 percent of Global 276 firms, and 13.7 percent of Global 276 revenues. Its share of FDIUS, however, is much higher, at 18.8 percent. The orientation of the Netherlands toward FDIUS is even more striking. The Netherlands accounts for 2.6 percent of OECD GDP net of the United States, 5.1 percent of the Global 276 head count, and 7.7 percent of Global 276 revenues, but 11.5 percent of FDIUS. So although Britain and the Netherlands put less of their total investment into FDIUS, they make FDIUS to a much greater degree than either France or Germany relative to their ability to make FDI in general. The lower share of FDIUS in the total stake of Britain and the Netherlands in the U.S. economy reflects neither indifference toward the U.S. market nor a passive orientation but, rather, even more oversized portfolio equity holdings than the Repressed Rich hold.[13]

Figure 3.5 presents just the information on FDIUS to show the relative over- or underweighting, based on the potential of each country for making FDIUS. Zero represents FDIUS in proportion to the share of the Global Fortune 276 of each country in 2006. A score of 2 represents FDIUS at twice the level predicted by the country share of the Fortune Global 276; –2 indicates FDIUS at one-half the level predicted. There are a few anomalies here. First, Austria, which on the basis of all other metrics should be in the Repressed Rich category, displays an anomalous and slight overweighting of FDIUS by virtue of its positive valve; however, Austria

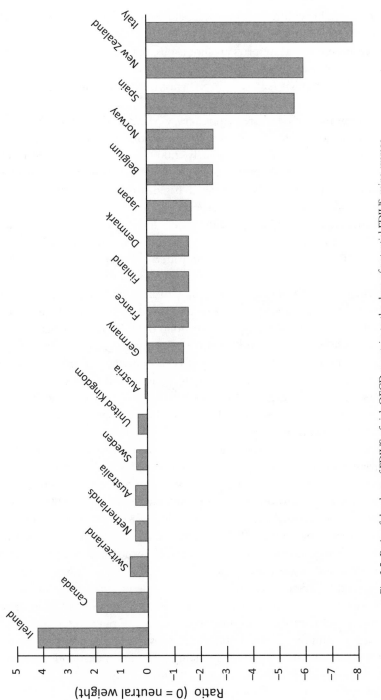

Fig. 3.5. Ratio of the share of FDIUS of rich OECD countries to the share of potential FDIUS, using average levels for 2000–2006. FDIUS, foreign direct investment into the United States; OECD, Organisation for Economic Cooperation and Development.

Source: Data from Bureau of Economic Analysis, http://www.bea.gov; Fortune Global 500.

overall is underweight with respect to investment into the United States. Second, New Zealand, which similarly on the basis of all other metrics should be in the Americanized Rich category, displays an anomalous and slight underweighting of FDIUS. But New Zealand is also one of the poorest of the rich OECD countries on a per capita basis and has few really large firms. Both factors limit its ability to generate any kind of overseas investment. In New Zealand, a *big firm* is defined as one with more than one hundred employees, whereas in the United States the largest census category is for firms with 100 times that number of employees. Altogether New Zealand had approximately 2,000 firms with more than 100 employees in 2006, which is about the same number of U.S. firms with more than 5,000 employees, and the only New Zealand–based firm with consistently more than NZ$1 billion in exports is its dairy export cooperative. The Danish economy is similarly populated by small and medium firms, despite my children's demands for more LEGOs. In any case, these economies are small, as is their FDIUS stake.

What about portfolio holdings? Does the pattern of over- and underweighting match the pattern for FDIUS? Carol Bertaut and Linda Kole argue that all OECD portfolio investors are significantly underweight with respect to overseas diversification.[14] But their aggregate analysis conceals differences among euroland countries and considers only equities, not portfolio debt. Moreover, what matters for us is not the level of "home bias" (which, after all, is very high even for the United States) but the degree to which a country has a disproportionately large or small stake in the United States and what kinds of investment make up that stake. We can assess the relative degree of over- or underweighting in a much more straightforward manner than we did before for FDI by simply using the share of rich-country GDP (net of the United States) of each country to measure the over- or underweighting of their portfolio investment. Most of the rich OECD have a fairly comparable GDP per capita, even on a non–purchasing power parity basis. Per capita income in these countries ranges from roughly $16,000 for Portugal and $25,000 for New Zealand to almost $55,000 for Switzerland and $60,000 for oil-rich Norway, but the unweighted standard deviation of $11,000 from the average of $37,000 per capita encompasses all the other cases. Because portfolio investment requires only cash in hand rather than sophisticated corporate structures capable of management at a distance, each economy should be able to generate portfolio investment into the United States in roughly the same proportions as its overall share of the rich OECD economy GDP. In fact, portfolio investment from these countries displays substantial deviation from this pattern, as figure 3.6 shows.

Figure 3.6 replicates the exercise in figure 3.5, substituting the ratio of holdings of equities and portfolio debt for FDIUS holdings. The interpretation is the same as in figure 3.5 except that it scales the share of the holdings of U.S. equities and portfolio debt of each country against its share of OECD GDP net of the United States. A score of 2 indicates holdings of portfolio debt or equities at double the share predicted by the share of OECD GDP of a country; –2 holdings indicates

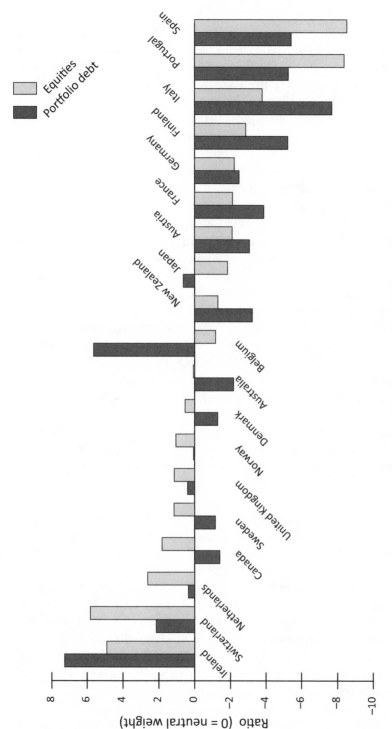

Fig. 3.6. Ratio of portfolio equity and debt holdings to share of OECD GDP, using average levels for 2000–2006. OECD, Organisation for Economic Cooperation and Development.

Source: Data from U.S. Treasury Department, Treasury International Capital, http://www.treas.gov/tic/shlhistdat. csv; International Monetary Fund, http://www.imf.org/external/ns/cs.aspx?id=28.

holdings at one-half the share predicted. The Americanized Rich all have overweight, sometimes substantially overweight, portfolio holdings of U.S. equities, and sometimes overweight positions in portfolio debt. Once more, New Zealand is an exception. By contrast, the Repressed Rich (Belgium and Japan aside) have underweight holdings of both portfolio equity and portfolio debt. For Belgium and Japan, the overweight holdings are of debt securities, not equities.

Figure 3.7 divides the dollar value of equity holdings by the dollar value of all long- and short-term debt to present the ratio of equity to debt holdings for these countries. Here the interpretation differs from the two previous figures. A score of 2 indicates that a given country held twice as many equities by value than bonds, compared to a neutral position (which indicates holdings proportional to the mix of equities and bonds in the U.S. market); –2 indicates a country held one-half as many equities by value as bonds compared to a neutral position. For comparison, the chart also displays U.S. foreign portfolio holdings scaled against the mix of equities and bonds available outside the United States and in the middle the neutral U.S. market at zero. The figure thus measures the degree of risk that investors from these countries are willing to tolerate because equities have greater risk than debt.

Recall from chapter 2 that one of the characteristics distinguishing the pattern of U.S. investment overseas from foreign investment into the United States was that the United States held roughly twice as much portfolio equity investment as it held portfolio debt. By contrast, foreigners *in toto* held twice as much U.S. portfolio debt as they held portfolio equities. Figure 3.7 shows that the distinction between Americanized Rich and Repressed Rich is not absolute. Again, however, the Americanized Rich as a general rule tend to resemble the United States by having a higher ratio of equity to debt in their overseas holdings. In Figure 3.7, the New Zealand affinity for a U.S.-like investment pattern finally emerges in a relatively high preference for U.S. equities over U.S. debt; similarly, the Belgian affinity with the Repressed Rich emerges in a preference for debt that exceeds even the Japanese currency-manipulation-bloated holdings of U.S. Treasury notes. Overall, in absolute terms, the Americanized Rich have a ratio of 1.55 for equity-to-debt holdings, whereas the Repressed Rich have only a 0.36 ratio. Stripping out the outsized holdings of Japan only raises this ratio to 0.52.

We combine both of the indicators of affinity for and aversion to a U.S.-like pattern of investment in figure 3.8. Figure 3.8 shows a fairly clear and statistically significant correlation between the overweight positions for FDIUS and overweight positions with respect to holdings of U.S. equities for the Americanized Rich and the reverse for the Repressed Rich. Note that in this and the two subsequent figures underweight holdings have been rescaled as the reciprocal. This is logically consistent. A country that holds half as much FDIUS (or U.S. equities), as a neutral weighting by GDP predicts, is equivalent to a country that has twice as much as we would expect. The bubble sizes in figure 3.8 reflect the absolute size of the total investment position in the United States of each country.

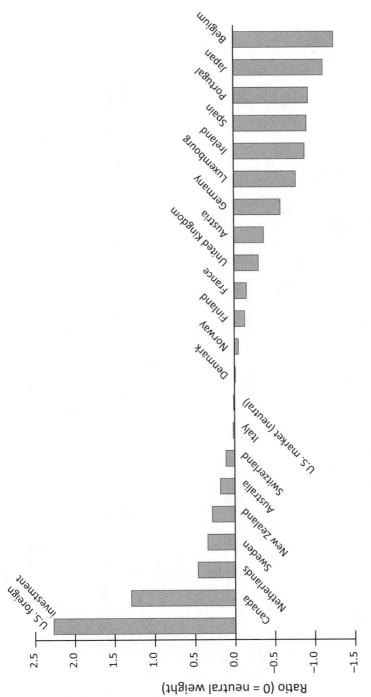

Fig. 3.7. Ratio of portfolio equity holdings to portfolio debt holdings for selected OECD countries, using average levels for 2000–2006. OECD, Organisation for Economic Cooperation and Development. *Source:* Data from U.S. Treasury Department, Treasury International Capital, http://www.treas.gov/tic/shlhistdat. csv; International Monetary Fund, http://www.imf.org/external/ns/cs.aspx?id=28.

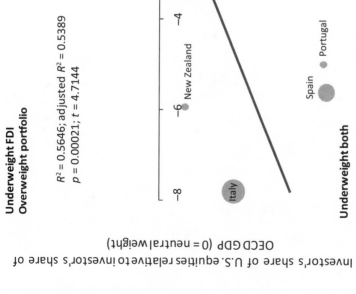

Fig. 3.8. Share of direct and portfolio investment of selected OECD countries into the United States in relation to underlying ability to invest, 2000–2006. Circles are proportional to the average value of total investment. Underweight holdings have been rescaled as the reciprocal. OECD, Organisation for Economic Cooperation and Development.

Source: Data from U.S. Treasury Department, Treasury International Capital, http://www.treas.gov/tic/shlhistdat. csv; International Monetary Fund, http://www.imf.org/external/ns/cs.aspx?id=28.

The Americanized Rich are disproportionately invested in the United States compared to the Repressed Rich. U.S. investment into those countries returns this favor. Figure 3.9 reverses figure 3.8 to display USDIA and U.S. holdings of foreign securities. In figure 3.9, the degree to which USDIA is over- or underweight is assessed against the share of global GDP net of the United States of each country, whereas U.S. portfolio holdings are scaled against the size of the relevant securities market. This helps us control for the fact that some economies have relatively small equities or bond markets in relation to their GDP. It allows us to capture the degree to which the United States has over- or underinvested in that market given the size of that market rather than the size of the economy as a whole. Figure 3.9 includes Mexico, Singapore, and Korea for the sake of comparison, but removing them does not affect the significance of the findings. (It does suggest that Singapore is the U.S. Ireland in Asia). Figure 3.9 shows that the United States mostly overinvests in the Americanized Rich and underinvests in the Repressed Rich. The small size of the Danish and Finnish economies, and the ease of supplying each from Sweden or Germany, perhaps explains the low level of USDIA in each; Nokia, meanwhile, accounts for a huge share of U.S. portfolio holdings of Finnish equities.

The findings shown in figure 3.9 are slightly less statistically significant than those in figure 3.8, but they still suggest that U.S. firms must have some nonrandom aversion to entering the Repressed Rich economies or some attraction to the Americanized Rich, or both. All other things being equal, the relatively equal levels of GDP per capita and the large size of France or Germany, for example, should make these markets as attractive to U.S. firms as smaller non-English-speaking economies such as the Netherlands and Sweden. And yet they are not. The standard theories about MNCs suggest one reason why all things might not be equal. Charles Kindleberger argues that a naïve understanding of the relative benefits of exporting versus producing overseas suggests that MNCs should not exist.[15] Firms making FDI experience additional coordination costs plus the "cost of being foreign" while potentially losing scale economies. So, perhaps U.S. firms prefer English-speaking economies (including the linguistically adept Netherlands) because the costs of being foreign are lower than in Germany or France. But if this is so, why do rational passive investors not balance their portfolios by overweighting their holdings of German and French equities rather than going overweight on both active and passive outward investment? The same is true for Repressed Rich investors, but in reverse.

Kindleberger also argues that firms actually making FDI must possess some additional competence to enter foreign markets because, otherwise, local firms free of the additional costs of coordination and of being foreign will outcompete them. This suggests that economies that are overweight on USDIA should be underweight on FDIUS because the presence of many U.S. MNCs is a signal that local firms are relatively uncompetitive. The reverse should also be true—countries with relatively high levels of FDIUS should show low levels of USDIA. Yet figure 3.10 shows exactly the opposite. There is a strong correlation between overweighting

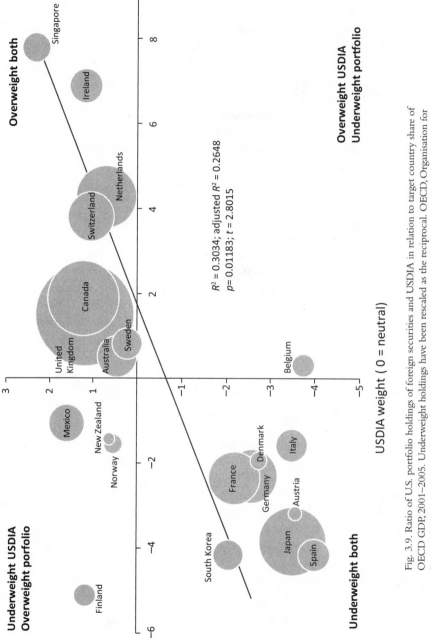

Fig. 3.9. Ratio of U.S. portfolio holdings of foreign securities and USDIA in relation to target country share of OECD GDP, 2001–2005. Underweight holdings have been rescaled as the reciprocal. OECD, Organisation for Economic Cooperation and Development; USDIA, U.S. (foreign) direct investment abroad.

Source: Data from U.S. Treasury Department, Treasury International Capital, http://www.treas.gov/tic/shlhistdat. csv; International Monetary Fund, http://www.imf.org/external/ns/cs.aspx?id=28.

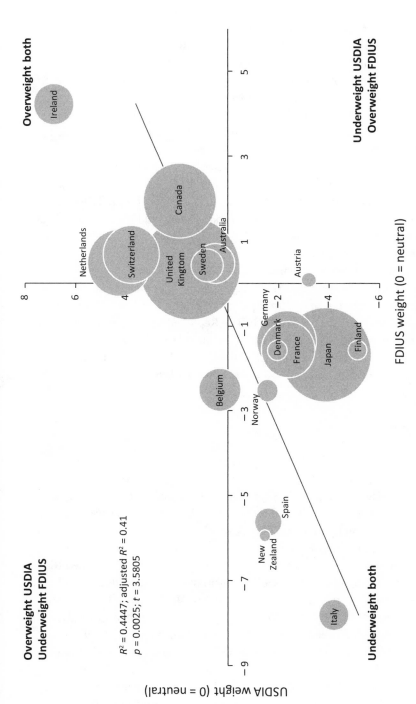

Fig. 3.10. USDIA share versus FDIUS shares for non–U.S. OECD countries, 2000–2006. Underweight holdings have been rescaled as the reciprocal. FDIUS, foreign direct investment into the United States; OECD, Organisation for Economic Cooperation and Development; USDIA, U.S. (foreign) direct investment abroad.

Source: Data from U.S. Treasury Department, Treasury International Capital, http://www.treas.gov/tic/shlhistdat. csv; International Monetary Fund, http://www.imf.org/external/ns/cs.aspx?id=28.

in both directions by the Americanized Rich and underweighting by the Repressed Rich. This suggests that firms in the Americanized Rich are not uniformly uncompetitive (and thus subject to U.S. investment into their economies) and that the Repressed Rich are not uniformly highly competitive (and thus able to fend off U.S. investment while investing into the U.S. economy). It is also consistent with arguments that trade and finance flow together.[16]

As we have seen, investment flows into and out of the United States divide the rich countries into two distinct groups. The Americanized Rich countries display investment patterns that mimic that of the United States—compared to a neutral portfolio, they are relatively overweight on FDI and equities while being underweight on passive holdings of debt. At the same time, the Americanized Rich have a marked preference for investing in the United States. They hold U.S. investments in preference to a neutral global basket, and they display a greater affinity for U.S. securities than do the Repressed Rich countries. U.S. investors display similar preferences for investment in the Americanized Rich. They hold relatively larger positions in the local equity markets of the Americanized Rich than they do in the equity markets of the Repressed Rich, and they prefer to locate USDIA in the Americanized Rich compared to the Repressed Rich. The Repressed Rich, meanwhile, display the opposite pattern—they underinvest in the United States in absolute terms and across most subcategories of investment, and the United States underinvests in them relative to the size of their economies and securities markets.

Moving Forward

In this chapter, I have continued the disaggregation of foreign investment positions into and out of the United States to show that U.S. creditors have different stakes in the United States and thus in U.S. growth. Putting aside the politically insignificant Corporate Shells, three broad groups exist. The Lockboxes have an almost entirely passive position in the United States, holding portfolio debt and not much else. The Repressed Rich have substantial FDIUS but a stake that is underweight relative to their potential for making FDI in general. Similarly, the Repressed Rich have substantial portfolio holdings of U.S. securities but holdings that, overall, are underweight relative to the size of their economies. Within these holdings, they have an overweight stake in U.S. government securities, compared to a balanced portfolio that also could include U.S. equities and U.S. corporate debt. By contrast, the Americanized Rich have substantial stakes in all three possible instruments: FDIUS, corporate debt, and government and agency debt. Their FDIUS stakes are overweight compared to their ability to make FDI. Their portfolio holdings are overweight relative to the size of their economies, and within their portfolios, they have relatively large holdings of equities and corporate bonds compared to U.S. Treasuries.

Comparing the investment of Britain and Germany in the United States relative to their underlying GDP shows this difference clearly, although it compares economic stocks to economic flows. British holdings in the United States amounted to nearly two-fifths of British GDP in 2005, whereas German holdings amounted to only one-seventh of German GDP. Overall the holdings of the Americanized Rich in relation to their own GDP are roughly double those of the Repressed Rich. Put simply, the Americanized Rich have more at stake in the health of the U.S. economy than the Repressed Rich, and they benefit more from a rapidly growing U.S. economy than the Repressed Rich. At the same time, both sets of rich countries have a different stake than the Asian Lockboxes because different kinds of debt create different constituencies supporting U.S. policy. Large volumes of FDIUS from rich countries mean that corporations have a direct stake in the U.S. economy. Among the Lockboxes, the overwhelming concentration of investment in the hands of central banks and SWFs means that corporations have a small and indirect stake. Central banks and, thus, politicians speak more loudly than firms.

How do these different stakes matter? Even though we are still at the beginning of our journey through the cycle of flows that energized U.S. differential growth, these different stakes bear on some of the manifestations of those at the end, namely the overseas growth of U.S. MNCs and the role of the U.S. dollar as a reserve currency. This reserve-currency role facilitates—indeed underpins—the flow of funds we have discussed in our two chapters on arbitrage. Susan Strange's distinction between top and negotiated currencies provides some analytic traction here.[17] Recall that for Strange a *top currency* is one that has a natural economic attractiveness for private actors considering overseas investment and public authorities thinking about the composition of their international reserves. This attractiveness necessarily stems from superior economic performance in terms of productivity and profit growth, as well as stability with respect to inflation. But, as I stress in chapter 1, superior performance is a *relative* matter. By contrast, a *negotiated currency* is one whose status as the international reserve currency emerges from explicit or tacit political considerations by both the issuer and the holder of that currency. These considerations obviously vary according to time and place.

The different patterns of investment by our three groups thus suggest differing degrees of attachment along a spectrum stretching from top to negotiated currency. For the Americanized Rich, the U.S. dollar appears to be a top currency. By contrast, the Repressed Rich have underweighted investment into the United States, which suggests that they find the U.S. dollar and the United States as an economic entity considerably less attractive than other options. For both, the relatively faster GDP and employment growth that the United States experienced in the long 1990s made U.S. dollar-denominated investments an attractive option and the United States an attractive location for investment, reinforcing the dollar as a top currency. By contrast, the Lockboxes have almost purely public holdings, which suggests that private actors are unable or unwilling to hold dollars or invest in the

United States, making the dollar a negotiated currency for them. In chapter 2, I have already suggested a plausible set of political considerations on the part of the Asian Lockboxes in the DFG Bretton Woods 2 argument. We cannot assume, however, that this reflects private preferences. Many of the Asian countries have capital controls of one form or another, many are relatively poor countries in which the bulk of firms are unable to make FDI, and many have relatively poor populations that are unwilling to take on the unknown risks of overseas investment. The first consideration, and to a certain extent the second one, reflects deliberate efforts by Asian governments to pursue statist development strategies. These statements take on even stronger force when we consider that China accounts for most of the Asian Lockbox holdings and population.

In the next chapter, I show that the differences between the Americanized Rich and Repressed Rich extends to their housing finance markets, with important consequences for employment and GDP growth. The United States was not alone in experiencing above-average growth in GDP and employment. The Americanized Rich also enjoyed better-than-average growth to varying degrees, whereas the Repressed Rich experienced below-average growth. The split among rich countries matters because it helped to prevent the emergence of the euro as a plausible competitor to the U.S. dollar as a top currency. Now, it could be argued that some countries will always exhibit above-average growth and others below-average growth—this is inherent in any average and, by itself, is meaningless. What makes the split among the rich countries meaningful, that is, more than just an artifact of the act of calculating an average? As discussed in chapter 4, the different housing markets in the Americanized Rich and Repressed Rich translated global capital flows and disinflation into growth differently. How did this happen?

4. Homes Alone?

Housing Finance Markets and Differential Growth

What we observe is not nature itself,
but nature exposed to our method of questioning.

Werner Heisenberg

Until the cascading crises of 2007–2008, nothing seemed more distant from a discussion of U.S. global economic power than housing. Most explanations for differences in growth rates between the United States and other economies focused on differences in systems of corporatist intermediation or social protection. Housing, or more properly housing finance systems, are not intrinsically the pivot of the international financial system. But over the past two decades, housing finance systems have become central to global financial flows. The central point of this chapter is that U.S. housing finance institutions translated global capital flows into U.S. MBSs and, thence, into more aggregate demand and thus differential growth for the United States. Housing finance systems in the Americanized Rich also generated differential growth for them. But housing finance systems in the Repressed Rich did not function this way.

How did this happen? Put simply, different housing finance systems had different capacities for translating disinflation and U.S. global arbitrage into increases in aggregate demand and, thus, economic growth. Disinflation rewarded countries with housing market financial institutions like those in the United States with above-average growth in employment and GDP. In turn, this above-average growth made investment in the United States and the Americanized Rich more attractive to private actors in repressed euroland and Japan. Those actors shifted capital from their economies into the faster-growing Americanized Rich, reinforcing their own relative stagnation and facilitating U.S. global financial arbitrage. The housing-driven differential growth machine required continual disinflation and recycling of U.S. trade deficits to work. By the mid-2000s, inflation in basic commodities undermined this growth mechanism, causing it to run in reverse.

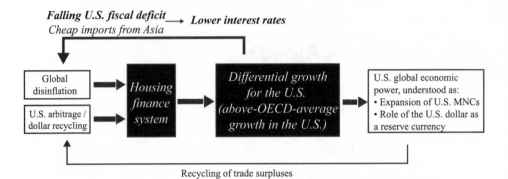

Fig. 4.1. Chapter 4: analytic focus.

The recycling of trade surpluses became more politicized, which also put upward pressure on interest rates. As interest rates rose, overextended households began defaulting on mortgages, causing overleveraged banks to fail in August 2007. My core task in this chapter, highlighted in figure 4.1, is to demonstrate the connection between housing finance systems and U.S. domestic differential accumulation. In later chapters, I consider the expansion of U.S. MNCs, that is, external growth, the issue of recycling, and the current crisis.

This chapter stresses the importance of microeconomic institutions, just like the conventional wisdom on employment and GDP growth in Europe and Japan. That conventional wisdom looks at corporatist wage-bargaining systems, labor market rigidities, and different varieties of capitalism to explain macroeconomic outcomes. Those arguments largely focus on supply-side institutions, are actor centered, and ignore aggregate demand. In contrast, here I focus on the sources of aggregate demand in institutions that are largely beyond actors' control. For reasons of economy, my analysis focuses on corporatist wage bargains that exchange wage restraint by workers for additional investment by capital.

Put simply, I revisit the division between the Americanized Rich and the Repressed Rich to show that wage restraint arguments suffer from omitted-variable bias. The Americanized Rich shared not only a bigger investment stake in the U.S. market but also U.S.-style housing finance systems and, therefore, better economic outcomes in the long 1990s. The Americanized Rich encompass both the usual liberal economies characterized by flexible employment practices and weaker unions and a fair number of corporatist, rigid, coordinated economies. The strong correlation between housing finance systems and differential growth reveals that arguments that stress only the causal significance of corporatist wage bargaining suffer from omitted-variable bias and fail to distinguish among corporatist economies with different pathways to aggregate demand formation. Arguments assigning causality to labor market rigidities and the varieties of capitalism share this problem. The reader can thus anticipate my critiques of these two analyses (although in chapter 6, I consider the varieties of capitalism argument in a different light).[1]

This chapter has four parts. First, I establish that the United States and countries with similar housing finance systems had better-than-average employment and GDP growth in the long 1990s. Then, I consider the alternative corporatist wage restraint explanation for this growth. In the third section, I show how international capital flows interacted with housing finance systems, and in the last section, I connect employment and GDP gains to housing finance systems.

One cautionary note before starting: I am not arguing that housing-based growth accounts for *all* GDP or employment growth in the rich countries. Rather, differences in housing finance systems plausibly explain the *difference* in growth rates (adjusted for population growth) among the United States, the Americanized Rich, and the Repressed Rich. The rich countries shared five similar growth impulses in the 1990s: (1) all experienced the mobile telecoms/deregulated telecoms revolution; (2) all experienced the internet boom; (3) all experienced the supply chain revolution; (4) all enjoyed cheaper manufactures from Asia; and (5) all, save Japan, had stock market booms.[2] Arguably, European countries in general did better from the first two growth impulses—they had and have better broadband and more mobile phones. Meanwhile, the United States did better from the third and fourth growth impulses. Finally, all had roughly similar real interest rates (and real interest rates matter for business investment, if we take the standard nonhousing view of the world). So, arguably, all three sets of economies should have grown at roughly the same rates. Yet they did not. This chapter points to housing finance systems as the source of the *difference* among these three economic groups, not the absolute *level* of growth.

Differential Growth in the Long 1990s

Power derives from *relative* gains, not just *absolute* gains.[3] Who were the relative winners in the OECD during the long 1990s, and why? Figure 4.2 charts the relative growth in absolute employment and GDP per capita from 1991 to 2005 for seventeen rich OECD economies. It shows the degree, in percentage terms, by which a given country either outperformed or underperformed the average level of performance for the nineteen rich OECD countries (excluding Luxembourg). Figure 4.2 was constructed by taking the average rate of growth of GDP weighted by size of the economy and the percentage increase in the actual number of employed people for these OECD countries, adjusting both for the change in the local population, and then measuring the percentage deviation from that average for individual countries. Negative values in figure 4.2 could thus correspond to *absolute* gains in 1991–2005. The point is to show *relative* gains, however. I adjusted

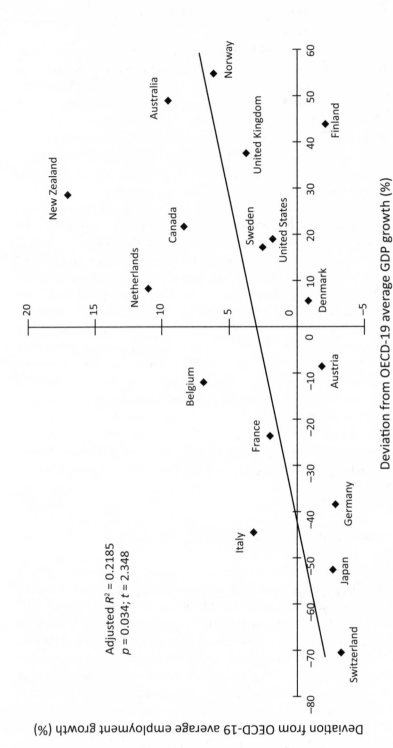

Fig. 4.2. Deviation from weighted average level of GDP and employment growth for seventeen OECD nations, 1991–2005 (percentage points). OECD, Organisation for Economic Cooperation and Development.

Source: Data from OECD national accounts, http://www.SourceOECD.org.

for population to control for the very different rates of population growth across these countries because rising population alone could account for the increased employment numbers or GDP. In particular, strong natural population growth plus immigration might otherwise account for much of the outsized GDP growth of the United States, Canada, Australia, and Britain.

I used actual employment, that is, the head count of people in employment (not the unemployment rate), to capture job creation. Whereas the unemployment rate conveys some information about the ability of an economy to create jobs, the more direct measure is the change in the number of people who actually do have jobs, after adjusting for population growth. The unemployment rate, by contrast, both excludes the discouraged unemployed who are no longer seeking work and includes those who register to collect benefits. A low unemployment rate could coexist with very low job creation and low rates of labor force participation, and a high unemployment rate could coexist with high labor force participation. By contrast, the United States combined high levels of labor force participation and job creation with a low unemployment rate, whereas Germany combined a smaller proportion the labor force at work with high unemployment. Again, I adjusted the data for population growth to control for outsized population growth and immigration into the English-speaking economies, even though high rates for both of these also pose an absorption challenge for labor markets.

I used weighted rates of growth because these more accurately capture the distribution of gains and losses across the OECD countries. It would not be surprising if a small economy achieved (or suffered) large relative gains (or losses) because there is always going be some stochastic variation in growth and smaller economies are more likely to show these random sector-specific effects. Consider Finland, which experienced huge losses, largely attributable to the collapse of the Soviet market, and then huge gains, largely attributable to the success of Nokia in the cell phone handset market. By contrast, it is harder for a huge, sectorally varied economy like that of the United States to secure substantially better or worse performance than the rest of the OECD. This alone makes U.S. performance in the 1990s remarkable.

All these adjustments are analytically conservative choices. From the point of view of the private actors, whose behavior drives investment flows and confirms a currency as a top international currency, what matters is simply the absolute difference in growth and profit rates rather than those rates adjusted for population growth. So the fact that the United States still had relatively higher rates of GDP and job growth than Germany or Japan even after we strip out population changes means that U.S. growth really was *relatively* outsized.

Figure 4.2 excludes Ireland as an extreme outlier. Irish GDP and employment each rose at roughly three times the average rate of the other countries. Spain and Portugal are not displayed because fully comparable data on employment growth are not available. And I exclude Luxembourg because it is a Corporate

Shell economy. These exclusions are also conservative because they remove data points that would tend to confirm our analysis. Finally, I use the period 1991–2005 because it captures most of the long post–Cold-War economic cycle, starting with the collapse of the Soviet Union and the reunification of Germany and ending with the beginning of the housing downturn. The argument here explains the origins of the downturn in the exhaustion of disinflation and dollar recycling.

Figure 4.2 reveals that the Americanized Rich and the United States did relatively better in terms of employment and GDP growth in 1991–2005 than did the Repressed Rich. In Figure 4.2, the two main axes are defined by the average rate of growth—that is, zero represents the average for these countries. So, first, figure 4.2 shows an unsurprising but nonetheless meaningful correlation ($R^2 = 0.2185$; $p = 0.034$) between above-average employment and GDP performance. More people working generally speaking means more GDP, although high rates of productivity growth can also cause higher GDP without increases in employment. Most of our Americanized Rich countries populate the upper right-hand cell, whereas the Repressed Rich populate the lower left-hand part of the figure.

This pattern raises three questions. Was growth in the Americanized Rich and the U.S. real growth, or was it only about outsized and unsustainable increases in debt financed consumption? If this growth really was housing-led, did housing crowd out manufacturing growth, as some critics argue? And, finally, was growth really connected to housing finance markets? The second section in this chapter deals with the last question; I address the others here. Put briefly, the answer is that the Americanized Rich experienced real increases in output that outstripped those of the Repressed Rich. Although the Americanized Rich overconsumed, they also overproduced and overinvested (as the more detailed analysis in chapter 5 also shows for the United States).

Table 4.1 displays more detailed economic data about relative performance in some of the rich OECD economies to address the issue of consumption versus output in the Americanized Rich. Table 4.1 displays only the G-7 countries plus Australia and the Netherlands only because a table with twenty countries is unwieldy. The numbers indicate the degree to which a country over- or underperformed compared to the average for all twenty rich OECD countries in percentage terms (Spain, Portugal, and Ireland are included), ranked by their unmisery index, which I explain later. Thus, in the first cell, 52 percent means that Australian economywide real gross value-added increased 52 percent more than the population-adjusted average increase in these twenty economies. This corresponds to an absolute real 67.5 percent increase. In the cell directly below, −68 percent indicates that despite the Australian overperformance with respect to economywide gross value-added, Australia underperformed by 68 percent with respect to manufacturing value-added. This will not surprise Australians, who watched entire labor-intensive industries collapse or retool in the face of Asian competition during the 1990s. Equally so, the extremely large jump in metals

TABLE 4.1.
Relative economic performance in select OECD economies, 1991–2005

Relative change	Australia	United Kingdom	Canada	United States	Netherlands	France	Italy	Germany[a]	Japan
Real GVA (%)	52	49	19	21	5	-23	-46	-30	-48
Manufacturing GVA (%)	-68	-79	24	71	-35	-35	-99	-79	-47
Real GFCF (%)	119	33	18	66	-32	-52	-70	-94	-128
Metals and machinery GFCF (%)	297	-28	4	60	-5	-62	-86	-81	-77
Housing GFCF (%)	-9	1	-3	90	-32	-69	-90	-96	-159
Employed (%)	10	4	8	2	11	2	3	-3	-3
Real GDP (%)	49	38	22	19	8	-24	-44	-38	-53
Un-misery index[b]	5.9	4.1	3.0	2.1	1.9	-2.2	-4.1	-4.1	-5.5

Sources: Data from OECD national accounts, http://www.sourceOECD.org.
Notes: Adjusted for changes in population and ranked by un-misery index. Data are the percentage deviation from the OECD-20 weighted average. Performance is judged against all twenty rich OECD economies. GFCF, gross fixed-capital formation; GVA, gross value-added; OECD, Organisation for Economic Cooperation and Development.
[a]Federal Republic of Germany.
[b]Un-misery index = 10 × (Relative change in number of employed + Relative change in GDP), to construct a normalized -10 to 10 index.

and manufacturing gross fixed-capital formation in Australia—almost three times the average increase—captures the high rates of substitution of capital for labor as Australian firms struggled to survive import competition.

Table 4.1 allows us to dispel certain myths about the 1990s boom. One such myth is that the U.S. boom was only about consumption—gas-guzzling sport utility vehicles (SUVs), flat-panel TVs, and McMansions. This is not borne out in the data. The U.S. and other "winner" Americanized Rich economies typically had above-average growth in economywide gross value-added (GVA), in manufacturing GVA, in gross fixed-capital formation (GFCF), in housing GFCF, and—significantly—in metals and manufacturing GFCF. These additional indicators show that GDP and employment gains were not solely about housing construction. On the contrary, the hollowed-out U.S. economy experienced substantially larger increases in gross fixed investment than the typical Repressed Rich economy. Even in the narrower category of metals and machinery manufacturing investment, in absolute terms the United States experienced a doubling of investment. Meanwhile manufacturing powerhouses such as Germany and Japan each saw only a one-fifth increase in metals and machinery manufacturing investment over the whole fifteen-year period. Manufacturing value-added in the United States also expanded much faster than in Germany or Japan, with a 71 percent relative increase and an absolute increase of 78 percent. Lower rates of investment growth in Japan and Germany do not indicate rapid productivity growth that conserved capital. Relatively speaking, Japanese and German productivity gains lagged those in the United States in our period (see tables 5.1 and 5.2). Table 4.1 also shows that, relatively speaking, the United States had well above-average increases in housing GFCF. But this reflects the stagnation of the German and Japanese housing markets, which saw absolute falls in real prices as well as absolute declines in housing GFCF in Japan and only a 5 percent increase in housing GFCF in Germany over this entire period.

Although housing construction surely played a strong role in the economic booms of the winners, in almost all of the Americanized Rich the evolution of the absolute level of housing GFCF actually was smaller than the overall growth of GFCF. Thus, if we turn from relative to absolute data, real GFCF in metals and manufacturing in the United States more than tripled, whereas U.S. housing GFCF only doubled, in 1991–2005. Indeed, in the United States the housing share of GFCF actually fell from roughly 65 percent in 1991 to 48 percent in 2005 before abruptly jumping up again. This pattern is replicated across most of the Americanized Rich. Thus, housing was not the only thing that grew during the long boom. Instead, housing had strong Keynesian multiplier effects across a wide range of industries, spurring a virtuous cycle of outsized growth in real production, investment, and employment. It must be admitted, however, that powered by the extension of cheap mortgages to subprime borrowers in 2006 and 2007 housing investment in the United States did jump well above trend after our period. Housing GFCF rose almost 2 percentage points to approximately 7 percent of

U.S. GDP in 2006. But this, of course, is why the boom came to an end—the need to chase subprime borrowers to originate new mortgages indicates that the resources needed for further growth had been exhausted.

The last row of table 4.1 presents a synthetic index that combines the degrees of over- and underperformance for each country into one metric. It combines the degree of deviation from the average evolution of population-adjusted employment with the similar deviation in GDP gains in 1991–2005. This index simply adds the relative change in GDP per capita and employment and then multiplies by 10 in order to get a kind of reverse misery, or "un-misery," index scaled from −10 to 10. The misery index of the inflation era combined change in the consumer price index with the open unemployment rate to determine how badly an economy was doing. The un-misery index inverts this to tell us roughly how *well* an economy is doing in terms of generating output and employment. The un-misery index is used later (in figure 4.4), when we confirm the relationship between housing finance systems and growth.

We have confirmed the faster relative growth of the United States and Americanized Rich. What explains that outcome?

Explaining Differential Growth

What explains the pattern of differential growth we have been discussing? I must first clear away alternative explanations for the employment and growth outcomes before elaborating my own. The conventional explanations for the employment outcomes in Europe stress corporatist social pacts that exchanged wage restraint for investment and a bigger social wage. The issue in these arguments is whether corporatism, employment protection for workers, and large welfare states affect employment and GDP growth. The analysis that follows suggests that this view omits an equally important *microinstitutional* cause affecting aggregate demand and thus suffers from omitted-variable bias. The overlooked variable is the institutional structure of the domestic housing finance system, which affected how disinflation was translated into increased aggregate demand in 1991–2005. Thus, much of the European debate on institutional rigidities misses the point, namely that aggregate demand still matters for growth.

Crucially, the differences in housing systems do *not* line up along the usual liberal versus corporatist or LME versus CME dichotomies that are the meta-categories for most work in this genre.[4] This allows us to say something novel and interesting to the usual arguments about the causes of high unemployment in the core of euroland. If housing finance systems had lined up with the usual LME versus CME dichotomy, we would be left with yet another situation of overdetermination and analytic opacity. Next, I consider the corporatism arguments; after that, I elaborate an alternative analysis that stresses housing finance as an alternative explanation.

Social Pacts and Growth

Many European economies and Japan had dismal employment and unemployment records during the long 1990s. They created relatively few jobs, thus consigning labor market entrants to unemployment, exchanging older workers for younger ones, or deterring female labor market entry. Euroland unemployment averaged around 10 percent at the beginning of the 1990s and declined slightly to around 8 percent by 2000, before ending at 8.6 percent in 2005. Given the slow population growth in euroland, underperformance reflects a failure to create jobs. Although the Repressed Rich account for approximately 46 percent of the rich OECD population and the Americanized Rich (net of the United States) account for only 20 percent, each group generated almost the same number of new jobs in 1991–2005 (table 4.2). Moreover, the Repressed Rich traditionally have relatively low rates of labor force participation compared to the Americanized Rich; they have higher unemployment even though fewer people are active in the labor market.

These dismal euroland averages conceal important national differences in employment performance that show up in our distinction between the Americanized Rich and Repressed Rich. Some European countries that fall among the Americanized Rich, such as Ireland, Denmark, and the Netherlands, saw sharp falls in unemployment and substantial gains in employment. Others such as Germany, France, and Belgium, saw only small employment increases during the long 1990s. Analysts looking for policies with which to battle unemployment naturally looked for policy explanations for the employment-miracle countries. Although everyone conceded that economic cycles mattered, the conventional wisdom in these analyses pointed to corporatist bargains that exchanged wage restraint and labor market reforms for business investment as one source of employment gains. In other words, analyses of the success stories stressed the contribution of old or newly created labor market institutional structures to employment revival.[5]

The conventional wisdom on European macroeconomic stability and growth has always stressed corporatist bargaining and wage restraint as a master variable. Although the target for these analyses has shifted from growth to inflation to

TABLE 4.2.
Comparative job creation: Change in total employment in the United States, Americanized Rich, and Repressed Rich, 1991–2005

	Population, 2005 (thousands)	Share of OECD Population, 2005 (%)	Net Job Creation, 1991–2005 (thousands)	Share of OECD New Jobs (%)
United States	296,677	34.1	23,117	50.0
Americanized Rich	169,345	19.5	11,484	24.8
Repressed Rich	404,317	46.5	11,672	25.2

Source: Data from OECD national accounts, http://www.SourceOECD.org.
Notes: OECD, Organisation for Economic Cooperation and Development.

employment over the past forty years, they identify willingness and ability of unions to commit to wage restraint as the major causal factor for macroeconomic balance.[6] Thus Lars Calmfors and John Driffill's statistical analyses show that either high levels of coordination or very low levels of labor market regulation were optimal for low inflation and unemployment outcomes. In the former, unions could not externalize the costs of wage militancy; in the latter, unions were absent.[7] Fritz Scharpf provides a game theoretic explanation of the actor behavior behind the Calmfors and Driffill argument.[8] Lane Kenworthy provides the best recent exposition of this argument, suggesting that economies characterized by corporatist wage restraint, and the increased latitude for employment promotion this gives states, delivered better employment outcomes in the 1980s than did less coordinated economies.[9] Precisely this contrast motivates David Soskice's effort to link microeconomic behavior by households to macroeconomic outcomes.[10] Whether or not these analyses are causally correct—and I am somewhat agnostic on this issue, as explained next—the tradition of looking to corporate actors and their bargains as the cause of positive macroeconomic outcomes continued at the end of the 1990s when analysts began looking for explanations for the euroland employment malaise.

This orientation toward corporatist intermediation or coordination naturally pointed both analysis and policy prescriptions toward social pacts as sources of better employment outcomes. Put simply, analysts argued that employment revival hinged on explicit corporatist bargains in which unions conceded wage restraint and labor market reform, employers promised investment in return, and the state rewarded this good behavior with forbearance with respect to intervention in collective bargaining and tight monetary policy. These new social pacts thus would generate new jobs by combining increased investment with more (because cheaper) exports and by permitting states to reduce labor market regulation. In a very visible International Labour Organisation (ILO) publication, Peter Auer argues pointedly that corporatist pacts explained employment successes in the Netherlands, Ireland, Austria, and Denmark. Auer argued that it was countries "which have retained, while adapting, their [corporatist] institutions, which now see their economic success spilling over into the labour market. It is therefore not the flexibility of the market, but the existence and adaptability of institutions and regulations which explain success in the cases reviewed."[11]

Similarly, Martin Rhodes identifies a new competitive corporatism as the cause of economic success in Spain, Italy, and the Netherlands.[12] In a variety of publications, Rhodes, Bernhard Ebbinghaus, and Anke Hassel discern competitive corporatism and pacting in Germany, although most conceded that the Alliance for Jobs had limited effect.[13] Niamh Hardiman attributes employment success in Ireland to an even broader pact encompassing social-service agencies and their clients.[14] Rhodes explicitly delineates the content of these corporatist social pacts: "All...social pacts...since the mid-1980s seek to combine wage moderation, the quest for lower social charges and greater flexibility of work conditions. The latter two objectives in particular imply (a) reform to social security systems (often with greater equity as a goal) and (b) a response to employers' demands for new productivity trade-offs."[15] The core assumption in all these analyses is a conviction that reducing wage costs improved competitiveness and boosted employment.[16]

By contrast, Andrew Martin dismisses the utility of contemporary social pacts and argues that macro-policy mattered more than fundamentally microeconomic institutions. Martin identifies the restrictive monetary policy practiced by the Bundesbank and European System of Central Banks (ECB) as the barrier to any sustained employment revival. According to Martin, the restrictive monetary stance of the ECB precluded a growth spurt sustained enough to absorb the backlog of the unemployed. He argues that labor market institutions alone could neither explain the persistence of European unemployment nor offer a solution. Instead, we have to look to the evolution of aggregate demand and the dampening of aggregate demand in Europe by the ECB. There was, he maintains, "no institutional mechanism by which aggregate demand in Euroland as a whole can be managed so as to pursue the goal of employment as well as price stability."[17]

Martin correctly identifies the crucial role of aggregate demand. Wage restraint, at best, simply changes the composition of aggregate demand from wages to investment or, at worst, reduces domestic aggregate demand, as in Soskice's New Keynesian analysis. Investment may have greater multiplier effects than wages, but it only does so if the investment occurs at home. Yet wage restraint at home depressed local demand, driving investment overseas. Thus, continent-wide wage restraint could have exactly the opposite effect predicted by the competitive corporatism arguments, triggering a downward spiral of demand and yet more unemployment. Yet the Americanized Rich in Europe *did* generate more growth and employment, including ones firmly anchored in the euro. If macroeconomic policy was uniform across euroland and strongly influenced monetary policy in Scandinavia and Britain, how did they grow?

In this context, it is worth returning to Kenworthy's interesting and balanced analysis. He notes that corporatist countries generated the same (slow) level of employment growth in the 1990s that they generated in the 1980s. This steady-state stability proved inadequate to the demand for new jobs in the 1990s but nonetheless preserved the old ones. In Kenworthy's analysis, what changed was not job creation in the coordinated economies but, rather, job creation in the noncoordinated ones. They suddenly proved more adept with respect to employment growth in the 1990s than they had been in the 1970s and 1980s.

What changed in the 1990s? The social pact literature would incline us to look at local wage-bargaining institutions and microeconomic issues such as labor market regulation. Soskice attempts a macroeconomic explanation based on microeconomic institutions. He argues that excess household saving and decreased consumption were an unintended consequence of threats to substantial welfare protections for skilled workers. For him, unemployment generates yet more un-employment:

> Thus in comparative terms, the insecurity-driven slowdown of consumption in Germany (and Japan and Italy) plays an important part in understanding differ-ent employment performance between the liberal market Anglo-Saxon economies and the large CMEs. The specificity of skills [in Germany and Japan], aggravated by uncertainty about the future of the protective welfare state, itself generated by the consensus nature of the political system, is the analytic tool which enables us to understand this.[18]

Soskice's analysis, however, seems circular. Rising unemployment feeds on itself subsequent to an external shock. But, German reunification aside, this argument can-not explain disparate performance between the CMEs and LMEs and, as we have noted, *among* the CMEs. At the same time, Soskice's explanation does not explain why workers in LMEs did not similarly discount their future stream of income and cut back consumption. The United States saw widespread defaults on traditional defined-benefit corporate pensions with cuts much greater than those proposed for European public pensions. And U.S. fiscal policy arguably was more stringent than that in Repressed Europe, which saw larger deficits all through the 1990s.

Our position, by contrast, is that the corporatism-centered analyses are looking at the wrong microinstitutional basis for macroeconomic outcomes and, thus, also misconstrue one large environmental shock. Housing market financial institutions can play a major role in creating aggregate demand. Thus, the usual corporatist analyses also misconstrue the environmental effect of falling interest rates. They focus too much on *real* interest rates, which admittedly remained high over the 1990s, and ignore the dramatic drop in *nominal* interest rates. Different housing finance institutions translated disinflation—a huge environmental change—into increased aggregate demand in differing degrees, which in turn caused different levels of job creation.

Housing Finance Markets and Growth

How then did housing market finance institutions matter? Put simply, housing market financial institutions that were most like those in the U.S. market had the greatest capacity to translate the disinflation of the 1990s into increased demand and rising employment; those that were least like the United States, had the least capacity. Additional aggregate demand operated through the normal Keynesian multiplier mechanisms—it stimulated additional employment though both de-mand and supply channels. Much of that additional employment was the entry of women into the service sector and low-skilled men into construction, decreasing unemployment precisely in the labor pools that typically experience higher levels of unemployment, longer unemployment, and labor market drop out. Countries with housing finance market institutions least like those in the United States, and which in addition stifled the growth of aggregate demand through wage restraint, did not experience rising aggregate demand and employment. Instead, in a disinflationary environment, financial repression and wage restraint were a self-inflicted wound that hindered growth and forced wage-restraint countries to rely on exports for growth. Countries with mixed institutions had mixed outcomes.

The 1990s was a period of profound disinflation everywhere in the OECD. Unlike the 1970s and 1980s, long-term *nominal* interest rates fell. Euroarea long-term interest rates fell from 11.2 percent in 1990 to 3.5 percent by 2005. U.S. long-term rates similarly fell from 8.7 to 4.0 percent in 1990–2003.[19] Although real interest rates did not fall, studies show that housing prices are much more sensitive to nominal rates than real rates.[20] Disinflation potentially could have released new purchasing power into the hands of consumers and companies. Why did the global disinflation aided by the Clinton administration conservative fiscal policy not benefit all OECD economies equally? Put bluntly, even though every debtor felt falling nominal interest rates, not every debtor could take advantage of the falling rates to reduce interest payments and free up cash for other consumption. Instead, debtors in countries with U.S.-style housing finance systems were able to use falling nominal interest rates to refresh their purchasing power.

Four key features characterize U.S. housing finance markets:

1. Relatively high levels of private individual homeownership.
2. Relatively high levels of mortgage debt in relation to GDP.
3. Easy and relatively cheap refinancing of mortgages, as well as cash out of home equity.
4. The ability of banks to securitize loans and move them off their books.

These four institutional features determined the degree to which falling rates translated into new aggregate demand because the level of homeownership determines how many households are affected by changes in housing costs and housing prices, the level of debt in relation to GDP determines how much purchasing power can be activated if debt payments are reduced, and low transaction costs for refinancing and the possibility of securitization determine whether it is actually possible to reduce those payments.[21] Thus, these features can be thought of as the sources for the breadth, depth, and likelihood of increased aggregate demand. When all four features were present, sometimes with an additional fillip from tax subsidies for mortgage interest, they enabled a relatively straightforward process of Keynesian demand stimulus to operate. When they were not present, disinflation did not trigger increased aggregate demand.

As nominal interest rates fell in countries with U.S.-style housing finance institutions, homeowners refinanced mortgages, shifting considerable purchasing power away from rentier interests and toward individuals with a higher propensity to consume goods, services, and housing. This consumption, in turn, generated new employment through standard Keynesian multiplier effects. Much of this new employment involved married women entering service-sector labor markets in order to sustain increased consumption. This new employment sustained the expansion by helping shift the federal budget into surplus and thus enabling the Fed or the local central bank to continue lowering interest rates. Much the same happened in equity (stock and share) markets, but for the average person, the housing market was a more important source of new consumption power because in the OECD more people own houses than own equities and because the average person has more housing equity than stocks. Granted that the United States is an extreme example, the top income decile in the United States owned 75 percent of all stocks by value in 2004 but only 36 percent of net home equity, whereas the bottom 90 percent owned only 25 percent of stocks but 64 percent of home equity.[22] Studies show that people spend unrealized home equity at four times the rate of stocks. At the same time, roughly half of the average European's net worth was home equity.[23] Home equity was thus potentially more important for creating new aggregate demand.

Mortgage refinancing released new purchasing power into the economy through two channels: reduced monthly payments and mortgage equity withdrawal. Consider an incumbent homeowner with a $100,000 mortgage at a 10 percent interest rate. To simplify matters, assume that he or she makes no principal payments and has no property taxes and that the mortgage represents 100 percent of the value of the property. The homeowner's housing costs are the interest payment on this mortgage, which amount to $10,000 per year. Now suppose that open-market mortgage interest rates fall to 5 percent. If our homeowner can easily and costlessly refinance the mortgage, he or she will save $5,000 per year in interest payments. This is the first channel.

Falling nominal interest rates on mortgages also drive up house prices because many—probably most—people buy on the basis of a given monthly payment, not on the basis of their total debt. Thus, if a home-buying household could afford $10,000 in annual interest when interest rates were 10 percent, they would buy a house with a $100,000 mortgage. But if interest rates fell to 5 percent, this household would start bidding for a $200,000 house. The original owners of the house would thus experience windfall gains if they sold. Incumbent owners typically used those gains to buy a more expensive house higher up the property ladder, thus bestowing similar gains on those above them, who also moved up, and so on, inflating housing equity across the entire income distribution. (Keep this in mind when we turn to the housing bust in chapter 7.)

Although the total stock of houses is not for sale in any given year, the valuation of houses is always a function of the most recent sales for those houses that are actively traded, just as it is for equities. If this wealth—fictitious capital—could be tapped, it might represent a new source of aggregate demand in the economy. Households that did not sell—easily the majority—could tap this notional increase in home values by taking out a home equity line of credit (HELOC) or home equity loan, which is collateralized by the owner's equity in his or her house. These loans are effectively second mortgages secured on the owner's existing equity and most often used to remodel the house, purchase durable goods, or repay more expensive credit card debt. Approximately one-fourth of U.S. homeowners have a HELOC or similar housing-related debt, amounting to just over $1 trillion, or a bit over 10 percent of total U.S. mortgage debt. The bidding-up process combined with a rising population to increase the nominal value of all U.S. residential real estate equity from roughly $6.5 trillion in 1991 to over $20.5 trillion in 2005.[24]

The institutional structure of housing finance determines whether these two channels will operate. Falling nominal interest rates will trigger a self-sustaining upward spiral when the transaction costs involved in mortgage origination and refinancing are low, when prepayment penalties are low, and when banks can securitize mortgages and HELOCs to move them off their books. These conditions characterize the United States and our other Americanized Rich countries but not the Repressed Rich. For example, stamp duties on mortgages in Belgium start at 10 percent, and many EU countries impose a substantial value-added tax (VAT) on house sales. In the U.S. state of Virginia, the equivalent of the "stamp duty" recently doubled—to 0.1 percent. (See table 4.3 for detailed information on housing market systems in the OECD.)

Similarly, the ability of banks to securitize loans allows them to move interest rate risk off their books and earn money from increased transactions rather than an increased spread. This gives them an incentive to continue lending regardless of the movement of interest rates. The volume and share of all asset-backed securities (ABSs) relative to U.S. GDP and total financial-sector debt indicate their importance to U.S. economic expansion in 1991–2005. In 1990, all ABSs amounted to 4 percent of GDP, roughly $250 billion, but by 2007, they amounted to 30 percent, or $4.3 trillion. Similarly, ABSs accounted for 9 percent of total U.S. financial-sector debt in 1990, but rose to 27 percent by 2007.[25] The majority of ABSs are MBSs. Thus, ABSs and the securitization process were crucial to the expansion of both the nonbanking sector and of the credit cycle in general.

Retrospective analyses confirm that the release of home equity in various forms mattered much more than the rising share markets for the net increase in real personal consumption in the OECD in 1996–2006, both because the propensity to consume out of home equity was much higher than the propensity to consume rising capital gains and because of the larger salience of home equity in the average person's portfolio.[26] Without any easy way to tap that equity, the latent additional purchasing power in home equity remained exactly that—latent. Thus, countries needed to combine widespread ownership with high levels of mortgage debt and easy refinancing to get economic leverage from disinflation.

TABLE 4.3.
Housing market characteristics for nineteen OECD countries

	Owner-Occupation (% of Households)[a]	Social Rental (% of Households)[a]	Private Rental (% of Households)[a]	Change in Owner-Occupation, 1980–Latest (% of Households)[b]	Residential Mortgages, 1992 (% of GDP)[b]	Residential Mortgages, 2004 (% of GDP)[b]	Typical Loan-to-Value Ratio, 2002 (%)[b]	Maximum Loan-to-Value Ratio, 2002 (%)[c]	Typical Loan Term, 2002 (Years)[c]	Mortgage Securitization Possible?	Home Equity Release Possible?
Austria	56	21	20	+6	~5.0	20.3	60	80	20–30	No	No
Belgium	74	7	16	+9	19.9	31.2	83	100	20	No	No
Denmark	51	19	26	-2	70.1	88.4	80	80	30	Yes	Yes (1993)
Finland	60	14	16	0	37.1	37.8	75	80	15–18	No	Yes
France	54	17	21	+9	21.2	26.2	67	100	15	Yes but limited	Not used
Germany	40	7[d]	50[d]	+5	41.0	52.2	67[d]	80[d]	25–30[d]	As covered bonds	Yes, but not used
Ireland	78	9	16	+1	20.3	52.7	66	90	20	Yes but limited	Yes but limited use
Italy	69	5	11	+16	3.2	15.3	55	80	15	Only recently	Not used
Netherlands	53	36	11	+13	43.2	111.1	90	115	30	Yes	Yes
Norway	78	3			46.1	56.0	83	80	15–20	Yes but limited	No
Portugal	64	3	25	+23	~20.0	52.5	70	90	15	No	No
Spain	85	1	10	+9	12.9	45.9	70	100	15	New but rising	Yes but limited use
Sweden	41	27	13	+4	50.8	51.6	77	80	<30	Yes	Yes
United Kingdom	69	22	9	+11	52.8	75.3	69	110	25	Yes	Yes
Australia	72	n/a	n/a	n/a	78.0	301.0	65	n/a	25	Yes	Yes
New Zealand	70	n/a	n/a	n/a	146.0	267.0	n/a	n/a	n/a	Yes but limited	No
Canada	64	n/a	n/a	n/a	42.7	43.1	75	n/a	25	Yes	Yes but limited use
United States	68	n/a	n/a	+5	45.0	65.0	78	100	30	Yes	Yes
Japan	60	n/a	n/a	n/a	25.3	36.8	80	n/a	25–30	No	No

Sources:
[a] Judith Allen, "Welfare Regimes, Welfare Systems and Housing in Southern Europe," *European Journal of Housing Policy* 6 no. 3 (2006): 251–77; EU Housing Statistics 2004 (years vary); Pietro Catte, Nathalie Girouarde, Robert Price, and Christopher Andre, "The Contribution of Housing Markets to Cyclical Resilience," *OECD Economic Studies* no. 38 (2004/1): 138 for non-EU countries.
[b] European Mortgage Foundation, *Hypostat 2006* (Brussels, EMF 2006).
[c] Duncan MacLennan, John Muellbauer, and Mark Stephens, "Asymmetries in Housing and Financial Market Institutions and EMU," *Oxford Review of Economic Policy* 14, no. 3 (1998): 70.
Notes: n/a data not available. OECD, Organisation for Economic Cooperation and Development.
[d] West Germany only.

A brief comparison of three major European housing markets with the U.S. market shows this. Keep in mind that housing costs amount to from one-fifth to one-quarter of disposable income in most European economies, so that falling interest rates have considerable potential for releasing new aggregate demand.[27] Italy, the first example, has widespread ownership; more Italian households own their homes than U.S. households. But these households largely hold no mortgage debt because the difficulty of foreclosure and the absence of securitization until recently mean that banks were reluctant to extend credit to consumers. Mortgages amounted to approximately 12 percent of GDP in 1992. The absence of mortgage debt nullifies any immediate advantage to consumers from falling mortgage interest rates. Refinancing has no purpose and home equity remains latent. Falling interest rates thus do not generate greater purchasing power.

France also has widespread homeownership and has nearly double the Italian level of mortgages in relation to GDP. But costly and difficult refinancing means that homeowners cannot translate falling nominal interest rates into a smaller interest burden. Here, too, home equity remains latent, even though prices rose strongly in the mid-2000s. Moreover, in both Italy and France, the aspiring homeowners' need to save for large down payments appears to depress aggregate demand.[28]

Germany, in contrast to Italy and France, has a relatively high level of mortgage debt relative to GDP. In 1992, it was only a few percentage points different from the U.S. level. But Germany has one of the lowest levels of homeownership in the OECD—approximately 42 percent in 2002—and refinancing is difficult and expensive. Most mortgages are securitized through *Pfandbriefe* ("covered bonds"), which remain on bank balance sheets. Consequently, banks impose hefty prepayment penalties to compensate for lost interest. Rentier interests thus prevail over debtor consumption. German housing prices actually fell despite ever lower interest rates in the 1990s.

By contrast, in the United States widespread homeownership, high levels of mortgage debt in relation to GDP, easy refinancing, and a huge volume of securitization permitted housing market Keynesianism to operate. The U.S. Federal Reserve Bank estimates that 80 percent of the increase in U.S. mortgage debt in the 1990s can be accounted for by mortgage equity withdrawal (MEW) and that MEW ran at roughly $0.3 trillion annually in 1991–2000 and at roughly $1 trillion annually in 2001–2005 ($530 billion, on average). MEW flowed through three channels. Roughly one-half of home equity borrowing was used to pay down higher-interest-rate consumer debt (usually credit cards), freeing up cash for future consumption. One-fourth was used for home improvements, which typically are very labor intense and thus have immediate employment effects. And one-fifth flowed directly into other consumption.[29] Although MEW came late to Britain, it rose from virtually nil to £13.2 billion, or 6.1 percent of disposable income, by the first quarter of 2007 and totaled £256 billion in 2001–2006.[30]

Finally, it is worth repeating that falling interest rates also ramified through liquid housing markets to create fictitious capital that banks and investment houses could repackage as MBSs to sell to domestic and foreign investors. So disinflation, caused in part by falling import prices and foreign purchases of U.S. securities, helped create even more securities to be sold overseas, allowing the recycling/arbitrage system described in chapter 3 to function. Mortgage securitization created a vehicle through which the fictitious capital in housing could be liberated, priced, and validated in the market.

Global Finance, Local Mortgages

Recall the global arbitrage analyzed in chapters 2 and 3. The United States borrows short term at low interest rates from the rest of the world and then reinvests long term for higher returns. Here I show the direct connections between foreigners' inward portfolio investment and housing markets. At one level, the connection is direct and obvious. Much of the portfolio debt that the United States sold overseas during the long 1990s was various flavors of MBSs. Together with U.S. Treasury debt, those sales helped drive down interest rates on U.S. mortgages, energizing the U.S. housing boom. In figure 4.1, this is shown by the arrow linking the arbitrage box and the housing finance system box.

The interest rate on the ten-year U.S. Treasury bond serves as the reference rate or benchmark for nearly all U.S. mortgages because the typical mortgage runs between seven and ten years, despite a thirty-year amortization schedule. Lower interest rates on U.S. Treasury bonds thus flow through immediately to new mortgage originations and somewhat more slowly to adjustable-rate mortgage resets. Sixty percent of foreign investment in U.S. portfolio debt as of December 2006 occurred as purchases of U.S. government and government-guaranteed agency debt. At that time, foreign investors held 52 percent of outstanding marketable U.S. Treasury securities and 16.8 percent of outstanding agency debt.[31] Agency debt comprises MBSs issued by the two government-sponsored financial giants, Fannie Mae and Freddie Mac.[32] In chapter 7, I explain how MBSs work in more detail; for now, we need only note that foreigners bought them in large quantities.

Foreigners' outsized foreign holdings of U.S. Treasury and agency debt helped to drive down interest rates on U.S. mortgages during the long 1990s. Current estimates suggest that recycling of Asian trade surpluses during the late 1990s and early 2000s depressed yields on ten-year U.S. Treasury debt by approximately 90 basis points, or almost 1 percentage point, and by as much as 150 basis points in 2005.[33] There are no estimates of the consequences of European or oil-exporter recycling, but plausibly they should have had much the same effect in the early to mid-1990s, when these groups were the primary funders of the U.S. trade deficit.

Foreign purchases of agency debt have an even more direct effect on housing. As already mentioned, agency debt is composed of MBSs originated by Fannie Mae and Freddie Mac. The U.S. federal government created Fannie Mae in 1938 to make housing more affordable by nationalizing the flow of funds in the mortgage market. Fannie Mae was privatized in 1968–1970, leaving the Government National Mortgage Association (Ginnie Mae) behind to finance public housing. Savings and loan banks (i.e., the U.S. version of *sparkassen* or building societies) got Freddie Mac, their own version of Fannie Mae, in 1970; it was fully privatized in 1989. The market belief in an implicit government guarantee for the firms—validated in August 2008 when the U.S. Treasury and Fed placed both firms into conservatorship and said it would accept their MBSs as collateral—provided both Freddie Mac and Fannie Mae with an advantageous position in the creation of MBSs because they could borrow in credit markets at rates below even the best rated banks.

Fannie Mae and Salomon Brothers essentially invented the modern MBS market in 1981 and also pioneered the overseas sale of these securities.[34] Freddie Mac invented the collateralized mortgage obligation (CMO), a derivative that slices up principal and interest payments into different tranches so that investors can buy bonds with maturities and returns that vary from the underlying individual mortgages in 1983. (Collateralized debt obligations, CDOs, encompass CMOs and other derivatives backed by different forms of debt; that is, CMOs are a subset of CDOs.) Securitization allows banks to move mortgage loans off their books by letting banks sell those mortgages to the capital market and thus replenish their capital. This allows banks to originate yet more loans while earning the bulk of their income from fees. This contrasts with the pre–financial liberalization model, in which banks held mortgages to maturity and made money from the interest rate spread between deposits and loans. Securitization removes interest risk from the books of the banks by shifting the risk presented by changing interest rates to the buyer of the MBS or CMO/CDO. Securitization technically does not shift credit risk per se because banks are sometimes required to guarantee the underlying mortgages.[35]

As late as 1989, savings and loan banks still provided 27 percent of consumer debt, mostly for home mortgages and mostly held in their own portfolios. By 2004, specialized mortgage lenders accounted for 39.4 percent of consumer debt, mostly by taking market share away from those savings and loan banks.[36] Unlike savings banks, private lenders typically securitize their loans and were responsible for the rapid growth of the subprime MBS and CDO market in 2004–2007. Figure 4.3 shows the growth and relative market shares of the three government-sponsored enterprises (GSEs) and nongovernment originators of MBSs from 1988 to 2006. The spike in mortgage debt and the huge post-2004 volume of subprime MBSs is quite visible.

Fannie Mae and Freddie Mac are both intermediaries and principals in the securitization process. They buy residential mortgages from the original mortgage lender, pool those mortgages in MBSs, and sell them directly or as derivatives to

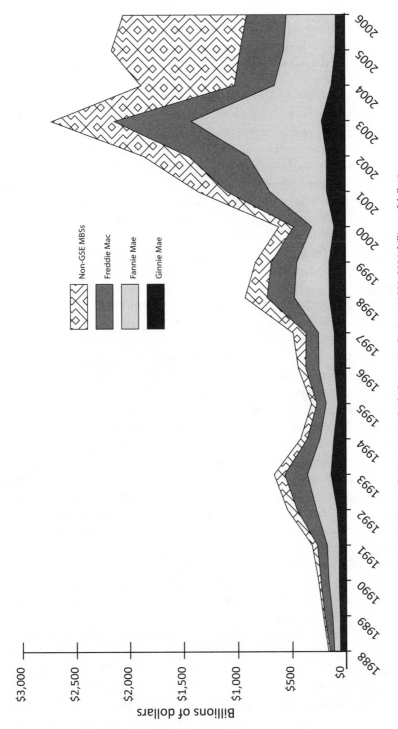

Fig. 4.3. Origins of U.S. mortgage-backed securities by issuer, 1988–2006 (billions of dollars).
Source: Data from Calculated Risk, http://calculatedrisk.blogspot.com.

the secondary market. Securitization allows investors to buy a bond whose income stream is defined by the aggregated principal and interest payments made by individual homebuyers. Pooling mortgages averages out the risks of default and prepayment, creating a predictable stream of payments. In addition, mortgages with similar risk characteristics can be packaged and sold at interest rates that reflect those risks, or they can be blended to create new derivative securities with the characteristics sought by investors. The primary domestic purchasers of agency debt are insurance funds and pension plans seeking to offset predictable long-term liabilities with equally predictable long-term assets. Fannie Mae and Freddie Mac also hold some MBSs to maturity. By 2007, Agency MBSs accounted for one-half of an outstanding U.S. mortgage debt of roughly $10 trillion, split 5:4 between Fannie Mae and Freddie Mac. A further one-quarter of the outstanding mortgage debt was privately securitized, and the last one-quarter resided with the lending institution as a discrete loan.[37]

Fannie Mae and Freddie Mac are the major conduits connecting international credit markets to the domestic U.S. housing market via securitized mortgages. In 2001, foreign holdings of agency MBSs amounted to $133 billion. By 2007, foreign agency holdings exceeded $1 trillion, with foreign official institutions (i.e., Asian Lockbox central banks) holding the majority.[38] Japan and China accounted for 45 percent of foreign MBS holdings—plus more private ABSs—and 52 percent of foreign U.S. Treasury holdings by 2006.[39] Private placement of ABSs was a minor but riskier conduit, although one that swelled in importance in 2004–2007 when the subprime mortgage business came into its, er, prime (see figure 4.3). The structured investment vehicles (off–balance sheet entities) of European banks appear to account for most of the non-Asian foreign purchases, albeit often on behalf of oil exporters, but Chinese purchases also appeared to have increased in 2007.[40]

Although the foreign share of securitized agency debt is *relatively* lower than its share of Treasury debt, the *absolute* amounts are not as disparate because there was almost twice as much agency debt in circulation at the end of 2006 as there was Treasury debt. Indeed, agency debt typically constituted one-third of all marketable U.S. debt securities, public and private. Consequently, foreign purchases of U.S. debt energized a giant circle: foreign purchases of U.S. Treasuries depressed the reference rate for mortgage interest rates, causing the issuing of new mortgages through refinancing or purchase; the new mortgages were then bundled into MBSs and sold to foreigners; and their eager purchases further depressed mortgage rates, enabling banks to fund yet more mortgage debt.

So far in this chapter, I have shown that the United States and the Americanized Rich had above-average employment and GDP performance and that they offered a housing pathway for the translation of falling interest rates into increased aggregate demand. I have also shown the connection between U.S. global arbitrage and the U.S. housing financial system. The last piece of the puzzle is connecting housing financial systems back to above- or below-average economic performance.

Housing and Growth

As I argue in the second section, we can characterize housing finance systems according to the degree to which homeownership is widespread, the level of mortgage debt in relation to GDP, the relative ease of refinancing, home equity withdrawal or mortgage origination, and the degree of securitization. These broad features all varied over the 1990s but to differing degrees. The last two changed the least, and the second changed the most. Table 4.4 provides comparative data on the structure of mortgage finance systems for the same G-9 countries displayed in table 4.1, plus group averages for the Americanized Rich and Repressed Rich. (More comprehensive data on all twenty rich OECD countries can be found in table 4.3.)

I use five indicators to capture the four features related to the housing market Keynesianism described here. These indicators are (1) the level of transaction costs related to property acquisition, (2) the degree to which securitization of mortgages is both possible and used, (3) the average level of home equity withdrawal as a percentage of GDP in 1990–2002, (4) the level of mortgage debt in relation to GDP in 1992 (at the beginning of the boom), and (5) the share of households who were owner-occupiers in 1990 (again at the beginning of the boom).

These choices are driven by both pragmatism and the model used here. Ideally, we want to have several measures for transaction costs. One would be a blended measure of transaction costs that first discriminated between the different levels of cost for originating new mortgages, refinancing, and HELOCs and then combined them synthetically in proportion to their share of total mortgage debt. A second measure would capture the differences between costs created by realtors (estate agents) and those imposed by the state or banks. As it turns out, in low-transaction-cost countries realtor fees account for the bulk of transaction costs, whereas in high-transaction-cost countries taxes account for the bulk of costs, which reinforces the easiness of refinancing in the Americanized Rich and the United States.

Alas, constructing such an index for the entire OECD would be a research project in itself. Consequently, I use the Global Property Guide's[41] assessment of the transaction costs involved in the purchase and sale of property. This is a round-trip measure, so I divide it by 2 because first-time homebuyers and HELOC borrowers are involved in only one transaction. This indicator captures the ease of refinancing and thus homeowners' ability to translate rising prices into more consumption. I modify this measure by adjusting the transaction-cost figure up or down by 0.5 (out of 10), depending on whether prepayment penalties are widespread in mortgage contracts. In Germany, as previously noted, prepayment penalties are the norm— most borrowers are required to compensate lenders for the early retirement of a mortgage. By contrast, in the United States, prepayment penalties are rare, giving borrowers a one-way bet on mortgage interest rates; if they fall, borrowers can refinance with no penalty. I also cross checked this indicator against the similar IMF "mortgage completeness" indicator.[42] I normalized the transaction-cost measure by

TABLE 4.4.
Comparative housing finance market characteristics of selected OECD countries

	United Kingdom	Australia	United States	Canada	Americanized Rich, Average[a]	OECD Countries, Average[b]	Repressed Rich, Average	Japan	Germany[c]	Italy	France
Relative transaction costs for property acquisition (% of total cost)	4.8	3.8	0.6	2.8	3.3	0.0	-4.1	1.2	-1.9	-7.7	-6.9
Is mortgage securitization possible?[d]	10	10	10	10	6.0	4.4	0.7	0	4	0	0
Home equity withdrawal, 1990–2002 (% of GDP × 10)	7	7	5	2	4.7	3.2	0.3	1	0	1	0
Mortgage debt, 1992 (% of GDP)	64.3	50.8	58	43.1	53.4	44.7	32.2	36.8	54	11.4	22.8
Owner-occupied housing, 2002 (%)	68	70	69	66	64.7	64.6	63.9	60	42	80	55
Synthetic housing index[e]	7.00	6.59	5.65	5.13	4.9	3.2	0.9	2.37	2.34	0.49	0.17

Sources: For relative transaction costs, Global Property Guide, "Housing Transaction Costs in the OECD," http://www.globalpropertyguide.com/articleread.php?article_id=95&cid= . For mortgage securitization, Pietro Catte, Nathalie Girouard, Robert Price, and Christophe André, "The Contribution of Housing Markets to Cyclical Resilience," *OECD Economic Studies* no.38 (2004/1): 125–56. For home equity withdrawal, OECD National Accounts, http://www.sourceOECD.org; Kostas Tsatsaronis and Haibin Zhu, "What Drives Housing Price Dynamics: Cross Country Evidence," *BIS Quarterly Review* (March 2004): 69–70; Massimo Giuliodori, "The Role of House Prices in the Monetary Transmission Mechanism across European Countries," *Scottish Journal of Political Economy* 52 no. 4 (September 2005): 523–24. For mortgage debt, Catte et al., "Contribution of Housing Markets," 138; Swedish National Board of Housing, Building and Planning (Boverket), *Housing Statistics in the European Union 2004* (Falun, Sweden: Intellecta Strålins, 2005); data supplied by European Mortgage Foundation. For owner-occupied housing, data supplied by European Mortgage Foundation.

Notes: Ranked by synthetic housing index. OECD, Organisation for Economic Cooperation and Development.

[a] Excludes the United States.

[b] All twenty OECD countries.

[c] Federal Republic of Germany.

[d] Yes = 10; no = 0; partial = 4 or 5.

[e] Synthetic housing index is calculated by normalizing all data to a 1–10 range, adding all five indicators, and then averaging.

taking the average across my cases and then subtracting the average, so as to divide countries into high- and low-cost groups.

Securitization captures the lenders' side of things. Banks that cannot securitize loans cannot originate as many loans and cannot shift interest risk on to the secondary market. This typically makes them more conservative in all senses about extending mortgage credit to consumers. This explains part of the very low level of mortgage debt in relation to GDP in Italy and the very high proportion of outright owners—87 percent.[43] Italian banks cannot easily securitize debt, and foreclosure can take up to six years, much longer than in the rest of Europe. Consequently, banks extend credit only to homebuyers who put up a very large down payment—often over 50 percent—which creates a substantial barrier to a liquid house market.[44]

Home equity withdrawal as a percentage of GDP is included for straightforward reasons—it captures the degree of economic stimulus that actually occurred in 1990–2002. I use these years because there is an inevitable lag between withdrawal and the full multiplier effects of spending from equity. For the index, I have multiplied equity withdrawal as a percentage of GDP by 10 to make its weight in the index the same as the other five elements. Home equity withdrawal is a more accurate proxy of the actual Keynesian stimulus emerging from the housing finance system than the rise in real estate prices across this period, which only tells us about the volume of *potential* equity withdrawal. Finally, the share of mortgage debt in relation to GDP and the percentage of owner occupiers are also straightforward measures of how exposed the average individual is to interest rate changes on mortgage debt. I have divided these measures by 10 to norm them to the 10-point scale for the other measures.

The first thing worth noticing in table 4.4 is the clear difference in the average levels of the Americanized Rich and Repressed Rich on all indicators except owner occupancy. The second is the degree to which the table captures much of our commonsense understanding of reality. Britain and Australia sit on the far end of the scale, suggesting a high sensitivity to changes in housing prices and interest rates. This is borne out in the politics of each country over the past two decades; voters have frequently turned out parties whose tenure coincides with high or rising nominal interest rates. On the other end, two of the four countries to the right of the overall average had falling housing prices for much of the long 1990s.

I used the data in table 4.4, plus similar data about the countries omitted from that table, to construct a synthetic measure of the degree of liquidity in the mortgage markets by adding these five indicators and then dividing by 5 to get a 0–10 index, where 10 indicates a very pro-cyclic housing market. This index is crude, but it captures the essentials about the likely influence of a housing finance system on aggregate demand. It also confirms that the Americanized Rich are Americanized, not just with respect to their overseas holdings but also with respect to the nature of their housing finance systems. Every one of our Repressed Rich countries has a synthetic housing index below the overall average. Nearly all of the Americanized

Rich have one above it. The two outliers—New Zealand and Finland—are precisely the countries that the analysis in chapter 3 indicates were in some way at the border between the categories. The analysis behind the synthetic housing index thus corroborates the assignment of country labels in chapter 3.

Figure 4.4 combines our un-misery index with the synthetic housing index to chart the relationship between housing finance systems and relative employment and GDP outcomes. It shows a statistically significant and thus nonrandom correlation between these two indicators.

Three interesting conclusions emerge from figure 4.4. First, it suggests that pacting probably is not the dominant explanation for good employment outcomes in the long 1990s. The poster cases for the pacting argument—Auer's Denmark, Ireland, Austria, and Netherlands—do not exhibit similar levels of employment and GDP growth performance. Austria is a clear underperformer, whereas the macro-performance of Denmark is only weakly above average and that of Ireland is literally off the chart. Moreover, three of Auer's success stories are essentially in the middle of the pack with respect to our un-misery index. If they did well on employment, this did not translate into increased GDP growth. On the other hand, all of Auer's stars did do well relative to the mass of corporatist economies. Although corporatist intermediation characterizes all of the Repressed Rich and some of the Americanized Rich, the differences in housing finance systems cut across the usual coordinated-liberal dichotomy. Earlier analyses thus probably incorrectly average the relatively good 1990s economic performance of corporatist economies with liquid housing markets and the bad performance of those with illiquid markets and then contrast that with the more variable performance of the liberal market economies.

This averaging or conflation probably explains the puzzle in the Kenworthy analysis, noted previously. Lane Kenworthy has shown that the relative job-creation abilities of coordinated and liberal market economies inverted around 1990–1992, with liberal economies underperforming during the 1970s and 1980s.[45] Because Kenworthy is caught in the usual dichotomous (coordinated vs. liberal) view of world he is unable to explain the inversion in the relative job-creation ability of corporatist and liberal economies.

Our analysis suggests an explanation. During 1970s and 1980s, nominal interest rates rose in tandem with inflation. Interest rates on prime thirty-year U.S. mortgages hit 18.3 percent in 1982; Australian rates, which were not deregulated until the mid-1980s, hit 17 percent in 1988. The high levels of mortgage debt relative to GDP and widespread homeownership in liquid housing markets would have translated these increases much faster than in illiquid ones, reducing aggregate demand and thus both GDP and employment growth. It is equally plausible, as Scharpf argues, that in the 1970s and 1980s corporatist wage restraint was a positive factor for employment. Wage restraint assured that central banks would not have to raise interest rates to punitive levels to control inflation. Thus, I am not arguing that at all times and under all circumstances U.S.-style housing markets are more likely

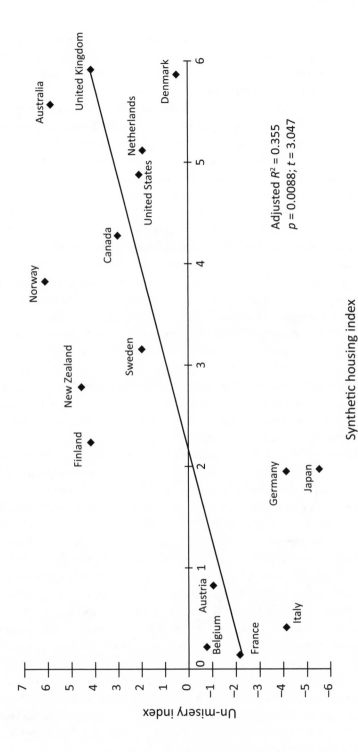

Fig. 4.4. Relationship between housing finance systems and the un-misery index for sixteen OECD countries. (See Fig. 4.2 and table 4.3.) OECD, Organisation for Economic Cooperation and Development.

to lead to above-average growth. Indeed, the analysis suggests that reverse can be true—inflation may percolate through U.S.-style housing markets in differentially *detrimental* ways, the same way that disinflation percolates through positively. This is precisely the problem that emerged after the housing bubble burst in 2005. But, either way, the analysis here suggests that housing finance systems may be an important omitted variable in most analyses of the relationship between coordinated wage bargaining or corporatism and employment/GDP growth.

The differential effects of inflation and disinflation on liquid and illiquid housing markets point us to a second important conclusion: U.S.-style housing finance institutions are not a perpetual-motion machine. The financial flows that drove U.S. growth contained two internal contradictions that ultimately choked off this cycle of growth. First, the positive feedback loop between U.S. and Asian-Chinese growth required deflation/disinflation to continuously free up more purchasing power in the United States. The more successful China was at running export surpluses, the more it could recycle funds into U.S. Treasuries and agency debt and the more downward pressure there was on U.S. interest rates. From 1991 through July 2007, prices for exports from developing Asia to the United States fell 27 percent, the same amount that developed-country export prices rose.[46] But the Chinese export successes also implied rapid Chinese growth and, thus, increasing Chinese calls on global raw materials and in its own supplies of semi-skilled labor. Raw materials prices started rising in 2004, and Chinese wages started rising in 2007. China, thus, began exporting inflation rather than deflation. This forced U.S. interest rates up, undoing the virtuous circle of disinflation, lower interest rates, more aggregate demand, and more disinflation.

Second, the pool of potential new entrants or upgraders in the housing market eventually had to dry up because lending markets chased less and less creditworthy buyers and homeownership rose 4 percentage points above the historical norm. Absent a large increase in incomes at the bottom of the market, this last tranche of new homeowners would necessarily find themselves stretched when it came to affording even an average house after a decade of rapid increases in housing prices. And without new entrants at the bottom, those in the middle would have no one to sell to and thus no unrealized equity to finance their own movement up the property ladder. But because the growth model relied on increasing volumes of imported Asian goods, workers in the bottom half of the income distribution eventually faced downward pressure on wages. Their real incomes fell continuously after 2000. Increasingly expensive houses could not be bought by increasingly impoverished workers, unless buyers and lenders were willing to engage in varieties of fraud in order to sell "toxic waste" MBSs (see chapter 7) to investors. The whole cycle thus gave out in 2005–2007 as the pool of creditworthy buyers gave out, leading to increased house prices via disproportionate increases in credit risk from buyers. Marxists will see this as a typical contradiction; Schumpeterians will see it as the typical process of growth to exhaustion.

Finally, the salience of housing for growth suggested by figure 4.4 points us to an important substantive difference between the classic processes of wealth and job creation in the era of the post–World War II Keynesian welfare state (KWS) and the current era. This difference is not the use of classic Keynesian multiplier effects triggered by loose(r) monetary policy. Central banks increased liquidity in both eras to boost employment and growth. What is different is the way in which increased aggregate demand is formed.

In the Bretton Woods or KWS era, lower interest rates mostly ramified through the economy via increased investment in the manufacturing sector. This, in turn, led to higher levels of employment and wages. Manufacturing investment led to more hiring of unionized workers, and more hiring of unionized workers led to higher wages. Union wages typically were linked to the productivity gains generated by the new investment. The broad increase in wages then validated ex post the original increase in investment. Growth thus ultimately rested on broad and equitable increases in income. But the typical consumer's relatively low level of debt and the illiquidity of mortgages before the 1970s meant that most wage earners were not affected directly by interest rate changes. By contrast, investment was interest rate sensitive. So, changes in interest rates had to flow through business investment to affect the economy.

But in the current period, interest rates directly affect consumption through workers' personal exposure to capital markets through their mortgages, car loans, and credit cards. HELOCs, defined contribution retirement plans, and mutual fund holdings are prevalent. Thus, increased consumption does not emerge from increased business investment that then percolates up through economywide collective bargaining and wage increases. Instead, a wide range of households are directly affected by falling interest rates because they both own a wide range of marketable assets and owe a variety of liquid debts. Falling nominal interest rates boost the value of marketable assets, including the newly marketable value of domestic housing, while also reducing debt payments. The historically new ability of households to capture and sell that increase in asset values allows households with rising home prices to expand their consumption. But because housing equity, unlike collectively bargained wages, is highly unequally distributed, both consumption and wealth continue to be uneven even as the economy grows. Indeed, growth magnifies the inequities by endowing housing-market insiders with huge amounts of nominal equity and, thus, equally huge amounts of potential consumption. Meanwhile, those who did not have a foot in the housing market or who had only a tenuous grasp on property at the time prices began rising are shut off from this process of wealth formation.

Housing and Macroeconomic Outcomes

There was an important positive feedback loop between housing market financial institutions and differential growth favoring the U.S. *domestic* economy. U.S.

housing markets translated the 1990s disinflation and global arbitrage into relatively faster growth for the U.S. economy compared with the Repressed Rich; essentially similar processes occurred in the Americanized Rich. Private actors everywhere responded to faster growth in the economies characterized by U.S.-style housing institutions by increasing their investment in those economies. In turn, this propelled the U.S. dollar into top-currency status and facilitated the recycling of U.S. trade deficits as new lending to the United States, reinforcing housing-led differential growth.

The Repressed Rich, by contrast, were forced into a variety of suboptimal wage policy choices. If they opted for wage restraint—or were forced into by the Bundesbank and then the ECB—they essentially tied themselves to export demand from the United States or the Americanized Rich. Wage restraint at home meant not just slower growth but, in particular, less investment, which hurt the capital goods–producing German economy.[47] Consumer goods and agricultural producers in the Repressed Rich lacked any internal dynamism, and the shift of medium-technology industries eastward into central Europe also put downward pressure on wages and employment.

The Repressed Rich also faced a set of suboptimal investment choices. To the extent that they responded to faster U.S. growth with increased (but still underweight) volumes of FDIUS, they received below-average returns on their investment (see chapter 5) while at the same time lowering the volume of capital invested in their home markets and substituting offshore production for domestic production. In their search for greater returns to offset these below-average returns, they often chased portfolio yields precisely when markets were about to collapse. The German *Landesbanken* bought large chunks of U.S. CDOs backed by subprime debt in their search for better returns than those found in their traditional market, the small and medium family enterprises that are at the heart of the German economy.[48]

Although I demonstrate a link in this chapter between housing finance systems and differential growth in the United States and, to a lesser extent, the Americanized Rich, I document this differential growth only at a macroeconomic level. But what about the microeconomic level? The burgeoning U.S. trade deficit and the 2007–2008 financial crisis suggest that the 1990s boom was wholly artificial. Both Marxist and realist analysts have argued that U.S. manufacturing was in a steep absolute decline in the long 1990s. Recall from chapter 2 that Giovanni Arrighi (a Marxist) argues that U.S. manufacturing is declining just as British manufacturing declined in the nineteenth century. Robert Gilpin (a realist) similarly argues that offshore investment by U.S. MNCs hollowed out the U.S. economy while creating differential growth favoring U.S. rivals (see chapter 5).

Although this chapter has shown that the United States enjoyed differential growth in quantitative terms, it leaves the question of quality unanswered. This qualitative or microeconomic side is the subject of the next chapter. The qualitative side of growth matters because the only way for the United States to close its trade deficit and thus validate the debt used to generate differential growth is by increasing tradable exports. For better or worse, most tradables are still manufactured goods—no manufacturing, no sustainable current account deficit; no sustainable current account deficit, no durable U.S. power. In later chapters, I consider other aspects of the trade deficit in relation to the accumulated stock of U.S. foreign debt, returning us to macroeconomic processes.

5. U.S. Industrial Decline?

> Do you know the only thing that gives me pleasure? It is to see my dividends coming in.
>
> John D. Rockefeller

In chapter 4, I document differential growth in the United States and the Americanized Rich during the long 1990s at a macroeconomic level. Was this growth a mirage? Recall that some realists and Marxists have argued that the 1990s were a period of long-term U.S. economic decline, focusing on the shift from a manufacturing to a service economy and using the nineteenth-century British industrial decline as an analogy. But both arguments misappropriate this analogy. In this chapter, I pick up the threads I start in chapters 2 and 3 and look at the external microeconomic consequences of U.S. global arbitrage and differential growth; this chapter thus complements the macroeconomic and domestic argument in chapter 4. The finer-grained analysis here shows that U.S. firms gained relative to their foreign competitors during the long 1990s, expanding U.S. overseas control over commodity chains. These gains matter because in the long run a country that cannot produce goods that people want, at prices they are willing to pay, can neither honor its debts nor possess power. Put differently, Gourinchas and Rey's metaphor of the United States as a highly leveraged global venture capitalist requires successful investment to justify the leverage.[1] I use in this discussion the analogy to Britain because, as Eichengreen says, this is the only other comparable data point.[2]

In this chapter, I deal more with the microeconomic "so what" of foreign investment than with its causes. Recall that one manifestation of U.S. global economic power was the absence of constraint on the United States. The United States could invest at home, consume at home, and invest abroad without facing the usual trade-offs. Thus, this chapter dissects the international side of U.S. global arbitrage. Also, it shows that USDIA expanded rapidly during the long 1990s. Rising USDIA indicates huge differences in the underlying competitiveness of

U.S. MNCs vis-à-vis their foreign competition. This addresses the arguments that financialization reflects a declining U.S. competitiveness; on the contrary, arbitrage helped competitive U.S. firms expand their control over overseas production and markets, particularly in the service sector. This expansion does not necessarily translate into increased U.S. exports, but it does show why borrowing short and investing long creates positive investment income. Just as U.S. global arbitrage aided U.S. domestic differential accumulation, it also aided overseas differential accumulation by U.S. firms.

Unlike with housing, however, there was no one-for-one correspondence between capital flows into the United States and capital flows out, except in a mechanical accounting sense. The connection is more diffuse than that identified in chapter 4, and frankly, it is impossible to match every dollar inflow with a corresponding outflow. The diffuse connection is a function of Verdoorn effects. As Jake Verdoorn, an economist, showed, rising output is almost always correlated with rising productivity. Most MNCs still do the majority of their business in their domestic market. The exceptions are MNCs from small countries, such as the Swiss giants Novartis and UBS. Foreign-funded differential growth favoring the United States gave U.S. MNCs a robust and expanding domestic market. This helped them generate the productivity gains that allowed them to compete overseas and the profits they needed to fund that expansion. By contrast, Repressed Rich MNCs faced stagnant domestic markets that hindered expansion into the United States compared to the Americanized Rich. Just as U.S. MNCs increased their overseas production relative to FDIUS, the ratio of FDIUS by the more dynamic Americanized Rich to that of the Repressed Rich increased from 1.4 to 1.6 in 1997–2005.

The chapter thus further examines the differences in productivity growth signaled in chapter 4. If differential growth is a source of U.S. power, then it is important to establish that U.S. differential growth opened up not just a quantitative but also qualitative lead over its rich-country rivals, even if all we can establish is a correlation. This issue is at the heart of the realist and Marxist misplaced analogy with British nineteenth-century economic decline, which also rests on a correlation between overseas investment and domestic stagnation. Nineteenth-century Britain missed the boat with respect to new industries and productivity-improving processes. By contrast, U.S. firms continue to define best practice not only in a wide range of manufacturing industries but also in much of the service sector. Here, too, U.S. firms benefited from faster domestic growth because of the close connection between aggregate growth and productivity growth that Verdoorn identifies. Finally, this chapter discusses the role of the U.S. dollar as an international reserve currency. (See figure 5.1 for the core analytic targets for this chapter.)

The expansion of U.S. MNCs and the widening productivity gulf matter for U.S. global economic power. Put simply, if the United States cannot make anything anyone wants to buy at a price that allows the United States to maintain a

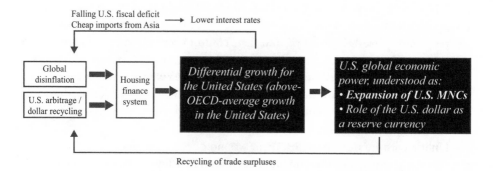

Fig. 5.1. Chapter 5: analytic focus.

politically acceptable standard of living, then differential growth in the long 1990s was a mirage and the realist and Marxist critics are right. The logical consequence of this mirage is a permanent collapse of the top currency position of the U.S. dollar, one proxy measure for U.S. power.

In this chapter, I first consider the analogy with the British industrial decline both directly and through a brief comparison of the nineteenth-century role of the sterling with that of the dollar today. I then move to a longer consideration of manufacturing, arguing that the reserve currency analogy is accurate but the manufacturing analogy is misplaced. The current era has its own dynamics because of the difference between industry and control that we have already highlighted. Unlike British firms, U.S. firms deploying leading-edge technologies have been able to create and control overseas subsidiaries. To confirm this, I disaggregate FDIUS and USDIA to show that not only do U.S. firms overseas generate higher rates of return than foreign firms in the United States but that the U.S. firms with above-average rates of return are precisely those that represent the core of the new economy. Indeed, considerable evidence points to U.S. MNCs as possessing a competitive advantage in foreign markets, just as the microeconomic theory of MNCs predicts. U.S. financial arbitrage thus funds both higher growth at home and high rates of expansion for U.S. industry abroad. I next consider the dismal U.S. export performance; to rework a phrase, if the United States is so competitive, how come it cannot export? Dismal export performance is the obverse of successful USDIA, which has substituted offshore production for exports as well as the explosive unrequited consumption of imports. And, ironically, U.S. exports have suffered precisely because, unlike nineteenth-century Britain, the United States lacks a territorial empire and cannot rigorously enforce property rights globally. U.S. exports thus face two barriers largely erected by other states: the absence of enforcement of intellectual property rights (IPRs) and the export of public-sector capital goods whose purchase is highly politicized. In the first, natural economic processes have shifted U.S. production into higher-valued design and research activities that require a rigorous defense of IPRs for profitability. Information is easier to copy than physical goods whose production often requires considerable tacit knowledge. Absent IPR enforcement, imitation will reduce export revenues. In the second, the United States exports public-sector capital goods whose purchase is highly politicized; this hinders U.S. exports while encouraging offshore production. By contrast, the decision to buy consumer goods—the bulk of U.S. imports—is dispersed and thus less susceptible to state control. The U.S. problem is excess imports, not insufficient exports. In this regard, we can see yet another internal contradiction, paralleling the one uncovered in chapter 3. Above-average U.S. growth attracted inflows of foreign capital that funded U.S. domestic and overseas expansion but that also funded excessive U.S. consumption. As with the housing motor, the consumption motor inevitably ran out of gas when this credit was extended to uncreditworthy consumers. Yet the accumulated foreign claims on the United States inevitably must return as purchases of U.S. goods, and this means a rise in both net U.S. exports and domestic production over the long run. Indeed, by mid-2008 U.S. goods exports had already risen by $370 billion compared to 2005, roughly double the increase in non-oil imports. At that time, energy imports made up over one-half of the trade deficit in goods.

The United States in Decline?

Both Marxist and realist "declinists" ground their analogy between the British decline and U.S. decline on the parallel shift of resources from manufacturing to the service and, especially, financial sectors at the end of the nineteenth and twentieth century, respectively. Giovanni Arrighi (a Marxist) states flatly:

> As in Britain's case at a comparable stage of relative decline, escalating US current-account deficits reflect a deterioration in the competitive position of American business at home and abroad. And as in Britain's case, though less successfully, US capital has partially countered this deterioration by specializing in global financial intermediation. Unlike Britain, however, the US has no territorial empire from which to extract the resources needed to retain its politico-military pre-eminence in an increasingly competitive world.[3]

Arrighi argues that British hegemony in the nineteenth century unraveled when Britain ceased to be a competitive manufacturer, missed the boat for new (twentieth-century) technologies, and instead shifted into unproductive financial activities. Capital, which could not find productive manufacturing outlets in Britain, instead spilled over into international markets as passive investment. Indeed, from Arrighi's point of view, things are worse for the United States today. Whereas Britain could finance its deficits on the backs of colonial Indian taxpayers, the United States must compete in international capital markets for funds. Arrighi thus makes an explicit link to the arbitrage and recycling mechanisms in our model.

Robert Gilpin (a realist) made a slightly different but still relevant argument thirty years ago.[4] He argues that USDIA accelerated U.S. relative decline by promoting more rapid industrialization in the key U.S. economic rival, Europe. In this respect, Gilpin freely borrows from the usual Marxist arguments about uneven development and attaches them to the core realist argument about the importance of relative gains. Gilpin sees U.S. relative decline as a perverse outcome of U.S. government policy supporting the expansion of U.S. MNCs abroad. The contemporary equivalents of Gilpin's 1970s MNCs are U.S. retail giants, such as Wal-Mart, Target, and Home Depot, that contract with Chinese exporters of simple manufactures. Imports by these retail giants created the physical flow of goods that accounts for one-quarter of the U.S. trade deficit. They also have helped power Chinese industrial expansion, closing the gap between China and the United States. Gilpin's argument remains relevant because our arbitrage argument hinges on the high returns that USDIA generates and because his core argument is that U.S. MNCs promoted differential growth favoring U.S. rivals, not the United States.

British Financial Arbitrage and Sterling versus U.S. Arbitrage and the Dollar

Do these analogies with Britain hold up? The financial analogy barely holds; the manufacturing analogy does not. Let us explore finance first, and briefly. Both Britain and the United States did structure the global financial system in surprisingly similar ways that favored each. Like the United States today, Britain systematically borrowed short and lent long at the macroeconomic level.[5] The British version reflected the apparent greater creditworthiness of British banks, which in turn rested on the absolutely and relatively high levels of productivity in British manufacturing, as well as on the superior ability of British banks to call on masses of money from the British countryside and from Europe. Both helped maintain the pound sterling as a top currency.

How did British financial arbitrage work? Non-British banks and internationalized British banks that were nominally located outside of Britain all maintained a presence in London in order to clear trade-related payments. These colonial banks parked the great seasonal flood of credits for raw material exports to Britain in London banks as short-term deposits, called commercial bills of exchange. These are comparable to the contemporary asset-backed commercial paper (ABCP) that backed the subprime CDOs at the heart of the current crisis. These bills were on call to settle payments on the equally massive and equally predictable ebb tide of British exports back to the formal and informal British empire. By 1908, the parked funds of foreign and colonial banks amounted to roughly one-third to one-half of total bank funds in Britain, a proportion comparable to U.S. foreign portfolio debt.[6] As Britain took in colonial short-term deposits, it also lent back long term to those colonial areas so that they could finance lumpy, long-maturing investments in railroads and other infrastructure. Britain thus borrowed foreign money at low interest rates on a short-term basis while lending that money back to peripheral countries at higher interest rates that reflected the longer term of the loan. Unlike the United States, nineteenth-century Britain was not a net debtor; like the U.S. dollar, the pound was a reserve currency, which facilitated global arbitrage.

Recall Susan Strange's distinction of *top, negotiated,* and *master currencies.*[7] For Strange, top currencies are attractive on their own economic merits, much like the U.S. dollar for most of the 1990s; negotiated currencies are those whose international role rests on implicit or explicit political deals between the countries involved; and master currencies are imposed by force. We can operationalize these qualitative distinctions further by mapping them on to the distinctions among competitive, oligopolistic, and monopoly markets. Master currencies, like monopolies, allow consumers (i.e., foreign buyers of securities) no choice. The essential feature of a top currency is that, as in a competitive market, no consumer has any ability to influence the output (the volume of currency in circulation) or price (the exchange rate) of that currency. Politically, this implies that holders of those assets can exert little pressure on the emitter of the top currency. Negotiated currencies are those in which some consumers, generally political actors, have concentrated holdings big enough to affect the price and output of the international reserve currency. Thus, the emitter of that currency has to take these consumers' preferences into account when it sets price and volumes.

We can also approach a quantitative measure of these differences by applying the Herfindahl-Hirschman index (HHI) and the usual four-firm concentration ratio to creditor-country holdings of securities denominated in an international reserve currency. The HHI is calculated by taking the sum of the square of the percentage shares of a given market of all firms; here, we use the shares of foreign-held securities held by all countries. The four-firm ratio (CR-4) is the share of the four largest firms. Conventionally, an HHI over 1,000 indicates an oligopolistic market, as does a CR-4 over 40 percent. The usual domestic trigger for an antitrust investigation is an HHI of 1,800.

At the beginning of the long 1990s, the U.S. dollar looked like a negotiated currency.[8] Its share of global currency reserves had fallen to approximately 50 percent, whereas the currencies later composing the euro accounted for 21 percent of reserves. Japan and equally so the Japanese central bank accounted for 21 percent of foreign-held dollar-denominated securities, pushing the HHI for foreign-held securities in 1989 to 1,000 and the CR-4 (Japan, Britain, Canada, and Germany) to 48.9 percent. This HHI seems high enough to validate the widely felt contemporary concern about the ability of Japan to influence the market for U.S. securities, even though it does not rise to the legal level used in antitrust cases; the CR-4 clearly signals an oligopolistic market. On this basis, it is reasonable to speak of the U.S. dollar as a negotiated currency in 1991, with the Japanese having considerable power to influence the dollar market.

U.S. differential growth in the 1990s reversed these trends. The share of foreign exchange reserves of the dollar had risen to 68 percent, whereas the share of the euro had slipped to 18 percent. On various measures, the trade-weighted exchange rate value of the dollar was up, between 34 and 47 percent in 1991–2002.[9] And the HHI for foreign holdings had fallen below 600, reflecting a huge diversification of asset holders and a crowding in of private investors. On this basis, assigning top currency status to the dollar also seems reasonable. Yet, as U.S. growth waned and the subprime crisis erupted, all these indicators once more went into reverse. Based on the official U.S. Treasury data for 2007, the HHI for foreign holdings was still below 600 for 2007, but the CR-4 (combining Japan, China/Hong Kong, Britain, and Canada) had risen to 37 percent. Unfortunately, the most accurate U.S. Treasury data on foreign holdings tends to arrive quite late in the day; Brad Setser has made a useful career out of reading the Treasury data as tea leaves, hoping to anticipate later revisions. These revisions all tend to magnify the shares of China and the oil exporters. This implies that the HHI and CR-4 for 2007 understate the degree to which the dollar has once more become a negotiated currency. And given current trends these numbers should worsen.

Ultimately, a top currency requires an ability to validate the holdings of that currency through the production of goods and services that holders of reserve currency assets plausibly might desire. Theoretically all that matters is that everyone be willing to use the international reserve currency to park their net export earnings. But offshore holders with substantial net holdings of reserve currency–denominated assets ultimately can liquidate those assets only in exchange for exports from the issuing country. This characteristic distinguishes a top currency from a negotiated currency, where asset holders accept some possibility of substantial losses in exchange for other, possibly nonmonetary gains.

We can get a sense of what is at stake by looking at the responses to British arbitrage, which, like U.S. arbitrage, disadvantaged the economically weak. Just as China has sought to propel itself into an industrial power, nineteenth-century Germany also sought to modernize. British arbitrage provoked Germany to found the Deutsche Bank in 1870 to help shift the financing of German foreign trade from a sterling to a Reichsmark basis, much as U.S. arbitrage is provoking creation of SWFs (see chapter 8). And although British financialization largely worked to the benefit of Britain, the arm's length relationship between British banks and British manufacturers meant that those banks were happy to lend colonial developers money that could be spent on U.S. or German exports. The same has been true of U.S. money-center banks today. It is also true of U.S. retailers, the contemporary counterpart to Gilpin's 1970s MNCs. But the fact that major U.S. industrial firms are able—because of financialization—to extend commercial credit to their customers assures a more direct connection between lending and the purchase of goods sourced from U.S.-controlled firms. So, although the first part of Arrighi's analogy is partially correct, the second is not. Ultimately, the issue is whether U.S. manufacturers are in decline.

The Decline of British Manufacturing

Is contemporary U.S. manufacturing in decline, unable to compete with the output of low-wage Asian labor or high-quality European firms in the same way that British manufacturers failed to compete with rising U.S. and German firms? Britain did miss the boat with respect to the new technologies of the late nineteenth century. But both sides of an analogy have to be correct for the analogy to hold, and U.S. firms are not missing the boat with respect to new technologies and production processes. In fact, the opposite is true, as the growing productivity gap between U.S. firms and their rich-country rivals in the aggregate evidences. The counterpart to U.S. macroeconomic differential growth in the long 1990s is microeconomic differential growth.

The late nineteenth and early twentieth centuries and the late twentieth century both experienced significant technological innovation. New nineteenth-century products included Bessemer steels, aniline dyes, fertilizers, bicycles, and electrical goods such as the telephone. Production-process improvements, including the replacement of steam/prime mover–powered machinery with electrically driven machines, better logistics that permitted a much larger scale of production, and the hierarchically organized corporation, were just as important. Finally, the period also saw financial innovations such as the use of publicly listed stock to control the direction of large enterprises, the formation of cartels to control output and stabilize prices, and the capitalization of goodwill and brand names.

British output of these new goods and its adoption of these new production and control forms lagged behind that in the United States and Germany. In some cases, even absolute levels of British output of older goods were lower than U.S. and German output by 1890. By 1900, both the United States and Germany were using FDI in these new industries to enter markets in Britain itself. By contrast, as Arrighi correctly argues, Britain withdrew into imperial markets instead of competing head on with the United States and Germany in these new technologies. Britain continued to produce the older wave of manufactured goods—iron and textiles—for the less-discerning imperial market, including and, most important, greater India, a large but unsophisticated market.

The export and production statistics show this clearly. The British share of world trade fell from approximately 30 percent, its mid-nineteenth-century peak, to 14.1 percent in 1913, whereas the U.S. share rose from 8.8 to 11.1 percent and the German share from 9.7 to 12.2 percent.[10] This shift reflected a huge difference in underlying productivity. U.S. labor productivity grew by 2 percent per year from 1890 to 1907, compared to British growth of 0.1 percent; by 1909, U.S. labor productivity was over 2.5 times as high as British productivity in fifteen major industries. From 1870 to 1913, U.S. GDP grew 4.9 percent annually and German GDP grew 3.9 percent, well ahead of the British 2.6 percent.[11] Britain was on the wrong side of rich-country differential growth.

Why did or could Britain not innovate to compete? Although Veblen reminds us that business, the search for control over profits, and industry, the search for more efficient production techniques, are different things, they are not wholly separate.[12] Three control-related factors dominated the relative decline of Britain because British manufacturers faced obstacles to *profitable* investment in the new technologies. First, British manufacturers could not reorganize labor relations in ways that would have made increased investment in the new production processes profitable. Although the new production technologies permitted huge increases in productivity, any effort to introduce new production technologies would have provoked crippling strikes by well-organized British workers. Unlike corporately owned U.S. firms, British firms were generally family-owned and operated only one plant, so a strike would eliminate that revenue and profitability of the firm.[13]

Second, Britain lacked education institutions capable of generating the kind of workforce the new firms needed. The new organizational formats both required new and different kinds of trained professionals. Britain lacked institutions for upgrading the skills of shop foremen, for producing trained engineers, and for creating professional managers. The United States and Germany had both in excess. The Germans pioneered the systematic training of skilled workers via apprenticeship programs; in the United States, Rensselaer Polytechnic was founded in 1824 and MIT in 1865.[14] Formal business-school institutions proliferated in the United States before World War I, with Wharton, Tuck, and Harvard Business schools all founded at that time.

Third, British firms could not generate new corporate forms to control the ownership of the new technologies. British lenders were able but unwilling to capitalize British firms using and producing the new technologies and goods. British banks had sufficient funds but lacked any political mechanism to assure themselves that the state or some other actor would ameliorate the maturity-mismatch risks that banks assumed by using short-term deposits to fund long-term investments in the new technologies. By contrast, both the United States and Germany had these mechanisms. The German state stood behind its big four banks.[15] In the United States, the Morgan bank stood behind the amalgamation of firms into trusts and stabilized panicked financial markets in 1907.

The issue of control becomes particularly salient when we turn to USDIA versus FDIUS (in the next section). Control matters for both Arrighi's and Gilpin's arguments, although both conceal this. Arrighi's implicit counterfactual argument is one in which UK-based manufacturing firms continued to dominate their markets by producing in and exporting from Britain. But suppose, instead, that British manufacturers had been able to transform their existing cash flow into control over nascent U.S. and German industry through FDI or passive equity stakes. Certainly the history of the British decline would have been written differently. We can imagine British-controlled firms rationalizing the global steel market by allocating market shares to regional subsidiaries. This would have protected the British market share and put many of the new technologies under the control of British firms. In fact, historically, the reverse happened. Rather than British firms in the new technologies expanding outside Britain, by 1912 the nascent multinationals General Electric, Westinghouse, and Siemens controlled two-thirds of the strategic electrical equipment industry *inside* Britain.[16] Gilpin similarly underrates the importance of the control of U.S. firms over offshore production.

U.S. Manufacturing Today

If Arrighi and Gilpin are right about a U.S. relative decline paralleling that of Britain, then we would expect to see U.S. firms locked into older production processes and products, poor human capital formation, and a rising importance of industry as compared to control. If Gilpin is right, we would expect to see European and Japanese levels of productivity converging on the U.S. level. Neither set of claims fully holds. U.S. firms have shifted low-end production offshore to developing countries while pursuing more advanced technologies and activities. Human capital formation in the United States concentrates on occupations with higher value-added. And the productivity gap between European economies plus Japan and the United States is growing in most cases despite the relatively higher productivity of U.S. firms operating in Europe.

U.S. manufacturing investment outpaced that in the Repressed Rich in both *relative* and *absolute* terms in the long 1990s. In absolute terms, U.S. GFCF doubled, from roughly $1 trillion in 1991 to $2.1 trillion in 2005; the manufacturing component of GFCF tripled, to $600 billion.[17] This brought GFCF from 14 to 19 percent of GDP. By contrast, in euroland (which includes some of our Americanized Rich), GFCF rose only €330 billion, not quite enough to maintain the GFCF share of euroland GDP at 21 percent. Aggregate data for euroland GFCF in manufacturing are not available, but Germany saw only a 22 percent increase and Italy 18 percent.

The distribution of investment increases and decreases in U.S. manufacturing also suggests a shedding of low-value activities in favor of higher-value activities. Large increments to GFCF in durable goods manufacturing investment more than offset disinvestment in nondurables. Leather goods, textiles and clothing, and foods and beverages—10 percent of manufacturing GFCF—saw absolute declines. By contrast, machinery and equipment, transportation equipment, and electrical and optical equipment—40 percent of GFCF—all saw both substantial absolute and relative increases. Because value-added in U.S. manufacturing grew by 50 percent, even after adjusting for population growth, a rising share for the three strong categories cannot simply reflect the collapse of manufacturing in the weak categories. On the other hand, manufacturing employment did not increase as rapidly. But this is precisely the point: rising value-added with a stable head count reflects increased productivity, which implies that U.S. manufacturing cannot be in an absolute decline.

But we have stressed *relative* change in this book. What about U.S. productivity relative to its rich-country competitors? In fact, economywide U.S. productivity increased faster than all of its OECD G-7 competitors except Britain and from a higher baseline in 1991–2006, both at an economywide level (table 5.1) and more narrowly in manufacturing (table 5.2). U.S. manufacturing productivity increased faster than all major U.S. competitors in 1991–2006 save Taiwan, Korea, and Sweden. Given that Taiwan and Korea still had ample room for catchup growth and that the U.S. economy is considerably larger than all three of these countries, U.S. manufacturing performance is remarkable.

Tables 5.1 and 5.2 rely on U.S. Bureau of Labor Statistics data because they are the most up-to-date. But the state of the art on global productivity differences comes from the KLEMS Project at Groningen University.[18] The project data corroborate Gilpin's interpretation of the 1950–1990 period. In those decades, most European countries experienced productivity growth at twice the U.S. rate, allowing the EU-15 to nearly close the output-per-hour-worked gap. But in the 1990s, this pattern reversed, and nearly all European economies and Japan lost ground to the United States in terms of both economywide productivity and manufacturing. U.S. output per hour worked rose 50 percent faster than in the EU-15, despite ample opportunities for catchup by the new EU members.

This disparity caused the EU-15 output per hour to decline 10 percentage points relative to the United States. Granted, some specific European countries, such as the Netherlands, have either productivity or capitalization levels well above the U.S. level. But it is also probably true that individual U.S. states or regions have levels comparable to the Netherlands because the U.S. average reflects a continental

TABLE 5.1.
Real GDP per employed person (2002 dollars, PPP adjusted)

	United States	Canada	Japan	Germany[a]	France	Italy	United Kingdom	OECD Average[b]
1991	61,733	51,130	47,462	48,813	60,671	57,886	48,553	51,074
2006	81,454	63,311	57,794	59,870	73,134	65,477	65,684	65,101
Change (%)	31.9	23.8	21.8	22.7	20.5	13.1	35.3	27.5

Source: Bureau of Labor Statistics, ftp://ftp.bls.gov/pub/special.requests/ForeignLabor/flsgdp.txt.
Notes: OECD, Organisation for Economic Cooperation and Development; PPP, purchasing power parity.
[a]Data are for postunification Germany, so the base level is not affected by unification.
[b]Includes Americanized Rich, Repressed Rich, and South Korea.

TABLE 5.2.
Real output per hour in manufacturing and total output (1991 = 100)

	United States	Canada	Japan	Germany[a]	France	Italy	United Kingdom	OECD Average[b]
Real output per hour in manufacturing (productivity)								
1991	100	100	100	100	100	100	100	100
2006	206	146	164	168	182	116	161	171
Total manufacturing output (output volume)								
1991	100	100	100	100	100	100	100	100
2006	174	158	115	116	132	105	110	152

Source: Bureau of Labor Statistics, ftp://ftp.bls.gov/pub/special.requests/ForeignLabor/prodsuppt01.txt.
Notes: OECD, Organisation for Economic Cooperation and Development.
[a] Data are for postunification Germany so the index level is not affected by unification.
[b] Includes Americanized Rich, Repressed Rich, South Korea, and Taiwan (and therefore is biased *against* the argument that the United States was above average because of rapid productivity growth in Korea and Taiwan).

economy, just as the EU-15 figures do. The KLEMS Project attributes most of the U.S.–EU-15 gap in productivity growth rates to multifactor productivity, not to additional inputs of capital or labor. Multifactor productivity is the unallocated residual, and it usually reflects better management of capital and labor inputs. At a sectoral level, the KLEMS Project identifies market services and information and communication technology equipment production as the major sources of the more rapid U.S. productivity growth (as well as that in the Americanized Rich group). Each of these factors runs contrary to the British decline analogy.

U.S. manufacturers have been able to reshape their labor force in ways that British factory owners could only dream of, with consequent increases in productivity and profitability. With union cooperation when possible, and over the heads of the unions when not, U.S. metal-bashing and machinery firms have recast their production practices to make them more responsive to customers and to drastically lower inventories of work in progress.[19] Similarly, the reshaping of the high-tech labor market that Microsoft pioneered—masses of contingent workers, stock options rather than defined benefit plans to assure loyalty, and a strong emphasis on teamwork—continues apace as more and more firms take on high-tech characteristics with respect to their output.

Second, unlike nineteenth-century British educational institutions, contemporary U.S. educational institutions remain more than adequate with respect to training the kind of workforce that high-skill-using industrial firms need; indeed, the United States is a net exporter of this talent via foreign students.[20] The upper quartile of U.S. universities specialize in the production of corporate administrators, engineers, scientists, and highly skilled technicians in law and medicine. Consider technical education, which is clearly of some importance for long-term economic growth. Reports that, for example, China produces nine to ten times as many engineers as the United States are based on data that include the equivalent of community college graduates in the total Chinese head count and then contrast them to U.S. engineers who have graduated from four-year college; rebased data that compare apples to apples show that the United States produces 50 percent more engineers per unit of population than China and three times the number produced in India.[21]

Adjusting for quality shifts the gap farther in favor of the U.S. educational system. A McKinsey Global Associates survey of MNCs found that these firms assessed 81 percent of U.S.-trained engineers as employable, against only 25 and 10 percent for India and China, respectively. Although Europe is certainly capable of producing competent technical cadres, and indeed produces more than the United States, roughly 75,000 of them are working in the United States, which is the equivalent of one-tenth of one year's output of science and engineering students by the European Union. It is important to note, however, that educational levels are a moving target. Carsten Holz estimates that the average number of years of schooling for Chinese workers will rise from roughly 8.5 in 2005 to approximately 10.8 by 2025 and points out that China has an efficient system for identifying the bright children of elites.[22]

Finally, financialization has enabled U.S. firms to retain control over their commodity chains. Arrighi's analysis contains an antinomy—whereas Britain retreated into financialization because it was capital rich and had no other domestic outlet for funds, the United States has retreated into financialization because it is capital short and needs financing from overseas. Arrighi's understanding of financialization rests on the classic Marxist interpretation of finance as something that is epiphenomenal to the real world of manufacturing. But what if financialization is, instead, an indicator of state strength and U.S. hegemony, as Panitch and Gindin argue?[23] What if financialization enables U.S. firms to be more competitive?

Unlike nineteenth-century British industrial firms, many contemporary U.S. industrial firms are also financial institutions. For example, GE (General Electric) is both a differentiated producer of industrial machinery and, via GE Commercial Finance (part of GE Capital until 2002) and GE Money (née GE Consumer Finance), a major financial firm offering, on the one side, mortgages, insurance, aircraft leasing, and receivables and, on the other side, ABSs, initial public offerings (IPOs), and other investments. GE financial operations accounted for 35 percent of the annual profit of GE in 2006, whereas its industrial operations (with four times as many employees) accounted for only 8 percent. The issue is how we interpret this fact, given that GE Capital is involved in financing the sale of GE products.[24]

Advocates of financial repression, including the varieties-of-capitalism literature, would argue that optimal levels of growth occur when finance is subordinated to manufacturing. Like Rudolph Hilferding (a Marxist), they see finance as parasitic on real economic activity. For Hilferding, finance capital represented a situation of "dependence of industry on the banks" in which "[a]n ever-increasing portion of the industrial capital does not belong to the industrialists who use it. They only receive the disposal over it from the bank, which, as far as they are concerned, represents the owner."[25]

Veblen, in contrast, points us to the issue of control over different parts of the value chain or, as Marxists would have it, the circulation of capital. Firms such as GE and Sony present a fusion of finance and industry in which some industrial firms have colonized finance in order to free themselves from a dependence on banks. These firms deal directly with capital markets and have internalized some of the purely financial parts of the value chain. This fusion does not characterize all firms.

The point, however, is that the nature of financialization varies from firm to firm and from economy to economy. This implies two things: (1) we have to analyze the particular performance of different sorts of firms to understand whether financialization helps or hurts manufacturing, and (2) the decline analogy founders on the third issue of whether or not capital markets support the creation and expansion of competitive U.S. firms.

In the next section, I deal with the first issue in more depth, showing that U.S. firms in sectors of the global economy that arguably could be characterized as being part of the current Schumpeterian growth wave were able to expand their global operations and that these more advanced sectors were among the most profitable sectors with respect to USDIA. By contrast, foreign firms investing in the United States are noticeably absent in advanced sectors and tend to have low levels of profitability in their operations in the United States.

The Relative Profitability of USDIA versus FDIUS

As I note in chapter 2, the observed return on equity for USDIA is much higher than for FDIUS. This disparate level of profitability for USDIA compared to FDIUS runs against the British decline analogy. Disaggregating the data on income from USDIA shows three important things that are consistent both with broader economic theory and with our argument that U.S. manufacturing is not in a terminal decline. First, the most profitable sectors for USDIA differ from the most profitable sectors for FDIUS, indicating some complementarity in the competitiveness of the firms that engage in FDI. Second, the most highly profitable USDIA is concentrated in the new leading sectors—the dynamic service sectors and in high-technology sectors—and not in older, mature sectors. Third, the volume of U.S. overseas production has been growing faster than the world economy as a whole, suggesting that U.S. firms control an increasing share of world output, even though they do not necessarily export that output from the United States.

By contrast, USDIA in *financial* sectors has, at best, average profitability, indicating not only that financialization certainly is no panacea for any alleged U.S. deindustrialization but also that Arrighi is wrong to see financialization as a symptom of deindustrialization. It is implausible that U.S. firms that are primarily nonfinancial could be uncompetitive and yet also be so highly profitable. So, although the United States runs enormous trade deficits in manufacturing, this more likely represents overconsumption generated by above-average growth than it does a lack of competitiveness on the part of U.S. firms. Indeed, as we have seen, the available data point toward higher levels of productivity growth in the United States than in Japan and Europe in the aggregate. This most likely reflects not only the earlier adoption of new information technologies but also the earlier reconfiguration of production practices to make the best use of those technologies. It is not consistent with the British decline analogy.

Tables 5.3 and 5.4 present disaggregated average return on investment data for the major sectors used by the BEA to classify USDIA and FDIUS. This allows us both to contrast the ROA for USDIA with that for FDIUS and to identify sectors that have either above- or below-average income during the periods 1998–2006 for USDIA and 1997–2005 for FDIUS.[26] The first thing to note is the huge disparity between the returns for USDIA and FDIUS. Over the near-decade for which we have comparable data, USDIA had an average ROA amounting to 9.5 percent, whereas FDIUS returned only 4.3 percent. This disparity is somewhat larger than that reported by Raymond Mataloni for the period 1988–1997.[27] He reports the ROA for FDIUS as either 5.1 percent using current cost estimates or 5.7 percent using historic cost estimates for assets. But our disparity is also somewhat smaller than Rebecca McCaughrin's estimate of a 6-percentage-point gap between ROAs for USDIA and FDIUS in the few years before 2004.[28] Despite the disagreements, this triangulation suggests that USDIA returns are roughly double FDIUS returns.

Equally significant, Mataloni reports that the ROA for FDIUS was 2 percentage points lower than the corresponding average ROA for U.S.-owned firms operating in the U.S. economy during his decade, although the gap had narrowed to only 1 percentage point by 1997. Weaker foreign ROA was not a statistical artifact caused by weak performance in just a few sectors in the United States. Foreign firms were invested in almost all sectors, and these investments generated below-average ROAs in two-thirds of all investment sectors. In other words, foreign firms underperformed not only U.S. firms operating overseas but also U.S. firms operating in the U.S. economy.

This finding presents a considerable puzzle. As Daniel Gros notes in his scathing critique of the Hausmann and Sturzenegger's dark matter argument, it is unlikely that foreigners would accept a rate of return lower than the risk-free return from by buying the bonds of their own governments.[29] Gros suggests that systematic tax avoidance, both by foreign firms investing in the United States and U.S. firms investing in Europe, explains the difference in ROAs. Both behaviors, he argues, are driven by lower corporate taxes in Europe; the United States has the second-highest nominal corporate tax rate the OECD. But, although transfer pricing and tax avoidance may plausibly explain 1 or 2 percentage points of the gap, it is doubt-ful that they explain the entire gap.

First, Gros's argument is based on nominal corporate tax rates, not the effective tax rates. The effective U.S. rates, at 24 percent, are higher than the OECD average of 20 percent.[30] Nonetheless, they are lower than those in major competitors such as Germany or Japan. And the share of corporate income tax revenues relative to GDP provides ambiguous evidence—corporate tax revenues in relation to GDP are much lower in the United States than in most of Europe. This could mean that effective U.S. rates are low and thus produce lower revenues or that firms prefer to declare taxable income in Europe because the effective rates are low and this produces higher overall revenues in Europe. A further complication is that effec-tive rates differ depending on the funding source for new investment. U.S. tax law very much favors debt-financed investment, with effective rates well below those in Europe until the huge 1986 tax reform and then somewhat below European rates after that.[31] In other words, U.S. tax laws favors the kind of arbitrage that the U.S. practices at a macro-level.

Second, aside from a steep fall associated with the first few years of the Latin American debt crisis of the 1980s, the foreign portion of the profits of U.S. firms has been steady from 1960 to the present, despite changes in the tax code. Relative corporate tax rates changed considerably as a consequence of the 1986 U.S. tax re-form. Before 1986, statutory U.S. corporate tax rates were a bit below the OECD average. After 1991, they were somewhat above the OECD average but below the G-7 average. Yet the proportion of income that U.S. firms declared overseas did not change. This suggests that the gap is not an artifact of recent efforts to dodge taxes by shifting profits to overseas subsidiaries.

Other factors suggest that that tax avoidance does not explain the entire gap. Harry Grubert compared partially owned (25–50 percent) and wholly owned sub-sidiaries of foreign companies operating in the United States.[32] His study found no difference in the level of reported profitability between these two types of firms. This suggests that tax avoidance via transfer pricing was not responsible for the bulk of the discrepancy because the minority owners of the partially owned firms presumably would have been vigilant about the diversion of profit to the parent firms. Grubert's study, which looks at the *willingness* of firms to avoid taxes, is par-tially confirmed by Mataloni, who looks at the *ability* of firms to avoid taxes via transfer pricing.

Mataloni notes that the median ROA gap between foreign manufacturing firms and their U.S.-based competitors rises from 3 to 4 percentage points as the share of intrafirm imports in final sales rises from less than 10 percent of sales to more than 70 percent.[33] Firms with higher levels of intrafirm imports should have greater opportunities to use transfer pricing to adjust their taxable income. Yet the decline in ROA is not commensurate with the increase in intrafirm sales and is smaller than the baseline gap of 3 percentage points on ROA. Instead, Grubert suggests that most of the ROA discrepancy is explained by differences in age, debt loads for firms, depreciation, and the payment of dividends between foreign- and U.S.-owned firms. Dividends and royalties already accounted for 53 percent of the net income of U.S. manufacturing firms by 1993. Grubert locates approximately half the difference in profitability in these causes.[34] This suggests that the competitive advantage of U.S. firms lay in their intellectual property, which is consistent with standard economic theory about MNCs.

Mataloni also provides a second clue that helps explain the difference in ROA. Foreign firms in the U.S. market in 1992 that had a market share in excess of 30 percent of the relevant market had rates of return close to the U.S. average.[35] Firms with market shares under 20 percent had rates of return 2 percentage points lower than the U.S. average. This suggests that profitability is related to the ability of firms to control their market via a degree of oligopoly or oligopsony. This finding is also consistent with standard economic theory about MNCs.

Standard economic theory argues that firms establish foreign subsidiaries only when they possess some production or technological advantage strong enough to overcome the additional costs of coordination at a distance and of operating in a foreign environment compared with simply exporting from their home market.[36] The below-average ROA of foreign firms in the United States indicates that these firms do not possess any overwhelming competitive advantage; instead, it suggests the operation of one or all of three possible motivations for investment in the United States. First, contrary to Gros, foreign firms may accept returns that are below average because they feel they cannot be a globally competitive firm unless they are operating in the U.S. market, which accounts for approximately one-quarter of global GDP, a larger share of global growth over the long 1990s, and in many market segments a substantial proportion of final sales. Second, firms may invest in the United States to hedge against the risks of exchange rate shifts that make exporting unprofitable. Third, the low ROA of foreign firms in the United States may be higher than their ROA on their own home market operations. If domestic financial repression produced a relatively lower cost of capital, they might accept a lower rate of return in the U.S. market. But these firms are more profitable elsewhere in the world, so why would this be?

A lack of broader comparable ROA data makes it difficult to assess the importance of the third motivation, although the KLEMS studies show that capital productivity is lower in Europe than in the United States. But the first two motivations imply that foreign firms are willing to pay a "tax" in order to get into the U.S. market, where the "tax" is their inferior ROA compared to U.S. firms.[37] An analysis of profitability in specific sectors suggests that this franchise fee interpretation is plausible. And the franchise fee interpretation tends to confirm our broader argument that U.S. manufacturing has shifted into advanced sectors rather than remaining bogged down in declining ones, a la nineteenth-century British manufacturing.

Table 5.3 shows that the most profitable sectors for USDIA (in relation to underlying investment) are largely high-technology or dynamic service-sector firms. In the table, values above 1.00 in the last column indicate above-average profitability, values below 1.00 indicate below-average profitability, and 1.00 indicates average profitability.

For contrast, table 5.4 provides comparably calculated data on return on investment (for 1997–2005) for FDIUS. Note that these estimates of return on investment are fairly conservative with respect to the USDIA data. Because the denominator is historic cost data, it tends to understate the profitability of firms in sectors with more recent investment while overstating profitability in firms with less recent investment. This bias favors the older automobile and metal bashing industries while penalizing the newer high-technology and wholesale trade sectors. If replacement-cost estimates (i.e., current cost) were available, they would probably magnify the differences between these different generations of firms rather than reducing them.

Scanning through sector by sector comparisons (e.g., between USDIA and FDIUS in transportation equipment, largely automobiles) confirms our naïve intuitions about profitability and competitiveness. In transportation equipment, foreign car firms manufacturing in the United States are much more profitable than U.S.

TABLE 5.3.
Average return on assets for USDIA, 1998–2006

	Share of All USDIA (%)	Average Return on Investment (%)	Relative Performance (ratio)
All industries		9.52	1.00
Mining and oil	5.7	14.7	1.54
All manufacturing	21.1	10.4	1.09
Food	1.4	12.6	1.32
Chemicals	5.4	11.5	1.21
Primary and fabricated metals	1.0	8.0	0.84
Machinery	1.3	11.5	1.21
Computers and electronics[a]	3.2	10.9	1.14
Electrical equipment, appliances, and components[a]	0.7	8.4	0.89
Transportation equipment[a]	2.3	6.7	0.71
Wholesale trade	6.9	15.4	1.62
Information[a]	3.1	6.8	0.71
Depository institutions	2.8	2.8	0.29
Finance (except depository institutions) and insurance	20.3	6.3	0.66
Professional, scientific, and technical services	2.4	9.9	1.04
Holding companies (nonbank)[b]	29.8	10.9	1.14
Other industries	7.8	8.4	0.89

Source: Data from Bureau of Economic Analysis, http://www.bea.gov.
Notes: USDIA, U.S. (foreign) direct investment abroad.
[a]Data for 1999–2005 only.
[b]Data for 2003–2006 only.

TABLE 5.4.
Average return on assets for FDIUS, 1997–2005

	Share of All FDIUS (%)	Average ROA (%)	Relative Performance (ratio)
All FDIUS	100	4.23	1.00
All manufacturing	33	5.74	1.36
Food	1	6.14	1.45
Chemicals	9	6.22	1.47
Primary and fabricated metals	2	5.54	1.31
Machinery	3	2.14	0.51
Computers and electronic products[a]	3	0.06	0.01
Electrical equipment, appliances, and components[a]	1	2.15	0.51
Transportation equipment[a]	5	7.35	1.73
Wholesale trade	14	7.33	1.73
Retail trade	2	5.45	1.29
Information[a]	9	−0.15	−0.03
Depository institutions	8	4.48	1.06
Finance (except depository institutions) and insurance	13	1.44	0.34
Real estate and rental and leasing	3	3.75	0.88
Professional, scientific, and technical services	3	1.18	0.28
Other industries	17	2.47	0.58

Source: Data from Bureau of Economic Analysis, http://www.bea.gov.
Notes: FDIUS, foreign direct investment into the United States; ROA, return on assets.
[a]Data for 1999–2005 only.

car firms manufacturing abroad, as we would suspect from comparing Toyota-USA to GM-Europe. Similarly, even more finely disaggregated data show that the Japanese manufacturers of transportation equipment in the United States are half again as profitable as the European ones. Just so, although U.S. computer equipment manufacturers overseas underperform their peers in the USDIA universe, they are substantially more profitable than computer firms making FDIUS. This is consistent with a naïve appreciation of the relative long-term competitiveness of, say, Dell compared with Toshiba and with the cutthroat pricing of electronics equipment in general.

Finally, returns for firms in the wholesale and retail trade sectors also confirm our naïve impressions. Competition from Wal-Mart in the United States caused a tremendous increase in productivity in the U.S. distribution sector. McKinsey Global Institute estimates that the U.S. wholesale and retail sectors accounted for more than half the jump in economywide productivity in the United States in 1995–2000.[38] So it is no surprise that U.S. wholesalers overseas have an ROA that is well above the average for USDIA and that foreign distributors that are capable of holding their own in the U.S. market also have an ROA above the average for FDIUS. Nonetheless, these foreign distributors have an ROA half that of their U.S. counterparts. This reflects the sophistication of European firms, such as Carrefour and Ahold, that have been able to add their own innovations to those pioneered by Wal-Mart.

The central point is that the general pattern of ROA is consistent with what we would expect if we scaled a granular sense of the firms involved up to the sector level. Tax arbitrage may or may not affect the overall level of declared income. But there is no reason to suspect that specific sectors have a greater or lesser propensity to engage in tax arbitrage. If we arbitrarily reduced USDIA income while increasing FDIUS income by 1 percentage point each to account for tax avoidance, this would not change the distribution of that income across different sectors. And that distribution of income is consistent with the argument that, rather than declining, U.S. firms have been able to expand their control over leading sectors in world markets.

More direct evidence of expanding U.S. MNC control can be found in the BEA and UNCTAD data on overseas sales and value-added for foreign affiliates of MNCs.[39] These indicate a steady increase in the ratio of U.S. overseas sales to sales in the United States by firms making FDIUS. In 1995, U.S. MNC affiliates (i.e., USDIA) sold $132 overseas for every $100 sold in the United States by affiliates of foreign firms (i.e., FDIUS). By 2005, the affiliates of U.S. firms were selling $150 for every $100 sold in the United States by affiliates of foreign firms. Value-added evolved in a similar way, rising in real terms from nearly $590 billion in 1995 to $824 billion in 2004, while turnover nearly doubled to $3.2 trillion. Service-sector growth, particularly wholesale and retail trade, was even faster, with services value-added increasing from 25 to 40 percent of total value-added. Despite this faster service-sector growth, U.S. overseas manufacturing value-added increased relative to foreign manufacturing production in the United States. Note that the substantial drop in the value of the dollar relative to other currencies did not occur until after 2004–2005, so these increases are not an artifact of favorable currency movements. On the contrary, given the relative stagnation in the Repressed Rich compared to the U.S. market, the overseas performance of U.S. firms is all the more remarkable. In short, even while foreign firms vastly increased their investment in the United States, U.S. firms expanded their overseas sales faster than did foreign firms. This evolution of sales and value-added is inconsistent with arguments about declining competitiveness for U.S. firms.

We can now connect the points made in the first section of this chapter with those in this section. Two different factors appear to explain this difference in performance. Put simply, unlike British firms in the nineteenth century, U.S. firms have been highly active with respect to product, process, and organizational innovations. Because civil airframe exports typically constitute 5 percent of U.S. goods exports and because airframe manufacturing is manufacturing and not just a service-sector activity, a quick comparison of Boeing and Airbus will be helpful here. Boeing lost market share to Airbus during the 1980s and 1990s because of the earlier shift of Airbus to new technologies such as fly-by-wire, innovative wing and cockpit designs, generous government launch subsidies, and a shift toward smaller planes subsequent to the adoption by airlines of a hub and spoke model for moving passengers. The main Airbus victims, however, were the technically stagnant and undercapitalized Douglas and Lockheed, both of which disappeared from the civil airframe market. After some hesitation caused by stock market pressures, at the end of the 1990s Boeing responded to the Airbus threat with a comprehensive set of product, process, and organizational innovations.

Whereas Airbus remains wedded to an aluminum panel-on-rib design for its fuselages, employing this technology even when using composite fiber panels, Boeing has moved comprehensively into the new composite technology.[40] After experimenting with composite materials (and computer-aided design, CAD) in the B777, Boeing made the leap to an integral composite body for the B787 airframe. This means that the fuselage tube is built up completely from composite fibers without any internal spars. This permits a more rigid, yet lighter and more fuel-efficient aircraft. It also permits a huge reduction in the number of parts, and thus in time and labor, required to build the plane. By contrast, although the Airbus huge bet on the very large A380 aircraft appears to give it a monopoly on aircraft seating over five hundred passengers, it also locks Airbus into the older panel-on-rib technologies.

Boeing also made a successful organizational shift. Unlike Airbus, which was essentially a creature of four EU states before being folded into the binational European Aeronautic Defence and Space Company (EADS), Boeing was a publicly held firm subject to share market pressures for immediate profitability. This limited the ability of Boeing to fund research and development (R&D) and to launch new aircraft. For the B787 program, Boeing adopted a new organizational format made possible by the successful use of CAD for the B777 program. The company brought its subcontractors in as risk-sharing partners, integrating their production processes using CAD systems. The risk-sharing partners invested their own capital into Boeing R&D and the B787 launch. Doing so removed the share market pressures on Boeing, although it also generated some of the same sorts of difficulties integrating subcontractors that hurt Airbus. In addition, it had the subtle effect of lessening the willingness of subcontractors to share technology with Airbus, for fear of reducing their own profits from the Boeing venture.

The success of Boeing in incorporating CAD and new materials into its production processes is not an isolated phenomenon. U.S. firms have been better at incorporating information technology (IT) into their production across the board. The most compelling evidence comes from a series of fine-grained analyses by Nick Bloom and various colleagues. In a series of papers, they compare the adoption of new IT-based production and management practices in Europe and the United States to explain why the trend toward converging U.S. and European productivity abruptly reversed after 1995. They compare a wide range of MNCs operating in Britain.[41] This allows them to hold labor markets and the final market constant and, thus, compare MNCs and British firms in a variety of sectors on a level playing field.

If the change in productivity rates were only about weaker U.S. labor unions or other factors native to the U.S. market, then U.S. firms would not be able to duplicate productivity increases overseas and foreign firms in the U.S. market would be able to attain levels of productivity and thus profits similar to those of U.S. firms. Instead, Bloom and colleagues find that U.S. MNCs in Britain have higher levels of productivity than both non-U.S. MNCs in Britain and native British firms. They statistically trace this to better productivity from and returns to IT investment by U.S. firms. Indeed, when U.S. firms acquire other firms in Britain, IT productivity rises, but the same does not occur when non-U.S. firms acquire other firms in Britain. Finally, because the most heavily IT-using sectors are service-sector firms, Bloom and colleagues dismiss the transfer pricing argument as a spurious source of higher productivity; the opportunity for transfer pricing is limited in services.

If there is an analog to nineteenth-century Britain, it is more likely to be found in the EU than the United States. Although the EU produces substantially more science workers than the United States, it produces substantially less in terms of patents and cited output.[42] Throughout the long 1990s, EU-25 R&D spending was one-fifth lower than U.S. R&D spending as a share of PPP-adjusted GDP, and one-third lower absolutely. Much of that was concentrated in the Americanized Rich. EU output of high-technology manufactured value-added also has substantially lagged behind U.S. and Asian output since the mid-1990s. The EU share of global high-tech value-added fell from 28 percent in 1990 to 18.4 percent in 2003. The IT revolution can also be seen in the quite vigorous defense by the U.S. state of the intellectual property rights of U.S. firms. U.S. firms received a greater share of royalties and licensing income than did foreign firms investing in the United States. In 1989, royalties and licenses accounted for only 2.1 percent of U.S. exports of goods and services.[43] By 2005, they were 3.3 percent, down somewhat from 3.6 percent in 2003.

U.S. firms in general are more efficient and more profitable at home and abroad. Arrighi's argument about uncompetitiveness in manufacturing thus seems to be off the mark, as does Gilpin's concern that U.S. MNCs will enable Europe to close the gap with the United States. And both are certainly off the mark about the service sector, where U.S. firms have shown vastly better productivity performance than European firms. From 1994 to 2004, total factor productivity in the U.S. service sector rose 1.3 percent annually, whereas productivity in Germany and Italy declined by 0.6 percent annually and in France barely rose.[44] Yet this leaves us with one important and obvious question: If U.S. firms are so good, why are there no exports? Or, more precisely, why are there not enough exports to balance the books?

U.S. Exports in World Markets

U.S. exports face three fundamental barriers in world markets. The first stems from the fact of differential growth, which affects the distribution of growth in global markets. Put simply, because the United States is growing faster than rich economies characterized by illiquid housing markets and wage restraint, it necessarily consumes more of what it produces and imports more from those economies. The problem is partly excess imports not insufficient exports. Second, the composition of U.S. exports affects the relative propensity of foreigners to buy U.S. sourced output (as opposed to local production by the affiliates of U.S. firms). Put simply, the United States makes things that governments buy, but it imports things that consumers buy, and governments have strong preferences for locally produced goods. This perhaps explains the well-known H. S. Houthakker and Stephen Magee finding that U.S. imports rise by 1.8 percent for every 1 percent increase in global GDP.[45] Third, although U.S. productivity growth is stronger than many of its rich-country competitors, much of that growth is concentrated in services, which have limited tradability. U.S. productivity gains in services tend to be exported via direct investment, as shown in our discussion of USDIA.

To briefly review the relevant points from chapter 4, the United States had both absolutely and relatively faster growth than the Repressed Rich in 1991–2005. Japan and Germany (both Repressed Rich nations) together constitute roughly 30 percent of OECD GDP net of the United States, whereas the universe of Repressed Rich countries constitutes 57 percent of OECD GDP net of the United States. Both Germany and Japan experienced extremely slow GDP growth in the long 1990s. Absolute German GDP grew only 21 percent and Japanese GDP only 17 percent during those years, whereas U.S. GDP grew 56 percent. Exports—both directly to the United States and indirectly via China—accounted for the bulk of economic growth for both Germany and Japan. Slow growth in the Repressed Rich could not be offset by the relatively faster growth among the Americanized Rich, which amount to only 25 percent of non-U.S. OECD GDP. Slow growth in the rich countries hurt U.S. exports precisely because U.S. exports are largely high-technology, high-design goods intended for rich sophisticated markets. By contrast, the larger Repressed Rich countries relied heavily on net exports for their GDP growth; in the 1990s, net exports accounted for approximately three-eighths of German growth from 1994 onward and one-quarter of Japanese growth.[46]

In additional, income polarization in the United States worked against U.S. producers of consumer goods. Income inequality grew considerably in the United States in the long 1990s, with the lion's share of income gains going to the top 20 percent and, within that group, to the top 5 percent. Stagnant incomes among the bottom half of the U.S. population favored imports of cheap consumer nondurables from developing Asia and particularly China. Despite cumulative inflation of roughly 50 percent from 1991 to 2006, the price of developing-Asian imports to the United States hardly changed at all, making stagnant incomes more bearable but making it impossible for U.S. firms to compete through on-shore production of labor-intensive goods. On the winning side of the U.S. income distribution, rising incomes favored producers of high-quality, high-prestige consumer durables, above all imported luxury cars. Germany exported roughly $25 billion worth of cars to the United States in 2005; Japan exported $50 billion worth. The bulk of these were BMWs, Lexuses, and Mercedes. The middle of the income distribution, where U.S. firms traditionally had strength, shrank during this period. The changing distribution of income is the hinge connecting the housing boom and the trade deficit because home equity gains were largely concentrated at the top of the income distribution (see chapter 7.)

The composition of U.S. exports also hinders export growth. U.S. exports are concentrated in sectors where the buyer is either the state or strongly influenced by the state: aircraft, pharmaceuticals, semiconductors, civil engineering equipment, telecommunications switching systems, agricultural products, and a variegated collection of service-sector exports such as the management of large-scale construction projects and systems integration for complex computer systems. These public-sector capital goods constitute approximately one-third of U.S. merchandise exports. But their sales are highly politicized. It would not be surprising if states chose to award contracts to local producers rather than to import or that they influenced private-sector purchasing decisions. For example, the Chinese state must approve all aircraft imports. Public health systems purchase most U.S. pharmaceutical exports. And the EU Common Agricultural Policy is a monument to state micromanagement of agriculture.

Jeffrey Immelt, the CEO of GE, which gets more than 50 percent of its revenues from overseas sales, laid out the situation very clearly in an interview in late 2007:

> In China, the government is the customer. . . . When I go to China I go to a combination of the department of energy, transportation, health and human services all rolled into one. The leader sits there and says: "You know what, Jeff? Your train order—you know—you've got to be more competitive. The turbine installation you had in the north is going well." And he's going down and beating me up like a purchasing manager at GM.[47]

Contrast this situation with the consumer goods that Americans largely import. The probability of overt or covert state interference is not absent, but it is certainly lower. The desires of states to promote native industry or local employment hindered U.S. exports during the long 1990s, despite consistent and sometimes successful U.S. pressure to liberalize trade in agriculture and public-sector contracting. Nevertheless, the United States does not lack competent and competitive exporters. The depreciation of the U.S. dollar in 2007 caused a sharp reversal of export and import growth, even though the dollar largely shifted only against the euro through December 2007. But, even before the dollar declined, U.S. exports covered a larger percentage of the U.S. net foreign debt in 2006 than they had in 2000. And in 2008, exports grew at nearly a 10 percent annual rate and accounted for nearly all U.S. economic growth.

Finally, a standard ricardian model suggests that increases in U.S. exports should come from sectors that have experienced relatively high productivity gains compared with other countries because this increases their comparative advantage. Yet U.S. productivity growth in the long 1990s disproportionately occurred in the service sectors. Total nonfarm U.S. productivity grew approximately 2.5 percent per year in 1995–2005, a rate that could not have been possible had service-sector productivity gains significantly lagged behind manufacturing gains.[48] The service sector accounted for 75 percent of total productivity growth, and within that, multifactor productivity growth (organizational changes rather than additional capital or labor inputs) accounts for the lion's share. Many services, however, are difficult to export directly. Instead, firms with the requisite tacit knowledge invest offshore to increase the returns to that knowledge, substituting offshore production for direct exports.

The yawning U.S. trade deficit could be understood as evidence of a massive decline in the competitiveness of U.S. manufacturing akin to that which plagued British manufacturing after 1880. Declining U.S. competitiveness in manufacturing would suggest that increased financialization, either directly by the incorporation of financial activity into a given corporation or by increased U.S. intermediation of global financial flows, was a second-best response to declining competitiveness. Thus, although U.S. arbitrage might have benefited the U.S. domestic economy, it perhaps has simultaneously harmed the external position of U.S. firms.

To the contrary, in this chapter I have shown that differential growth favoring the United States at a macroeconomic level was matched by differential growth at the micro-level. Differences in housing financial systems in the long 1990s translated global disinflation and U.S. global financial arbitrage led into better-than-average gains in GDP and employment in the U.S. domestic economy. Similarly, the availability of cheap capital enabled U.S. firms to expand production at home and abroad, increasing the productivity gap between themselves and the average rich-country competitor. Far from fleeing into financial activity as a way to escape a declining manufacturing sector, competitive U.S. manufacturers and service providers took control over the financial segments of their value chains, successfully absorbed advances in IT into their production processes, and translated this into a growing share of foreign production and markets.

The fine-grained data on income from foreign direct investment shows that the U.S. external economy benefited economically from financial flows moving cheap capital into the U.S. economy while allowing exports of capital from the United States at a higher return in the form of FDI. Here there is a similarity to the original Bretton Woods system. Then, an overvalued dollar allowed U.S. MNCs to expand into European markets more easily. Now, arbitrage made it cheaper to do so, easing overseas expansion by a diversified set of U.S. manufacturing firms, as well as new service firms. This analysis allows us to dismiss the Arrighi and Gilpin analogy to the nineteenth-century British decline. Far from liquidating overseas assets (and thus surrendering a share of overseas growth) while also failing to invest in new domestic industry, the United States is selling claims on future U.S. production while expanding control by U.S. firms of global markets. Given a declining dollar after 2005, both of these presage increased production by U.S. firms and by foreign firms located in the United States.

U.S. differential growth in the long 1990s was not a mirage. U.S. arbitrage returned domestic and offshore benefits to the U.S. economy, or more precisely to U.S. corporations and the top 10 percent of U.S. income earners that own 75 percent of the shares of those firms. U.S. arbitrage thus generated benefits for a slice of the U.S. public while saddling the bulk of the taxpaying public with a larger national debt. U.S. arbitrage also generated these benefits by offering foreigners pieces of paper—claims on future U.S. production—that were vulnerable to a drop in the exchange rate for the U.S. dollar. Why, then, did those on the losing end of U.S. arbitrage acquiesce in this arbitrage? What might make them change their own policies supporting U.S. differential growth? In chapter 6, I explain why the internal arbitrage of foreigners inclines them against any race to the exit; in short, the next chapter is a discussion of how political power elsewhere sustains U.S. differential growth.

6. The External Political Foundations of U.S. Arbitrage

[The Chinese economy is] unstable, unbalanced, uncoordinated, and unsustainable.

Premier Wen Jiabao, March 2007

[We are] calling upon [the] social partners to show a high level of responsibility....[I]t is clear that if one is not satisfied with the present level of unemployment, wage moderation should remain of the essence....[I]f you are in a position where there are doubts about your present level of cost competitiveness, then of course wage moderation remains absolutely of the essence.

Jean-Claude Trichet, April 12, 2007

We have only one needle in our compass. That needle is price stability, our definition of price stability.

Jean-Claude Trichet, August 7, 2008

The Dollar as a Collective Good?

Why did foreign investors tolerate and even abet U.S. global arbitrage and differential growth; why might they continue to do so? In chapter 4, I show that the housing finance systems in the United States and the Americanized Rich translated global disinflation and capital inflows into greater local aggregate demand and differential growth. As the primary recipient of global capital flows, the United States benefited disproportionately from this process at the macroeconomic level. The United States never absorbed less than 60 percent of net global capital outflows from 2000 through 2006; even in 2007, the United States absorbed nearly 50 percent of net outflows. In chapter 5, I show that these benefits extended to U.S. MNCs, which expanded their already considerable share of global production and value-added faster than their rich-country competitors in the aggregate.

For their part, the foreign investors that abetted this process by purchasing passive U.S. debt got very low interest rates and, as it turned out, considerable paper capital losses as the trade-weighted value of the U.S. dollar dropped by nearly one-third from mid-2002 to mid-2008. Yet through mid-2008 foreign investors added nearly $700 billion to their holdings of dollar-denominated securities. Why did and do foreign investors tolerate their massive exposure to a falling dollar? This chapter returns to the domain of chapters 2 and 3 (the lower left-hand box in figure 1.1) to reconsider the political issues that determine the quantity and quality of foreign investment in the United States.

This chapter is thus both retrospective and prospective. To signal this, the lower left-hand box in figure 6.1 and the analytical-focus schematics in subsequent chapters are recoded to show how the positive feedback loops powering the differential growth of the U.S. economy turned into negative feedback loops from roughly 2005 onward. In this case, figure 6.1 asks whether the dollar has shifted from a top currency to a negotiated currency. Retrospectively, we want to know how political structures induced the accumulation of ever larger quantities of U.S. dollar-denominated assets before the 2007–2008 crisis erupted. Prospectively, we want to know how that crisis is likely to affect old holdings of and new flows into U.S. assets.

Put simply, the foreign governments that now matter most to U.S. financial arbitrage tolerated and continue to tolerate that arbitrage because they were unwilling to change the political structures in their *own* countries that sustained it. Political elites used extant political structures to privatize the gains from acquiescing in U.S. financial arbitrage while socializing potential losses, which makes dollar recycling in their interest. Foreign elites consequently supported the dollar as a negotiated currency even as the U.S. economy began slowing in 2007. Recall that *negotiated* does not imply an explicit political deal but, rather, that the attractiveness of the dollar derives relatively more from political than from narrowly economic considerations. In turn, the fact that decisions about the dollar are political makes it more likely that enough countries will collectively support the dollar despite incurring capital losses from the falling dollar exchange rate in 2007 and early 2008. This acquiescence thus parallels the grudging acquiescence Lloyd Gruber documents about trade accords.[1] In this chapter, I thus close the circular mechanism laid out in the first chapter, connecting the differential growth documented in the previous two chapters to the recycling of U.S. trade deficits into U.S. financial arbitrage. The chapter has two tasks. First, it notes that the financing of the U.S. and thus of global aggregate demand is a collective good; why would an individual country not be tempted to dump its dollar holdings and let other countries carry the burden and risk? Second, it looks at the political rationales that override economic ones to produce acquiescence, even in the face of the 2008 crisis.

These issues can be understood as the financial equivalent of the growth and trade decoupling debate, whose central issue was whether Europe, and to a lesser extent Asia, could grow in the absence of sustained U.S. growth. Dollar recycling and rising exports were clearly a substitute for domestic growth in Asia (excluding Japan) and China, where investment fell by 9 percent of GDP in 1996–2004, and in Latin America, where it fell by 3 percent of GDP.[2] These countries chose to

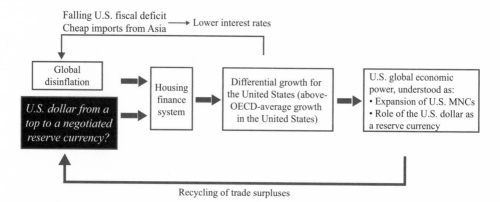

Fig. 6.1. Chapter 6: analytic focus.

prop up U.S. demand rather than invest at home. But the German 7.6 percent of GDP current account surplus in 2007 surely also suggests an economy that could not grow on its own; exports expanded at three times the rate of GDP that year, and throughout the 2000s, German GDP growth was generally negative except for exports. As the U.S. economy stalled, slowing the Chinese economy, Germany reverted to negative GDP growth for the second quarter of 2008. Equally telling, global equity markets followed U.S. markets downward in autumn 2008.

Political support for dollar recycling also goes to the heart of the continued operation of the housing machine that drove U.S. differential accumulation in the long 1990s before it crashed into the brick wall of subprime defaults. The degree to which this machine can run in reverse matters for the durability of U.S. global economic power. The end of the housing boom means that U.S. growth will slow. But the key issue for U.S. power is how much the U.S. growth slows relative to that in Asia and Europe, not the absolute slowdown in growth. Put simply, if Europe and Asia cannot decouple (i.e., grow on their own without exports to the United States), then continued acquiescence in U.S. global arbitrage makes sense as a second-best choice.

Looking backward from 2007, Morgan Stanley estimated that a 1 percent decline in U.S. growth translated into anywhere from a 1 to 7.2 percent decline in the growth of Asian economies (excluding Japan) one year later.[3] If Asia and Europe cannot decouple from the United States, then a U.S. growth slowdown will erode but not eliminate the relative gains the United States made in the long 1990s. If Asia and Europe can decouple, then in the long run the differential gains the United States made in the 1990s will disappear as many countries in these areas surpass a United States hobbled by the financial fallout from its housing market excesses. By 2009, decoupling appeared unlikely. In the first part of this chapter, I argue that, as a practical matter, financial decoupling is difficult if not impossible.

But the more important argument is that decoupling would entail unbearable political costs, which is why we see so little of it.

Before exploring political motivations, note that foreign MNCs (i.e., FDIUS), which accounted for 20 percent of U.S. foreign debt net of bank loans in 2006, cannot afford to exit the single largest world market. Even though the dollar has fallen, shifting the ratio of nominal GDP between the United States and Europe in favor of Europe, the European market remains fundamentally divided in ways that the United States and North American markets are not, and on a PPP basis, the United States remains a bigger market. Half of the global profits of Toyota, Honda, and Nissan are made in the U.S. market. To the extent that the cost basis of foreign MNCs in the United States is *not* dollar denominated, because of imported components or products, a falling dollar will induce them to step up purchases of U.S. sourced components, reducing the U.S. trade deficit, and to step up investment in North America, increasing demand for dollars. The falling dollar motivated a number of important European firms to announce new or expanded production in the United States. For example, in 2008 Volkswagen announced plans for a new $1 billion factory in Tennessee to produce vehicles based on a mid-size sedan platform designed solely for North America and using a largely North American component base.

Given the immobility of FDIUS, will portfolio investors flee? The key players here are mostly foreign central banks, which are fully political creatures. This is particularly true for the Japanese and Chinese central banks, which possess the largest holdings of U.S. securities (at roughly 12 and 10 percent each), particularly U.S. Treasury debt (at 26 and 18 percent). Indeed, from mid-2006 through mid-2007, there was no new net private investment into the United States.[4]

We start our examination of the political bases for support for U.S. arbitrage and thus dollar recycling by considering the question of exit as a practical matter and then turn to specific systems of arbitrage. Although considering exit appears prospective, it also reveals the history of U.S. arbitrage by tracing out a nonevent, namely the absence of sustained expansion of foreign securities markets. The financial repression that inhibited real growth in the Repressed Rich also inhibited the growth of financial markets. In the first section, I note that this repression made and makes the expansion of the supply of non–U.S. dollar-denominated securities difficult. Absent a crisis, only incremental expansion of the pool of securities will occur. In the second section, I examine the motivations of elites in specific countries, showing that the primary barriers to an expansion of the supply for or price of non–U.S. dollar-denominated securities are political in nature. They derive from elites' arbitrage against their own subjects. These elites benefited from the very wage restraint and financial repression that made their economies rely on exports for growth during the long 1990s. Will the elites impose costs on themselves to avoid capital losses that fall on the masses?[5] I consider three of the main U.S. creditors—the Repressed Rich, Japan, and China—both in relation to their collective action problem around the dollar and their domestic political structures.[6] The oil-exporter Lockboxes are considered in the discussion of SWFs in chapter 8. Oil looms large from 2006 on, when the price per barrel shot up from $60 to $150. But Europe and Asia still accounted for the bulk of dollar recycling in the 1990s and 2000s, respectively. Indeed, even in 2006–2007, Asia accounted for three times as much dollar recycling as all the oil exporters combined.[7] And as the oil prices declined after 2008, oil exporters became correspondingly less important. The Americanized Rich, as we have seen in chapter 4, have a mutually beneficial economic relation with the United States and already have something close to a U.S. level of financialization.

No Exit?

Put simply, continued financial repression both motivated an export orientation during the long 1990s and then limited the supply of alternative investment vehicles when the U.S. boom burst. This made and makes a wholesale flight from the dollar and dollar-denominated investments difficult. In this section, I focus on the absence of exit options when U.S. growth began slowing, but I also suggest the limits that operated during the U.S. upswing in the long 1990s. Here I analyze the long-term institutional and political basis for this situation. As a practical matter, foreign investors in the United States have weak exit options, given that marketable U.S. equities and bonds represent approximately two-fifths of the world supply of these vehicles by value. The data presented here are largely drawn from 2006 and were the best available at the time of writing. The simultaneous collapse of global equities markets in 2008 changed only the absolute amounts and not the relative proportions. Figure 6.2 shows the relevant regional shares of the $51 trillion in global equity capitalization at the end of 2006. Figure 6.3 shows the relevant regional shares of the $69 trillion in public and private debt securities as of year end 2006. As of 2007, foreigners held in excess of $8 trillion in U.S. securities, or roughly 7 percent of the total global supply of negotiable securities, suggesting that any wholesale flight would precipitate costly losses. Indeed, both figures already reflect part of the post-2002 slide in the relative value of the U.S. dollar; at the most recent exchange rate peak of the dollar in late 2001, U.S. equities accounted for 50 percent of total global equities and U.S. debt securities accounted for 45 percent of total global debt securities.[8] Barring a total collapse of the dollar, these figures represent something close to the floor on the share of U.S. dollar-denominated securities of the global securities markets in the medium run. They also reflect over a decade of accumulation of U.S. securities by foreigners.

But even though it is true as a matter of mathematics that *currently* the supply of alternative investment vehicles is too small to accommodate a shift away from U.S. securities, this might not be true in the future. This has both a supply and

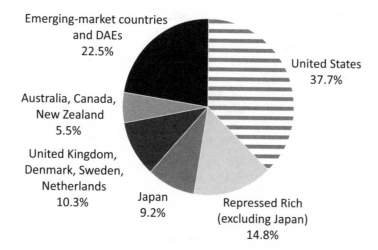

Fig. 6.2. Share of global equities capitalization by region, 2006. Emerging markets and DAEs = Hong Kong, Korea, Singapore, and Taiwan province plus Israel and middle-income developing economies. DAEs, dynamic Asian economies.
Sources: Data from International Monetary Fund, *Global Financial Stability Report, September 2007,* IMF, Washington, D.C., 138; World Federation of Exchanges website, http://www.world-exchanges.org/statistics; Statistics Australia, http://www.abs.gov.au/; Reserve Bank of New Zealand website, http://www.rbnz.govt.nz/statistics/.

price component. Asset markets are inherently elastic because prices can rise with demand. Yet, given the current limited supply of liquid assets, nondollar asset prices would rapidly rise if holders shifted out of dollar-denominated assets, with politically deleterious consequences. Alternately, the Repressed Rich could generate more assets, allowing diversification away from U.S. assets without forcing extravagant increases in existing asset prices. And, indeed, their modest shares of global equities and private debt markets (see figures 6.2 and 6.3) suggest there is plenty of room for expansion. But could this be done? To help set up later arguments relating to the political barriers, we need to disaggregate global securities markets the same way that we disaggregated investment into the United States.

Table 6.1 compares the size of total financial assets for the major economic blocks by totting up all equities, public and private debt securities, and bank loans and comparing this sum to GDP. It reveals, at first blush, a surprising finding, considering that analysts such as Giovanni Arrighi have made so much of the financialization of the U.S. economy (see chapter 5). The surprise is that the United States is one of the least financialized rich countries, at least in terms of the ratio of total financial assets to GDP. The Americanized Rich—primarily because of the large weight of Britain in their subtotal—are the most financialized. But the Repressed Rich are also somewhat more financialized than the United States. Nonetheless, all of the rich countries are close to the standard set by Fernand Braudel, who once

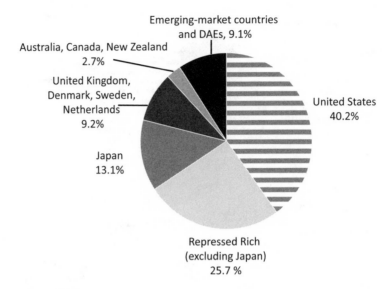

Fig. 6.3. Share of global public and private debt securities markets by region, 2006. Emerging markets and DAEs = Hong Kong, Korea, Singapore, and Taiwan province plus Israel and middle-income developing economies. DAEs, dynamic Asian economies.
Sources: Data from International Monetary Fund, *Global Financial Stability Report, September 2007,* IMF, Washington, D.C., 138; World Federation of Exchanges website, http://www.world-exchanges.org/statistics; Statistics Australia, http://www.abs.gov.au/; Reserve Bank of New Zealand website, http://www.rbnz.govt.nz/statistics/.

observed that a four-to-one ratio of capital stock to GDP was typical in rich economies.[9] Differences emerge when we consider the degree of financialization with respect to liquid assets, however. Illiquid bank loans constitute a near-majority of financial assets in euroland and, more precisely, among the Repressed Rich. By contrast, in the Americanized Rich and the United States, liquid assets constitute a huge majority of assets, with equities having the heaviest weight. Furthermore, the liquid financial assets of the Repressed Rich are in turn heavily weighted toward public debt, complicating new issues of liquid debt securities.

Figure 6.4 provides a breakdown of the distribution of financial assets by region and class of asset. It shows that the U.S. financial market is disproportionately composed of equities and private bonds, which is why the U.S. share of global equity and especially private debt markets is larger than the U.S. share of global GDP. The United States is underweight in public debt and, even more so, bank assets (i.e., loans). This reflects years of securitization of bank loans and particularly of mortgages. The Americanized Rich are similarly overweight equities and considerably underweight public debt, reflecting decades of fiscal prudence in Australia and New Zealand and more lately in Britain. Again, the concentration of banks in Britain and the Netherlands biases the bank asset ratio of the Americanized

TABLE 6.1.
Ratio of total financial assets to GDP in selected countries, 2006

	GDP (billions of dollars)	Assets (billions of dollars)[a]	Ratio of Assets to GDP
United States	13,194.7	56,509.4	4.28
Americanized Rich	6,244.4	35,335.2	5.66
Repressed Rich[b]	9,493.2	45,138.5	4.75
Japan	4,366.2	19,930.5	4.56
Emerging markets plus DAEs[c]	14,078.5	29,020.1	2.06
Memo: Global total	48,204.4	190,422	3.95

Sources: Data from International Monetary Fund, *Global Financial Stability Report, September 2007* (Washington, D.C.: IMF, 2008), 138; World Federation of Exchanges website, http://www.world-exchanges.org/statistics; Statistics Australia, http://www.abs.gov.au/; Reserve Bank of New Zealand website, http://www.rbnz.govt.nz/statistics/.
Notes: DAEs, dynamic Asian economies.
[a]Total of equities, debt securities, and bank assets.
[b]Excluding Japan.
[c]As defined by the IMF plus Hong Kong, Israel, Korea, Singapore, and Taiwan Province.

Rich upward, reflecting less securitization than in the United States. By contrast, the Repressed Rich display the opposite pattern. Their financial assets are heavily weighted toward bank assets and public debt, both of which have larger proportions than their share of global GDP. Public debt is even more salient for Japan, reflecting nearly two decades of fiscal deficits after their bubble burst. The U.S. financial bailout could change this situation.

Figure 6.5 carries this one step further to show how overweight Japan and the Repressed Rich are with respect to the $43 trillion global public debt market. Whereas the U.S. share of global public debt securities is somewhat smaller than its share of global GDP, Japan and a euroland diminished by exclusion of the United Kingdom, Denmark, Sweden, and the Netherlands each have public debts absolutely as large as that of the United States. And while the U.S. public debt notionally captures some of the contingent liabilities involved in U.S. public pensions (because the federal Social Security pension-program Trust Funds hold roughly $2 trillion of the U.S. public debt securities), the same is not true for most euroland public debt.[10] Including the contingent liabilities built into public pensions in the Repressed Rich would considerably increase their share of an even larger total global public debt.

Finally the global distribution of bank lending is heavily weighted toward the Repressed Rich and, within them, the European Repressed Rich. Figure 6.6 displays the regional shares of global bank assets, including domestic lending, in December 2006. (It also includes the rest of the world, as other countries have a significant share). The relatively underweight U.S. share is immediately evident in figure 6.6, as is the equally overweight position of the Repressed Rich, including Japan. Whereas the United States accounts for 27.4 percent of global GDP but only 14.4 percent of bank lending, the Repressed Rich account for 28.8 percent of global GDP but 39.4 percent of bank lending. In short, the Repressed Rich are very

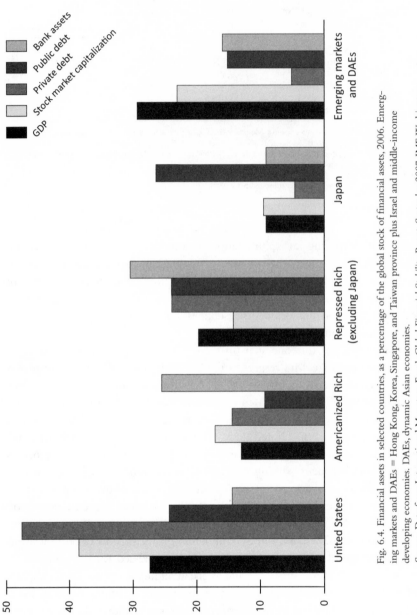

Fig. 6.4. Financial assets in selected countries, as a percentage of the global stock of financial assets, 2006. Emerging markets and DAEs = Hong Kong, Korea, Singapore, and Taiwan province plus Israel and middle-income developing economies. DAEs, dynamic Asian economies.

Sources: Data from International Monetary Fund, *Global Financial Stability Report, September 2007*, IMF, Washington, D.C., 138; World Federation of Exchanges website, http://www.world-exchanges.org/statistics; Statistics Australia, http://www.abs.gov.au/; Reserve Bank of New Zealand website, http://www.rbnz.govt.nz/statistics/.

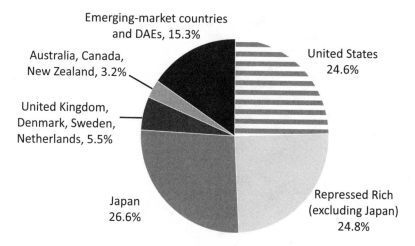

Fig. 6.5. Share of global public bond markets by region in selected countries, 2006 (%). Emerging markets and DAEs = Hong Kong, Korea, Singapore, and Taiwan province plus Israel and middle-income developing economies. DAEs, dynamic Asian economies.
Sources: Data from International Monetary Fund, *Global Financial Stability Report, September 2007*, IMF, Washington, D.C., 138; World Federation of Exchanges website, http://www.world-exchanges.org/statistics; Statistics Australia, http://www.abs.gov.au/; Reserve Bank of New Zealand website, http://www.rbnz.govt.nz/statistics/.

much overweight in public debt and bank lending and are underweight in private debt and even more so equities.

The structure of the global securities markets thus reflects long-standing financial repression and makes it difficult for large holders of U.S. dollar-denominated securities to shift to alternative investment vehicles. The Repressed Rich, and even more so Japan, are committed to reductions rather than expansions of their public debt, not an expansion to accommodate flight from the dollar. Governments in these countries face unprecedented demographic shifts that will impose large fiscal burdens over the next twenty years, burdens that considerably exceed those in the United States. It is doubtful they will add to those burdens by expanding deficit spending now. Furthermore, the EU Stability and Growth Pact (SGP) also inhibits any expansion in public debt. The SGP in theory protects banks and northern European governments from the imprudence of Club Med governments, although in practice the first violations came from the colder countries with hotter spending. Nonetheless, the SGP makes any rapid expansion of fiscal deficits, and thus public debt, difficult. A rapid and asymmetrical expansion of public debt inside the European Union would probably threaten the stability of the euro, driving investors back to U.S. dollar-denominated securities.

What about expanding the supply of equities and private debt? The data in table 6.2 on the size of equity and debt markets shows that the United States *is*

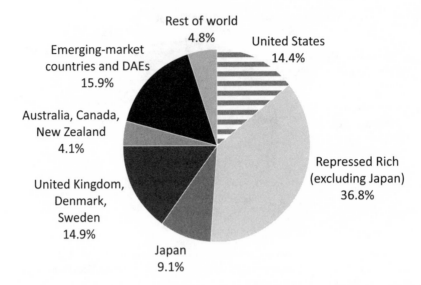

Fig. 6.6. Share of global pool of bank assets by region, 2006. Emerging markets and DAEs = Hong Kong, Korea, Singapore, and Taiwan province plus Israel and middle-income developing economies. DAEs, dynamic Asian economies.
Sources: Data from International Monetary Fund, *Global Financial Stability Report, September 2007,* IMF, Washington, D.C., 138; World Federation of Exchanges website, http://www.world-exchanges.org/statistics; Statistics Australia, http://www.abs.gov.au/; Reserve Bank of New Zealand website, http://www.rbnz.govt.nz/statistics/.

much more financialized than other countries in the sense that the ratio of liquid, marketable financial assets relative to GDP is higher than for any other country or group of countries (save the Netherlands). This reflects the fact that U.S. financial engineering has converted more U.S. streams of income into liquid assets than is the case in any other major country. In addition to mortgages, the pool of securitized debt also includes commercial receivables, credit card receivables, automobile purchase loans, and educational loans.

Table 6.2 also unveils the salience of bank loans in the asset pool of the Repressed Rich. Unlike in table 6.1, in which the Repressed Rich appear to be more financialized than the United States, in table 6.2 their level of financialization suddenly drops well below that of the United States, not to mention the United Kingdom and the Netherlands. The disproportionately large U.S. share of global private debt and equities markets reflects the prior shift of illiquid bank loans into liquid debt securities via the securitization of mortgages and other receivables. Assetwise, the Repressed Rich countries possess scads of bank loans and public debt. But bank assets cannot be sold unless they are securitized, and the 2008 crisis will hamper all but the most transparent forms of securitization for the foreseeable future. Even in financial fair weather, however, the securitization of bank loans or a

TABLE 6.2.
Ratio of liquid securities to GDP in selected countries, 2006

	GDP (billions of dollars)	Stock Market Capitalization (billions of dollars)	Total Debt (billions of dollars)	Stock Cap Plus Total Debt (billions of dollars)	Ratio of Securities to GDP
United States	13,195	19,569	26,736	46,305	351
Americanized Rich (total)	6,244	8,689	8,595	17,284	277
United Kingdom	2,395	3,794	3,298	7,092	296
Netherlands	667	725	1,700	2,425	364
Repressed Rich (total)[a]	9,493	7,221	16,424	23,645	249
France	2,252	2,313	3,495	5,808	258
Germany	2,899	1,638	4,851	6,489	224
Japan	4,366	4,796	8,719	13,515	310
Emerging markets plus DAEs[b]	14,079	11,692	6,056	17,749	126
Memo: World totals	48,204	50,827	68,734	119,561	248

Sources: Data from International Monetary Fund, *Global Financial Stability Report, September 2007* (Washington, D.C.: IMF, 2008), 138; World Federation of Exchanges website, http://www.world-exchanges.org/statistics; Statistics Australia, http://www.abs.gov.au/; Reserve Bank of New Zealand website, http://www.rbnz.govt.nz/statistics/.
Notes: DAEs, dynamic Asian economies.
[a] Excluding Japan.
[b] Emerging Markets and DAEs defined as in Figure 6.2.

vast expansion of equity markets in the Repressed Rich would create political and economic difficulties, as we discuss later.

On the other hand, the emerging markets are considerably underweight with respect to all forms of financial assets, particularly private debt. Here, too, a wholesale shift into local securities would create political and economic difficulties. Put aside concerns about whether most emerging markets have corporate governance structures that will instill confidence in most investors. Although real, these pale beside the immediate consequences of a shift from dollar assets to local currency assets—an appreciation of that local currency that would price exports out of U.S. markets and perhaps trigger a serious deflation.[11]

To sum up matters so far, decades of financial repression have limited the exit options for refugees from U.S. securities. Both the supply and composition of securities on the other side of the transaction make exit problematic. The European Repressed Rich are long on illiquid bank loans and short on equities and private debt. Japan, aside from ultimately being too small as a market, is similarly long on bank loans and on low-yielding public debt. And although the Americanized Rich do have large supplies of equities and private debt, they (like Japan) are too small to absorb much capital fleeing U.S. dollar-denominated securities. The only way to change this equation is to change the supply and composition of the securities markets in euroland, Japan, and key emerging markets all at once. This would lower the costs of exit from dollar-denominated securities. But political costs, not economic costs, inhibit this outcome. The composition of securities in different markets reflects both political choices and the patterns of domestic arbitrage that ultimately help sustain the larger U.S. global arbitrage. Nonetheless, for analytic reasons, let us put aside the issue of domestic political motivations for a moment. If we do so, foreign holders of U.S. securities clearly face a typical prisoners' dilemma–based collective action problem. We should see investors racing to the exits to avoid capital losses. Each country should, rationally, seek to shed its holdings, yet exit will precipitate the very losses they seek to avoid. Why have we not seen massive exit? We next consider the investors' collective action problem.

Investors' Collective Action Problem

Recall the Dooley, Folkerts-Landau, Garber (DFG) Bretton Woods 2 argument, which suggests that developing countries will continue to absorb dollar-denominated securities because of the growth benefits that this generates. In the Bretton Woods 2 argument, the periphery holds dollars to permit export-led growth. Maintaining the exchange rate of the dollar is a public good. Although it is collectively in the interest of the periphery to sustain peripheral growth by accumulating dollar reserves, any given individual peripheral country has an incentive to defect and sell its dollar reserves so as to also avoid losses from a depreciating dollar. This suggests that the gains from holding dollars offset the losses for the periphery as an aggregate. There is some evidence supporting the idea that the periphery collectively holds dollars. The dollar became a top currency, largely held by dispersed private actors, in the 1990s. But, after 2004, dollar-denominated holdings became much more concentrated by country as well as concentrated into the hands of political actors such as central banks and SWFs; the dollar became a negotiated currency.

Barry Eichengreen argues that holders of dollars face a classic collective action problem that undermines the Bretton Woods 2 argument.[12] The dollar holdings of the periphery have already imposed billions of dollars of capital losses on central banks and expose those banks to billions of dollars more in potential capital losses if the exchange value of the dollar continues to fall further. Why will any individual country not defect from the provision of this public good?

Maintaining Bretton Woods 2 is actually not a classic collective action problem in which each individual has an equal stake in maintain the collective good. Instead, the uneven distribution of holdings creates what Russell Hardin calls a privileged (or K) group—a core group with so great a stake in the benefits from the public good that the group provides it regardless of free riding by smaller players.[13] The distribution of dollar-denominated portfolio holdings as of mid-2007 reveals this privileged group because current holdings, not the averages used in previous chapters, define the relevant actors. As of mid-2007, four actors controlled the bulk of U.S. overseas portfolio debt: Japan (12.2 percent), China (10.3 percent in the official statistics, but surely more), select European economies, and the oil exporters (again, officially 3.2 percent, but surely an underestimate and rising rapidly).[14] The adherence of any individual economy to dollar recycling thus needs a specific local explanation, not a collective one, and moreover one that attends to the members of the privileged K group. In short, the explanation needs to rest on the *private goods* that lie behind the *public good* of maintaining the dollar as a reserve currency and holding dollars as reserves. Here the private good is not just the equally public good of maintaining growth in the economies of dollar holders, but also elites' desires to leave intact the political structures that privilege themselves. Decoupling from the dollar would force an unraveling of those local political structures.

Foreign elites benefit from domestic systems of arbitrage—private goods—that are nested within the larger structure of U.S. global financial arbitrage. These systems benefit those elites by socializing potential losses from a collapse of the dollar and forgone gains from open access to global financial markets while privatizing the gains from elites' access to those global financial and goods markets. These systems require a degree of financial repression, which in turn limits the volume of available securities. Creating plausible exit options would require political elites to dismantle much of their own systems of power and arbitrage. Exit from or attraction to the dollar thus rests as much on political foundations as it does economic foundations. Political considerations constrain the creation of non–U.S. dollar-denominated securities and, thus, limit exit options. Let us now consider the important players.

Political Barriers to Exit

The European Repressed Rich

Blockholding and Social Protection   Earlier we saw that bank loans constitute a large share of the available assets among the Repressed Rich economies. We know from the U.S. economy that bank lending can be securitized. So technical barriers clearly do not prevent securitization, although mixing streams of income from different countries is problematic given the legal heterogeneity of Europe.[15] What political and economic barriers prevent securitization or an expansion of the supply of equities? What prevents use of the euro as a reserve currency and as a step toward decoupling from the United States? Continental European production systems rest on two mutually supporting pillars: the systems of corporatist intermediation (see chapter 4) and financial repression. These pillars simultaneously help create export competitiveness for continental European firms while inhibiting an expansion of the pool of liquid securities or the use of the euro as a true international reserve currency. Put simply, changing the financial system would undermine export competitiveness in politically powerful industries characterized by differentiated quality production.

Consider the analysis of European capitalism presented by the *Varieties of Capitalism* school. *Varieties* argues that the continental European CMEs require financial repression to make their economies work.[16] Financial repression is an essential complement of institutional solutions to five key coordination problems associated with profitable production: corporate governance or the continued capitalization of the enterprise, skills formation, relationships with suppliers and buyers, wage bargaining, and relations among employees. Strategic actors in CMEs typically resolve these issues through negotiation rather than via hierarchies or, as in the LME type, via the market. *Varieties* argues that institutional solutions to these problems cannot be chosen a la carte but, rather, need to form a coherent whole to work well. Institutional coherence makes firms competitive in the long run, but disturbing one feature undermines the workings of the other features.

The institutional feature that most concerns us is the use of financial repression to manage problems of corporate governance and the related issue of capitalization of the firm as an ongoing enterprise. Relational banking, that is to say, a long-standing commitment on the part of a single or small number of banks to fund the long-term investment of a firm, characterizes CMEs.[17] Relational banking works by matching maturities and reducing bank credit risk. Firms need long-term capital to fund long-maturing investment as well as to retain their skilled workforce during downturns in the economic cycle. Because funding comes from banks rather than capital markets, firms are insulated from short-term market pressures for profitability, particularly during downturns. For their part, banks are concerned with protecting their loans from bankruptcy. An ongoing concern provides better protection than one in receivership. Banks monitor the performance and long-term prospects of firms by placing bank agents on their boards. By assuring firms of credit and then monitoring those firms to prevent the inevitable moral hazard created by credit guarantees, banks can reduce their credit risk. Moreover, holding loans to term reduces the dangers from mark-to-market accounting.

Speaking empirically, rather than theoretically, about Germany, Peter Hall notes that "Extensive cross-shareholdings that protected companies from hostile take-overs allowed [German firms] to privilege investment over profitability, and strong employers associations promoted the close ties among firms that facilitate collaborative research and development," and he later notes that "German firms continue to draw more heavily on long term bank-based finance than British firms, and hostile takeovers are much less frequent in Germany and Sweden than Britain."[18] A similar provision of long-term capital, in this case from the state, characterized France up until the 1990s.[19] After that, the state typically used controlling stakes and a similar system of interlocking corporate ownership to protect firms from hostile takeovers, particularly from the foreign investors that owned a substantial but passive share of the equities of the forty largest firms populating the CAC40 index. Interlocked large firms and family-owned small and medium firms, rather than publicly capitalized firms, similarly characterize Italy.

By contrast, open capital markets characterize *Varieties* LMEs. These capital markets fund new firms through equity issues (IPOs) and discipline old firms by allowing actors that wish to contest managerial control to buy shares in an open market. Falling share prices for firms that underperform in terms of profit expose those firms to a takeover by anyone with sufficient cash to buy a controlling block of shares. Thus, unlike banks in CMEs, actors in capital markets are under constant pressure to generate above-average returns and keep their shares at a level sufficient to dissuade a takeover threat.[20] Institutional investors—whose performance is constantly monitored because regulations require them to mark to market daily and who manage a huge proportion of the equity float—are willing to pay a share price premium of approximately 20 percent for above-average performance by the firms in which they are invested, reinforcing the disparity between the share prices of under- and overperforming firms.[21] Banks, meanwhile, can carry their loans at book value as long as debtors are current on interest payments.

This classic closed system of corporate governance eroded during the 1990s. But, even at the end of our period, most CMEs still had considerably less market contestation for control over firms than was the case in the LMEs. Table 6.3 shows that only the largest German firms had relatively small controlling blocks of shares, although these were still larger than corresponding blocks in the United Kingdom or United States. This is consistent with recent research by Martin Höpner and Lothar Krempel, which shows that the tight interlinks among German firms had loosened, but not disappeared, during the 2000s.[22] Loosening occurred after the Social Democrat government passed corporate governance reforms, weakening blockholder protections and eliminating capital gains on sales by banks of their holdings of industrial equities in the late 1990s.

Table 6.3 mostly lists relatively large firms. But smaller firms show the same or greater degree of blockholding. Mark Roe sampled the first twenty listed firms with capitalization just over $500 million in each of several European countries and the United States to determine the proportion of firms with a controlling block of at least 20 percent. In the average Repressed Rich economy, 83 percent of sampled firms had such a block, compared to an average of 69 percent in the Americanized Rich.[23] Given that most of the Americanized Rich are relatively smaller economies whose medium-size firms are large in the local context, this is a significant difference. All things being equal, we would expect the largest local firms to have the greatest public shareholding.

Blockholding insulates firms from capital market pressures, according to Roe. If the *Varieties* arguments are correct, then increasing the volume of equities by taking private firms public or by opening block shareholdings to a free float or by increasing the volume of marketable private securities by securitizing bank loans would expose continental European firms to market pressures that arguably would be detrimental to their production model. These capital market pressures would undermine their ability to foster and retain labor with firm-specific, nontransferable skills. Export firms and their associated unions would be expected to resist any such expansions.

Bank-based finance also reinforces an absence of marketable securities and equities through a different channel. Banks locked into long-term loans at fixed interest

TABLE 6.3.
Controlling blocks of shares in major European economies and the United States, 1999

Country	Number of Listed Firms	Median Largest Voting Block[a]	Mean Largest Voting Block[a]	Share of Medium-Size Firms with a 20% Controlling Block (%)[b]
Austria	50	52	54.1	100
Belgium	121	50.6	42.1	80
Bel20	20	45.1	38.3	n/a
Germany	374	52.1	49.1	90
Dax 30	30	11	17.3	n/a
Spain	193	34.2	40.1	n/a
France				
CAC40	40	20	29.4	100
Italy	216	54.5	48	100
Netherlands	137	43.5	42.3	90
United Kingdom	250	9.9	14.4	40
United States				
NYSE	1,309	> 5% disclosure threshold	3.6	n/a
NASDAQ	2,831	> 5% disclosure threshold	3.4	10

Sources: Columns 2–4: Maria Maher and Thomas Andersson, *Corporate Governance: Effects on Firm Performance and Economic Growth* (Paris: OECD, 1999), 15; Column 5: Mark Roe, *Political Determinants of Corporate Governance* (New York: Oxford University Press, 2003), 19.

Notes: n/a, not available; NYSE, New York Stock Exchange.

[a] As percentage of listed industrial companies.

[b] First twenty firms with capitalization over $500 million as of 1995.

rates are especially vulnerable to inflation. This inclines them to support a cautious monetary policy as a supplement to active supervision of their debtors to reduce credit risks. In addition, David Soskice argues that CMEs require a disciplined central bank to prevent inflationary tendencies that arise from relatively centralized collective bargaining.[24] The ECB and its genetic predecessor, the Bundesbank, both display this strong anti-inflationary bias. Indeed, the ECB actually raised rates while the 2008 crisis was unfolding. Increasing the supply of marketable securities presents a dual threat to this anti-inflation bias. First, an increase in the volume of marketable securities allows nonbank firms to create credit by creating derivatives based on those securities. Marketable securities thus permit both an expansion of the money supply and an increase in the velocity of money unsanctioned by the ECB. Instead, both the Bundesbank and the ECB strongly prefer wage restraint as the path to higher profits.

Second, a crisis scenario in which investors flee U.S. dollar-denominated securities for euro-denominated securities implies falling real interest rates in the ECB domain as investors bid up the price of those securities. Higher securities prices would induce more consumer spending through wealth effects. The ECB response most likely would be a rerun of the Bundesbank brutal postunification interest rate hikes. This would make the euro even more expensive relative to the dollar, punishing the export industries at the heart of the CME institutional complex. The ECB anti-inflation bias thus militates against the creation of too much in the way of new assets.

A similar dynamic limits use of the euro. To be an international reserve currency, a currency must circulate. This implies that euroland as a whole must run a trade deficit. But if corporatist wage restraint remains a political pillar of euroland polities, then trade deficits imply job losses. The euroland damp squib of an economic revival in 2004–2007 surely owes something to the diversion of Chinese exports from a slowing U.S. economy to a Europe whose currency had risen sharply against the yuan. When the dollar started falling against the euro in 2002, Chinese trade and euroland trade were roughly in balance. By 2007, with the yuan down by roughly 40 percent against the euro, China was running a €160 billion, or $230 billion, surplus with Europe, a bit larger than its surplus with the United States. Although the $170 billion increase in the EU current account deficit in 2006–2008 matched the $125 billion decrease in the U.S. current account deficit, it seems improbable that the European Union would tolerate even the $400 billion deficit that the United States normally runs, let alone the $800 billion peak deficit in 2006.

Arbitrage   Why should we characterize the combination of blockholding and finance via bank loans as a system of arbitrage? Mark Roe argues that the larger economic environment determines whether blockholding has positive or negative effects.[25] If we assume that the management of a given firm is opportunistic—an assumption generally verified by the U.S. experience—then blockholders can check managerial opportunism and rent seeking in a way that dispersed shareholders cannot. In oligopolistic markets, this check can prevent inefficiency and self-dealing. But blockholding provides no special advantage in today's increasingly competitive global markets. Instead, markets discipline managers, along the lines already discussed for the LME case. Our discussion of the superior IT management of U.S. MNCs (see chapter 5) suggests that competitive capital and product markets together can force management to reduce slack.[26] By contrast, blockholders, and particularly family-based blockholders, are less likely to introduce tighter managerial practices, as the nineteenth-century British experience shows.

Why do I characterize these practices as ultimately political? The *Varieties* school argues that even in competitive markets blockholding permits a hoarding of skilled labor. But this argument also implies the creation of insider-outsider labor markets (because skilled labor does not circulate and entry-level positions are not created), as well as a hesitancy to enter new markets (because banks cannot transfer the credit risk involved in entrepreneurial activity and management is composed of administrators, not entrepreneurs). Blockholding thus has political consequences through its effects on the distribution of employment, income, and ownership.

The European Repressed Rich experience these effects three ways. First, the use of wage restraint in the pursuit of macroeconomic balance keeps demand low and, thus, slows economic growth (see chapter 4). Relentless wage restraint has assured that the wage share of GDP in Repressed Europe is lower than in both the United States and the Americanized Rich as a whole. From 1991 to 2005, the share of compensation of employees in GDP in Germany, Austria, and Italy fell by roughly 4.4 percentage points each, while in the United States, Britain, and Australia, it fell by only 1.5 percentage points. The average fall in the OECD was 2.6 percentage points.[27] Although financial repression delivers employment stability and social insurance to insiders, it does not deliver employment-generating growth to outsiders. German manufacturing firms, for example, had consistently good productivity growth, albeit below U.S. levels (see table 5.2). Yet without increased aggregate demand Germany could not translate that productivity growth into job creation. And even though financial repression may guarantee profitability for firms and security for banks, a rising share for gross operating surplus does not seem to translate into either increased domestic investment or employment. GFCF in the European Repressed Rich actually fell in relation to GDP, especially in Germany. What wage restraint did do was repress European growth and reinforce dependence on external sources of demand, particularly from upper-income Americans, and encourage banks in the Repressed Rich to invest in U.S. securities.

A consideration of the housing finance markets reinforces this. The Repressed Rich mortgage requirements of large down payments and quick amortization induce higher levels of personal savings in those who wish to buy their housing. Banks then channel this cash to local firms. But given the risk aversion of the banks, little of this funding is available for start-up firms. Moreover, European banks are relatively less profitable despite their secure positions in their domestic markets. Instead, European banks sought greater returns in the 1990s and 2000s by coming late to a variety of booms. Contrary to what we might expect on the basis of geography or export markets, European banks, not Japanese or even more so U.S. banks, had the greatest exposure in the 1997 Asian financial crisis, and they turned out to have a surprisingly large exposure to the subprime ABS and CDO crises as well.[28]

Second, conventional wisdom and the *Varieties* school give great credit to the old European pattern of house banks and family-owned firms, particularly for small and medium enterprises. Unlike the United States, where the NASDAQ stock exchange and a vibrant venture-capital infrastructure have permitted and promoted IPOs that make it possible for owners to cash out part of their gain while also recruiting professional management, the combination of retained loans and family ownership means that management is often recruited from within the family. Shallower stock markets in continental Europe make it difficult for families to cash out, as in the United States. Anecdotally, we might be persuaded from the Porsche experience that family ownership and management are not detrimental to long-term performance. After all, the Porsche minnow essentially swallowed the Volkswagen whale after the European Union ruled that the lopsided Volkswagen voting structure illegal. But more systematic data suggest that family ownership accounts for a substantial portion of the performance gap between U.S. firms and those in Europe, partly because family firms account for 30 percent of European firms versus only 10 percent of U.S. firms.[29] Family firms with nonprofessional management typically have less efficient managerial practices.

Third, the core components of corporatist bargains in Repressed Europe used to be an exchange of wage restraint for investment and later became an exchange of wages now for deferred wages received as an expanded social wage, the promise of a well-compensated early retirement if that became necessary, and generous public pensions.[30] But securitizing bank loans would create a large set of long-maturity obligations whose only obvious landing spot would be the private pension firms. Repressed European banks managed their maturity mismatch by accepting these long-dated assets in return for a place on the boards of the firms to which they lent money. Pension funds, by contrast, are naturally interested in matching long-term liabilities to customers with a set of long-maturing assets to fund those liabilities.

In contrast, the Americanized Rich private pension funds—often mutual funds or unit trusts—constitute some of the largest holders of securitized assets and equities. Indeed, some private pension funds in the United States are as large as the funded public pensions of some European states. In 2007, the five biggest private U.S. pension funds—General Motors, IBM, General Electric, Boeing, and ATT—were all in the top thirty largest discrete pension funds in the world, controlling $378 billion in assets.[31] Individually each was larger than the Singaporean Central Provident Fund, and collectively they were twice as large as all German funds in the top three hundred. Altogether, the top three hundred pension funds controlled $10.4 trillion at the end of 2006, which was 40 percent of the total global pension market and 9 percent of total global liquid securities. U.S., Dutch, British, and Canadian pension funds accounted for 61 percent of these assets, with the United States alone accounting for 43 percent. By contrast, Repressed Europe accounted for only 7 percent of total pension assets, with German funds accounting for 1.5 percent.[32]

Pensions are not missing in Repressed Europe; rather, they are mostly public and mostly on a pay-as-you-go basis instead of being capitalized. This different construction of property rights around pensions matters for our argument. If banks expand European debt markets by securitizing their loans, the natural constituency for this debt is the pension funds. Yet, as the bruising battles over the Swedish ATP funds in the 1970s showed, business has no desire to create and confront a massive state-run agency controlling huge volumes of corporate debt and equities.[33] On the other side, unions rightly fear the kinds of lightly regulated privately run pensions that abused their clients in Britain after the shift from the state-run State Earnings Related Pension Scheme (SERPS) to private plans. Finally, the mass public in Repressed Europe is unlikely to countenance a direct assault on its public pension rights. Because both first- and second-tier pensions have historically been tax funded and public, few individuals have saved any sizable amounts for retirement, although fears about the sustainability of public pensions have lately induced an upturn in savings. The transitional double-payment problem would be more grievous in Europe than in the failed proposals to privatize the U.S. Social Security Old Age Pension. And the European public is unlikely to support further privatization of pensions after the 2008 financial debacle.

The interest of businesses in preserving a functioning production model and the interest of the mass public in retaining public pension rights thus create formidable barriers to the securitization of bank loans in Repressed Europe. Securitization is the only way for Repressed Europe to expand the supply of securities to cope with an influx of money fleeing dollar-denominated securities. Yet removing financial repression would undermine managerial strategies for inducing the formation of labor with firm-specific skills. It would subject management to pressure from both capital and product markets, making it harder to share rents among managers and workers inside the firm. Consequently, actors in Repressed Europe are unlikely to push for securitization.[34] If they did so, it would break down the insider-outsider barriers that privilege incumbent firms and their employees; reduce the ability of employer organizations and unions to determine wages via collective bargaining, and thus reduce their political power; and surely increase pressures for more market liberalization as firms confronted increased competitive pressures and sought to lower their costs. Meanwhile, the costs of stagnant employment growth are passed on to the fisc and the public via welfare state spending.

Japan

Blockholding and Social Protection   Repressed Europe is unable to generate securities or abandon dollar-denominated securities without undermining the sources of its economic competitiveness and disturbing the position of political elites, but what about Japan? Japan combines the reasons of both Repressed Europe and China for diffidence about disturbing its reliance on dollar recycling. Japan also faces an increasingly perilous national security environment as the Chinese economy grows while the Japanese population ages. This was not true at the beginning of our period. Then, a flood of excited books proclaimed Japan as an economic superpower whose currency was already supplanting the dollar. But the use of the yen as a reserve currency crested in 1991, and the yen-dollar exchange rate peaked in 1995.[35] Instead, after a crash whose similarities with current U.S. circumstances surely troubles members of the Federal Reserve Bank Open Market Committee, Japanese financial power ebbed as its enormous pools of stock market and property wealth drained away during a multidecade stagnation.

Like Repressed Europe, and perhaps even more so, Japanese economic success rested on a system of financial repression mediated by political elites and favoring manufacturing. Like wage restraint in Repressed Europe, the Japanese system of social protection compressed domestic demand, making Japan reliant on external demand for growth. But a direct attack on that system of social protection in the name of higher real incomes was and remains politically impossible because the ruling Liberal Democratic Party (LDP) is funded by inefficient industries and elected by voters enjoying a range of direct and indirect subsidies. Thus, the Japanese state opts for the decidedly second-best option of accumulating dollar-denominated securities to keep the yen at an exchange rate consistent with enough exports to keep the economy from recession.

As with many late developers, the Japanese state combined targeted finance and trade protection to promote and expand novel industries in which Japan had little obvious contemporary comparative advantage.[36] The state used tax laws to induce private savings to flow into the Postal Savings System and then channeled these funds through the various fiscal investment and loan programs (FILPs) into favored industries and projects. The Ministry of Finance directly controlled these off-budget vehicles, whose cash flows amounted to one-half the official budget. Bank lending followed public and private signals—administrative guidance—on which sectors had the official blessing to expand. Because the most important banks sat at the center of loosely affiliated networks of industrial firms (keiretsu) their choices about the direction of finance mattered. Until the 1980s, industrial firms drew most of their finance from bank loans rather than capital markets. As in Repressed Europe, banks could monitor the behavior of firms by sitting on their boards, use monthly meetings of keiretsu executives as information channels, and rely on dense networks of corporate share crossholdings—including their own 20+ percent share—to discipline errant management. But because competition forced each keiretsu to enter any emerging sector, they had a tendency to create overcapacity, trapping bank funds in low-yielding enterprises.

Partisans of the view that this industrial policy was a success perhaps overstate their case. But there is no question that what some analysts call convoy capitalism characterized the Japanese economy and polity.[37] Japanese convoy capitalism combined many of the same elements of the Repressed European coordinated market economies but with different emphases on state or private regulation in specific areas. European CMEs used public welfare states to secure compliance from workers, making risky investments in firm-specific skills. The Japanese CME used private, occupational welfare (called kaisha-shugi), although legislation introduced more universal elements in the 1990s. Lifetime employment at steadily rising wages guaranteed private-sector workers a stable return on their skills. In addition, firms provided housing, health care, postretirement employment, and recreation to core male workers. In these sectors, targeted finance and employee loyalty produced world-class firms with levels of productivity well above their nearest rivals.

But in other sectors, protection and the complex web of cross-subsidy created by keiretsus, the state largess, and corruption combined to leave firms well below world-class productivity levels. Although Japan has a formal, public welfare state, public social policy actually operates more through trade protection that shelters inefficient Japanese small firms and farms. If we index U.S. productivity levels by industry at 100, in 1987 productivity in the Japanese shipbuilding industry was 135, the automobile industry was 95.1 (but Toyota and Honda were at 125), and rubber products was 109. By contrast, productivity in Japanese food processing was 32, clothing 46, and furniture 21.[38] Americans naturally see only the best Japanese producers in the form of increased imports, but laggard Japanese industries pulled its overall manufacturing average down to only 66 percent of the U.S. level. Protection kept agriculture and service-sector productivity below world benchmarks.

The awkward combination of firms that set world benchmarks and firms that fell well below them created half of the conditions for the disastrous 1990s for Japan.[39] High-cost production in agriculture, services, and some local manufacturers sucked up consumer purchasing power at the same time that targeted finance and huge productivity gains in the winner industries led to enormous increases in output. With demand deficient at home, extra production flowed overseas as exports, particularly to the United States. Much like China today, Japan faced a choice as successful exports led to the accumulation of huge dollar reserves—allowing these export receipts to flow into the local economy would lead to yen appreciation and hurt politically powerful export firms; recycling these surpluses as purchases of U.S. dollar-denominated securities would preserve an undervalued yen but risk huge capital losses if the yen ever appreciated against the dollar.

Arbitrage   One way out of this dilemma would be gradual liberalization of the laggard sectors, not only to bring them closer to world benchmarks but also to free up domestic purchasing power.[40] U.S. deregulation of the service sector induced similar liberalization in Europe and Australia by pitting tradables firms against the nontraded sector.[41] The 1986 Maekawa report suggested similar reforms for Japan.[42] Although significant telecommunications and transport deregulation occurred in the 1990s, Maekawa and similar reports were stillborn. Instead, Japanese exporters opted to flee Japan through FDI rather than fight for the reform of high-cost nontraded producers at home.[43] During the late 1980s and 1990s, export-oriented Japanese firms created new capacity in North America and Southeast Asia. At the same time, the laggard firms, conscious that they would be bailed out if their own investments failed, also overinvested and diversified domestically. The key semiconductor industry, for example, created new domestic capacity that was 30–50 percent in excess of projected demand in the early 1990s.

The sudden appreciation of the yen after 1986 created the other half of the conditions for Japanese post-1990 stagnation. Consumers suddenly found themselves flush as import prices fell, and companies were flush with export profits. Both factors led to a rapid appreciation of land and share prices. Japanese shares briefly had price-earnings ratios over 70, and the Imperial Palace grounds in Tokyo had a notional value equal to all the land in California. But both bubbles also had a short shelf life because they prevented any change in the underlying structural factors dampening demand. Indeed, they exacerbated overinvestment by both sets of firms. When the Japanese central bank responded to the twin bubbles by raising interest rates, Japanese growth slowed to the imperceptible levels mentioned in chapter 4, leaving both sets of firms with stranded investments and falling profits.

Japan thus entered a debt–deflation trap much like the 1930s U.S. Depression.[44] Firms had built too much capacity by borrowing too much money using inflated land values as collateral; banks had loaned too much money in the belief that land prices never fell. Both were wrong. Falling land prices and falling prices for goods trapped firms and banks in bad loans. Banks could not cut off loans to "zombie" firms whose collateral was land that was now valued 30–40 percent below its 1990s market level because this risked losing the entire loan and forcing the bank itself into bankruptcy. Firms would not invest in the presence of overcapacity. Workers understandably chose not to spend, given the sudden rise in their perception of economic insecurity and, as the decade wore on, the latent fiscal crisis of the state. Big manufacturing firms shifted jobs offshore and resorted to more temporary workers (who did not qualify for occupational benefits), further depressing local demand and inducing an insecure public to spend less.

In this context, only two sources of growth remained: government-sponsored construction, which had the additional political benefit of large kickbacks for the LDP, and exports. And exports relied on a cheap yen, which in turn meant systematic intervention by the Bank of Japan and Ministry of Finance in foreign exchange markets. Thus, as R. Taggart Murphy notes, the Japanese state came to identify "its own survival with the continuous build-up of (Japan-owned) dollars in the American banking system," because "[t]here was, in fact, never any real possibility that Japan's power holders would commit political suicide by abandoning control over the economy to markets that they did not trust."[45]

Like Germany in the 1990s, reforms changed some parts of the corporate governance structures behind Japanese convoy capitalism. Banks reduced their holding of corporate equities to roughly 6 percent by 2003, changing places with foreigners, who increased their holdings to over 20 percent. Foreigners were allowed to take over Japanese firms, including major players like the Long Term Credit Bank, Nikko Securities, and, de facto, Nissan Motors. But all this pales beside the unrequited Japanese accumulation of U.S. Treasury and agency securities. In 1989, Japan held $150 billion in long-term U.S. government and agency bonds; in 2006, it held $720 billion. The increase corresponds roughly to the Japanese cumulative goods and services trade surplus with the United States over those years.[46] Although China has lately emerged as the major Japanese trading partner in both directions, much Japanese export of industrial machinery to China represents indirect trade with the United States because Chinese-assembled Japanese brands are exported to the United States.

Japanese divestment of U.S. securities would thus undermine the current sources of Japanese growth by hampering exports to both the United States and China.

It would undermine the system of corporate interlocks and lifetime employment that produces skilled labor for export firms. It would also force a massive redistribution of labor time away from manufacturing and toward new service sectors that would require wrenching changes in the Japanese system of social protection. And as in Repressed Europe, all these changes are politically unacceptable. The public cannot organize to attack trade protection, although they do vote with their yen when offered the chance. Among other things, Japanese housewives are a major source of cash for the carry trade (described in chapter 2), and they are major consumers of cheap Chinese clothing when stores offer such goods.

The expansion of yen-denominated securities would undermine some of the sources of Japan competitiveness in the same way as we noted for Repressed Europe. Although the current domestic portfolio of Japan is less heavily weighted toward bank loans and more toward equities than that of Repressed Europe, the bulk—34 percent—of Japanese securities is public debt. Firms are in a position to issue new debt because the market is not overflowing with corporate bonds. But the ability of firms to service this debt is questionable; many firms are still working off the excess capacity installed in the bubble years. What purpose would new debt serve? Like Repressed Europe, Japan remains locked into a world in which U.S. and Chinese growth permits local political arrangements and power structures to continue, and political elites thus countenance the recycling of local trade surpluses into dollar-denominated securities held by the state. Nothing has changed since 2002, when Akio Mikune and Taggart Murphy wrote that "the elite certainly has no intention of risking its hold on power by instituting any kind of fundamental structural change, while the wider public displays little appetite for the economic and political upheavals that would be the inevitable price of a real shift in existing power arrangements."[47]

China

Finally, Chinese elites similarly have private reasons to support the public good that U.S. dollar recycling provides, even though they have less ability to increase the supply of yuan- or renminbi-denominated securities. Put simply, the Chinese business elite has a disproportionate influence on the Communist Party because the elite is largely composed of party members and their relatives. In turn, the party controls the fully politicized People's Bank of China (PBOC). This allows Chinese elites to socialize their risks and privatize their gains to a much greater degree than their European and Japanese counterparts. China provides the pure case for the DFG Bretton Woods 2 argument.[48] DFG argue that China as an entity is engaged in a political exchange with the United States. In return for absorbing U.S. debt (which is equivalent to subsidizing U.S. consumption), China retains access to U.S. markets for its exports, thus assuring continued employment growth and domestic political stability. The Chinese Academy of Social Sciences believes that a 1 percent change in U.S. growth causes a similar change in Chinese growth.[49] China needs to generate roughly 20–24 million new jobs per year to absorb both the current overhang of 200 million or so excess workers in agriculture as well as new labor market entrants.[50]

DFG clearly state that their stylized model only *assumes* that the government has as its goals the elimination of underemployment and the creation of a capital stock capable of surviving in competitive markets. Both of these are public goods from the point of view of the Chinese population. But we need to discern the private goods behind these public goods because the Chinese accumulation of U.S. securities worth more than $1 trillion or so makes this political exchange economically dangerous. Moreover, the pattern of Chinese growth in the past three or four years has diverged away from the employment-generating growth of the classic Bretton Woods 2 years (1991–2003/2004). Instead, China is now on an export-dependent, job-stagnant growth trajectory that involves unsustainable accumulations of U.S. dollar assets.[51]

Why? Successful Chinese industrialization ultimately must cause the renminbi to rise against the dollar. Rising Chinese productivity should cause rising wages and, in turn, a rising cost for Chinese-produced goods relative to U.S. goods. At the same time, successful Chinese industrialization creates such a large call on dollar-denominated global commodities that it too adds to the cost of Chinese goods unless the renminbi appreciates against the dollar. On the other hand, a rising renminbi would permit China to buy newly cheapened U.S. goods, lowering total production costs. The 21 percent appreciation of the yuan against the dollar from mid-2005 to mid-2008 has already imposed considerable capital losses on the Chinese stocks of U.S. dollar-denominated debt, threatening the stability of the PBOC.[52] At that time, China was committing roughly one-eight of its GDP to the purchase of all foreign bonds. Ronald McKinnon argues that a rapid renminbi appreciation might also plunge China into a Japanese-style deflation.[53] What makes these risks reasonable at an economic level?

The DFG argument is based on a simple thought experiment. Suppose exports directly and via multiplier effects generate half of the 9 percent annual growth of China, a reasonable assumption given that exports ballooned from 20 percent of Chinese GDP in 2000 to 35 percent in 2006. Even netting out imported content leaves exports at 17–18 percent of Chinese GDP in the late 2000s.[54] Suppose further that accumulating $4 trillion of U.S. securities over twenty years (1999–2019) is needed to keep the renminbi at a level that sustains this level of exports. Over twenty years, Chinese GDP will expand from roughly $1.35 trillion to $8 trillion, assuming the dollar-renminbi exchange rate stays the same. If the dollar, instead, falls by 50 percent relative to the renminbi, China will lose a stock of wealth worth $2.5 trillion one time in exchange for creating a constant flow (GDP) that is $3.3 trillion higher than it would otherwise be. This analysis lies behind DFG's assumption that Chinese leaders are in the business of producing public goods, first and foremost economic growth. And the experience of the prior decade partly supports this thought experiment—the nominal Chinese GDP nearly tripled in 1997–2006 while the stock of international reserves rose similarly from 15 to 41 percent of GDP.

But private goods lie behind every public good. Three private goods motivate the Chinese adhesion to the dollar. The first, as DFG point out, is that economic stability preserves the power of the Chinese Communist Party. But it cannot, therefore, be assumed that the party is able to steer growth in a stability-maximizing direction. The second private good, running against the first, is the maldistribution of the fruits of growth toward the princelings of that party, the children of party elite. The third private good is that, as in the United States, the risks of arbitrage are socialized via the central bank while the benefits are privatized into the hands of the princelings.

Although the Chinese Communist Party unquestionably prizes stability, there is some reason to doubt that the current pattern of growth actually contributes to long-term stability in so far as this stability requires the constant absorption of labor market entrants. This is why it is important to discern the private goods behind a DFG-style explanation for Chinese decisions about reserves. Although the party elite prizes stability, the connection between growth and stability is not a given, nor is it correct to assume that the party has some magic formula assuring growth. Two issues arise here: rising income inequality and capital-intense growth.

The rapid growth of China has certainly led to rising incomes everywhere in China. Even the slowest-growing province, Hubei, nearly doubled its per capita GDP in 1997–2007.[55] But the distribution of that growth is highly uneven. China now has large income disparities between urban and rural incomes and also among provinces. The three most urban provinces, the cities of Beijing, Shanghai, and Tianjin, all have per capita incomes three times the national average and five times the average income of the nearly one-half trillion people living in the fourteen poorest provinces. The top three nonurban provinces by per capita income account for approximately one-sixth of the Chinese population but over one-quarter of Chinese GDP, almost as much as the provinces that account for the bottom half of the population. Throwing the three city-provinces back in increases the GDP share to 40 percent, versus a population of share of 20 percent. And these are the official figures. At the same time, the center lacks the taxation capacity to redistribute direct income and, instead, relies on levies on provincial treasuries to fund an increasingly tattered social safety net. These income disparities have motivated millions of people to relocate illegally to take advantage of higher urban incomes. But intraprovincial inequalities are probably as high as interprovincial ones, creating considerable social tension. The literature on social revolution suggests that unrest is more often associated with changes in income levels than with low income levels per se.

The second issue is an emerging disconnect between export growth and employment growth. At the beginning of the 1990s, China was primarily an exporter of labor-intensive, low-value goods and a processing center adding labor content to a wide range of goods by doing the final assembly (these included the classic textile/garment, toys/housewares, and cheap electronics exports of the now-mature dynamic Asian economies, DAEs). The former set of goods were generally wholly made up, whereas the latter were usually processing exports. Clothing and toy exports typically used locally produced inputs. Electronics exports typically used local labor to process imported components into a finished commodity. As late as 1997, textiles/garments still composed 28 percent of Chinese exports, with toys/housewares and light electronic equipment each accounting for an additional 10 percent.[56] Overall, processing declined from 30 percent of exports to 10 percent by 2006.[57] Both of the Chinese export streams absorbed huge numbers of workers displaced by agricultural reform in rural China. From 1990 to 2005, the share of primary production in total employment fell 15 percentage points, paralleling a 10-percentage-point decline in the sector share of GDP. Meanwhile, secondary production increased its GDP share by 12 percentage points.[58]

But by 2005–2007, the Chinese export composition had changed considerably, with a marked reduction in processing trade and a marked increase in the sophistication and capital intensity of production. By 2005, the categories had changed places, with electronics accounting for 35 percent of exports (of which automatic data processing, ADP, equipment was a full 10 percent), and textiles/garments and toys/housewares accounting for only 18 and 11 percent, respectively.[59] At the same time, the import intensity of exports declined considerably, with more value-added locally.[60] This certainly represents a successful development story. But it also casts two large shadows over the DFG Bretton Woods 2 logic.

First, the employment-generating capacity of exports is declining, in part because of dollar recycling. Eswar Prasad argues that overly cheap capital and land have skewed Chinese investment in a capital-intense direction.[61] Recycling trade surpluses with the United States pushes down the cost of borrowing for Chinese firms, inducing them to substitute capital for labor. As the central bank buys up excess dollars with renminbi, it expands the money supply. In turn, a larger money supply increases inflation, further reducing the cost of capital relative to labor. More capital has increased productivity by approximately 21 percent annually.[62] Prasad notes that nonagricultural output is now growing three times faster than nonagricultural employment.[63] But these productivity gains come at the expense of employment. From 1995 to 2004, absolute manufacturing employment fell by a head count of 17 million, although this should be seen against total, but decelerating, employment gains of approximately 330 million in 1978–2001.[64]

Second, the increased local content of Chinese exports means that both the United States and non-China Asia will find it harder and harder to balance their accounts with China. This puts even more pressure on China to continue dollar recycling in pursuit of exports. As the import intensity of Chinese exports declined, China accumulated larger and larger trade surpluses in 2005–2007 and, thus, bigger and bigger piles of dollars. The yawning trade gap with the United States is well known, but from 2004 on the Chinese trade deficit with the rest of Asia also declined in relation to the Chinese GDP. In this sense, the Chinese export success has reached its own limits. Just as the U.S. mortgage-led boom used up the supply of creditworthy borrowers, China has used up its supply of political cover in the United States and is now experiencing the unexpected consequences of export success. Export receipts no longer can be easily recycled into passive assets and, instead, need to be invested more actively, with all the obvious potential for political friction that brings. Exports themselves are a source of political tension, as U.S. congressional threats about new tariffs indicate. So, even if the DFG Bretton Woods 2 argument once made sense, by 2007 it had exhausted its necessary preconditions. If Chinese elites acted as a unitary political actor whose goal is the public good of maximizing employment to maximize stability, we would have expected a shift in policy sometime after 2004–2005. But this kind of shift was not evident. Why?

The emerging disconnect between export growth and employment growth suggests the second major private good behind the growing Chinese trade surplus and thus dollar reserves. The largest economic benefits from growth have gone to the children of the party elite, who have constituted themselves as a new economic elite. Just as in postcommunist Russia, the ownership of the means of production has fallen into the hands of those who can exploit the right political connections to assure the security of their ownership in a system lacking in any serious legal protection for property rights.[65]

The composition of the cohort of Chinese centi-millionaires—people with a personal wealth over 100 million yuan—shows this. This level of wealth makes them U.S. dollar deca-millionaires (100 million yuan = $13 million) at the exchange rate current in late 2007. There are 3,220 such Chinese, of whom fully 2,932 (or 91 percent) are the children of high-level Communist Party officials.[66] These children also hold 85–90 percent of the key positions in the five most important industrial sectors: finance, foreign trade, land development, large-scale engineering, and securities. Their control over these positions has assured their wealth in a society in which markets largely function via contacts, not contracts.[67] From their point of view, profitability ultimately rests on exports rather than on a brutal struggle to maintain prices in a Chinese market characterized by no brand loyalty, no product differentiation, and workers' emerging ability to push wages up. Pegging the renminbi against the dollar has helped exports remain buoyant, and even expand as the dollar fell against other currencies in 2006 and 2007, because it shifted exports to Europe. By 2008, the Chinese trade surplus (in dollar terms) with Europe was larger than with the United States. Although Europe and the United States absorb roughly equivalent volumes of exports from Asia, European growth is also hostage to U.S. growth. So the Chinese capitalist elites have reasons to pressure the party to pressure the PBOC to maintain the renminbi–U.S. dollar link.

But, at the same time, pegging has unleashed inflationary pressures that the central bank cannot control, precisely because its commitment to the peg precludes the effective use of monetary policy to control inflation. So the party princelings continue to pocket export profits while the Chinese macroeconomically destabilizing accumulation of dollars continues. If inflation forces a maxi-revaluation of the renminbi against the dollar, it is the central bank and the public that bear the losses on existing dollar assets. The princelings have privatized the profits from growth while socializing the risks and losses via the central bank. On the other hand, if the state slows the appreciation of the renminbi, this will increase inflationary pressure, hindering further employment gains from adding more Chinese value to exports.

Finally, the third private good behind the public good of Chinese adhesion to Bretton Woods 2 explains why the central bank has been somewhat insouciant about this accumulation of dollars. The PBOC, after all, is a large professionally trained bureaucracy, whose economists surely understand the dangers inherent in continually expanding the U.S. dollar reserve holdings. Why does the PBOC accept pressure from the party to continue absorbing dollars? The PBOC engaged in a hugely profitable arbitrage against Chinese households and banks until 2008. The privileged position of the PBOC in the Chinese market accounts for these profits. Although interest rates shifted against the central bank by 2008, the financial crisis made capital preservation and the economy more pressing issues for the bank than arbitrage. A return to normalcy would restore arbitrage.

In order to manage the Chinese currency peg against the dollar, the PBOC sterilizes the Chinese trade surplus by buying up the foreign currency receipts of exporters with yuan and then uses new issues of bonds to try to mop up the increase in liquidity. The PBOC thus accumulates assets denominated in dollars—creating exchange rate risk—while creating yuan-denominated liabilities. The PBOC invests its dollars in U.S. Treasury and agency bonds, but at higher nominal interest rates than it pays for its own liabilities. Because Chinese inflation is also probably running at a higher rate than U.S. inflation, the real gap between earnings on assets and payments on liabilities is even larger. As the *Economist* notes, the PBOC "earned an estimated 343 billion yuan on its foreign reserves last year. On the other side of the ledger it had to pay interest of 90 billion yuan on banks' reserves held at the central bank and on bills it issued to absorb excessive liquidity (largely caused by the surge in foreign-exchange reserves)." The *Economist* reports that the PBOC had larger profits than Citibank in 2006, at 29 billion dollars.[68] The PBOC steadily increased reserve requirements for banks in 2007 and 2008 in an effort to dry up excess liquidity. Reserve requirements shift about two-thirds of bank profits to the PBOC because banks, in effect, lend the central bank $1 trillion at roughly 2 percent interest.[69]

Why did Chinese savers not evade this arbitrage? Because China still has currency and capital controls and because the range of financial instruments available to the average person is substantially limited, the Chinese state can force household savings into banks at low interest rates. These savings are then either reloaned to the enterprise sector or used to absorb PBOC bond issues in the course of sterilization. The savings behavior of Chinese households is thus highly rational, given that they have limited savings vehicles and no trust in state-provided social protection. Households save a huge proportion of their income, amounting to roughly 14 percent of GDP, or approximately 40 percent of national saving; Chinese gross saving is roughly 10 percentage points of GDP higher than expected, with high household savings accounting for most of this. Ninety percent of these household savings end up in banks.[70] The Chinese banking sector, which does 80 percent of all credit intermediation, redirects these savings to politically connected Chinese enterprises, where it accounts for one-half of all investment funds.[71] (Retained earnings account for the rest.) But banks pay extremely low interest rates to households—paradoxically another inducement to higher savings because people are trying to accumulate enough savings to ride out predictable emergencies and have no other access to credit. Nominal interest rates range from less than 1 percent for demand deposits to approximately 3.5 percent for a one-year time deposit (i.e., a U.S. certificate of deposit, CD).

Firms meanwhile have been using accrued profits to self-finance their expansion rather than paying dividends. The share of domestic saving of firms jumped by 7 percentage points of GDP from 2000 to 2006.[72] This tends to suppress domestic consumption and means that the share market does not serve as an alternative vehicle for savings but, rather, as a casino for speculators. The shaky governance structures of firms exacerbate this. All savings flow inexorably toward enterprises that, in turn, use these funds to create new productive capacity. As in Japan, the resulting excess production can only flow overseas, generating—in the medium run—ever increasing trade surpluses and yet more monetary expansion as export receipts make their way to the central bank.

The PBOC thus finds itself trapped between two sides of the classic Mundell-Fleming trilemma. The PBOC can focus either on containing inflation or on maintaining (or very gradually unwinding) the renminbi peg against the dollar. The PBOC could contain inflation by dramatically revaluing the renminbi; this would cheapen imports, reduce export receipts, and discourage excess investment. But revaluation would also cause massive capital losses on its roughly $1.4 trillion in foreign currency–denominated reserve assets, losses that would inevitably fall on the mass public and not on the Chinese princelings. And, as McKinnon argues, it might trigger a profound deflation as firms try to find a price point at which domestic demand absorbs the resulting excess capacity in manufacturing.[73] Maintaining the dollar peg continues the status quo, but at the cost of continued growth in the money supply and inflationary pressures. This would induce even more speculative investment, as in the 1990s Southeast Asian financial crises. Given that bank funds in China are loaned on the basis of connections, not inherent creditworthiness, much of this investment is probably not remunerative in the medium run. Here, too, the inevitable unwinding of this overinvestment would concentrate losses on the banks holding the savings of the mass public of China.

As with the Southeast Asian central banks in the 1990s, either choice forces the PBOC to confront elites and give precedence to national macroeconomic interests rather than the elites' particular interests in profitability. As in the 1990s, it is doubtful that central banks whose independence is purely nominal will act against elites' short-term interests. By contrast, it is all too easy to imagine the PBOC delaying, given that the costs will fall on the public and not the princelings. Boosting domestic consumption is an obvious way to square the Mundell-Fleming triangle. Domestic consumption currently accounts for only 35–40 percent of the Chinese GDP. But, as in Japan and Europe, this would require redistributing income away from enterprises and their owners and toward the Chinese public. The same is true for a policy change that allowed free capital movement to address the third leg of the Mundell-Fleming trilemma. Giving Chinese savers access to global capital markets would inevitably lead them to abandon the PBOC, China Investment Corporation, and Chinese enterprises as intermediaries and to lend directly to relatively safer and more remunerative global financial institutions. This would force the Chinese princelings and enterprises to borrow at interest rates that reflect their poor corporate governance and lack of creditworthiness.

No Exit

European and oil-exporter holders of dollar-denominated assets suffered substantial unrealized capital losses after 2002 as the dollar fell against the euro, and the Chinese also suffered from the gradual, if gentle, revaluation of the renminbi from mid-2005. Foreign absorption of dollar-denominated assets abetted a process of differential accumulation in which the lion's share of growth among the rich countries went to the United States and in which the United States was able to enjoy consumption out of proportion to its underlying production. Yet, even as the dollar fell and as the U.S. economy visibly slowed in late 2007, foreign central banks stepped up purchases of U.S. dollar assets.[74] This phenomenon repeated itself during the autumn 2008 crisis, although the crisis drove up the exchange rate of the dollar. Foreign lenders—and in particular China—helped precipitate the nationalization of Fannie Mae and Freddie Mac (see chapter 7), first by stopping their purchases of agency bonds and then by reducing their holdings. Yet the absence of exit options meant that the net sales of agency bonds produced net purchases of U.S. Treasury bonds as a substitute. In July 2008, foreigners sold $58 billion in agency bonds, but bought $34 billion in U.S. Treasuries; in October 2008, China announced it would be buying an additional $200 billion in Treasuries.[75] Why did foreigners accumulate dollar-denominated assets and why did they not abandon them as the dollar fell? Why did foreign states abet outsized U.S. growth and consumption? Why did foreign economies remain coupled to the U.S. economy?

Steering a different course would have required painful changes in the domestic political structures of U.S. foreign creditors in addition to changes in economic policy. These creditors practice different forms of domestic financial repression and wage restraint that have benefited local elites. Such practices systematically reduce domestic demand and thus make local firms reliant on external demand for growth above and beyond simple demographic or stationary growth. The United States supplied that external demand in the long 1990s. Even in recession, the United States continues to supply much of global growth directly and indirectly via its deficit with China. Nothing shows this more clearly than the abrupt deceleration of European and Chinese growth in 2008 and the collapse of share prices on the Shanghai and Russian stock markets as U.S. growth stalled and oil prices plunged.

Financial repression benefited specific business elites in Europe, Japan, and China. A reduction in financial repression through an expansion in the supply of local currency–denominated securities would reduce the political power of those elites while exposing those elites to more market pressures. Similarly, changes in local regulations and practices that might enhance consumer demand would also reduce elites' ability to control the financial system in ways that benefit themselves. Elites in the largest U.S. creditors thus have reasons to continue to accumulate dollar-denominated securities. Although continued accumulation creates the possibility of continuing capital losses, those loses are largely borne by outsiders or by the mass public. The gains, meanwhile, fall into insiders' hands, particularly in China.

Because dollar holdings are increasingly concentrated, the individual economies considered here constitute a privileged, or K, group in the provision of the collective good of dollar recycling. The Chinese continued and outsized accumulation of dollar-denominated assets in 2008 is the best evidence for the behavior of this K group, but even small countries such as Thailand and Malaysia, which should be among the potential free riders or defectors from the dollar pool, added roughly $30–40 billion to their dollar holdings in the last quarter of 2007. This makes the collective action problem smaller than it otherwise would be.

This pattern also reveals how financial repression outside the United States and financial innovation inside the United States are symbiotic processes. The United States has inadvertently locked China, Japan, and Repressed Europe into a set of bad choices that favor the United States. Elites there can avoid massive capital losses only by accepting equally massive changes in the levers they use to control their own economies. Alternatively, they can continue to subsidize U.S. consumption by recycling dollars, which puts a floor under the U.S. economy and sustains the central role of U.S. assets in world markets, or they can redeem their dollar holdings by increasing their consumption of U.S.-sourced goods. The last two choices clearly reinforce U.S. differential accumulation over the long term; the first choice might do so as well because a period of economic reorganization would slow growth in the medium term. All the choices make an abrupt end to dollar re-cycling unlikely.

Indeed, the response of foreign creditors to the crisis actually reinforced some as-pects of U.S. global financial arbitrage. In the year before the crisis, foreign entities bought $205 billion in U.S. Treasuries, $285 billion in agency bonds, and $750 bil-lion in U.S. corporate securities (including private-label MBSs) and equities. In the year after the crisis (July 2007–July 2008), foreigners bought $475 billion in Treasuries, $150 billion in agency bonds, and $265 billion in corporate bonds and equities.[76] What went missing was inflows into U.S. equities, with their higher, long-term potential returns, and corporate bonds, with their higher interest rates. So although foreigners did reduce their net holdings, pressuring U.S. interest rates upward, they exacerbated the structural imbalance between returns on U.S. foreign assets and liabilities (see chapter 3).

This chapter asks why three large creditors continued their dollar recycling even as the housing bubble burst. In that sense, it considers the final step in the housing-led differential growth argument laid out in chapter 1, in both senses. It closes the loop from differential growth as an outcome back to the sources of dif-ferential growth, but it also represents the final step, in that dollar recycling is now in question.

Thus, we now turn fully to the housing bust. The last two chapters of this book deal with the U.S. housing bust and financial crisis, and with the oil exporters omitted from this chapter. As these chapters show, despite continued recycling the U.S. housing-led differential growth is over, even though differential growth is not necessarily over. Successful housing-led global growth in the long 1990s consumed the basis for its own success.

7. Boom to Bust

Housing, Politics, and Financial Crisis in America

Under the placid surface, at least the way I see it, there are really disturbing trends: huge imbalances, disequilibria, risks—call them what you will. Altogether the circumstances seem to me as dangerous and intractable as any I can remember, and I can remember quite a lot.

Paul Volcker, Stanford University, February 16, 2005

Anytime is the best time to buy.

Kieran Quinn, chairman of the Mortgage Bankers Association, April 5, 2008

The market can stay irrational longer than you can stay solvent.

Attributed to John Maynard Keynes

Question to Treasury Secretary Henry Paulson:
"Is the worst over?"
Paulson: "The worst is just beginning."

Press conference to announce Project Lifeline, February 12, 2008

What went wrong? Why did the housing bust happen? In this chapter, I argue that the housing bust grew endogenously out of the same dynamics that produced the housing boom. Joseph Schumpeter argues that all economic booms require some cheap "raw material" to fuel growth: new production processes that lower labor or capital costs, cheaper energy, cheaper transport, or abundant primary commodities.[1] In earlier chapters, I identify the cheap raw materials fueling the housing boom as disinflation and U.S. arbitrage. During the 1990s, U.S. multinational and retail firms off-shored more and more labor-intense production to low-cost Asia, producing a flood of ever-cheaper nondurable goods. Net, this lowered official inflation rates and thus the corresponding interest rates for mortgages. Simultaneously, European and Asian recycling of trade surpluses allowed U.S. arbitrage in global financial markets. This, too, lowered interest rates for mortgages. The U.S. housing finance machine transformed these inputs into extra aggregate demand and thence into differential growth.

But macroeconomic phenomena per se neither have interests nor act on them. In this chapter, I examine the operators of the growth machine—home buyers and financial firms—to understand why the bubble burst and subsequent political and economic conflicts. Falling interest rates by themselves could neither produce nor terminate a boom. As already noted, the U.S. housing finance system tended to translate falling rates into increased aggregate demand more quickly and strongly than dissimilar systems. This process required a steady stream of buyers at the bottom of the housing ladder. By buying houses at the bottom, new housing market entrants freed up equity held by purchasers above them, allowing those purchasers to also move up the housing ladder. This generated trillions of dollars of fictitious capital gains for incumbent homeowners. For their part, financial firms devised a relatively simple system for profiting from this activity. They acquiesced in the origination of trillions of dollars of new mortgages to validate homeowners' capital gains and then set up a seemingly simple carry trade designed—so they thought—to yield them enormous safe profits.

The very success of U.S. differential growth exhausted the sources of that growth. First, the housing machine required disinflation to work, and one of the most powerful fuels for disinflation was the reduction of prices for consumer nondurables through the offshoring of labor-intensive production to Asia. But, on net, new home buyers by definition tended to be lower-income, lower-skilled workers for whom the lower interest rates had made housing affordable. The more that labor-intensive production moved offshore, the fewer potential housing market entrants there could be as incomes stagnated at the bottom. Initially, the relatively high proportion of nondurable goods in the consumption package of those unskilled workers offset their falling real wages.[2] Yet eventually the two blades of the scissors of falling wages and rising house prices had to meet, cutting the fuel line for the housing boom. Offshoring does not account for all income stagnation at the bottom, but it was nonetheless a powerful force repressing wage growth.

Second, successful offshoring to China and other developing countries produced multiplier effects there, powering their economic growth but also creating new inflationary pressures. Given their initial low level of development, economic growth necessarily involved greater and greater calls on global raw material supplies, including, and most important, oil. Development meant creating an entirely new infrastructure—roads, buildings, power generation, and telecommunications—and thus huge inputs of cement, steel, copper, and energy. For example, Chinese iron-ore imports, which in aggregate equaled half of Brazilian total iron-ore exports in 1996, rose to three times the larger level of Brazilian exports in 2006. All told, Chinese imports of oil, soybeans, and copper were about thirty times higher in 2008 than they were in 1995.[3] The calls on global resources by developing nations reversed the disinflation that characterized the long 1990s, motivating central banks in developed countries to begin raising interest rates in 2005.

Third, the very nature of housing and credit markets meant that the last entrants into the market would be the least creditworthy, raising the risks of lending to them. From 1995 to 2005, the U.S. homeownership rate rose by roughly 5 percentage points, pushing the homeownership frontier out into the terra incognita of the uncreditworthy.[4] The majority of loans made in 2004–2006 were of the subprime or Alt-A variety, indicating the lack of a down payment (purchase money) and then, problems with the borrower's creditworthiness or with a wildly overpriced house. These loans were generally at high and variable interest rates, making debtors vulnerable to any up-tick in the reference interest rate. Thus, they were designed to be refinanced into lower, fixed-rate loans after a few years of house-price appreciation had generated some equity for the owner.

Finally, the huge volumes of U.S. dollar-denominated securities piling up in central banks began motivating those banks to seek higher returns. The major oil exporters already had SWFs, but by 2007, many other countries began setting them up. For now, it simply suffices to note the threat to U.S. financial arbitrage (see chapter 8 for more details). In short, by 2006, the housing boom had exhausted its homebuyer and disinflation inputs, and arbitrage was starting to fade away. The housing-led differential growth machine then began to run backward, slowing the U.S. economy. This threw the apparently simple, but extremely risky, arbitrage system run by financial institutions into crisis. Inflation ticked up, making it more difficult for homeowners to service their mortgages. Interest rates ticked up, dampening and then reversing house-price appreciation. And debtors with subprime and Alt-A loans began to default on those loans. By mid-2008, delinquency on all mortgages made in 2007 ran at three times the level for 2005 vintage mortgages, with 15 percent of 2007 vintage subprime mortgages, 7 percent of Alt-A mortgages, and 1 percent of prime mortgages delinquent.[5] With $1.56 trillion outstanding in subprime and Alt-A loans, this threw highly leveraged financial firms into a crisis of their own making.

In this chapter, I examine the bursting of the housing bubble and the consequent end of this period of U.S. differential accumulation. Because disinflation was the central input into the boom, inflation has become the central focus of postboom politics. I thus focus on a critical but unexpected divide between debtors and creditors around inflation. Generally, debtors favor inflation; creditors favor deflation. Yet the current conjuncture has reversed that pattern with respect to short-term preferences. Let me repeat this because it is a source of some confusion: *short-term* preferences. In the first section, I examine debtors to understand the exhaustion of new housing market entrants and the sudden short-term preference for low inflation by incumbent owners facing interest rate resets, and in the second section, I turn to creditors to understand their preference for more liquidity and thus a higher probability of inflation. In the third section, I examine U.S. government policy responses to the crisis to understand a second reversal, the renationalization of mortgage finance that effectively ended what had been an era of neoliberal

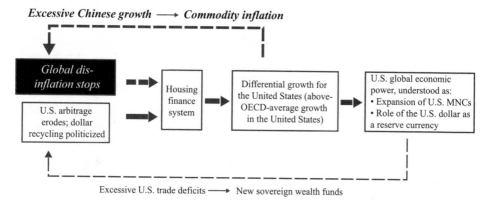

Fig. 7.1. Chapter 7: analytic focus.

deregulation and privatization. (See figure 7.1.) I treat foreign creditors and SWFs (a second source of restatization or nationalization) separately in chapter 8.

The Old and New Politics of Homeownership

The U.S. housing bubble and the more-than-just-housing financial crisis that it triggered have created two counterpoised political pressures over inflation and liquidity as actors fight over who should bear the losses from the crisis.[6] And the potential losses are big—subprime and Alt-A mortgages alone totaled roughly $1.56 trillion in early 2007, and the collateral damage from related credit default swaps and bankruptcies was potentially larger.[7] These pressures reflected an unusual reversal of typical creditor-debtor interests. On the one side, indebted homeowners had an interest in *lower inflation* in the short and medium run. Put simply, these households had barely enough cash flow to service their mortgages, so any additional pressure on their budgets from rising prices dramatically increased their personal risk of foreclosure. Inflation prompts rising interest rates via mortgage rate resets or via increasingly costly claims on their income from non-housing-related expenses, particularly food and fuel.

On the other side, the financial community had an interest in *more liquidity,* even at the risk of higher inflation in the short and medium term. Higher liquidity keeps institutions with large bad bets on MBSs and other securitized debt afloat by allowing them to avoid having to mark those dodgy securities to their current depressed market value. Financial institutions hope that increased liquidity will keep them solvent long enough for higher inflation to bring nominal incomes and nominal house prices back in line. In short, creditors hope to redeem their loans at their nominal par value and thus avoid bankruptcy by avoiding write-offs for those loans. And on the third side, the parts of the U.S. state most concerned with the financial sector have become massively involved in the housing market, effectively renationalizing housing finance.

These pressures represent reversals of prior political preferences around inflation, which, as we have seen, matter for the housing-growth machine. In the 1980s and 1990s, the financial community and elite income groups constituted the social base for very low inflation and a global push for independent central banks, often at the expense of employment levels. These communities pursued a parallel political policy of financial and market deregulation and fiscal restraint. By contrast, unions and lower-income groups preferred looser monetary policy, more government spending, more regulation of financial markets, and more trade restraint. Yet, at least in the short run, the current crisis inverted these preferences. Lower-income homeowners and the mass of recent housing market entrants had a structural preference for lower inflation and taxes, whereas the financial community pressed for massive state intervention in financial markets and huge injections of liquidity. What explains this shift?

Put simply, the interests that drive short-term policy preferences have shifted. On the one hand, the combination of historically low nominal interest rates, high rates of homeownership, and high but eroding housing prices in 2007–2008 inclined some members of core groups in the voting public in the United States and similar countries toward a preference for low inflation and low taxes. Homeowners now fear foreclosure should rising inflation lead to higher nominal interest rates and, thence, to higher and unaffordable mortgage payments. Given stagnant incomes, rising food and fuel prices combine with higher property taxes to reduce homeowners' abilities to service their mortgages. Finally, homeowners fear capital losses should they be forced to liquidate their home in a broadly declining market. Thus, all other things being equal, these groups have reason to favor more conservative politics. Not *all* homeowners will display these preferences. The current conjuncture shifts the preferences only of those most vulnerable to rising interest rates and to declines in home equity. But a shift in the preferences of only 5–10 percent of voters can be electorally decisive, and by late 2008 one-sixth of U.S. homeowners had negative equity.

On the other side, the financial community, including and especially SWFs, banks, and hedge and private equity funds, finds itself trapped in illiquid, hard to value, losing bets on subprime mortgages and their associated CDOs. These actors needed additional liquidity and were willing to countenance inflation and higher interest rates later to avoid certain losses or bankruptcy now. They preferred a public bailout of the housing market, even if that caused expanded deficits and risked an expanded state presence in one of the largest sectors of the economy. They also needed direct state intervention in credit markets to overcome their collective action problems around credibility and to erect a firewall to stop panic sales from leaping to securities whose market value would otherwise be stable. All other things being equal, as chapter 4 suggests, higher inflation erodes U.S. differential growth.

For reasons elaborated here, rising interest rates lead to falling home prices. Falling home prices have eliminated the notional equity that collateralizes mortgage debt, thrown 15 percent of homeowners into negative equity, and put large volumes of mortgage-backed bonds into default. The key question in the subprime mortgage–spawned financial crisis was precisely who would lose as prices fell: homeowners? investment banks? hedge funds? the state? foreign creditors? As of mid-2008, the flood of foreclosed properties had already substantially depressed unrealized home equity and motivated unprecedented federal government intervention into the mortgage and financial markets. This distributional battle creates the tension around interest rates and inflation previously described. Lower interest rates would help maintain housing prices by allowing buyers who cannot make their current payments to either refinance or sell their house to buyers with better credit. But, if central banks supplied the liquidity needed to keep interest rates low, they risked driving up long-term inflation. This is why, for example, the ECB resisted lowering rates until October 2008. Let us look at the homeowners' interests first.

Homeowners, Inflation, and the Housing Market

The classic arguments about housing suggest that private homeownership creates a politics inimical to a universal welfare state because mortgages crowded out taxes early in the life cycle of a household.[8] Jim Kemeny and Francis Castles both argue that the need to accumulate a down payment and then to service a mortgage inclines homeowners against higher taxes for public services. The classic arguments largely address the early post–World War II period. We must thus supplement these classic arguments with one salient fact reflecting current realities: there is a lot of wealth and money to be lost if housing prices fall. Total outstanding U.S. mortgage debt totaled $11.1 trillion at the end of 2007, and market prices at that time implied that homeowners had approximately $11 trillion of nominal equity in their houses.[9] The fear of foreclosure and equity evaporation is what creates the tension around interest rates and inflation. Lower interest rates would help maintain housing prices, validating creditors' assets, by allowing subprime buyers who cannot make payments to sell their house to buyers with better credit.

Why have debtors' short-term interests around inflation reversed? Put simply, many households at all income levels had shoehorned themselves into crippling mortgages homes at boom-era prices. This left them with little cash flow to handle the sudden jump in food and fuel prices, and these jumps dramatically increased their personal risk of foreclosure. Inflation also threatened buyers who used adjustable-rate mortgages (ARMs, i.e., variable-rate mortgages) with rising interest rates once their mortgage rate reset. Nearly $1 trillion of subprime and Alt-A ARMs were scheduled for resets in 2007–2008.[10] And the cascade of foreclosures that would result from interest rate resets also affected older, incumbent borrowers through their variable-rate home equity loans.

Consider typical subprime households. Subprime borrowers typically had bad credit scores and low income relative to their debt. The heads of these families were in their early thirties, had approximately $37,000 of disposable income after taxes, and accounted for much of the 5-percentage-point rise in the homeownership rate in the United States that occurred from 1994 to 2005.[11] As late housing market entrants, these families, on average, paid a high price relative to their incomes—borrowing $200,000 on average—because housing prices rose well ahead of incomes. This high debt-to-income ratio meant that most of these mortgages were ARMs. ARMs accounted for approximately 20 percent of mortgages in the 1990s. But during the housing bubble the share of subprime and Alt-A mortgage originations jumped from 2 percent in 2002 to 20 percent in 2006, and 92 percent of these were ARMs. The typical Alt-A buyer, with good credit and an excessively large loan in relation to income, was in much the same position because 68 percent of these loans were ARMs. The typical subprime ARM in 2007 was resetting from approximately a 7 or 8 percent annual interest rate to something closer to 10–10.5 percent.[12]

Even older, incumbent borrowers were vulnerable to interest rate resets. At around $50,000 or $55,000, the average posttax incomes for heads of households ages 45–54 in the fourth income quintile are approximately one-third higher than for heads of households ages 25–34. These families typically had some equity in their house and generally had a fixed-rate loan. But this is precisely the group that used MEWs to extract cash through HELOCs or closed equity loans.[13] HELOCs are effectively a second mortgage secured on the owner's existing equity and are most often used to remodel the house, purchase durable goods, or repay more expensive credit card debt. Approximately one-fourth of U.S. homeowners have a HELOC or similar housing-related debt, amounting to just over $1 trillion, or a bit over 10 percent of total mortgage debt. HELOCs and other forms of MEWs accounted for approximately 6 percent of disposable income from 2001 to 2007, up from the 2 percent level prevailing before 2001, and thus were a major contributor to excess U.S. consumption and the trade deficit.[14]

Rising inflation and taxes are a triple threat to these debtor families. Although inflation erodes the real long-term cost of their mortgage, this only helps if these families can hang on to their house in the long run. In the short run, inflation almost immediately increases mortgage payments as the nominal interest rate resets on ARMs. As of 2006 (before food and fuel prices really shot up), 20 percent of homeowners (*homeowners,* not households) in the bottom half of the income distribution were already spending more than half their income on housing. A further 19 percent were spending between 30 and 50 percent of their income on housing. All together, homeowners at all income levels spending more than 30 percent of their income on housing constitute 30 percent of all homeowners and 20 percent of all U.S. households, including renters.[15]

Inflation also indirectly reduces homeowners' equity as interest rates rise. Rising nominal interest rates depress housing prices. This threatens new homeowners with negative equity—owning more on their house that the market says it is worth. Rising interest rates depress the market price of houses because potential buyers confront higher monthly payments at any given price point. By June 2008, housing prices had already fallen 18 percent from the peak, leaving an estimated 13 million homeowners with negative equity and obliterating the typical equity in 2005 and 2006 vintage subprime and Alt-A mortgages. The 30–35 percent decline from 2006 levels that is needed to bring housing prices back into line with traditional price-to-income ratios or price-to-rental ratios would leave nearly 30 percent of U.S. homeowners, or 23 million households, with negative equity.[16]

Declining home equity matters not just because households with negative equity are more likely to be foreclosed. Declining home equity also threatens the balance sheet of the average household. Home equity accounts for one-third of the assets of the average U.S. household. But in the bottom six income deciles, median net worth is only $38,000, and it is almost exclusively home equity. Households in these deciles own only 6 percent of all U.S. stock holdings, whereas those in deciles 7 and 8 hold only 11 percent. By contrast, the top 10 percent by income owned 58 percent of stocks in 2006.[17] Put differently, households in the bottom six income deciles had $1 trillion in net worth in 2006, but falling home prices will almost certainly take away the entire $1 trillion.

Finally, the run up in housing prices has probably made all of our groups hostile and vulnerable to rising taxes. Higher housing prices mean higher property taxes (i.e., "rates" in British parlance), which squeezes other revenue sources. In the United States, property taxes are fundamentally a local revenue source that pays for education, policing, and some social services. They account for roughly 70 percent of local government revenues and 10 percent of total revenue at all levels, and their dollar volume increased at twice the rate of all taxes in 2000–2005.[18] In 2001–2004, the average property tax bill rose 21 percent in the United States. By 2007, property taxes accounted for 3.4 percent of total personal income.[19] Because rising housing prices have fed into higher property taxes through rising assessments, it has become harder to increase other tax burdens for national purposes such as broad social programs. Citizen protests in 2006 and 2007 forced changes to and, in some cases, caps on both the level of and rate of increase for property taxes in twenty U.S. states.[20]

These dynamics reverse the usual debtor preference for inflation. Indeed, 1960s and 1970s housing market incumbents generally preferred inflation, which rapidly and unambiguously reduced the real debt burden while inflating the nominal value of homes. Home buyers in the 1960s and 1970s typically used fixed-rate, long amortization (thirty-year) mortgages and did not have HELOCs. And they typically had reasonably secure jobs with the expectation of a long tenure and inflation adjustments to their wages. These conditions made inflation a one-way bet, favoring debtors. Imagine a typical Californian buying a $20,000 tract house in 1960 using a 1.75 percent Veterans Housing Authority fixed-rate loan. And even today we might imagine that long-incumbent homeowners who refinanced into fixed low-interest-rate mortgages after the Asian financial crisis or 9/11 might prefer a bit of inflation *if* their incomes keep pace. But that is a large *if,* given that many high-income jobs in the financial and real estate sectors evaporated during 2008 and that incomes are no longer inflation-adjusted. If incomes failed to rise in the relatively benign economic environment of the 2000s, why would they rise in the postbust era?

To summarize, the large number of debtors with ARMs or with tight budgets should exhibit a preference for low inflation in the short run. The current conjuncture directly shifts only the preferences of those most vulnerable to rising interest rates and declines in home equity. But a shift in the preferences of only 5–10 percent of voters can be electorally decisive. And subprime and Alt-A mortgages are geographically concentrated in electorally important states such as California, Virginia, Florida, and Texas, the first three of which also have relatively expensive metropolitan housing. It could be argued that a targeted bailout might relieve indebted homeowners, but the scale of such a bailout would be quite inflationary.

Capital Fright and the Renationalization of the Mortgage Market

On the other side of the inflation equation is the entire global financial industry, which wields tremendous political influence and, in essence, collapsed in autumn 2008. The credit market shutdown also implicated foreign central banks in Asia and Europe, directly through their holdings of U.S. assets and indirectly because of exposures of private banks to those assets. As of June 2007, central banks held approximately $750 billion in agency debt. Their potential losses have already been partially realized in the market via the fall in the dollar against the euro, although not yet in local currency terms. But a further slowdown in the U.S. economy could lead to more losses. European banks were particularly exposed to problems emanating from subprime mortgages because they had bought CDOs at the peak of the housing boom (much as they did before the 1997 Asian financial crisis) and parked these investments in highly leveraged structured investment vehicles (SIVs)—off-balance-sheet entities created by banks to escape the Basel II capital-adequacy regulation. Estimates of global exposure in SIVs ranged from $300 billion to around $1.2 trillion in 2007; meanwhile, residential mortgages, mostly from the U.S., backed 56 percent of the global total of $1.3 trillion in CDOs.[21]

In 2007 at the start of the crisis, financial firms feared a wave of defaults on subprime mortgages that might cumulate into a broader wave of defaults and foreclosures on Alt-A and prime loans. Although subprime mortgages accounted for only 6.5 percent of all U.S. mortgages by number, they were more than six times as likely to go into foreclosure as prime mortgages.[22] This liquidation would upset the balance of supply and demand in U.S. housing markets for several years, wiping out the collateral that backs mortgage bonds. In normal times, foreclosure often results in banks losing 20 percent of the money they loaned on a specific property; in the current climate, losses of 40–50 percent might become the norm.[23] Banks and investors trying to recapture their loans via foreclosure would thus take huge financial losses. Moreover, the depressing effect on prices from liquidating subprime-related foreclosures might very well extend losses to Alt-A and prime mortgages with thin equity cushions. As previously noted, one-sixth of U.S. home-owners already had negative equity (were "underwater") as of 2008. In those circumstances, life events such as job loss, health problems, and cuts in overtime might lead borrowers to walk away from properties or miss payments in the expectation that banks have little recourse and that they themselves have nothing to lose. Homeowners' illiquidity spelled insolvency for financial institutions.

Markets were already out of balance in the aggregate as of 2007, with roughly 1.5 million houses entering foreclosure, nearly double the 2006 rate, and delinquencies at three to four times the usual levels.[24] Historically, only 5–6 percent of U.S. owner-occupied residences sell in any given year, with the level floating between 4 percent (in recessions) and 7 percent (in the 2006 boom year) of the total stock. The inventory of homes for sale at any given time is approximately 3.5 percent of the stock, or six months of sales. But in April 2008, the inventory of homes for sale exceeded 6 percent of the stock of owner-occupied dwellings, or twelve months of sales, and one in three homes in the second quarter of 2008 were sold at a loss. More foreclosures would only swell inventories.[25] Given these problems, major financial institutions had already suffered roughly $500 billion in losses on subprime mortgage–related securities by mid-2008, driving major institutions into bankruptcy.[26] Table 7.1 gives a breakdown by country. The table does not include potential and actual losses on $1.1 trillion in Alt-A loans and roughly $10 billion in actual losses at Fannie Mae and Freddie Mac. Most Alt-A loans were due for interest rate resets in 2009 and 2010, after this book appeared.

How did these financial firms get themselves into such big trouble over mortgages, and how did the crisis come to involve nearly every credit market? Why did the Fed and ECB inject billions of dollars and euros of new liquidity into the market? To understand the difficulties of the financial firms and why they need huge volumes of liquidity to get out of them, we must delve into the seemingly complicated world of SIVs holding MBSs and CDOs. Although SIVs and CDOs are conceptually complicated, the basic issues are very simple. Indeed, they boil down to the same kind of arbitrage we saw at a global level with investment flows into and out of the United States. Put as simply as possible, banks used SIVs to borrow billions of dollars on a short term (90- to 180-day) basis at low interest rates. The SIVs then turned around and invested those billions into what looked like long-term securities—thirty-year mortgages—at higher interest rates. The large wedge

TABLE 7.1.
Cumulative write-downs and credit losses on subprime mortgages and
MBSs by banks, at August 2008 (billions of dollars)

	Write-downs and Losses	Capital Raised
U.S. banks	243.4	172.9
Belgian, Dutch, and Swiss banks	73.1	43
British banks	64.9	59.3
German banks	56.1	26.3
French banks	23.3	25.3
Asian and Middle Eastern banks	21.7	19.7
Other European banks	9.8	2.3
Canadian banks	9.6	2.8
Total	501.1	352.9

Source: Yalman Onaran, "Banks' Subprime Losses Top $500 Billion in Writedowns,"
Bloomberg, 12 August 2008, available at: http://www.bloomberg.com/apps/news?pid=2
0601087&sid=a8sW0n1Cs1tY&.
Notes: MBSs, mortgage-backed securities.

in figure 4.3 shows the rapid expansion of the private-label MBSs in 2004–2007 that constituted the raw material for SIVs.

In principle, this kind of maturity mismatch is very risky, and in practice, the fact that many of those mortgages went to high-risk subprime and Alt-A borrowers increased those risks. The banks, however, believed that they could avoid these risks. They thought that most of the ARMs behind the MBSs and MBS-based CDOs that their SIVs were buying would be refinanced after two years. This would allow bank SIVs to repay the short-term money they had borrowed. Banks did not believe that defaults might occur across the board instead of being contained to a few localities. What went wrong? The collapse in housing prices from 2006 onward made it impossible for subprime and Alt-A borrowers to refinance their loans, and inflation made it more and more likely that these borrowers would outright default. Those defaults caused the market value of CDOs to plummet, causing the financial crisis.

To understand what went wrong we need to understand how MBSs and CDOs work. Let us start with MBSs. In a precrisis, vanilla, pass-through MBS, Fannie Mae and Freddie Mac packaged mortgages with somewhat similar interest rates, maturities, and credit risks into a huge pool with an average interest rate payout, maturity, and credit risk. Investors bought a percentage of that MBS pool to get a pro rata share of principal and interest payments from the pool. Fannie Mae and Freddie Mac, acting as loan servicers, would "pass through" these payments to investors. If the pool experienced a 1 percent default rate, then all buyers of that pool shared the loss. To get a different interest rate, maturity, or level of risk, investors would need to buy a different MBS. Unlike more complicated derivatives, the mortgages in a pass-through MBS stayed intact; a defaulting mortgage affected only its MBS pool. Conversely, investors in that pool could foreclose defaulters without affecting other MBS pools.

Yet default was rare. The mortgages going into these vanilla MBSs had to conform to Fannie Mae and Freddie Mac underwriting standards—thus the adjective *conforming* in conforming mortgage. As previously noted, these standards required a potential homebuyer to possess a good credit rating, to document that his or her total postmortgage debt payments would consume no more than 34 percent of gross household income, to make a substantial down payment (usually over 10 percent), and (as of 2007) to borrow less than $417,000.[27] Furthermore, conforming mortgages could not go to multifamily units with more than four apartments.

These underwriting standards meant that the typical default rate (credit risk) on a pass-through MBS historically was lower than 0.5 percent. This earned the MBS an AAA (investment-grade) rating from the credit-rating agencies and allowed Fannie Mae and Freddie Mac to ensure payment to investors at a low cost, usually less than 25 basis points (0.25 percent). Indeed, the real risk with a vanilla MBS was not credit risk per se but, rather, that debtors would exercise their right to prepay the mortgage by refinancing or accelerating principal payments, thus effectively calling the bond. Astute readers will realize that vanilla MBSs in many ways are a classic product of the Bretton Woods or Fordist-era welfare state. They socialized the risks attendant on providing housing finance, implicitly homogenized the returns to investors, favored debtors (because principal prepayment was costless), and homogenized borrowers to a middle-class-family model buying single-family homes.

By contrast, private-label MBSs and CDOs are much more a product of the post-Fordist era. They took mortgages from nonconforming households (in all senses), allowed investors to speculate and earn differential returns, and shifted risks to debtors. Private-label MBSs did not offer investors a pro rata share of payments from a given pool of mortgages; instead, the underlying pool of mortgages was sliced up into tranches in order to offer investors differing degrees of risk and reward, as well as maturities at variance from the underlying mortgages. Private-label MBSs and CDOs are thus synthetic products containing bits and pieces of various mortgages. A defaulting mortgage can thus affect many different CDOs, and a specific set of CDO investors cannot foreclose without affecting other CDOs. The logic behind mixing different mortgages into a wide range of CDOs was to limit the risk from any single default. What mixing did, however, was allow one defaulter to contaminate many CDOs. This prompted the widespread "salmonella in the sausage" metaphor about bad CDOs.

Almost by definition, most of the mortgages going into the pool of non-GSE MBSs were nonconforming. If those mortgages had been conforming, they would have been offered to Fannie Mae or Freddie Mac on account of their superior insurance and servicing costs. Although not all nonconforming mortgages are subprime, almost all carry greater risks than do prime, conforming mortgages. The default risk for subprime mortgages was roughly five to six times that for prime mortgages. Yet CDOs composed of private MBSs routinely attracted the same

AAA-type credit ratings from the rating agencies as the Fannie and Freddie MBSs. How did financial institutions use CDOs to turn high-credit-risk debt into low-credit-risk debt?

Financial institutions gave CDOs differing degrees of legal priority over interest and principal payments to make an investment-grade bond out of dodgy nonconforming debt. Bankers took a pool of nonconforming mortgages, sliced them into different CDOs, and then assigned each CDO a specific priority over the underlying flow of payments from the pool. Regardless of which mortgages made interest payments or principal prepayments, those payments were assigned first to the CDO with the highest legal priority (called "super senior" tranches). This legal priority in claiming cash from the flow of payments is precisely what made this tranche apparently riskless enough to merit an AAA credit rating despite its underlying subprime mortgages. Once this highest tranche was paid, the next highest tranche received its payments, and so on. Each subsequent tranche thus had to wait on the tranche(s) above it to take its share of payments, so each subsequent tranche/CDO had a lower credit rating.

A pool of subprime mortgages of average BBB quality could thus back up some AAA-rated CDOs because those particular CDOs were guaranteed the first cut from the interest payments generated by the mortgages. The lowest tranche—called "toxic waste"—is the first to absorb defaults and the last to be paid interest, albeit at a very high-interest-rate payout. Where vanilla pass-through MBSs homogenized investor returns, private CDOs differentiated them by assigning different contractual priorities to the flow of mortgage payments. Financial firms incorrectly thought that risk could be concentrated into one specific toxic CDO to shield the others from risk.

Having manufactured an AAA-rated CDO bond from subprime dross, banks could then move this CDO debt off their books and into their SIVs. CDOs by themselves were not necessarily problematic. The combination of CDOs and SIVs, however, was toxic for the entire financial system because it combined risky assets and massive leverage. The simplest way to understand an SIV is to imagine it as a bank-run mutual fund for big investors. The bank and some big investors created and capitalized an SIV with their own money; this constituted the equity base for the SIV. The SIVs would then leverage their equity by borrowing anywhere from ten to fourteen times its equity. In a critical regulatory decision in 2004, the U.S. Securities and Exchange Commission (SEC) permitted the investment banks Lehman Brothers, Bear Stearns, Merrill Lynch, Goldman Sachs, and Morgan Stanley to exceed the normal twelve-to-one limit on leverage.

SIVs leveraged themselves by borrowing short- and medium-term money in commercial capital markets. SIVs did this by issuing short-term debt, ABCP, that matured in 90–180 days. SIVs had to refresh, or reborrow, this money every time its 90- to 180-day term came up. The SIVs used this borrowed short-term money to buy AAA-rated CDOs. The organizations lending short-term money to SIVs counted on the CDOs to provide collateral in the event of a default by the SIV. Global ABCP offerings doubled to $1.2 trillion annually in 2004–2007, based on demand from SIVs.[28] Banks used SIVs to engage in a carry trade, borrowing short-term cash to invest in nominally long-term CDOs. Banks relied on their creditors to refresh their short-term loans as they matured every three to six months.

How did the SIVs make money? The bank SIVs basically had the same credit rating as the CDOs, so banks could not profit from an interest rate spread based on apparent creditworthiness. Instead, SIVs profited from the spread created by the *apparent* maturity difference between the long-term CDOs that they held and the short-term and medium-term commercial paper they issued to fund the purchases of those CDOs. Longer-term debt generally carries higher interest rates than short-term debt, and longer-term CDOs did yield higher interest rates. And the SIV magnified this difference in returns through the massive leverage we have discussed.

This leverage was the source of great risk and great profits. By leveraging ten to fourteen times, SIVs could turn their own very small investment into very large profits. But the risks came because SIVs incurred what looked like a large maturity mismatch, borrowing short term to invest in long-term assets. Readers who made their way through chapter 2 will immediately notice the similarity to the aggregate U.S. foreign debt maturity mismatch. But SIVs do not have the privilege of printing money like the U.S. state. Instead, they had to roll over the ABCP funding their debt every three to six months. If short-term interest rates rose sharply, SIVs would find themselves paying out more interest on their ABCP debt than they received in interest from their CDO assets. Worse, if the creditors of an SIVs refused to roll over the ABCP, the SIV would have to liquidate its underlying assets—those CDOs—to repay its creditors. Although banks offered their SIVs an emergency credit line in case they could not fund their ABCP, no one expected to have to use these credit lines.

The insouciance of banks and SIVs about this maturity mismatch derived from their belief that their nominally long-term CDO assets were in reality short-term debt, despite being backed by nominally thirty-year mortgages. The mortgages backing a vanilla MBS take seven to ten years to mature on average, but they can take as much as thirty years to fully amortize. By contrast, most of the mortgages going into the CDOs were 2/28 ARMs; that is, the relatively low "teaser" interest rate lasted two years, and then for the next twenty-eight years the interest rate would reset annually or biannually. Everyone expected that these mortgages would be refinanced in year 2, before the ARM reset to a higher interest rate. Subprime and Alt-A homebuyers taking out 2/28 mortgages did so in the belief that house prices rising at a 5–10 percent annual clip would soon give them the equity they needed to qualify for a lower-interest-rate, conforming, fixed-rate mortgage. Banks believed that the short life of CDOs immunized them from the risk of rising interest rates in the ABCP market. If interest rates rose, SIVs believed they could use their emergency credit lines from their parent banks to shield them from any forced liquidation of the CDOs they owned while they awaited the inevitable refinancing that would quickly retire the CDO. No one expected these ARMs to reset, pushing cash-strapped buyers into foreclosure.

The investors in SIVs thus thought they had set up a basic carry trade, issuing apparently AAA-rated short-term paper while actually investing in not-really-long-term, not-really-AAA-creditworthy instruments that paid out long-term interest rates with no apparent risk. In fact, the rate of default on Baa-rated CDOs (the very bottom of investment grade) was approximately ten times the default rate on similarly rated corporate bonds.[29] The banks that created the SIVs also thought they had a great deal. Because SIVs were off–balance sheet investments, banks did not have to back the SIVs with their own regulatory capital or reserves until and unless the SIV had to draw on its emergency line of credit. Holding mandatory reserves for regulatory purposes decreases the profitability of banks; SIVs allowed banks to avoid this regulatory drag on earnings.

Crunch Time in Credit Markets

The proximate cause of the crisis was that banks and borrowers alike needed a continued 10 percent annual appreciation in housing prices to bring their bets into the money. But the arrival of subprime borrowers signaled the end of house-price appreciation. The supply of creditworthy new and trade-up buyers was exhausted, which is why banks began offering loans to less-creditworthy households. No new buyers meant that housing prices could not continue to rise indefinitely, yet the only available new buyers were people who could not actually afford their mortgages.

We can disaggregate the sources for this bad bet on the bank side. Three things went awry in the CDO gamble by SIVs: excessive faith in mathematical models, reliance on the historical default data behind those models, and a belief that housing prices would always rise. First, as new, over-the-counter, tailor-made, and complicated derivatives, CDOs could not be valued in a public, liquid market.[30] Instead, the regulatory agencies and the ratings agencies allowed SIVs and investment banks to value CDOs based on their internal models. This is called Level 3 pricing under the Financial Accounting Standards Board (FASB) Statement #157, promulgated in September 2006. Level 1 pricing involves marking-to-market, when a security can be valued using a recent sales price for the exact same security in public, ongoing trades. Level 2 pricing involves using publicly available data on similar but not exact copies of the derivative to guestimate—using the model—prices for relatively illiquid securities with no recent history of trades and thus no price quotes. In contrast, Level 3 marking-to-model involves pure guess work. The model says a unique derivative is worth a certain amount, and without any trades or public data, who is to say otherwise?[31] Marking-to-model instead of marking-to-market allowed SIVs to accumulate imprudently large quantities of essentially illiquid CDOs. But what if these models were wrong? What if they underestimated the probability of forced sales of many illiquid CDOs rather than a gradual or sporadic liquidation? What if people suddenly wanted to know what was behind an otherwise opaque CDO or to foreclose on a specific mortgage?

Second, and worse, the historical data behind those models did not reflect the radical change in the underlying population of subprime borrowers. The ratings agencies and the investment banks used data on subprime default rates in the 1990s to justify their assessment of current risks. But the population and environment behind these data changed in the 2000s. In the 1990s, subprime mortgages constituted a small niche product in the mortgage market, with default rates that were in the low single digits. Subprime mortgages provided a legitimate way for people with damaged but improving credit or who had varying or cash income to get into the housing market—at a price, of course; banks charged higher interest rates to reflect the lack of documented income or a weak credit score. Banks carefully screened subprime borrowers precisely because they were bad credit risks whose defaults would land on the balance sheets of these banks. And an environment of gently rising housing prices helped 1990s subprime borrowers refinance themselves into lower-interest-rate mortgages. All this mitigated the default rates for subprime in the 1990s.

But the influx of new subprime borrowers after 2003 changed the subprime population and its behaviors in ways that made retrospective models less accurate. First, mortgage brokers rather than banks screened subprime borrowers. Brokers made money by originating mortgages, not by holding them to term, and their compensation systems meant that they made more money when a buyer could be lured into a large high-interest-rate mortgage. Brokers faced no credit risk, so brokers had incentives to market as many dodgy mortgages as they could. Brokers made loans to otherwise un-creditworthy "NINJAs," who had "no income, no job, and no assets," as well as would-be yuppies aspiring to granite kitchen counters. In 1994, there were only $34 billion in subprime originations, mostly through banks; in 2004–2006, subprime originations averaged over $600 billion annually, mostly through brokers and specialist lenders.[32] The connection to the similar $600 billion jump in the ACBP market should be obvious. The influx of new, effectively unmodeled subprime borrowers changed the default probabilities dramatically, as did the end of house-price appreciation.

The historical data also did not capture a subtle shift from using subprime as an instrument for homebuyers with damaged credit to using subprime to speculate on rising home prices. For their part, borrowers were betting that continuously rising housing prices would bail them out of their subprime ARMs at the first reset. They contracted for 100 percent financing at higher-than-prime interest rates because they did not expect to be paying that rate forever. Instead, if housing prices continued to rise 10 percent or more annually, after two years our erstwhile subprime

borrowers would find themselves with 20 percent equity in their houses and qualify for a conforming, fixed-rate, thirty-year mortgage at a lower interest rate. They
could thus refinance their houses before the reset seriously affected their finances.
And reset they would because 78 percent of all subprime mortgages originated in
2006 were 2/28 ARMs, which meant an interest rate reset after two years.[33]

This set up the third problem in the SIV CDO gamble: What if housing prices
failed to rise annually at double-digit rates? What if no new creditworthy buyers
entered the market to release owners' unrealized equity and allow those owners to
trade up? Then overstretched borrowers would not have 20 percent equity and
would not be able to refinance into conventional mortgages at lower interest rates.
Instead, they would face a crippling interest rate reset that might force them into
default. And this is exactly what happened in late 2006 and 2007. The rising
tide of subprime mortgages met a sudden rise in interest rates as the Fed tried to
dampen emerging inflationary pressures from food- and fuel-price rises. Housing prices softened. Suddenly, refinancing was impossible, and the most recent
subprime borrowers, who were most reliant on rising prices to bail them out,
began to default at rapidly rising rates. Whereas only 4 percent of all 2004 vintage
securitized subprime loans were in default after nine months, 10 percent of 2006
vintage loans and 16 percent of 2007 vintage subprime loans were in default after
nine months. The reversal of housing-price appreciation plus the prior change
in subprime-borrower behavior turned the Level 3 marking-to-model into pure
make-believe. SIVs were holding dross, not AAA-rated assets. But they still owed
billions of dollars in ABCP collateralized by those CDOs.

As rising mortgage defaults percolated up into the CDOs of SIVs, those SIVs
found it harder and harder to roll over their short-term debt by issuing new ABCP.
Rising defaults compromised the value of their collateral for that ABCP. SIVs had
three options for repaying maturing ABCP: borrow new money to repay older
ABCP debts, liquidate their CDOs, or use their emergency credit lines. But who
would put up new money? Most banks were already invested in SIVs, so they all
knew that defaults were rising and thus that these CDOs were potentially worth-
less. Who would buy CDOs knowing that double-digit declines in value might
happen? The supply of hapless Norwegian villages or teachers' pension funds was
not infinite. Instead, SIVs turned to their patron banks for emergency loans. This
put those banks into a difficult position because they did not have enough cash to
cover the needs of their own SIVs.

But banks could not go into the open market to borrow either because who
would lend to them? Even if other banks were not similarly caught short, those
banks had good reason to suspect that any CDOs offered as collateral might dramatically fall in value. Indeed, banks were so worried about counterparty risk (the
risk that a bank that borrowed might default) that they stopped lending to other
banks against nearly all kinds of collateral, not just CDOs. Banks feared that the
unknown risks tainting CDOs also tainted other derivatives.[34] This fear produced

successive credit crunches in August and November 2007 and March, July, and September 2008. No one wanted to lend money to banks that might fail; no one could evaluate which banks were at risk because CDOs were totally opaque. Thus, financial markets began rejecting not only CDOs backed by student and automobile loans but also auction-rate securities issued by U.S. municipalities and commercial paper offered by "Main Street" firms in the normal course of business. The market rejection of CDOs caused the nominal value of SIVs to drop $150 billion from July to December 2007; ABCP issues declined $400 billion in the same period.[35]

Banks thus had to begin bringing their SIVs back on to their books, defeating the whole purpose for SIVs in the first place. Citigroup, for example, had to put $40 billion of CDOs from its own troubled SIVs back onto its own balance sheet. Bringing SIVs back on the books reduced the profitability from investing in CDOs because banks had to set aside regulatory capital for them. This requirement also had negative macroeconomic consequences. Bringing SIVs on board and setting aside capital for them would force banks to reduce their other forms of lending because they would have insufficient capital under the Basel II standards relative to their outstanding lending. (banks must hold sufficient capital to offset the possibility that loans going bad might force the bank into bankruptcy.) The origins of the successive credit crunches reduce to this simple math—banks lost approximately $500 billion through July 2008 while attracting only $350 billion in new capital. Given the usual level of reserve requirements, the $150 billion shortfall in capital implied that banks had to withdraw $2 trillion in lending.[36] The easiest way to withdraw that lending was to avoid lending to other, potentially risky banks.

Table 7.2 displays the degree to which major U.S. commercial and investment bank holdings of Level 3 assets—a proxy for CDOs—already impaired capital adequacy for those banks at the end of 2007. As with the 1982 Latin American debt crisis, these levels threatened the survival of banks, not just their ability to create credit, as the Lehman Brothers collapse in September 2008 shows. Financial firms that had concentrated on subprime and Alt-A mortgages, such as Countrywide Financial, IndyMac, and Fremont, collapsed.[37] And the problems extended beyond the banks themselves. First, the near-collapse of the ABCP market began affecting the ability of normal businesses to borrow to meet their ongoing obligations while waiting on payment from sales of their goods. Second, major insurance firms, such as AIG, had insured many subprime mortgages against default through credit default swaps (CDS). Defaulting mortgage bonds threatened AIG with bankruptcy through calls on those CDS, but a bankrupt AIG would force banks to call in yet more loans because they had used AIG CDS to evade capital adequacy regulations.

Banks once more had committed the fallacy of composition, believing that they could coin money from undercapitalized SIVs without experiencing any systemic risks or creating new behaviors in the market that might alter the behaviors on

TABLE 7.2.
Exposure of major U.S. banks to Level 3 assets, end of 2007

	Level 3 Assets (millions of dollars)	As Percentage of Total Assets	As Percentage of Equity Capital	As Percentage of Tangible Equity	Comments
Bank of America	21,640	1.37	16.0	39.6	
Bear Stearns	20,250	5.1	160.1	161.1	Bought by JP Morgan
Citigroup Inc.	134,840	5.72	106.3	212.9	
Goldman Sachs	72,050	6.91	200.0	235.9	
JP Morgan Chase	60,000	4.06	50.0	101.5	
Lehman Brothers	34,680	5.26	168.0	209.8	Bankrupt in September 2008
Merrill Lynch	15,390	1.43	41.0	45.4	Bought by Bank of America
Morgan Stanley	88,210	7.44	258.3	287.3	Bought by Wachovia

Source: Mark Killion and Natasha Muravytska, "Credit Crunch Threatens U.S. Financial Sector's Equity," available at: http://www.globalinsight.com/Perspective/PerspectiveDetail11004.htm.
Notes: Level 3 assets are marking- to-model under Financial Accounting Standards Board (FASB) #157.

which they had based their models. But investments that are safe for one bank alone are not necessarily safe for all of them. As banks piled into the CDO and ABCP markets, they exhausted the supply of credible subprime borrowers and reliable mortgage brokers. This changed the environment that had made CDOs a rational investment in the first place. The carry trade of banks on subprime-mortgage-backed CDOs went so disastrously awry that it threatened to bring down the major players in the global financial system. Once housing prices stopped being on fire, all the assumptions behind the SIV leveraged speculation in CDOs disappeared and capital markets froze as banks began refusing to lend to one another. Banks could not solve their own problems, so they turned to the state.

Government Intervention and the Renationalization of the Mortgage Market

Even though the crisis was ongoing at the time of writing, I must consider government responses to that crisis because these already had changed the structure of the housing market financial systems that generated differential growth. As in prior global financial crises, the U.S. Federal Reserve and U.S. Treasury took the lead. As in prior crises their initial responses reflected an initially optimistic understanding of the crisis as a liquidity rather than solvency crisis. The Fed initially assumed that banks were fundamentally solvent, that most CDO assets were fundamentally sound, and thus that the greatest danger was from a panic sale of CDOs that might bring down weaker banks and the financial system. Thus, the initial interventions were relatively small, even if they seemed extraordinary at the time, and mostly took the form of extra liquidity for banks and bond dealers. Central banks believed that more liquidity would enable banks to make good on their emergency lines of credit to their SIVs, easing the panic. Then markets could accurately price CDOs, enabling them to trade and thus enabling banks to do business with one another again and fund their SIVs with other people's money. This did not happen. Ultimately, it became clear that major institutions were insolvent, forcing finance ministries and central banks to nationalize major parts of the financial system. All these interventions tried to steer a course between too much and too little liquidity—too much would aggravate inflation, already at relatively high levels; too little would mean more failing banks. Indeed, in Europe the ECB raised rates in early 2008 precisely from fear of inflation.

Central bank and finance ministry interventions occurred in five waves, each triggered by a spike in the so-called TED spread (table 7.3). The TED spread measures the gap between the three-month U.S. Treasury bill and a three-month Eurodollar loan at LIBOR, the rate that banks charge one another. The TED spread measures the assessment by banks of the creditworthiness of other banks and thus the probability of bank failures. During the ten years prior to the crisis, this TED spread averaged approximately 42 basis points. In each crisis, the TED spread shot up well above this, hitting nearly 250 basis points in August 2007, 220 basis points in November 2007, just over 200 basis points in March 2008, 150 basis points in July 2008, and well over 400 in September–October 2008.[38] These spreads resemble the usual spread between developed-country and developing-country public debt.

Central bank and finance ministry interventions fell into three broad categories, corresponding to the three broad problems banks always face: liquidity, capital adequacy, and deposit stability. Banks were unable to borrow from one another because of counterparty risks and, thus, ultimately unable to lend either long or short term to the real economy. Defaults on MBSs threatened to wipe out bank capital, triggering cascading defaults through counterparty risk and calls on CDS, as well as declining share values for banks. Depositors ran for safer places such as government bonds, forcing banks to curtail not just long-term but also short-term lending. Governments responded at first only with emergency liquidity injections that soon became routine. When this failed, they sought to alleviate mortgage distress and thus the damage to bank balance sheets. This soon turned into a stealth or outright nationalization of financial institutions whose capital had evaporated. And, finally, governments began offering unlimited guarantees to depositors. Each step was intended to address a specific part of the crisis. Each seemed unprecedentedly large at the start, yet soon looked small relative to later interventions. Each round of the crisis expanded not only the dollar size of each tool but also its application to new areas of the financial system. Each, at the time of writing, seems unlikely to be unwound any time soon.

Let us start with liquidity injections, which were intended to keep banks solvent and lending. The immediate problem of financial firms in mid-2007 was their

TABLE 7.3.
Central bank and finance ministry interventions, August 2007 to October 2008

Institutions	Interventions	Institutions	Interventions
August 2007			
U.S. Federal Reserve	US$62 billion	European Central Bank	€156 billion
Bank of Canada	CA$ 1.64 billion	Bank of Japan	¥1 trillion
Reserve Bank of Australia	AU$ 4.95 billion	Swiss National Bank	SFr 2–3 billion
Monetary Authority of Singapore	SG$ 1.5 billion (~ US$1 billion)		
December 2007			
U.S. Federal Reserve	US$30 billion term auction facility	U.S. Federal Reserve, European Central Bank, and Swiss National Bank	US$90 billion currency swap arrangement
Bank of Canada	CA$ 3 billion		
March 2008			
U.S. Federal Reserve	US$200 billion term securities lending facility and primary dealer credit facility	European Central Bank	Extra US$10 billion into currency swap pool
		Swiss National Bank	Extra US$2 billion into currency swap pool
May 2008			
U.S. Federal Reserve	Term auction facility increased to US$75 billion	European Central Bank	US$20 billion per month extra into currency swap pool
September 2008			
U.S. Federal Reserve	Term securities lending facility auctions become weekly	U.S. Treasury Department	De facto nationalization of Fannie Mae, Freddie Mac, and AIG
G-7 plus Swiss central banks	US$427 billion currency swap arrangement		
October 2008			
G-7 plus Australian, Swedish, and Swiss central banks	Coordinated 0.5% rate cut	Denmark, Germany, Iceland, Ireland, United Kingdom, and United States	Deposit insurance caps raised, removed, or extended to new classes of deposits
OECD finance ministries	Loan guarantees: Austria: €85 billion France: €320 billion Germany: €400 billion Italy: €20 billion Netherlands: €200 billion Spain: €100 billion United States: US$700 billion	OECD finance ministries	Bank recapitalizations: Germany: €80 billion France: €40 billion United Kingdom: US$64 billion United States: US$250 billion

Notes: OECD, Organisation for Economic Cooperation and Development.

inability to value and sell their own CDOs or those of their SIVs and thus to bring their assets and liabilities into balance. Although central banks clearly thought this problem could become self-sustaining, they also thought the problem was limited to mortgage securities. The first interventions thus provided liquidity to banks in unusual volumes so they could absorb those CDOs. The Fed and the ECB coordinated what they thought would be a once-only, $200 billion-plus global liquidity injection in August 2007, lending cash against the usual collateral.

The rising tsunami of mortgage defaults and foreclosures in fall 2007 prompted a dawning recognition that resetting interest rates on ARMS in 2008–2009 would throw many more mortgages into default. This combined with the difficulties in disentangling exactly which mortgages made up the highly opaque CDOs on bank books to throw suspicion on other synthetic assets built from car loans, student loans, and corporate receivables. In other words, there was not just more bad debt but more bad debt everywhere. Consequently, the entire ABCP market began drying up again in late fall 2007 as private firms refused to lend to one another. The collapse of the auction-rate securities market, the parallel ABCP market funding municipalities, triggered a new round of intervention.[39]

This time, central banks changed the rules governing the kind of collateral they would accept and began accepting private-label residential and commercial MBSs in exchange for the liquid government debt they loan to banks. Normally, the U.S. Federal Reserve accepts only Treasury bonds and Agency (Fannie Mae, Freddie Mac, and Ginnie Mae) bonds as collateral. The vehicle used by the Fed for this intervention was the $30 billion term auction facility (TAF) in December 2007. Initially, TAF allowed banks access to cash on a twenty-eight-day rather than overnight basis, and its $30 billion was an order of magnitude larger than typical open-market operations. TAF disciplined banks by forcing them to bid for funds. This marketlike mechanism steered cash to the banks with the biggest problems but in an opaque way that reduced the possibility of a run on those banks. By August 2008, $200 billion of TAF cash was available on an eighty-four-day basis.

TAF soon spawned similar facilities for nondepository banks. At the third TED spike in March 2008, the Fed created two new facilities that accepted novel forms of collateral and permitted open-market operations on a twenty-eight-day basis.[40] The Term Securities Lending Facility of March 2008 allowed banks to use nonagency MBSs as collateral against U.S. Treasury bonds and cash. The Fed also created a parallel fund for broker-dealers (nonbank entities authorized to do business with the Fed), the Primary Broker Dealer Facility. TED spike four and the collapse of Bear Stearns provoked the Fed to begin accepting all kinds of ABSs, including AAA-rated but suspect CDOs, at the discount window under a Term Securities Lending Facility that was expanded to $200 billion.[41] Thus, from August 2007 to July 2008, the share of U.S. Treasury bonds on the Federal Reserve Bank balance sheet fell from 90 to just over 50 percent as banks and brokers sought liquidity to meet their obligations.[42] Finally, in September 2008 the Fed announced it would also begin backing depository banks' purchases of commercial paper (ABCP) through the ABCP Money Market Mutual Fund Liquidity Facility and guaranteeing the commercial paper of nonfinancial firms through the Commercial Paper Funding Facility. By September 2008, the Fed was providing approximately

$1.6 trillion in liquidity support to the U.S. and foreign financial systems through twelve different facilities.

The ECB similarly auctioned off funds in late December 2007, providing over €130 billion net at a 4.21 percent interest rate. This was higher than normal for ECB open-market operations but much lower than the prevailing LIBOR. The volume transacted was also the largest ECB auction since the ECB began operations.[43] From summer 2007 through August 2008, the average ECB open-market auction involved twice as much cash as in the auctions from 1999 to summer 2007. In December 2007, the major central banks also agreed to swap currencies to allow European borrowers with dollar liabilities to have access to dollars through channels that would not disrupt credit markets. This facility was expanded several times. And in October 2008, the major central banks made a coordinated rate cut.

These interventions failed to resolve the problem because by 2008 the problem clearly was that banks did not believe their counterparties were safe. No one really knew the quantity and quality of bad CDOs, MBSs, and CDS poisoning the books of a counterparty. (And, indeed, the auction of Lehman Brother's assets postbankruptcy revealed huge losses.) Thus, banks choked off lending to one another and, in doing so, began choking off credit to the real economy.

This problem could be addressed only by repairing capital base of the banks. Central banks thus tried to prop up housing prices, so as to limit foreclosures and prevent panic selling of foreclosed properties that would further damage MBS and CDO values. Research suggested that falling housing prices were a primary cause of foreclosures. Intervention took two forms: (1) new regulations and programs aimed at limiting or preventing interest rate resets on ARMs that might drive recent buyers into delinquency, and (2) public lending agencies ramped up their provision of capital for resale into mortgage markets to keep sales from collapsing as banks ran away from mortgage lending. The U.S. federal home loan banks (FHLBs) as well as Fannie Mae and Freddie Mac once more became the primary sources of U.S. mortgage finance. In addition, governments intervened directly in some mortgage contracts. When this failed, they were forced to nationalize failing financial firms.

The first intervention aimed to resolve part of the collective action problem of the banks around subprime mortgages. No single bank could forebear from resetting interest rates so as to avoid a massive and self-reinforcing wave of foreclosures. Each bank had an incentive to pursue foreclosure as quickly as possible to shift houses on to a small and shrinking pool of potential buyers with diminishing access to mortgage finance. But the state could induce *all* banks to waive their right to reset interest rates on ARMs to limit the flood of foreclosures. The Hope Now Alliance plan, announced in December 2007, represented a voluntary but ultimately ineffective agreement among banks to pursue an orderly freeze on interest rates for subprime mortgages that had some hope of staying current if rates did not reset. The plan was thus largely in the interests of the lenders because it tried to build a firewall between the foreclosures that were necessary, given the borrowers' true insolvency, and those for which borrowers faced insolvency only if their interest rate reset. The continuing drop in housing prices nullified the effects of this plan.

Instead, in July 2008 the Fed finally began pressing banks to acknowledge their losses on mortgages by reducing the principal balance for the roughly 12 percent of homeowners who then had negative equity. New regulations and legislation authorized the Federal Housing Agency to insure mortgages for which banks accepted a 15 percent write-off.[44] Once more, the point was to prevent any disorderly liquidation of houses in the hope that long-term growth would make the underlying loans good again and, by doing so, make good the foundation for distressed MBSs and CDOs.

In the second mortgage market intervention, public lenders stepped in to replace absent private lenders in mortgage markets. The various FHLBs, twelve banks chartered by the federal government during the Depression as a lender of last resort in housing markets, also eased access to credit for mortgage lenders. Countrywide Financial, a key mortgage lender, borrowed more than $51 billion from the Atlanta Federal Home Loan Bank that year. Overall the FHLBs provided nearly $750 billion to banks in the third quarter of 2007, helping total lending by the FHLBs in 2007 to rise by nearly $350 billion compared with 2006.[45] This reversed the privatization of mortgage finance characterizing the long 1990s.

The Fed also suggested that Fannie Mae and Freddie Mac sell part of their prime MBS holdings to make room for Alt-A MBSs purchased at the current distressed market prices and offer direct refinancing of subprime mortgages facing ARM resets, and it suggested that the Federal Housing Authority be permitted to do something similar.[46] In 2007, Fannie Mae and Freddie Mac absorbed billions of dollars of Alt-A MBSs, bringing them to 11 percent of the Fannie Mae total book by June 2008.[47] On the other side, investment banks off-loaded the dodgy MBSs without crippling losses and thus avoided collapse. Yet this weakened Fannie Mae and Freddie Mac, setting the stage for their de facto renationalization in August 2008. This nationalization signaled the beginning of direct efforts to bolster bank capital.

Bank nationalizations and politically engineered mergers had already started back in August 2007, when the Bank of England offered £8 billion in emergency loans to mortgage lender Northern Rock before nationalizing it. In the United States, the Fed also intervened directly to limit the collateral damage—literally and figuratively—from bank failures. In August 2007, Bank of America bailed out Countrywide Financial Corporation at the behest of the Fed. Countrywide was a key player in mortgage markets, originating nearly 10 percent of all new U.S. mortgages and handling payments on nearly 20 percent of all existing U.S. mortgages (including mine). Its collapse would have thrown the entire U.S. housing finance system into turmoil. Central banks also invited in capital from SWFs as a way to make an end run around any legislative barriers to direct action. SWFs provided roughly $70 billion of the $260 billion of new capital that core U.S. financial institutions needed in 2007 and 2008. (We turn to the SWF issue in chapter 8.)

Just as with the steady expansion of liquidity injections, each nationalization and capital injection increased in scale.

The slow-motion collapse of investment bank Bear Stearns provides the best example of why. Two Bear Stearns housing-based hedge funds collapsed in July 2007, causing $200 million in losses. As the Bear Stearns losses mounted, its counter-parties on both sides of the ledger began refusing to offer or accept deals from Bear. Even though its borrowings were secured by collateral, lenders feared this collateral could not be sold in open markets in the event of the collapse of Bear Stearns; its collapse would have pushed approximately $210 billion in MBSs and other securities into markets that were already unwilling to accept even one-tenth that amount. The sale of these securities would also have established a Level 1 or Level 2 price for many Level 3 securities with artificially high prices, forcing banks to write off huge losses and throwing them into bankruptcy. Consequently, the Federal Reserve Bank had to offer JPMorgan Chase an essentially unrestricted $30 billion line of credit to buy out Bear. The Bear collapse showed that the fail-ure of any large institution would bring down the rest by impairing their balance sheets. And in summer 2008, the very largest institutions were in trouble, including Lehman Brothers and its $400 billion in CDS.

By July and August 2008, default rates on the dodgy Alt-A mortgages that Fannie Mae and Freddie Mac had absorbed from the private sector began to rise, provoking doubts about their solvency. In July, Fannie Mae wrote off $5.35 billion in Alt-A mortgages. This caused both the TED spread and the spread between Fannie Mae and Freddie Mac funding costs and equivalent U.S. Treasury notes to rise by almost 70 basis points (0.70 percent). Foreign investors sold off $58 billion in agency MBSs, driving up mortgage interest rates and choking off what little home buying was occurring.[48] In September 2008, the Fed and U.S. Treasury put both firms into conservatorship, a polite word that meant Chapter 11 bankruptcy and an 80 percent government shareholding that meant de facto renationaliza-tion. Fannie and Freddie, along with the FHLBs, had become the only sources of new money in the mortgage market; their collapse would have shut down the en-tire housing market. Nationalization, by contrast, prompted an almost immediate 50-basis-point (0.5-percentage-point) decline in thirty-year fixed-rate mortgages, helping prop up the housing market.

De facto nationalization of the GSEs did not resolve the larger problems in the housing or financial markets. Generally, the peak home-selling season runs from March to August. As of September 2008, the supply of houses on the market remained at twice the normal level, and prices had fallen approximately 15 per-cent from their peak. Defaulting mortgages crippled Lehman Brothers, driving it into bankruptcy. They also depleted the capital base of insurer AIG, which had written $150 billion in CDS (insurance on bond defaults) for MBSs and paid out $25 billion in claims. The AIG $300 billion in CDS benefiting European banks apparently forced the U.S. Treasury to nationalize AIG; an uncontrolled AIG bankruptcy would have seriously damaged major European banks by forcing them to increase their regulatory capital or call in loans. AIG had allowed European banks to evade regulatory capital limits by writing $300 billion in CDS for them.[49] Once more, the U.S. Treasury stepped in to take an 80 percent ownership stake while the Fed offered an $85 billion credit line at penalty interest rates and then an additional $38 billion in October 2008.

These bank failures and fear of further bank failures motivated states to preempt bank runs by guaranteeing depositors' accounts. The first extraordinary instance of this occurred in the United States, where the Federal Deposit Insurance Corporation (FDIC) guaranteed all funds in money market accounts at nondepository institutions. Money market funds are a primary source of short-term working credit for businesses, and a flight from them to U.S. Treasuries would have crippled Main Street. In short order, the U.S. FDIC temporarily increased its insurance levels for depository banks from $100,000 per account to $250,000 while also providing an unlimited guarantee for funds currently in a money market account. Denmark, Greece, and Ireland guaranteed all deposits regardless of level; Britain and Sweden bumped coverage up to roughly $87,000 and $70,000, respectively; and bank regulators in the European Union pledged to raise the minimum coverage to €50,000.

By autumn 2008, none of these interventions had worked. Banks were refusing to lend to one another, short-term credit markets were frozen, and banks were chronically low on capital. The U.S. Treasury and Fed proposed and got the Emergency Economic Stabilization Act, whose $700 billion Troubled Asset Relief Plan (TARP) was initially oriented toward buying up dodgy assets in a rerun of earlier interventions. Instead, the TED spread breached 400 basis points in October 2008, compelling states everywhere to inject public capital directly into banks. Iceland prosecuted the first nationalizations as its overextended banks collapsed amid a currency crisis. But Britain, a major financial center, forced everyone's hand by taking direct stakes in major banks, including a majority controlling interest in the Royal Bank of Scotland and a controlling interest in a combined Lloyds TSB–HBOS. Germany, France, and Spain followed in quick succession, offering packages equal to between 2 and 3 percent of their GDP.

This induced the U.S. Treasury to "volunteer" nine major U.S. commercial and investment banks to accept a minority government share amounting to $125 billion, while putting another $125 billion on tap for further purchases of bank shares. The U.S. Treasury also guaranteed $1.5 trillion of the bank debt and $500 billion in business accounts. This boosted the total U.S. bailout by an additional $2.25 trillion, offset by any dividends received and the potential recovery in bank share prices. At the time of writing, it remained to be seen whether this intervention would be effective; the only remaining step would involve majority stakes and the true nationalization of the financial system.

These nationalizations are probably the only way to resolve the crisis because they directly bolster the capital base of the banks, enabling them to resume lending to the public while also reducing counterparty risk. The British intervention was roughly equal in scale to its annual budget; the U.S. intervention was roughly equal to the entire Social Security old age pension. The Irish guarantee was twice its GDP. For now, it is sufficient to note that OECD governments had incrementally moved toward the nationalization of the mortgage and financial markets with each response to the 2007 and 2008 crises. On the supply side of the U.S. market, the FHLBs and the renationalized Fannie Mae and Freddie Mac ended up providing the most new money for housing finance, and on the demand side, the Federal Reserve bank ended up holding billions of dollars of old MBSs on its books. And in the middle, the state acquired ownership of a wide swathe of banks.

Aftermath of the Crisis

In chapter 2, I show that foreign capital disproportionately flowed into U.S. housing during the long 1990s, and in chapter 4, I show that this capital energized differential growth in the United States and the Americanized Rich, compared to the Repressed Rich. Recall that mortgages constituted nearly one-half of the outstanding debt of the U.S. nonfinancial sector in 2007. Disinflation and declining nominal interest rates flowed through the U.S. housing finance system in ways that accelerated the recovery of aggregate demand. This enabled above-OECD average growth in the United States, sustaining the top-currency position of the dollar. No economic boom goes on forever, however, and the housing boom had exhausted its core inputs by 2005. Disinflation turned to inflation as Chinese wages began rising and, more important, the price of food and fuel jumped to unprecedented levels. Cheap mortgage finance exhausted the supply of new housing market entrants that was needed to enrich housing market incumbents, and banks increasingly made loans to borrowers who had little hope of ever making payments on what were increasingly large debts.

The bursting of the housing bubble revealed that the entire global financial system had also mortgaged itself to the fortunes of the housing market. The huge profitability of banks rested on their ability to disguise a simple but highly leveraged carry trade in which they borrowed money short term to buy their own seemingly long-term MBSs and CDOs. The bad bank bets started a slow-motion financial crisis marked by a series of increasingly extraordinary central bank interventions. The bursting of the bubble thus triggered a whole series of political and economic reversals.

Economically, the subprime-sparked financial crisis of 2007–2008 caused a massive and generalized financial crisis. With respect to our narrow—but important—housing arena, this means that mortgage credit is going to be difficult to get in the foreseeable future for borrowers who lack down payments and incomes sufficient to qualify them for a GSE-conforming mortgage. The GSEs, including the FHLBs, are likely to be the major sources of credit for U.S. mortgages, limiting the growth of the assets of U.S. financial institutions. Second, the housing finance growth machine is likely to run in reverse for some time, sucking aggregate demand out of the economy as illiquid households reduce their consumption to meet mortgage payments and as insolvent households fall (or rush) into foreclosure. Moreover, the reliance on conforming mortgages, although prudent, will force liquid households just entering the housing market into saving more of their income for a down payment. The crisis thus removes one engine of U.S. differential growth. It remains to be seen what the new one may be.

The second reversal emerging from the bust blends political and economic effects. Debtors and creditors still have conflicts over inflation and interest rates. But, at least in the short run, the crisis reverses their usual preferences because of the constraints facing illiquid and insolvent households and financial firms. Cash-constrained households across the income spectrum now have a significant stake in holding down taxes and interest rates in the medium term. This requires lower inflation. At the same time, rescuing the finance sector requires huge infusions of liquidity and puts enormous stress on central bank balance sheets and fiscal resources. The pursuit of lower interest rates by the Fed in 2007 and 2008 aimed at avoiding crippling resets on ARMs and also increasing the spread between the costs of bank borrowing and the mortgages that were still performing. But lower interest rates imply more liquidity and more inflation down the line. So, too, does the vast enlargement of the fiscal deficit to pay for the recapitalization of banks and to make good on loan guarantees. The Fed, thus, has to balance political pressures that neatly correspond to the various short- and long-term pressures it faces as it trades off financial stability against the position of the dollar.

The third reversal is more political. Politically, this crisis marks the high tide of the neoliberal erosion of the institutional structure of the Bretton Woods–era Keynesian welfare state in the United States.[50] Neoliberal deregulation came late to housing. Until the 1990s, housing finance had effectively been nationalized and regulated via the effective monopoly that the GSEs Fannie Mae and Freddie Mac had over mortgage securitization. During the long 1990s, private MBS securitization and the creation of nonvanilla MBSs undermined the GSE monopoly and accentuated the risks of borrowing for homeowners and lending for the beneficial owners of MBSs. Housing-related risk was desocialized, particularly after 2002, when nonagency MBSs began gaining significant market share (see figure 4.3). The George W. Bush administration (2000–2008) abetted this expansion of private-sector market share by relaxing regulatory standards and suggesting that Fannie Mae and Freddie Mac reduce their presence in the market.

This process impinged on U.S. power. Differential growth based on housing was central to U.S. global economic power. Leonard Seabrooke has argued that the GSE extension of credit to lower-income but "prime" credit-risk groups, and the subsequent broader (but riskier) expansion of credit to subprime by private entities, expanded the deposit base of U.S. financial institutions and made a larger pool of securities available for sale worldwide.[51]

The crisis has both renationalized and denationalized U.S. housing finance. By *denationalization,* I do not mean privatization. The crisis has effectively destroyed private issuers of MBSs; private MBS issues zeroed out in the third quarter of 2007. The minor players are bankrupt; the major players lack the credibility and capital to reenter this business. This leaves only the GSEs—Freddie Mac and Fannie Mae plus the FHLBs—standing as large-scale purchasers of raw mortgages and producers of credible MBSs.[52] In the year after the crisis started in summer 2007, these three institutions generated nearly all the new credit in the U.S. housing market. The FHLBs were particularly aggressive in supplying capital to mortgage lenders, on the one side, while Fannie and Freddie absorbed and packaged mortgages, on the other side. The role of the GSEs will only expand because of the legislated, albeit temporary, increase in the conforming loan limit to the low-$700,000 range and because they remain the only—if barely—credible issuers of MBSs. This shift of mortgage origination and securitization back to the GSEs constitutes the renationalization of U.S. housing finance.

At the same time, denationalization has occurred in the sense that the domestic market is absorbing a decreasing share of MBSs. At the end of 2007 and beginning of 2008, foreign central banks and their related SWFs were the major buyers of agency MBSs (as well as benchmark U.S. Treasuries).[53] U.S. housing finance became even more dependent on foreign investment, but with the maturity structure lengthening. This undoes the "borrow short, lend long" arbitrage that underpinned U.S. growth during the long 1990s. So does the rise of SWFs themselves.

8. Toward the Future

Arbitrage, Differential Growth, and Economic Power

[Sovereign wealth funds] are making investments that they probably think are O.K. but not spectacular.... There has to be a political objective over and above the rate of return.... You don't need to appoint two directors to a board to have influence [over target firms] when you own 10 percent of the company.

Felix Rohatyn, January 22, 2008

The United States grew faster than the Repressed Rich countries even on a population-adjusted basis during the long 1990s, increasing its economic power among the rich OECD countries and maintaining its share of global GDP despite rapid growth in developing Asia. U.S. differential growth relied on the availability of two crucial inputs: continued disinflation and the recycling of U.S. trade deficits via U.S. financial arbitrage. In chapter 7, I discuss the exhaustion of disinflation and how it flowed through to mortgage defaults and financial crisis. In this chapter, I examine the potential exhaustion of U.S. global financial arbitrage, the second key driver for growth, before offering up a conclusion. Arbitrage also bears on the recapitalization of troubled U.S. financial firms. With both main drivers for housing-led differential growth gone, can U.S. global economic power persist? What legacy does the U.S. growth spurt of the long 1990s leave for the United States and the world?

Disinflationary pressures initially came from the successful and profitable shifting of labor-intensive production offshore by U.S. multinational and retail firms in the long 1990s. This shift caused a significant decline in the price of consumer nondurables that helped interest rates fall and thus brought new entrants into the bottom of the housing market. But this offshoring also reduced the supply of new entrants into the housing market by holding down wages for unskilled and low-skill male workers. Eventually, new housing market entrants could be shoehorned only into houses with subprime and Alt-A mortgages (see chapter 7), setting up conditions for the financial crisis.

How did U.S. global financial arbitrage, the second key driver for growth, exhaust itself? Recall that arbitrage was both a cause for and a consequence of differential growth. Foreign purchases of U.S. Treasury bonds and MBSs from Fannie Mae and Freddie Mac depressed mortgage interest rates in the United States. The U.S. housing finance system translated falling interest rates into increased aggregate demand. Although this demand stimulated the U.S. economy, much also leaked out into the purchases of imported vehicles and consumer nondurables that drove growth in the Repressed Rich and in China. By the 2000s, successful industrialization in China and the proliferation of SUVs in the United States began pumping billions of dollars into the hands of oil exporters; these economies then recycled their trade surpluses passively into corporate and government bonds, driving interest rates even lower. But just as the disinflation-housing dynamic eventually grew large enough to exhaust its raw materials, the recycling dynamic eventually tested the willingness of U.S. creditors to accept below-average returns on increasingly larger holdings. In chapter 6, I argue that the political pain entailed in a wholesale flight from U.S. securities made flight improbable, but this argument ignores what might happen if the U.S. creditors diversified their holdings, moving them from passive investments and into more active, higher-return investments, or exercised their market power by abandoning selected securities markets.

Both events occurred simultaneously with the 2007–2008 financial crisis. First, the increasing concentration of foreign holdings of U.S. dollar securities gave increasing market power to discrete investors, particularly the Chinese. By 2008, China probably accounted for more than one-eighth of all portfolio holdings of U.S. securities. The refusal of the Chinese state to absorb more agency MBSs in summer 2008 was the proximate cause for the renationalization of Fannie Mae and Freddie Mac. Up until July 2008, foreign official investors were absorbing approximately $20 billion per month in agency debt. But in July and August, China actually shed $4.6 billion in agencies, and other foreigners sold $10.1 billion.[1] Fears that foreigners would sit out a $200 billion refinancing for Freddie Mac and Fannie Mae in September 2008 prompted the U.S. Treasury to impose its conservatorship on the two agencies. Nonetheless, foreign creditors had no place to go with their dollars. They dumped agencies, only to buy $71 billion in U.S. Treasuries instead.[2]

Second, the emergence of new SWFs in the mid-2000s signaled the limits to the tolerance of creditors for U.S. financial arbitrage, just as the proliferation of nonconforming mortgages signaled the limits to housing-price appreciation. Although central banks will remain the biggest players in U.S. dollar recycling in the short run, SWFs are a visible manifestation of an erosion of U.S. economic power as the dollar shifts from a top currency to a negotiated currency. (See figure 8.1.)

Does it matter? On the one hand, SWF investments might simply magnify the long-term inability of U.S. creditors to extricate themselves from a U.S.-centered global economy. A bigger stake in the United States makes SWFs and their parent states even more dependent on the health of the U.S. economy. On the other hand, a shift out of low-yielding Treasury and agency debt into equities or direct control

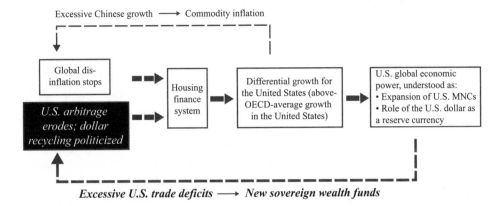

Fig. 8.1. Chapter 8: analytic focus.

over existing U.S. firms would undo U.S. global financial arbitrage, encouraging a long-term diversion of new investment out of the United States. In addition, the rising stake of SWFs in financial firms could have malign consequences. As noted in chapter 1, power in markets comes from control over critical nodes in the value (or commodity) chain. Well-capitalized entities are well capitalized because they control these critical nodes. The market capitalizes the income stream that these entities control, immunizing these powerful entities from takeovers. The most troubling consequence of the reversal of the housing growth cycle might thus be not the falling exchange rate of the dollar or the U.S. reliance on foreign central banks to fund the trade deficit—although these obviously matter—but the devaluation of the capitalization of formerly powerful firms, particularly in finance. This devaluation exposes these firms to takeovers by SWFs and other foreign entities.

SWFs thus present not just a threat to arbitrage but in addition a threat to the expansion of U.S. corporate control over global commodity chains. SWFs have taken minority stakes in the core broker-dealer financial firms and commercial banks that are involved in every corner of the economy, and they have access to proprietary information from nearly every firm. These financial firms thus offer an unparalleled point of access to the workings of the U.S. economy. SWF investments are thus inherently *unlike* those of the Japanese firms that acquired star properties such as Rockefeller Center and Pebble Beach Golf course, or even major Hollywood studios such as Columbia. Electronic eavesdropping at Pebble Beach offers much less in the way of control than, say, a 20 percent stake in Citigroup; and Columbia drained cash out of Sony for years. SWFs clearly matter, but the relative novelty of large-scale SWFs explains why my analysis of them is lodged here in the concluding chapter. Both the observations about SWFs and the conclusions about the future for U.S. differential growth after the long 1990s are necessarily speculative.

Sovereign Wealth Funds: Three Issues

Three issues are clear enough to discuss. First, SWFs are the counterpart to the U.S. trade deficit in more than just a mechanical, accounting sense. Second, even if we cannot accurately predict where the behavior of SWFs will range on a spectrum from passively benign to actively malign, the mere fact of substantial ownership stakes in key financial firms represents a stunning reversal of a major thrust in U.S. foreign economic policy. U.S. policy in the long 1990s aimed at opening up LDC financial markets to U.S. financial firms and allowing U.S. financial and nonfinancial firms not only access to those markets but an opportunity to control value chains. The housing bust and the emergence of SWFs instead expose the entire U.S. financial sector to the kind of capture that U.S. policy sought on behalf of its firms.

Third, in a second reversal, the ability of SWFs to rescue damaged financial institutions (and perhaps preference for doing so) represents a new version of the fusion of state and capital that Weber labels "political capitalism."[3] Regardless of their formal structure, at least half the SWFs by capitalization right now are the essentially private firms of the families and cliques that control the major non-OECD oil-exporting states. The fund with the greatest potential growth is the Chinese SWF China Investment Corporation (CIC). If the Chinese State Administration for Foreign Exchange (yes, SAFE) transferred only 20 percent of its current holdings to CIC, CIC would dwarf all other SWFs except Abu Dhabi's massive Abu Dhabi Investment Authority (ADIA). With all the SAFE holdings, CIC would be twice as large as any current SWF. And China remains a one-party authoritarian state. In this regard, SWFs are a huge step away from an international society based on rational capitalism and legitimate authority and toward one based on political capitalism and patrimonial authority. From the point of view of labor, the rise of SWFs might portend an unparalleled disaster that offsets the renationalization of housing finance. SWFs present a double concentration of power: personalized control over huge chunks of capital that is quite different from the control exercised by, say, pension or mutual funds.

Sovereign Wealth Funds and the U.S. Trade Deficit

SWFs are the counterpart of the U.S. trade deficit in more than just a mechanical, accounting sense. To be sure, they could not have arisen without some excess accumulation of foreign exchange. Most SWFs owe their start to a need to park excess export revenues of one sort or another in some secure form, offshore from the local economy. The continuous U.S. trade deficits of the long 1990s—over $6.3 trillion, although disproportionately since 2004—put funds into the hands of successful exporters, who then used their export receipts to capitalize their SWFs. Central bank recycling of export surpluses into U.S. Treasury and agency securities, and eventually the more sophisticated SWFs recycling of surpluses into passive or controlling holdings of equities and real estate, kept the exporter currencies stable against the dollar. This enabled them to continue export-led growth despite burgeoning U.S. trade deficits. If export-surplus countries had not deliberately recycled foreign exchange surpluses into purchases of financial assets, either their currencies would have appreciated, reducing their volume of exports, or they would have expended the money on more imports from the United States.

Until recently, most exporters parked their surplus receipts at the central bank. The novelty today is thus neither SWFs per se, which have existed since the 1950s, nor accumulations of foreign exchange by Asian and other central banks but, rather, the decision to merge the two. This is why SWFs are the counterpart to the U.S. deficit in more than a mechanical sense. They represent a political response to the rising costs of U.S. financial arbitrage for U.S. foreign creditors.

SWFs (i.e., state-owned financial institutions that invest the savings of a state offshore) arise in a narrow, technical sense from state capture of export revenues above and beyond the imports a country. Much of this revenue was initially derived as royalties on raw materials exports, particularly oil. The first SWFs emerged as places to park and accumulate those revenues. Kuwait started the first SWF in 1953, followed at a distance by the U.S. state of Alaska and the Canadian province of Alberta in 1976. Large commodity and oil exporters with small populations need SWFs to buffer their economies against price volatility, to diversify their economies, and to bank what is in essence a nonrenewable capital asset. Up until the 2007–2008 financial crisis, most SWFs were content with small equity stakes in a wide range of firms or passive investment in bonds and real estate.

The Asian surplus economies that account for more than one-half of the cumulative U.S. trade deficit do not confront these issues. These are noncommodity exporters whose excess foreign exchange earnings are relatively more stable across the business cycle, begin in private hands, and plausibly could be used for expanded imports. In many cases, they have low per capita incomes that might benefit from additional consumption.

Why, then, make an SWF? SWFs are a second-best solution to the political inability of Asian exporters to decouple from U.S. import demand. Elites could have chosen to allow more private consumption, undoing the political foundation for the excess savings that Ben Bernanke identifies as the cause of U.S. trade deficits. Instead, exporters transferred part of their accumulated surpluses to their SWFs. With the aggregate trade surplus of Brazil, Russia, India, and China (the BRICs) and the gulf states running in excess of $600 billion per year in 2006 and 2007, this caused a massive increase in the scale of the typical SWF. Secrecy, particularly on the part of the gulf state SWFs, makes a precise accounting impossible, but estimates for mid-2007 range from $1.5 trillion to $3 trillion.[4] This made SWFs as large as the global hedge-fund industry at that time. Projections put the aggregate size of SWF holdings at between $7 and $12 trillion in 2012 versus a current global asset base of roughly $120 trillion. (The upper limit assumed oil prices over $100 per barrel, however.) SWFs thus could end up holding somewhere in the region of 10 percent of marketable securities globally. Table 8.1 presents a list of the largest SWFs, as well as their interventions in OECD financial firms.

Changes in the scale of U.S. deficits also motivated the shift of accumulated funds to SWFs. Even though the United States ran more or less continuous deficits from 1991 on, these deficits were fairly manageable. Only $3.3 trillion of deficits accumulated in the twelve years up to 2004. Policy errors—the Bush administration (2000–2008) combined passion for tax cuts and high military adventurism—accumulated another $3 trillion of trade deficit in 2004–2008. These policy errors aggravated the normal workings of the housing finance machine to produce an outsized housing bubble and equally and consequentially outsized U.S. trade deficits. This magnified the costs of holding passive dollar assets, particularly because the dollar depreciated more or less continuously from 2004 through 2008. Rather than park funds in depreciating assets, creditor political elites decided to shift their portfolios into higher-yielding equity stakes and controlling interests in U.S. firms. This was a second-best choice compared to allowing a free flow of funds within their own economies and with the world. Entities with the ability to direct flows of capital create enormous political leverage, as well as enormous opportunities for private gain.

A U.S. Own Goal on Financial Power

Why does this matter? Why is this a reversal of U.S. policy goals an own goal? Many commentators, like the *Economist,* dismissed fears of the new SWFs by arguing that global pension funds, mutual funds, and insurance companies each accounted for roughly $20 trillion in holdings as of 2007.[5] This made each of them now as large as SWFs are projected to be in four or five years. But this misses the point. Pensions, mutual funds, and insurance companies are all tightly regulated, obliged to offer some degree of transparency, and generally speaking have clear fiduciary duties with respect to matching assets and liabilities. Indeed, unlike SWFs, pension funds and insurance companies have huge legally enforceable liabilities offsetting their assets. This makes them accountable and potentially vulnerable to millions of voters in the developed countries.

SWFs, by contrast, are doubly political creatures. As previously noted, they owe their existence to the politically motivated decision to peg exchange rates against the dollar even as trade surpluses and reserves cumulated past the point of a reasonable level of insurance against the kind of financial turmoil Asia saw in 1997. After all, even if the Asian and other states wished to hold down effective wages and personal consumption to retain a competitive position in world markets, they could have simultaneously directed new export receipts into upgraded infrastructure and other forms of collective consumption supporting productivity increases,

TABLE 8.1.
Sovereign wealth funds: Scale and recent acquisitions, 2008

Sovereign Wealth Fund	Estimated Value of Holdings (US$ billions)	Comment and Recent Acquisitions
Abu Dhabi Investment Authority (ADIA)	650–1,000	60% equities, 20% fixed income, 10% real estate; 4.9% stake in Citigroup ($7.5 billion)
Government Pension Fund—Global (Norway)	341	40 bonds:60 equities split; 5% maximum holding in any one firm; owns 1% of Rolls–Royce Engineering
Government Investment Corporation (Singapore)	330	$9.6 billion stake in UBS, equaling 11% of shares; $6.9 billion stake in Citigroup
Kuwait Investment Authority (KIA)	215–250	6.9% stake in Daimler; 1.7% stake in BP; €524 stake in Industrial and Commercial Bank of China; $3 billion share in $12.5 billion bailout of Citibank in January 2008 (with Saudi Prince Walid bin Talal); $2 billion share of $6.6 billion recapitalization of Merrill Lynch (with Korea Investment Corp. and Mizuho Corporate Bank)
China Development Bank	n/a	$3 billion stake in Barclays; technically not a SWF
China Investment Corporation	200	Founded in 2007; $5 billion stake in Morgan Stanley; $3 billion stake in Blackstone; $3–4 billion into financial firm J C Flowers; only one-third of investment will be overseas
Temasek (Singapore)	160	Stakes in Merrill Lynch ($4.4 billion); Barclays ($2 billion); Standard Chartered (3.7% stake, $1.4 billion); ICICI Bank (India); China Construction Bank (5.1% stake, $2.5 billion); Bank of China (5% stake, $1.6 billion)
Stabilization Fund (Russia)	141	Allegedly shifting into euro-denominated investments; $32 billion shifted to Future Generations fund in February 2008
Future Fund (Australia)	70	Essentially an offshore public pension fund
Qatar Investment Authority	50–70	8.7% stake in Lagardere (France); 20% stake in London Stock Exchange and 10% stake in OMX (Scandinavian bourse); 60% equities, 20% bonds, 20% nontraditional assets
Alaska Permanent Fund	38	Dividends paid out annually to Alaska citizens

TABLE 8.1.—(cont.)

Sovereign Wealth Fund	Estimated Value of Holdings (US$ billions)	Comment and Recent Acquisitions
Brunei Investment Corp.	30	Looking for a stake in financial firms
Khazaneh Nasional BHD (Malaysia)	25.7	Mostly holds Malaysian government shares of para-public corporations; also invests in Southeast Asia
Korea Investment Corp.	20	Put in $2 billion of $6.6 billion recapitalization of Merrill Lynch (with Kuwait Investment Authority and Mizuho Corporate Bank)
Investcorp (Bahrain)	10	A wide range of U.S. commercial properties, including hotels, offices, apartments, and shopping malls
State General Reserve Fund (Muscat)	10	
Istithmar (Dubai)	8	2.7% stake in Standard Chartered Bank (United Kingdom); hedge fund GLG; M&A specialist Perella Weinberg
Dubai International Capital	6	Stakes in Och-Ziff Capital Management (9.9%, $1.3 billion), ICICI (India), Daimler, EADS; Dubai's state airline is a major purchaser of Airbus aircraft
Abraaj Capital (Dubai)	4	Mostly investing in Pakistan
Arcapita (Bahrain)	3.8	£2.15 billion takeover of Viridian Energy (Ireland)
Mubadala Development	unknown	7.5 % stake in Carlyle group

Sources: James Mawson and Renée Schultes, "Tracking the Assets That Make the Gulf an Economic Powerhouse," *Financial News*, 2 August 2007, available at: http://www.financialnews-us.com/?page=ushome&contentid=2348431254; Tony Tassell and Joanna Chung "How Sovereign Wealth Funds Are Muscling In on Global Markets," *Financial Times*, 24 May 2007, available at http://www.ft.com/cms/s/ffcc6948-0a21-11dc-93ae-000b5df10621.html; Brad Setser and Rachel Ziemba, "Understanding the New Financial Superpower—the Management of GCC Official Foreign Assets," *RGE Monitor*, December 2007, http://www.cfr.org/content/publications/attachments/SetserZiembaGCCfinal.pdf; http://online.wsj.com/public/resources/documents/info-foreignSWFi08.html; company websites.

Notes: BP, British Petroleum; EADS, European Aeronautic Defence and Space Company; M&A, mergers and acquisitions; n/a, not available; SWF, sovereign wealth fund.

like Singapore but on a grander scale.[6] SWFs, instead, recycle cash back into deficit countries, albeit in search of higher yields than those offered by U.S. Treasuries and agency bonds. Second, they are political in that they have no offsetting liabilities, no transparency, and in general are controlled by a very small number of government and party officials in authoritarian states. This last feature exacerbates the lack of transparency, which, after all, is shared by the less-threatening private equity and hedge funds.

In chapter 1, I note that all politics was about power. The politics of the market is no different. Because politics is ultimately about power, the analysis of economic processes obliges us to pay attention to *differential rates* of growth and not just absolute growth. Markets are systems of power because the constitution and regulation of property rights determine the profitability of enterprises and because the differing positions of firms in a given value chain (or commodity chain) allow them to exert differing degrees of control over that chain. Controlling the architecture of a commodity or value chain conveys the ability to determine the distribution of profit within that chain. Firms thus struggle to secure the best possible price, both to grow faster than potential competitors and to immunize themselves against takeovers. As Jonathan Nitzan has argued, vulnerability to buyouts explains why firms always seek a profit rate above the average rate in their economy rather than simply seeking profitability.[7] Profitability per se does not assure continued control; rather, control assures higher profitability and thus continued control.

In the 1990s, financial firms in general, and U.S. financial firms in particular, asserted control over more and more nodes in global value chains. With this control came a greater and greater share of domestic U.S. profits and, in some cases, of global profit as well. In the United States, the financial sector accounted for 37 percent of all pretax domestic corporate profits by the 2000s, double their share in the 1980s.[8] The 2007–2008 crisis (see chapter 7) created a window of opportunity for some SWFs to inject themselves directly into the heart of the U.S. financial sector, although it probably also marks the end of excessively large financial-sector profits.

Compassionate U.S. conservativism reversed the usual pattern of emergency international financial bailouts by producing dispassionate foreign ownership of a huge swathe of U.S. investment capital. Ironically, developing-country SWFs provided the U.S. financial firms with more money—$24.8 billion—in the last quarter of 2007 than the IMF ever lent in any single quarter to bail out troubled LDCs. The peak IMF emergency lending amounted to $13.7 billion in the third quarter of 2001 and $13.4 billion in the fourth of quarter 1997 during the Asian financial crisis.[9] SWFs and central banks easily accomplished this outsized reverse lending using assets exceeding $2 trillion and $4 trillion, respectively, at year end 2007.[10]

All this means that SWF investment strategies can manifest what Max Weber calls political capitalism, in particular "continuous business activity generating profit through unusual deals with political authorities."[11] For Weber, political capitalism stands in contrast to rational capitalism, in which businesses oriented toward routine trade and production seek profit through exchange—while also making strenuous efforts at the creation of monopoly in the struggle over prices. So far, SWFs have sought stakes in well-connected and thus politically powerful firms such as Blackstone, Carlyle Group, Morgan Stanley, and Citigroup. A stake in these firms gives SWFs privileged access to the U.S. political system via the large and growing tribe of ex-presidents, senators, and secretaries of the Treasury collecting salaries from these firms.

Against this, we might argue, like Gregory Nowell, that SWFs were largely invited in by OECD governments seeking to shore up their shaky financial institutions without having to resort to the more complicated and time-consuming solution of parliamentary and public approval.[12] Thus, these bailouts follow the patterns set in 1982, 1994, and 1998, when the Fed and U.S. Treasury orchestrated bailouts and deployed their own funds to rescue their own banks and foreign governments from collapsing debt pyramids. According to this view, SWFs might well be marginalized from any truly critical decision making undertaken by investment banks and broker dealers; instead, these deals might take place in more domesticated shadow networks at some distance from the formal and internationalized corporate boards. Moreover, the political response to the 2008 crisis will certainly produce a sweeping reregulation of the financial sector that limits profit rates in that sector for the medium term.

A U.S. Own Goal on Market Liberalization

SWFs also represent something of an "own goal" for U.S. foreign economic policy. Put bluntly, U.S. foreign economic policy had been centered on opening foreign goods and especially financial markets to U.S. firms. The United States urged financial liberalization and destatization on a wide range of countries. But SWFs present a restatization of finance and, moreover, an intrusion of offshore states into the U.S. financial system, as previously noted. They thus represent a reversal of overt U.S. policy preferences during the long 1990s. Rather than U.S. financial firms inserting themselves into critical nodes in the value chain in LDCs, the reverse is occurring.

U.S. foreign economic policy since the 1970s has had two dominant impulses. The first was to open up foreign markets for specific U.S. export goods, and the second was to secure access for U.S. financial firms to foreign financial systems. The first started with the effort by the Richard Nixon administration to shift the United States toward a science-based economy and renovate the General Agreement on Tariffs and Trade (GATT) to encompass previously excluded goods and activities.[13] Nixon sought to expand the ambit of GATT to encompass agricultural goods, services (and particularly public services), and the protection of intellectual property rights. This impulse produced the WTO Uruguay Trade Round, which was ratified under the Clinton administration.

The Clinton administration launched its big emerging markets (BEM) strategy to seize the opportunities created by the new WTO.[14] The BEM strategy correctly identified the ten largest LDCs (China, India, Indonesia, Brazil, etc.) as the most likely sources of global growth in the next decades. The Clinton administration tried to get these countries to open up their domestic markets to U.S. service-sector exports, such as finance, telecommunications, and air transport—the kinds of public-sector capital goods we identify in chapter 2 and the kinds of capital goods that constitute approximately one-third of U.S. merchandise exports. The United States was a competitive producer of the public-sector capital goods that these infrastructure-deficient economies needed to integrate into the world economy. The BEM strategy fit perfectly with U.S. efforts to liberalize public-sector procurement and service-sector trade through the General Agreement on Trade in Services (GATS) and the WTO because these public projects were the ones most often steered to local firms. In the past, such steering enabled some European countries and Japan to generate their own competing producers of public-sector capital goods.

The second, more financial impulse quickly became the primary axis for policy under the Clinton administration, despite the orientation toward the BEMs. Getting U.S. financial firms a stake in foreign financial institutions or the ability to operate freely in foreign markets assured the United States of three permanent economic advantages. First, it would cripple or limit the ability of local states to use their financial systems to target industrial development and thus exclude U.S. public-sector capital-goods exports. Second, any successfully developing LDC was likely to have growth rates larger than that of the United States because it could exploit the stock of readily available technologies. U.S. financial firms that had access to foreign financial markets could thus get a "piece of the action," assuring that LDC prosperity contributed to U.S. prosperity and lessening differential growth in favor of those LDCs. Finally, an intermingling of U.S. and foreign financial interests plausibly might create a check on nationalist tendencies in those LDCs.[15]

Other countries grudgingly or willingly signed on to the WTO.[16] Greater trade integration might allow them easier export-led growth. But they largely resisted U.S. pressure for financial integration, understanding that the stakes were higher for the reasons already discussed. Even when states lacked a developmentalist ideology, the U.S. penetration of the financial sector would reduce the opportunities for the direct political use of finance, that is, corruption. External scrutiny of lending and the application of rich-country accounting norms would check the self-dealing rampant in economies in which banks were often simply appendages of industrial firms and those firms were simply appendages of people who ran or funded their own political parties.[17]

In the event, the United States used a series of financial crises to pry open foreign financial sectors. The U.S. price for emergency assistance during the 1994 Mexican peso crisis and the Asian financial crises of 1997–1998 was an opening of local financial sectors to U.S. firms.[18] By 2000, nineteen of the thirty largest Mexican financial firms were foreign-owned, and the foreign share of bank assets was even larger, at 79 percent.[19] The 1997–1998 Asian crises also provided opportunities for U.S. and allied firms to enter previously closed markets. The foreign share of Korean bank assets exceeded 20 percent by 2005. At the same time, foreign banks and investors bought 50 percent of the outstanding shares of Korean commercial banks, giving them effective control over much of the banking sector.[20] Much the same occurred in Thailand and Indonesia. Even when these foreign intrusions were not by U.S. financial firms, they reduced the ability of LDC governments to use their financial sectors as a tool for industrial policy. Conversely, they increased the probability that the United States would be able to export goods and services to a newly opened public sector using private finance to buy those goods and services.

But in 2007–2008, the wheel turned. The subprime difficulties of U.S. commercial and investment banks exposed them to the same kind of takeovers they had previously orchestrated. U.S. banks turned to SWFs for extra capital to shore up their balance sheets (see table 8.1). Firms such as Citigroup, Merrill Lynch, and Bear Stearns suddenly found themselves with Chinese, Singaporean, or gulf minority partners. Chinese net purchases of U.S. assets amounted to 3 percent of U.S. GDP in 2007, three times the peak Japanese inflow in the 1980s and 1990s, and all of it was from state-controlled firms.[21] The financial crisis thus reversed the destatization that the U.S. sought for the LDCs and, instead, inserted LDC states into its own political economy.

Race to the Sovereign Wealth Funds?

The commingling of developing-country SWFs and developed-country core financial institutions suggests the three usual Goldilocks scenarios, each corresponding to a line of analysis prevailing among pre–World War I Marxists. The first scenario is benign, at least from the point of view of capital—SWF stakes in western banks might create something akin to the ultra-imperialism Karl Kautsky sketched on a much smaller scale with regard to European financial integration circa 1914.[22] By taking stakes in developed-country banks, LDCs have made their investment returns hostage to developed-country economic success. This was nowhere more apparent than when CIC invested $3 billion in Blackstone and promptly saw more than $0.6 billion of that evaporate as Blackstone shares fell after their IPO.

More generally, Chinese desires to cultivate connections to the United States, as well as acquire expertise with respect to fixing up the nonperforming loan problem in their own banks, motivated them to permit minority stakes by U.S. banks in Chinese banks after 2000. Bank of America took a 9 percent holding in China Construction Bank, Citigroup took a 19.9 percent stake in Guangdong Development Bank, a Goldman Sachs–Allianz–American Express consortium took a 10 percent stake in the Industrial and Commercial Bank of China, HSBC took a 19.9 percent stake in the Bank of Communications, and the Royal Bank of Scotland took a 19.9 percent stake in Suzhou Trust. The Chinese government currently limits foreign stakes to 19.9 percent.

On this view, the more money SWFs invest in developed-country firms and equities, the greater their interest in a stable and trouble-free expansion of the global economy. Because the essentially political owners of SWFs will have direct access to political leaders, the commingling of interests in both directions creates channels of communication and influence that might reduce interstate economic conflicts. This portends yet another reduction in the power of labor relative to capital, but it might facilitate an orderly sharing out of global growth enhanced by the transfer of some production knowledge to LDCs. *Orderly sharing out* here means among different owners of capital. This scenario corresponds broadly to the Dooley, Folkerts-Landau, and Garber Bretton Woods 2 analysis.

The second scenario is less benign; it corresponds to Rudolf Hilferding's assessment of the prewar period.[23] Hilferding argues that the fusion of bank and industrial capital created giant combinations whose struggles for market share spilled over into trade wars and sometimes imperialist shooting wars. As we have seen, capitalism is a struggle for relative gains as firms seek monopoly or quasi-monopoly control over their value chain. Relatively higher, above-average rates and volumes of profit are always better than merely average profits. SWFs, like Hilferding's banks, would have large holdings in specific firms. This would make their own survival a function of the survival of those firms.

Struggles among politically connected giant combinations of SWFs, investment banks, and industrial firms over shares of the profit pool could easily deteriorate into the outright use of trade barriers, contract rigging, and industrial espionage to bolster returns. SWF access to government resources and policy via party officials or royal households will make this a tempting option. This struggle would exacerbate the usual volatility of the market.[24] This is particularly likely as the big LDC economies seek secure sources for raw materials for their material-intensive industrialization.

In addition, by taking large minority stakes in leading financial firms, SWFs may be able to not just exert undue influence on developed-country politicians but also buy up and transfer wholesale a variety of industries. The expertise embedded in financial firms is largely composed of tacit knowledge, making it the least susceptible to relocation. A buyer would have to move a large swath of personnel offshore. But high-technology firms are a somewhat different matter because they blend both tacit knowledge and knowledge codified in patents. Patents are an important source of control in high-tech value chains. SWF stakes in politically important financial firms would inoculate SWFs against political backlash.

The final scenario is yet more disturbing; it corresponds to Lenin's analysis of interimperialist war.[25] As politically controlled entities, SWFs might be easily tempted into accumulation via pure political capitalism if absolute gains turn negative, as they did in the Depression in the 1930s. Here SWFs represent the advance guard of a group of largely authoritarian states bent on the methodical expansion of their economic power. In the 1930s, trade barriers rose to exclusionary levels as the major powers carved out mutually exclusive imperial trading blocs. In the most malign versions of this, the Japanese spent the better part of the 1930s successfully conquering bits of China and unsuccessfully contesting for control over eastern Siberia. In the most benign version, the British offered trade preferences and barter to a wide range of peripheral economies. Thus, Argentina received a predefined quota for meat exports to Britain in return for a pledge to make good on its debts to Britain, and Denmark exchanged butter for British coal. SWFs might seek to carve out similar trading blocs by exerting pressure on politicians via their tame financial firms.

The point is not that SWFs by themselves could produce this outcome. Rather, they add to the pressure for this outcome because of their concentrated influence via financial firms, which typically have a direct line into the central banks and finance ministries of most countries. The SWFs of authoritarian countries give these countries two points of leverage against the largely democratic developed countries. First, their ability to shift large volumes of investment between the major currencies allows them to play various developed countries against one another. This does not necessarily have to take the form of depressing the value of a currency; indeed, a threat to appreciate a currency and thus harm exports might be just as compelling. The ability to whipsaw developed countries could reduce political pressure to liberalize both the politics and economics in the SWF owner. Second, SWFs give politicians in authoritarian countries a tool with which to buy support in their own country. SWF access to developed-country financial firms could be used to steer resources and market access to domestic firms in good odor with the local government. A stronger base of support reduces internal pressure for liberalization.

It is clearly too early to predict which scenario will transpire, although the middle of three Goldilocks scenarios always seems "just right." Certainly the general approach in this book suggests that the middle scenario is most likely. Moreover, central banks remain the largest holders of U.S. assets, not SWFs, suggesting strong pressure for a continuation of Bretton Woods 2 by other means and reinforcing the middle scenario. Nonetheless, SWFs clearly make the kind of U.S. arbitrage that sustained the U.S. growth model in the long 1990s less tenable. By shifting LDC surpluses out of low-yield assets and into longer-term, higher-yield investments, they undo the pattern of arbitrage identified in chapters 2 and 3. With this certainty in hand, and having closed the loop first sketched out in chapter 1, we can now venture some conclusions about U.S. global economic power and the possibilities for continued U.S. differential growth.

U.S. Global Capitalism, Past and Future:
Back to the Future Once More?

This book is about U.S. global economic power. I start by noting a central paradox about the United States in the long 1990s. During the 1990s, the United States accumulated historically unprecedented volumes of net foreign debt, and, even by nineteenth-century U.S. standards, fairly high levels of net foreign debt in relation to GDP. It is hard to imagine an economic superpower having a high level of foreign debt. Indeed, many critics saw that debt as the clearest evidence that U.S. global economic power has been in continuous decline since the 1980s. In somewhat the same way, these critics see the current subprime-spawned financial crisis as evidence of inevitable U.S. decline.

Power is an inherently elusive concept and essentially invisible to our usual techniques of measurement and quantification. These difficulties induce analysts to study what they can measure, which usually means looking at stocks rather than flows. Or analysts employ understandings of power that stress the deliberate efforts of actors to shape the behaviors of other parties. Both approaches lead to the conventional wisdom that we have noted: surely U.S. creditors must now be able to turn dollar liabilities into political and economic liabilities; surely the central international role of the dollar must give way if the United States is so heavily indebted.

This book offers a different interpretation of the evolution of U.S. net foreign debt during the long 1990s and of the current financial crisis. I use the flow of global capital into the United States and through the U.S. housing finance market system as a cloud chamber to reveal the effects of and manifestations of the otherwise invisible shape of U.S. economic power. This power emerged from U.S. differential growth, facilitated by the absence of constraints on the U.S. economy and the increased control over global production. The central position of the United States and the dollar in the world economy allowed the United States to avoid constraint and engage in global financial arbitrage, borrowing short term at low interest rates from the rest of the world and investing long term at higher rates of return back into the world. Oversized but short-term capital inflows combined with disinflation to drive down U.S. nominal interest rates in the long 1990s (see figure 1.1).

Nominal U.S. interest rates actually fell less than rates did elsewhere. But the U.S. housing finance market created more aggregate-demand bang for each buck of declining interest rates. This created differential growth favoring the U.S. economy and, to a lesser extent, economies with similar housing finance markets. The centrality of housing finance markets for differential growth meant that the most important action in the long 1990s occurred behind the backs of actors and that most of this action took the form of normal Keynesian macroeconomic processes. Existing OECD housing finance structures translated falling interest rates and disinflation into different levels of new demand among the Americanized Rich and Repressed Rich countries; more demand meant more growth, and less demand meant less growth. And because power is about differential growth, this process advantaged the United States relative to its most important rich-country competitors.

U.S. power manifested itself in the ability to consume and invest at home while also investing abroad. The structure of U.S. housing market finance enabled U.S. borrowers to borrow and *spend* more than consumers in economies characterized by less liquid mortgage and housing markets. U.S. housing finance markets thus helped generate more aggregate demand in the U.S. economy, powering it ahead of the Repressed Rich in terms of population adjusted GDP and employment. Above-average U.S. growth drew capital in from the Repressed Rich, reinforcing their reliance on external demand while sparking more U.S. growth. Japan and Germany, the next two largest developed economies, in effect ran this cycle backward. Housing prices fell, employment markets were weak, and physical investment faltered. Sluggish growth confronted German and Japanese banks with low domestic returns. Sluggish growth confronted German and Japanese households with increased insecurity about their employment and the ability of their state to make good on its pension and health liabilities. Both groups responded by saving more and exporting those savings in search of better yields abroad. In turn, this slowed their economies further, reinforcing the excess saving that Ben Bernanke uses to explain the U.S. current account deficits.

U.S. overseas borrowing mirrored the enormous expansion of fictitious capital in housing, as well as the enormous expansion of the physical stock of housing. The nominal value of U.S. home equity (net of mortgage debt) rose by nearly $7 trillion from 1991 to 2006. Growth and capital inflows bolstered the position of the dollar in world markets and central bank reserve holdings. This cycle was self-sustaining in the medium run, allowing the U.S. economy to escape constraint and combine domestic consumption growth with investment at home and abroad. The United States expanded its share of rich-country GDP at the expense of the Repressed Rich and held its share of global GDP constant, despite rapid growth in developing Asia. Moreover, U.S. firms expanded their direct control of overseas output considerably faster than foreigners expanded their control of U.S. output, and the U.S.-owned share of global equities more than doubled.

Like all booms, the 1990s U.S. boom ended when it exhausted its cheap inputs, in this case disinflation and U.S. arbitrage. Does this mean an end to U.S. differential growth in general or to merely this episode of U.S. differential growth? Does it mean an end to U.S. global economic power? To be true to the premises of this book, I offer two considerations. One is rooted in history and bears on the evolution of capitalism in general; the other looks at the specific institutional forms that drive macroeconomic growth processes, comparing our long 1990s to the original Bretton Woods period as well as to what might come. Both views suggest that reports of the demise of U.S. global economic power are premature, although by no means do I wish to suggest that all is well. And clearly, just as deliberate technology policy in the 1980s mattered for the 1990s boom, and just as deliberate fiscal policy mattered in the early 1990s for disinflation and arbitrage, deliberate efforts to put the U.S. fiscal house in order will matter for renewed U.S. differential growth. That growth will undoubtedly have a dynamic that is not housing-driven, yet it is likely to remain centered in the United States because the United States has been the primary (although not exclusive) source of new global growth in the same way that Britain was in the nineteenth century.

In chapter 5, I consider and dismiss the analogy between nineteenth-century Britain and the late-twentieth-century United States to show that the 1990s boom was not just about consumption and that it did not portend some collapse of U.S. manufacturing. Contemporary U.S. manufacturing was not in the same kind of terminal decline as late Victorian British manufacturing. Upgrading and technological dynamism characterize U.S. manufacturing, not an involution into empire and declining sectors. But a different analogy to nineteenth-century Britain is worth considering. This analogy bears on how the expansion of the British economy drove global capitalism in the nineteenth century.

Britain and the rest of the world experienced asynchronous but connected cycles of growth and stagnation in the late nineteenth century. Accurately assigning credit for all sources of growth is impossible, but British trade deficits surely mattered in the same way that U.S. trade deficits now matter for global demand. The United States and the rest of the world are locked into the same kinds of asynchronous but connected cycles of growth. U.S. growth integrates more areas of the world into global production through enormous U.S. trade deficits. Exporters then redeem their accumulated credits on the U.S. economy, stimulating U.S. growth directly or indirectly.

After 1800, the British demand for agricultural imports induced huge increases in the global volume of trade, migration, and capital flows. This British demand induced or forced the creation of capitalist agriculture worldwide. But this process did not proceed evenly; Britain and its agricultural periphery experienced partially asynchronous periods of expansion during the nineteenth century. A booming British economy stimulated increased exports of agricultural and other raw materials from the Western Hemisphere and Asia. These exports depressed agricultural prices in Britain, causing a massive shift of employment out of agriculture and either into manufacturing or offshore to grow more agricultural goods for export back to Britain. Booming global agricultural production also sucked capital out of Britain, raising interest rates and slowing the British economy. The British slowdown then reduced the demand for and prices of agricultural exports. Lower prices slowed growth in the peripheral countries and thus reduced their demand for capital and capital goods imports, as well as for immigrants. In turn, falling wages, smaller calls on capital and thus lower interest rates, and cheaper raw materials combined to stimulate British expansion anew. British boom and bust triggered colonial bust and boom, with interest rates and nominal commodity prices as the transmission mechanisms.

Oscillation was *not* instantaneous because creating new agricultural production capacity required both large-scale and lumpy infrastructure investment in railroads and harbors and, on a smaller scale, equally durable investments in family farms or plantations. Peripheral investors waited for credible shifts in relative prices before committing to production, but once they had committed, production could not be turned off if prices fell—and they did fall because uncoordinated peripheral investment always led to overinvestment, surpluses on the market, and falling prices. This, then, produced a financial crisis in the periphery as deflation made debt service difficult for exporters. Producers then moved farther outward geographically in search of cheaper land or upgraded their production to restore or sustain profits.

This oscillation also characterizes the United States and developing Asia (and to a lesser extent Latin America) since World War II. In the nineteenth century, the gold standard kept the value of the pound sterling constant, actual prices oscillated, and debt deflation was a constant threat; interest rate changes transmitted growth impulses. In contrast, fiat money and floating exchange rates characterize the current oscillation, changing the dynamic a bit. The present oscillation involves swings in the relative value of the dollar that transmit growth impulses. A strong dollar draws in massive volumes of low-grade manufactured products from select LDCs, inducing and validating durable investment in productive capacity in parts of the periphery. In 1987, the United States absorbed 22 percent of world manufactured exports, up from 11 percent in 1975; from 2000 on, despite Asian industrialization, the United States still absorbed 17.5 percent of global manufactured exports. Moreover, the United States also absorbed over 50 percent of LDC exports of manufactures in the 1980s and 24 percent in the 2000s. Despite having an economy one-half the size of the United States, Japan in 1987 absorbed only 4 percent of world manufactured exports, up from 2 percent in 1975. The Japanese share of global imports dropped during the 2000s, and despite its central position in Asian commodity chains, Japan absorbed only 5.3 percent of LDC exports.[26]

Just as in the nineteenth century, the uncoordinated rush to invest inevitably and quickly led to overproduction, falling prices, and a financial crisis in the periphery. The U.S. response historically was to keep the dollar strong to bail out LDC debtors and their U.S. creditors. A strong dollar enabled strong U.S. import demand and LDC recovery. But the increased volume of imports liquidated lower-grade U.S. manufacturing, displacing U.S. workers into services. The ensuing destruction of purchasing power in the United States then slowed the U.S. economy, causing the dollar to fall, and making investment in the United States once more attractive to both local and foreign capital.

In the nineteenth century, the process of oscillation and financial crisis around the British economy shifted agricultural production ever farther outward. The wheat frontier, for example, moved from Ireland to the U.S. Northeast, the U.S. Midwest, and finally western Canada and Australia over the course of the nineteenth century. Similarly, the labor-intensive production of garments and toys has shifted from Japan, to Korea and Taiwan, to Indonesia and Mexico, and finally to China over the past fifty years.[27] Oscillation and financial crisis have moved labor-intensive manufacturing ever outward, whereas the U.S. economy has moved on to more human capital–intensive manufacturing and services production (as well as a considerable amount of location-specific, labor-intensive services production). This oscillation involves the rich OECD countries as well, the Americanized Rich to a greater relative degree than the Repressed Rich. A declining U.S. dollar induces an inward rush of productive capital from the rich OECD, as firms establish subsidiaries to protect their U.S. market shares. This ties these countries even more firmly to a globalized economy by forcing firms that might otherwise content themselves with national or regional production chains to globalize those production chains.

Just as British economic oscillations expanded the global economy in the nineteenth century, U.S.-driven oscillation has expanded the global economy in the late twentieth and early twenty-first centuries. The current crisis—barring a 1930s-style financial crisis and trade collapse—thus represents the end of one more cycle of expansion. This cycle has brought economies containing approximately 2 billion people firmly into global circuits of capital. Unlike the British economy, which was largely a passive global investor, U.S. investors are positioned to capture a significant portion of future growth. From 1994 to 2006, the United States-owned share of the Morgan-Stanley MSCI All Country World (excluding the U.S. market index) rose from 10 to 24 percent of total market capitalization. The U.S. share of the purely emerging markets that compose this index remained substantially lower, at 5 percent, which, of course, implies that these truly are passive equity stakes, not a controlling interest.[28] But U.S. retailers and manufacturing firms control a substantial share of LDC output.

Each oscillation has increased the U.S. net foreign debt, but this debt is not purely and simply a source of U.S. weakness. Foreign creditors essentially have four options with respect to their claims on the United States. Two are implausible; two are not. The first implausible option is for foreign creditors to sell dollar assets at a great loss, temporarily depressing the U.S. dollar and bumping U.S. interest rates up. But, as discussed in chapter 6, all foreign creditors cannot exit at once. Selling dollar claims to Americans would leave creditors with dollars still in their hands. Could Asian creditors sell dollar assets to Europeans in exchange for euro assets? European states are unlikely to exchange control over their firms for dollars; indeed, in September 2008 the German government legislated limits on SWF ownership stakes. The reverse is also true—most Asian states will not allow Europeans to buy out their manufacturing sectors using dollar assets. The second implausible option is for U.S. creditors to exchange passive U.S. investments for more active forms—the SWF option. But this would tend to drive up the prices of the relevant U.S. assets, which would stimulate the U.S. economy through wealth effects. Meanwhile, creditors would be selling their existing holdings at low prices to buy other holdings at high prices, which is surely not beneficial and politically would be an embarrassment.

The two more plausible options already played out in the prior cycle of growth in the 1980s. First, creditors can continue to hold U.S. assets and finance U.S. growth. This was the Japanese option in the 1980s, leavened with some disastrous purchases of real assets such as the Pebble Beach Golf Club, and most of this book is about the consequences of this choice. Some developing countries have benefited from this choice, particularly China; nevertheless, it does permit the United States to continue to consume, invest at home, and invest abroad with fewer constraints than its peer competitors. This option thus continues the pattern of differential growth that favors the United States relative to Europe and Japan; this is a highly probable outcome. The second plausible option is to use dollars for new direct investment in the United States and for purchases of U.S.-sourced goods. In chapter 5, I dwell on the issue of deindustrialization precisely to show that the United States still has the capacity to produce for export. As with the prior option, this also tends to reinforce U.S. differential growth, albeit through a mechanism than other than housing.

The alternative to these options is, of course, more home-grown growth in other rich countries. Yet this seems unlikely to produce faster growth than in the United States. First, Repressed Europe and Japan were unable to decouple from the United States in 2007–2008. As the U.S. economy cooled, euroland growth tumbled from a 3.2 percent annual rate in the third quarter of 2007 to −0.8 percent in the second quarter of 2008, led by slowing growth in Germany. In Japan, one-fifth of whose exports still go directly to the United States, growth also turned negative by the second quarter of 2008.[29] This means that these economies will not experience the kind of differential growth that might unseat the United States from the center of the world economy. And, as noted in chapter 6, neither Japan nor euroland is politically willing to accept the trade deficits that necessarily accompany turning their currencies into a global reserve currency.

The huge U.S. net foreign debt is thus a structural feature favoring a continued central role for the United States and the U.S. dollar. Robust growth in emerging markets is certain to shift more trade in a south-south direction. But, at the same time, the pile of central bank–held dollars created by past and ongoing export-led growth will present only a larger and larger problem. As of early 2008, emerging markets and oil exporters were accumulating $150 billion per year, even as the U.S. economy slowed. Continued dollar accumulation and sterilization confront the export-surplus countries with a choice between inflation, which degrades their competitiveness in global export markets and risks social unrest, and revaluation, which degrades their competitiveness in global export markets and risks capital losses. Eventually, their central banks will have to release some dollars and increase imports from the United States, spurring U.S. economic growth. The money has to be spent somewhere, and even if everyone literally "passes the buck," eventually it will end up purchasing U.S. exports. Mark the original Bretton Woods system as the first round of post–World War II economic growth; mark our long 1990s as the second round. Even if the third large round of post–World War II global growth emerges from global demand for U.S. goods rather than the other way around, the United States will continue to grow faster than its rich-country rivals.

This leads logically to a consideration of the specific institutional bases that match supply and demand in the macroeconomy. In the first round of growth, the original Bretton Woods system, collective bargaining institutions assured that supply and demand would grow in tandem. Explicit deals linked increases in productivity to increases in pay.[30] In chapter 4, I dismiss these kinds of corporatist bargains as the sources of differential growth or employment outcomes in the long 1990s. But there is no doubt that they mattered for macroeconomic stability and outcomes in the earlier Bretton Woods period. The expansion of public-sector and other forms of sheltered employment similarly put a floor under aggregate demand, stabilizing private investment with its huge multiplier effects. Capital controls and the tight regulation of finance assured that local firms had access to cheap finance for that investment. Finally, the enormous U.S. economy served as the buyer of last resort when production outpaced local demand. Although housing was an important source of demand in this period, it was positioned toward the end of the causal chain. Stable and rising wages enabled people to buy houses on credit, which in turn fed back into stably rising aggregate demand. As in the long 1990s, the United States faced no external constraints and U.S. MNCs were able to expand freely globally.

The unraveling of the Bretton Woods system in the 1970s put supply and demand out of kilter and imposed constraints on the United States. The institutions linking wages to productivity, supply to demand, all came under assault in the 1980s and 1990s. In the United States, businesses broke the link between pay and productivity by shifting production offshore and breaking unions. In Europe, firms exposed to world trade joined with fiscal bureaucrats troubled by rising public debt to undo the automatic links between public- and private-sector pay.[31] Although European firms could not explicitly break the pay-productivity link, they sought greater world market shares by negotiating local wage restraints. These actions created a growing gap between supply and aggregate demand, which developing-country industrialization aggravated. Meanwhile, foreign pressure helped force the deregulation of the U.S. domestic oil market and, later, efforts to balance the budget.

What, then, led to renewed growth in the 1990s? Certainly a wave of innovations first planted in the 1970s and 1980s came to fruition in the 1990s: the Internet, supply-chain management, and mobile telephony. These underlay the shared growth impulses in Europe/Japan and the United States during the long 1990s. But what lifted the population-adjusted U.S. growth rates above those in its peer competitors was a new way of generating aggregate demand in the absence of stably rising wages. Financial deregulation enabled homeowners (as distinct from wage-earners) to access otherwise illiquid assets. First and foremost among these was housing equity. The structural features of U.S.-style housing finance systems translated disinflation into new aggregate demand by letting people access and spend their rising home equity. Aggregate demand derived from rising home prices helped power the entire global economy in the long 1990s, and it accounts for the differences in growth rates among the United States, the Americanized Rich, and the Repressed Rich. Although central banks and politicians abetted the decline in nominal interest rates, this new aggregate demand largely emerged behind the backs of actors.

Renewed U.S. global economic power in the 1990s was largely produced by a machine running on autopilot. This machine, like any other, was perfectly capable of running or being driven off the rails once people understood how it worked. Deliberate policy accelerated the rate at which the housing-growth machine exhausted its two major drivers: disinflation and arbitrage. But even without George W. Bush's income tax cuts and Greenspan's excessive cuts to the federal funds interest rate, the housing machine would eventually have run out of gas. Because the housing machine largely favored those who already had housing equity to begin with, it exacerbated the widening income and wealth disparities that had emerged with the collapse of the first Bretton Woods system. Ultimately, the housing machine ran out of buyers at the bottom for the same reason it ran out of disinflation.

Chinese export success ultimately reversed the disinflation input to the growth machine and the supply of new buyers. On the one side, continued Chinese growth led to larger and larger calls on limited supplies of global raw materials, particularly foods and fuels. This lifted raw materials prices to levels not seen for decades. On the other side, a continued flow of cheap imports helped undercut wages and employment at the bottom of the U.S. labor market, making it harder for people at the bottom to buy houses. Not only was their income compressed, but more of it was diverted to food and fuel and away from housing. Rising inflationary pressures ultimately motivated the Federal Reserve Bank to hike interest rates after 2005. This cut demand in the housing market and made refinancing and equity withdrawal more difficult. By 2007, the Fed was backpedaling on those hikes as the U.S. economy teetered on the edge of recession and then fell into financial crisis.

At the same time, U.S. global financial arbitrage, the second major driver of differential growth, relied on a steady supply of secure assets that could be sold into global capital markets. These new assets largely took two forms: new U.S. Treasury bonds and new MBSs. Even if these MBSs were ultimately packaged as CDOs, markets had to generate the raw materials for those CDOs. In turn, the supply of MBSs required a steady supply of new and *creditworthy* entrants into housing markets, as well as rising prices. But a steady supply of new creditworthy borrowers and rising prices are in direct conflict. If prices rose faster than incomes, fewer people would be able to afford houses. The pool of creditworthy borrowers in the housing market dried up because the great rush into ownership both exhausted that pool and pushed house prices up to unaffordable levels. For a while, the private-label producers of MBSs bridged the divide by lending to subprime homebuyers.

Subprime, recall, refers not just to poor people but more generally to people at all income levels who took on imprudent levels of debt. Their mortgages made sense only in an economic environment in which housing prices kept going up, enabling their mortgagers to refinance into a conforming mortgage at lower interest rates. But, of course, continuously rising house prices meant even more people were being priced out of the housing market, removing part of the demand that drove up housing prices. The exhaustion of the pool of new potential homebuyers limited the supply of new MBSs that could be flogged to foreign buyers of U.S. assets. As discussed in chapter 7, once those uncreditworthy buyers began defaulting on their mortgages, the whole structure of CDOs and SIVs collapsed. This motivated foreign asset buyers first to shift their purchases to longer-term and higher-yielding U.S. assets and then to flee U.S. assets at the margin. This flight confronted the U.S. triple play of domestic consumption, domestic investment, and offshore investment with a hard budget constraint as of 2008.

This constraint will force hard budgetary choices on households and governments, reopening the question of how to bring global supply and demand back in balance. But it is important to note that these choices are not absolute. The United States does not have to bring its external accounts into complete balance. As a purely mathematical exercise, it is plausible that the current U.S.-centric system could continue for some time if U.S. nominal GDP growth exceeds the nominal rate of interest on its foreign debt. Maurice Obstfeld and Kenneth Rogoff have calculated that reducing the U.S. current account deficit to roughly 3 percent of GDP—lower than today's deficit, but not inconceivably so—would require nominal appreciations of roughly 30 percent on the part of Asian and European currencies. The euro has already risen this much and more. A nominal annual U.S. GDP growth of 3 percent—slightly higher than today's growth but, again, well within historical parameters—would keep the ratio of debt to GDP perfectly stable.[32]

External constraints thus do not dictate the shape of a new U.S. macroeconomic growth regime. Instead, just as U.S. creditors face political difficulties changing their reliance on the U.S. market, the United States itself faces political barriers to any reform. U.S. elites themselves arbitraged against their own population during the 1990s. This domestic arbitrage lay behind the global arbitrage that benefited the U.S. economy. U.S. elites used U.S. global arbitrage to socialize their costs of borrowing while privatizing gains. Recall that low-cost capital inflows to the United States permitted high-return capital outflows. But the same parties did not contract these flows. Instead, claims on the fiscal base of the United States—U.S. Treasury bonds—permitted the creation of private claims on profits made at home and abroad. Rising U.S. foreign debt reflected both direct and indirect claims on taxpayers because interest on Treasuries comes from general revenues. Interest on GSE/agency MBSs comes from mortgage payments, and now, with Fannie Mae and Freddie Mac renationalized, from the taxpayers. Meanwhile, private firms and their nominal owners reaped the profits from off- and on-shore operations of U.S. MNCs.

The resulting distribution of costs and benefits among U.S. elites is hard to discern precisely. On the one hand, the top 10 percent of the population with respect to holdings of wealth is surely the greatest beneficiary of private claims on profits. This 10 percent holds a net worth of approximately $2.5 million per family unit (mean) or nearly $1 million (median), of which approximately one-half is housing wealth.[33] Even using the median figure, these families each have holdings roughly twice as large as those held by the other 90 percent, and they hold between 75 and 80 percent of all equities. Yet, at the same time, it is precisely this top 10 percent that is most exposed to income taxes and other taxes. Currently, the top 10 percent of income earners (a close proxy for the top 10 percent by wealth) accounts for approximately 68 percent of federal income taxes, and the top 5 percent accounts for 57 percent of income tax revenues. These federal revenues fund the interest on foreign-held federal debt; at the same time, these revenues are ultimately what will fund the Social Security pension system when it eventually has to redeem its vast Trust Fund holdings of U.S. Treasuries to meet its legal obligations to U.S. pensioners. The current conflict over limiting Social Security benefits or privatizing accounts is thus an effort to reduce claims on taxes that largely fall on the upper 10 percent.

I doubt the top 10 percent of income earners will politely acquiesce to a reversal of the three Bush tax cuts that so greatly benefited them. Yet a reversal of the mortgage catastrophe requires not just lower interest rates on mortgages but also additional income for the bottom 90 percent so that overindebted mortgagers can make their payments or reenter the housing market. It is an open question whether elites can make the connection between their own long-term interest in reenergizing U.S. growth and the need to restore mortgage-ability in the rest of the population. As Leonard Seabrooke argues, it was precisely the vast expansion of credit and income to the middle 40 percent of the income distribution that enhanced U.S. global financial power by expanding the pool of mortgage securities.[34]

On the other hand, the mortgage-driven 2008 financial crisis has rearranged all the pieces on the U.S. political chessboard by more than reversing twenty-five years of deregulation. Mortgage financing—which, recall, amounts to more than one-third of the U.S. securities market—is back in government hands. So, too, are many core financial institutions. The rest of the financial sector is crippled and is tethered to the state through an IV line to the Fed. Although a return to the

Bretton Woods–era capital controls and levels of financial regulation is unlikely, a political base for financial reregulation now exists. Indeed, the U.S. financial system increasingly resembles the German system, with its four large universal banks with market shares over 10 percent; a more numerous set of partially or fully national-ized firms, including the GSEs; and a plethora of local savings banks and credit unions (i.e., thrifts or *sparkassen*). It is unimaginable that political authorities will give the new banking giants the free rein that their smaller predecessors enjoyed.

The future thus hinges to a degree on the relative balance between positive action and action taken behind the backs of actors. Much U.S. global economic power is structural and inert, as the retrospective analysis of the role of hous-ing finance–driven differential growth shows. A rerun of housing-led differen-tial growth is entirely unlikely; the gains from future disinflation are also limited. But the 1990s allowed U.S. firms to expand their control over global commodity chains while saddling foreign investors with a variety of low-yielding assets. And it allowed at least some U.S. consumers to place themselves in sparkling new homes that will be with us for some time. The next cycle of U.S.-led growth will prob-ably involve the U.S. real economy, much as in the early 1990s. The clearest path to growth involves a somewhat broader distribution of income across the U.S. popu-lation, and positive steps to assure a broader distribution would go a long way to assuring that the United States remains the stable center of the global economy.

U.S. economic power derives from the willingness of other private and pub-lic actors to buy and hold U.S. assets. This willingness flows from differential growth that favors the United States and also helps create the conditions for that growth. U.S. power frees the U.S. economy from the normal constraints, and the reserve status of the dollar reflects and reinforces that lack of constraint. Differ-ential growth enables U.S. firms and investors to expand their control over global economic activity. U.S. economic power is, thus, less about the ability to compel the behavior of other actors than it is about the ability to create structures that induce behaviors favoring the United States. This definition may be too tame for those who see *power* only as domination and are concerned mainly with statecraft. But a definition of *power* in terms of domination and explicit statecraft makes it impossible to see how power operated through the market and behind the backs of actors in the long 1990s.

Notes

Preface

1. And it is worth remembering that British foreign investment and U.S. housing were also tightly connected in the nineteenth century; see Thomas Brinley, *Migration and Economic Growth* (Cambridge, UK: Cambridge University Press, 1973); Simon Kuznets, *Secular Movements in Production and Prices* (New York: Augustus Kelly, 1967).

1. Our Borrowing, Your Problem

1. On differential accumulation as a concept, see Jonathan Nitzan, "Differential Accumulation: Towards a New Political Economy of Capital," *Review of International Political Economy* 5, no. 2 (1998): 169–216; Jonathan Nitzan and Shimshon Bichler, "New Imperialism or New Capitalism?" unpublished paper, available at: http://bnarchives.yorku.ca/124/2004.

2. On feedback or reflexivity in social life, see George Richardson, *Feedback Thought in Social Science and Systems Theory* (Philadelphia: University of Pennsylvania Press, 1991); George Soros, *Alchemy of Finance* (New York: John Wiley and Sons, 1987).

3. Benjamin Cohen, "The Macrofoundations of Monetary Power," in *International Monetary Power,* edited by David Andrews, 31–50 (Ithaca: Cornell University Press, 2006).

4. Jane D'Arista and Stephany Griffith-Jones, "The Dilemmas and Dangers of the Build-up of US Debt," in *Global Imbalances and the US Debt Problem,* edited by Jan Joost Teunissen and Age Akerman, 53–86 (The Hague: Fondad, 2006), esp. 64.

5. Calculated from the EU-KLEMS database, http://www.euklems.net/, using purchasing power parity GDP in constant 1990 Geary-Khamis dollars, which controls for fluctuations in exchange rates and inflation.

6. Uwe Becker and Herman Schwartz, *Employment Miracles: A Critical Comparison of the Dutch, Scandinavian, Swiss, Australian and Irish Cases versus Germany and the US* (Amsterdam: University of Amsterdam Press, 2005).

7. Leila Heckman, "Insight: Refuge May Be Found via New Frontiers," *Financial Times,* 13 February 2008, available at: http://www.ft.com/cms/s/0/234aaafe-da4e-11dc-9bb9-0000779fd2ac.html.

8. United Nations Conference on Trade and Development, *World Investment Report, 2006* (New York: United Nations, 2006), 332–33; Bureau of Economic Analysis (BEA), "An Ownership Based Framework of the US Current Account, 1995–2005," *Survey of Current Business* (January 2007): 45; Organisation for Economic Cooperation and Development (OECD), *Measuring Globalization: Activities of Multinationals, II: 2008* (Paris: OECD, 2008), 378, 382.

9. Examples of the Americanized Rich are Britain, the Netherlands, Australia, Canada, and the Scandinavian countries.

10. Examples of the Repressed Rich are Japan, Germany, Italy, Austria, Belgium, Portugal, and Spain.

11. See Fareed Zakaria, *The Post-American World* (New York: W. W. Norton, 2008); Parag Khanna, *The Second World: Empires and Influence in the New Global Order* (New York: Random House, 2008). Exchange rate data are from the Federal Reserve Bank.

12. Cohen, "Macrofoundations of Monetary Power."

13. Robert Gilpin, *US Power and the Multinational Corporation* (New York: Basic Books, 1975); Joseph M. Grieco, "Anarchy and the Limits of Cooperation: A Realist Critique of the Newest Liberal Institutionalism," *International Organization* 42, no. 3 (summer 1988): 485–507; Christian Palloix, "Self-Expansion of Capital on a World Scale," *Review of Radical Political Economy* 9, no. 2 (summer 1977): 3–28; Nicos Poulantzas, "Internationalisation of Capitalist Relations and the Nation-State," *Economy and Society* 3, no. 2 (1974): 145–79.

14. Max Weber, *Economy and Society,* edited by Gunther Roth and Claus Wittich (Berkeley: University of California Press, 1978), 107–8, 638.

15. Oliver Williamson, *Economic Organization of Capitalism* (New York: Free Press, 1985); Thorstein Veblen, *The Theory of Business Enterprise* (Clifton, N. J.: A. M. Kelley, 1904 [1975]). See also Neil Fligstein, *The Architecture of Markets: An Economic Sociology of Twenty-First Century Capitalism* (Princeton: Princeton University Press, 2001); Harrison White, *Markets from Networks: Socioeconomic Models of Production* (Princeton: Princeton University Press, 2001).

16. Jonathan Nitzan, "Differential Accumulation," 173–74 (emphasis in original).

17. Giovanni Arrighi, "Hegemony Unraveling—I," *New Left Review* no. 32 (March–April 2005): 23–80; Giovanni Arrighi, "Hegemony Unraveling—II," *New Left Review* no. 33 (May–June 2005): 83–116.

18. There is a debate about how profitable Chinese firms are. See Song-Yi Kim and Louis Kuijs, "Raw Material Prices, Wages, and Profitability in China's Industry—How Was Profitability Maintained When Input Prices and Wages Increased So Fast," World Bank China Research Paper No. 8, October 2007 (Beijing, China).

19. Quoted in Calculated Risk, October 7, 2007, available at: http://calculatedrisk.blogspot.com/2007/10/citi-music-stops-prince-visits.html.

20. Weber, *Economy and Society,* 152.

21. The essays in David Andrews, C. Randall Henning, and Louis Pauly, eds., *Governing the World's Money* (Ithaca: Cornell University Press, 2002) provide typical actor-centered

analyses, as does Jonathan Kirshner, *Currency and Coercion: The Political Economy of International Monetary Power* (Princeton: Princeton University Press, 1995). Benn Steil and Robert Litan, *Financial Statecraft: The Role of Financial Markets in American Foreign Policy* (New Haven: Yale University Press, 2008) are probably closest to my view in their treatment of financial flows; the cast in the Andrews, Henning, and Pauly collection reprise their roles in David Andrews, ed., *International Monetary Power* (Ithaca: Cornell University Press, 2006), using a purely relational definition of *power*—"does actor A's monetary behavior influence actor B"—that could accommodate my treatment of power.

22. See Herman Schwartz, "Explaining Australian Economic Success: Good Policy or Good Luck?" *Governance* 19, no. 2 (April 2006): 173–205, for a full-scale consideration of actors and institutional change.

23. See Friedrich Hayek, "The Use of Information in Society" and "The Pretence of Knowledge," *Essence of Hayek,* edited by Chiaki Nishiyama (Stanford: Hoover Institution Press, 1984), 211–224, 266–280. See also Geoffrey Hodgson's characterization of Hayek's arguments in *Economics and Evolution: Bringing Life Back into Economics* (Ann Arbor: University of Michigan Press, 1993), 152–85.

24. Weber, *Economy and Society,* 38–40; Peter Breiner, "'Unnatural Selection': Max Weber's Concept of *Auslese* and His Criticism of the Reduction of Political Conflict to Economics," *International Relations* 18 (2004): 289–307; W. Garry Runciman, "Was Max Weber a Selectionist in Spite Himself?" *Journal of Classical Sociology* 1, no. 1 (2001): 13–32, quotation on 15.

25. Breiner, "'Unnatural Selection,'" esp. 292–94.

26. Weber, *Economy and Society,* 40.

27. BEA, "US Trade in Goods," table 2b, available at: http://www.bea.gov.

28. Eurostat, *External and Intra-European Union Trade, Statistical Yearbook—Data 1958–2006* (Luxembourg: Office for Official Publications of the European Communities, 2008).

29. For discussions of the United States as a "savvy investor," see Barry Eichengreen, "Global Imbalances: The New Economy, the Dark Matter, the Savvy Investor, and the Standard Analysis," University of California, Berkeley, March 2006; John Kitchen, "Sharecroppers or Shrewd Capitalists?: Projections of the U.S. Current Account, International Income Flows, and Net International Debt," *Review of International Economics* 15, no. 5 (November 2007): 1036–61.

30. Michael P. Dooley, David Folkerts-Landau, and Peter Garber, "An Essay on the Revived Bretton Woods System," NBER Working Paper no. 9971, National Bureau of Economic Research, Cambridge, Mass., 2003; Michael P. Dooley, David Folkerts-Landau, and Peter Garber, "The Revived Bretton Woods System: The Effects of Periphery Intervention and Reserve Management on Interest Rates and Exchange Rates Center Countries," NBER Working Paper no. 10332, National Bureau of Economic Research, Cambridge, Mass., 2004; Michael P. Dooley, David Folkerts-Landau, and Peter Garber, "Direct Investment, Rising Real Wages and the Absorption of Excess Labor in the Periphery," NBER Working Paper no. 10626, National Bureau of Economic Research, Cambridge, Mass., 2004; Michael P. Dooley, David Folkerts-Landau, and Peter Garber, "The US Current Account Deficit and Economic Development Collateral for a Total Return Swap," NBER Working Paper no. 10727, National Bureau of Economic Research, Cambridge, Mass.,

2004; William Cline, *The US as a Debtor Nation* (Washington, D.C.: Institute for International Economics, 2005); Ricardo Hausmann and Federico Sturzenegger, "The Missing Dark Matter in the Wealth of Nations and Its Implications for Global Imbalances," *Economic Policy* (July 2007): 469–518.

31. See the country case studies in Herman Schwartz and Leonard Seabrooke, eds., *The Political Cost of Property Booms,*special issue *of Comparative European Politics* 6, no. 3 (September 2008).

32. Arrighi, "Hegemony Unraveling—I"; Arrighi, "Hegemony Unraveling—II."

33. Gilpin, *US Power and the Multinational Corporation.*

34. Susan Strange, *Sterling and British Policy* (New York: Oxford University Press, 1971). See also Eric Helleiner's application of Strange's categories to the U.S. dollar in Eric Helleiner and Jonathan Kirshner, eds., *The Future of the Dollar* (Ithaca: Cornell University Press, 2009).

35. Dooley, Folkerts-Landau, and Garber, "The Revived Bretton Woods System"; Mikuni Akio and R. Taggart Murphy, *Japan's Policy Trap* (Washington D.C.: Brookings Institution, 2002).

36. Norway's Government Pension Fund-Global is the obvious exception to the rule; the experiences of Alberta's Heritage Trust Fund and the Alaska Permanent Fund are not entirely bad but also not entirely encouraging.

37. Barry Eichengreen, *Global Imbalances and the Lessons of Bretton Woods* (Cambridge, Mass.: MIT Press, 2007), 125–26.

38. In this regard, see Michael Shalev's perceptive article, "Limits and Alternatives to Multiple Regression in Comparative Analysis," *Comparative Social Research* 24 (2007): 259–308.

2. Global Capital Flows and the Absence of Constraint

1. Pierre-Olivier Gourinchas and Hélène Rey, "From World Banker to World Venture Capitalist: US External Adjustment and the Exorbitant Privilege," NBER Working Paper no. 11563, National Bureau of Economic Research, Cambridge, Mass., August 2005. See also Ricardo Caballero, Emmanuel Farhi, and Pierre-Olivier Gourinchas, "An Equilibrium Model of Global Imbalances and Low Interest Rates," NBER Working Paper no. 11996, National Bureau of Economic Research, Cambridge, Mass., 2006.

2. For example, many of Ronald McKinnon's superb analyses of the U.S.–East Asian dynamic end with pleas for actors on both sides to rewrite the rules governing capital flows, for the United States to increase U.S. savings in part by balancing the U.S. budget, and for developing countries to reform their financial systems so that prudential regulation becomes more effective. See Ronald McKinnon, "The World Dollar Standard and Globalization: New Rules for the Game?" in *The Future of the Dollar,* edited by Eric Helleiner and Jonathan Kirshner (Ithaca: Cornell University Press, 2009); Ronald McKinnon, *Exchange Rates under the East Asian Dollar Standard: Living with Conflicted Virtue* (Cambridge, Mass.: MIT Press, 2006).

3. Ben S. Bernanke, "The Global Saving Glut and the U.S. Current Account Deficit," Sandridge Lecture, Virginia Association of Economics, Richmond, Va., March 10, 2005. Bernanke was not yet chair of the Federal Reserve Open Market Committee at the time he gave this lecture, but he has reiterated this view since his appointment. See Richard Cooper,

"Understanding Global Imbalances," unpublished paper, Harvard University, May 2006, for a similar argument that emphasizes aging populations in Germany and Japan a bit more than Bernanke does.

4. David Soskice makes a similar argument in "Macro-economics and Varieties of Capitalism," in *Beyond Varieties of Capitalism: Conflict, Contradictions and Complementarities in the European Economy,* edited by Bob Hancké, Martin Rhodes and Mark Thatcher, 89–121 (New York: Oxford University Press, 2007), but in addition he links this to the firm-specific skill profile of the German and Japanese workforce by contrast with the general skill profile of the U.S. and British workforces.

5. The EU-25 countries are Austria, Belgium, Cyprus, the Czech Republic, Denmark, Estonia, Finland, France, Germany, Greece, Hungary, Ireland, Italy, Latvia, Lithuania, Luxembourg, Malta, the Netherlands, Poland, Portugal, Slovakia, Slovenia, Spain, Sweden, and the United Kingdom. The EU-27 countries are the EU-25 plus Bulgaria and Romania. The euroland-13 countries are Austria, Belgium, Finland, France, Germany, Greece, Ireland, Italy, Luxembourg, the Netherlands, Portugal, Slovenia, and Spain.

6. William Cline, *The US as a Debtor Nation* (Washington, D.C.: Institute for International Economics, 2005); Ricardo Hausmann and Federico Sturzenegger, "The Missing Dark Matter in the Wealth of Nations and Its Implications for Global Imbalances," *Economic Policy* (July 2007): 469–518.

7. Cline, *US as a Debtor Nation,* 48–66.

8. Ibid., 275–79.

9. Hausmann and Sturzenegger, "Missing Dark Matter."

10. Emile Despres, Charles Kindleberger, and Walter Salant, "The Dollar and World Liquidity: A Minority View," in *Changing Patterns in Foreign Trade and Payments,* edited by Bela Balassa, 144–56 (New York, W. W. Norton, 1970). Gourinchas and Rey, "From World Banker to World Venture Capitalist" in effect update this argument.

11. Barry Eichengreen, "Sterling's Past, Dollar's Future," The Tawny Lecture, Leicester, U.K., April 10, 2005.

12. Barry Eichengreen, "Global Imbalances: The New Economy, the Dark Matter, the Savvy Investor, and the Standard Analysis," University of California, Berkeley, March 2006, 9.

13. Giovanni Arrighi, "Hegemony Unraveling—I," *New Left Review* no. 32 (March–April 2005): 23–80, quotation on 69; Giovanni Arrighi, "Hegemony Unraveling—II," *New Left Review* no. 33 (May–June 2005): 83–116; Peter Gowen, *Washington's Global Gamble* (London: Verso, 1999).

14. Arrighi, "Hegemony Unraveling—I," 64.

15. Compare David Harvey, *The New Imperialism* (New York: Oxford University Press, 2003).

16. Giovanni Arrighi and Beverly Silver, *Chaos and Governance in the World System* (Minneapolis: University of Minnesota Press, 1999), 272.

17. Leo Panitch and Sam Gindin, "Finance and American Empire," *Socialist Register* (2005): 46–81; Leo Panitch and Sam Gindin, "Superintending Global Capital," *New Left Review* no. 35 (September–October 2005): 101–23.

18. Panitch and Gindin, "Finance and American Empire," 47, 73.

19. Panitch and Gindin, "Superintending Global Capital," 112–13.

20. Panitch and Gindin, "Superintending Global Capital."

21. Michael P. Dooley, David Folkerts-Landau, and Peter Garber, "An Essay on the Revived Bretton Woods System," NBER Working Paper no. 9971, National Bureau of Economic Research, 2003; Michael P. Dooley, David Folkerts-Landau, and Peter Garber, "The Revived Bretton Woods System: The Effects of Periphery Intervention and Reserve Management on Interest Rates and Exchange Rates Center Countries," NBER Working Paper no. 10332, National Bureau of Economic Research, Cambridge, Mass., 2004; Michael P. Dooley, David Folkerts-Landau, and Peter Garber, "Direct Investment, Rising Real Wages and the Absorption of Excess Labor in the Periphery," NBER Working Paper no. 10626, National Bureau of Economic Research, Cambridge, Mass., 2004; Michael P. Dooley, David Folkerts-Landau, and Peter Garber, "The US Current Account Deficit and Economic Development Collateral for a Total Return Swap," NBER Working Paper no. 10727, National Bureau of Economic Research, Cambridge, Mass., 2004. McKinnon, *Exchange Rates,* makes a parallel argument.

22. Nouriel Roubini and Brad Setser, "Will the Bretton Woods 2 Regime Unravel Soon?: The Risk of a Hard Landing in 2005–2006," unpublished paper, New York, 2005; Barry Eichengreen, *Global Imbalances and the Lessons of Bretton Woods* (Cambridge, Mass.: MIT Press, 2007), 1–34.

23. Andrea Goldstein, "The Political Economy of Industrial Policy in China: The Case of Aircraft Manufacturing," William Davidson Institute Working Paper no. 779, University of Michigan Business School, Ann Arbor, July 2005; John Newhouse, *Boeing versus Airbus* (New York: Knopf, 2007), 181–90.

24. The U.S. Treasury Department and Bureau of Economic Analysis (BEA) also began including derivatives in the Index of Industrial Production (IIP) data as of mid-2007. The reasons for doing this and the methodology for establishing valuations of gross fair value are elaborated at: http://www.treas.gov/tic/frbulmay2007.pdf. Roughly 85% of derivatives were with European-domiciled entities and 56% were with UK-domiciled entities. The inclusion of derivatives (which are excluded from the Cline, Hausmann and Sturzenegger, and Arrighi data) does not substantially affect net U.S. foreign debt. Consequently, I have also excluded them here.

25. Four-fifths of U.S. holdings of foreign securities are dollar denominated, so exchange rate changes have only a small effect; U.S. Treasury Department, *Report on US Portfolio Holdings of Foreign Securities, December 2005* (Washington, D.C.: U.S. Treasury Department, 2006), 11.

26. Ibid., 3, 12; U.S. Treasury Department, *Report on Foreign Portfolio Holdings of US Securities, June 2006* (Washington, D.C.: U.S. Treasury Department, 2007), 3, 16.

27. U.S. Treasury Department, *Report on Foreign Portfolio Holdings, June 2006,* 3, 16.

28. U.S. Treasury Department, *Report on US Portfolio Holdings of Foreign Securities, December 2004* (Washington, D.C.: U.S. Treasury Department, 2005), 3.

29. Rebecca McCaughrin, "Global: Rising Risk of US Debt Costs," *Morgan Stanley Global Economic Forum,* 19 July 2004.

30. Gerard Dumenil and Dominique Levy, "The Economics of US Imperialism at the Turn of the 21st Century," *Review of International Political Economy* 11, no. 4 (October 2004): 657–76.

31. Daniel Gros, "Foreign Investment in the US, I: Disappearing in a Black Hole?" Center for European Policy Studies Working Document no. 242, Brussels, April 2006;

Daniel Gros, "Foreign Investment in the US, II: Being Taken to the Cleaners?" Center for European Policy Studies Working Document no. 243, Brussels, April 2006.

32. Note that this figure differs from that in the previous paragraph because it uses different base years.

33. Raymond J. Mataloni Jr., "An Examination of the Low Rates of Return of Foreign Owned U.S. Companies," *Survey of Current Business* (Washington, D.C.: U.S. Department of Commerce, March 2000), 55–56.

34. Gros "Foreign investment in the US, I," 6.

35. Ibid., 7.

36. Mataloni, "An Examination of the Low Rates," 60, 63.

37. Charles Kindleberger, "Theory of Direct Foreign Investment," in *Transnational Corporations & World Order,* edited by George Modelski (San Francisco: W. H. Freeman, 1979); John H. Dunning, *Multinational Enterprise and the Global Economy* (Reading, Mass.: Addison Wesley, 1993).

38. I thank Anne-Marie Durocher for this suggestion; a Toyota executive allegedly boasted that Toyota "owned" more U.S. senators than GM did because Toyota had strategically dispersed production across the United States.

39. BEA, http://www.bea.gov.

40. Brad Setser, "Tokyo—Sao Paolo—Rio—New York—Washington…" April 23, 2007, available at: http://www.rgemonitor.com/blog/setser/. That said, for much of 2000–2005 period the spread between AAA-rated borrowers in the United States and emerging-market public-sector bonds was derisory. But the spread between emerging-market bonds and JPY interest rates was not derisory.

41. Stephen Jen, "'JPY Carry Trades': The Undeserved Scapegoat," *Morgan Stanley Global Economic Forum,* 9 March 2007.

42. Francis Warnock and Veronica Warnock, "International Capital Flows and US Interest Rates," NBER Working Paper no. 12560, National Bureau of Economic Research, available at: http://www.nber.org/papers/w12560.

43. See Ronald McKinnon's arguments that China helps stabilize Asian exchange rates in *Exchange Rates,* chap. 5.

3. Investing in America

1. Peter Hall and David Soskice, eds., *Varieties of Capitalism* (Oxford: Oxford University Press, 2001).

2. U.S. Treasury Department, *Report on Foreign Portfolio Holdings of US Securities,* June 2006, 8; Bureau of Economic Analysis (BEA), http://www.bea.gov. In private conversation as well as forthcoming work, Ronen Palan has argued that a substantial portion of investment flows into and out of the Netherlands, Switzerland, and the United Kingdom also represent this kind of corporate shell. It is impossible, however, to disentangle this investment from the more straightforward and probably more substantial flows from the same countries. Consequently, here I put only the more obvious corporate shells into this fourth, residual category. No one believes that the Cayman Islands is an economy capable

of generating billions of dollars of outward investment; it is easy to believe this of Britain or the Netherlands, however. Switzerland is somewhere in between.

3. Tim McGlaughlin, "Bear Hedge Fund Sank as Merrill Protected Clients," *Washington Post*, 3 August 2007: D1.

4. BEA, http://www.bea.gov.

5. See Ronen Palan, Richard Murphy, and Christian Chavagneux, *Tax Havens: At the Heart of Globalization* (Ithaca: Cornell University Press, 2009), for an effort to document the actual beneficial ownership of these flows.

6. United Nations Conference on Trade and Development (UNCTAD), *World Investment Report 2006* (New York: United Nations, 2006), 303.

7. Ramin Toloui, "Petrodollars, Asset Prices, and the Global Financial System," *PIMCO Capital Perspectives* (January 2007): 1–16.

8. Unless otherwise noted, the data in this paragraph come from ibid.

9. Ibid.

10. BEA, "U.S. Trade in Goods, Historical Trend Series IDS-0182," table 2b, available at: http://www.bea.gov.

11. Ibid., tables 2a and 2b.

12. Data from BEA, http://www.bea.gov.

13. And as Palan, Murphy, and Chavagneux, *Tax Havens*, argue, it may also reflect the use of Britain and the Netherlands as custodians by residents of other countries.

14. Carol C. Bertaut and Linda S. Kole, "What Makes Investors Over- or Underweight?: Explaining International Appetites for Foreign Equities," Federal Reserve Bank International Finance Discussion Papers no. 2004-819, Washington, D.C., September 2004.

15. Charles Kindleberger, "Theory of Direct Foreign Investment," in *Transnational Corporations & World Order*, edited by George Modelski (San Francisco: W. H. Freeman, 1979), 91–107.

16. Xun Cao, "Transnational Flows of Portfolio Investments: A Network Analysis 2001–2005," unpublished paper presented at the International Studies Association Annual Meeting, Chicago, 2007. Cao's clusters, which are based only on portfolio flows, do not line up precisely with those presented here, however. See also Philip R. Lane and Gian Maria Milesi-Ferretti, "A Global Perspective on External Positions," IMF Working Paper no. 05/161, International Monetary Fund, Washington, D.C., 2005.

17. Susan Strange, *Sterling and British Policy* (Oxford: Oxford University Press, 1971).

4. Homes Alone?

1. Herman Schwartz and Leonard Seabrooke, "Varieties of Residential Capitalism in the International Political Economy: Old Welfare States and the New Politics of Housing," *Comparative European Politics* 6, no. 2 (September 2008): 237–61, provides a critique of the varieties of capitalism argument.

2. The French CAC40 tripled in 1995–2000 from ~1,850 to ~6,500, the German DAX30 from ~2,100 to ~7,600, and the UK FTSE100 from ~3,300 to ~6,930. And let us not speak of the now defunct German Neuer Markt (a NASDAQ clone that exploded in 2001).

3. Jonathan Nitzan, "Differential Accumulation: Towards a New Political Economy of Capital," *Review of International Political Economy* 5, no. 2 (1998): 169–216.

4. See, for example, David Soskice's analysis of aggregate demand management regimes in "Macro-economics and Varieties of Capitalism," in *Beyond Varieties of Capitalism: Conflict, Contradictions and Complementarities in the European Economy,* edited by Bob Hancké, Martin Rhodes and Mark Thatcher, 89–121 (New York: Oxford University Press, 2007), which stolidly contrasts LME and CME capacity for managing aggregate demand to minimize unemployment.

5. See, for example, Peter Auer, *Employment Revival in Europe: Labour Market Success in Austria, Denmark, Ireland, and the Netherlands* (Geneva: International Labour Office, 2000); Niamh Hardiman, "From Conflict to Coordination: Economic Governance and Political Innovation in Ireland," *West European Politics* 25 no. 4 (2002): 1–24; Philippe Pochet and Giuseppe Fajertag, eds., *Social Pacts in Europe in the 1990s* (Brussels: ETUI, 1997, 2000); Martin Rhodes, "The Political Economy of Social Pacts: 'Competitive Corporatism' and European Welfare Reform," in *New Politics of the Welfare State,* edited by Paul Pierson, 165–94 (New York: Oxford University Press, 2001).

6. Classic statements can be found in Peter Lange, George Ross, Maurizio Vannicelli, eds., *Unions, Change, and Crisis: French and Italian Union Strategy and the Political Economy, 1945–1980* (New York: George Allen and Unwin, 1982); Peter Gourevitch, Andrew Martin, George Ross, Stephen Bornstein, Andrei Markovits, and Christopher Allen, *Unions and Economic Crisis: Britain, West Germany and Sweden* (Boston: George Allen and Unwin, 1984), esp. Andrew Martin's chapter.

7. Lars Calmfors and John Drifill, "Bargaining Structure, Corporatism, and Macro-economic Performance," *Economic Policy* 6 (April 1988): 13–61.

8. Fritz Scharpf, *Crisis and Choice in European Social Democracy* (Ithaca: Cornell University Press, 1991).

9. Lane Kenworthy, "Corporatism and Unemployment in the 1980s and 1990s," *American Sociological Review* 67 (June 2002): 367–88.

10. Soskice, "Macro-economics and Varieties of Capitalism," 90–91.

11. Auer, *Employment Revival in Europe,* 2.

12. Martin Rhodes, "Globalization, Labor Markets and Welfare States: A Future of 'Competitive Corporatism?'" in *The Future of European Welfare: A New Social Contract?* edited by Martin Rhodes and Yves Mény, 178–203 (London: Macmillan, 1998); Rhodes, "Political Economy of Social Pacts"; Bob Hancké and Martin Rhodes, "EMU and Labor Market Institutions in Europe: The Rise and Fall of National Social Pacts," *Work and Occupations* 32, no. 2 (2005): 196–228.

13. Bernhard Ebbinghaus and Anke Hassel, "Striking Deals: Concertation in the Reform of Continental European Welfare States," Max Planck Institut für Gesellschafts forschung Discussion Paper no. 99/3, Cologne, Germany, 1999; Anke Hassel and Bernhard Ebbinghaus, "From Means to Ends: Linking Wage Moderation and Social Policy Reform," in *Social Pacts in Europe—New Dynamics,* edited by Giuseppe Fajertag and Philippe Pochet, 61–85 (Brussels: European Trade Union Institute/Observatoire Social Européen, 2000); Anke Hassel, "The Politics of Social Pacts," *British Journal of Industrial Relations* 41, no. 4 (December 2003): 707–26.

14. Hardiman, "From Conflict to Coordinating."

15. Rhodes, "Political Economy of Social Pacts," 180.

16. Hassel and Ebbinghaus, "From Means to Ends," 4.

17. Andrew Martin, "Social Pacts, Unemployment, and EMU Macroeconomic Policy," in *Social Pacts in Europe—New Dynamics,* edited by Philippe Pochet and Giuseppe Fajertag (Brussels: ETUI-OSE, 2000), 369.

18. Soskice, "Macro-economics and Varieties of Capitalism," 119.

19. Organisation for Economic Cooperation and Development (OECD), "OECD Fact-book, 2005," available at: http://www.sourceOECD.org.

20. Richard Green and Susan Wachter, "The Housing Finance Revolution," unpublished paper presented at the Federal Reserve Bank 31st Economic Policy Symposium, Jackson Hole, Wyo., August 2007, 9.

21. Duncan MacLennan, John Muellbauer, and Mark Stephens, "Asymmetries in Housing and Financial Market Institutions and EMU," *Oxford Review of Economic Policy* 14 no. 3 (1998): 54–80, presents a slightly different analysis.

22. Calculated from Federal Reserve Bank, "Survey of Consumer Finance," 2001 and 2004, available at: http://www.federalreserve.gov/pubs/oss/oss2/2004/bulletin.tables.int.xls; Federal Reserve, "Recent Changes in US Family Finances," *Federal Reserve Bulletin* (2006): A8. Note also that to the extent that home market bias exists, it constrains the average European's access to equities anyway.

23. MacLennan, Muellbauer, and Stephens, "Asymmetries in Housing," 58.

24. Alan Greenspan and James Kennedy, "Sources and Uses of Equity Extracted from Homes," FEDS Research Paper no. 2007-20, Federal Reserve Bank, 2007, 43, 26.

25. Data from Contrary Investor, http://www.contraryinvestor.com.

26. Alexander Ludwig and Torsten Slok, "Impact of Changes in Stock Prices and House Prices on Consumption in OECD Countries," IMF Working Paper no. 02/01, International Monetary Fund, Washington, D.C., January 2002; Bank for International Settlements, *72nd Annual Report,* Washington, D.C., 2003, 130; Massimo Giuliodori, "The Role of House Prices in the Monetary Transmission Mechanism across European Countries," *Scottish Journal of Political Economy* 52, no. 4 (September 2005): 519–43; Claudio Borio, "The Structure of Credit to the Non-government Sector and the Transmission Mechanism of Monetary Policy: A Cross-Country Comparison," Bank for International Settlements Working Papers no. 24, Basel, 1995; Raphael Bostic, Stuart Gabriel, and Gary Painter, "Housing Wealth, Financial Wealth, and Consumption: New Evidence from Micro Data," unpublished paper, University of Southern California, December 2005; Karl E. Case, John M. Quigley, and Robert J. Shiller, "Comparing Wealth Effects: The Stock Market versus the Housing Market," NBER Working Paper no. 8606, National Bureau of Economic Research, available at: http://www.nber.org/papers/w8606; John Muellbauer, "Housing, Credit and Consumer Expenditure," unpublished paper presented at the Federal Reserve Bank 31st Economic Policy Symposium, Jackson Hole, Wyo, August 2007, 33–34.

27. MacLennan, Muellbauer, and Stephens, "Asymmetries in Housing."

28. Muellbauer, "Housing, Credit and Consumer Expenditure," 8.

29. Greenspan and Kennedy "Sources and Uses of Equity," 8–9, 17.

30. Carrick Mollenkamp and Mark Whitehouse, "Northern Rock May Point to U.K. Crunch," *Wall Street Journal,* 24 September 2007, A2; Ambrose Evans-Pritchard, "German Team Damn UK Economic 'Miracle' as a Sham," *Daily Telegraph,* 23 October 2007, 5; Muellbauer, "Housing, Credit and Consumer Expenditure," 24, 28, 34.

31. U.S. Treasury, *Report on Foreign Portfolio Holdings of US Securities, June 2006* (Washington, D.C.: U.S. Treasury Department, 2007), 3, 5.

32. In European parlance, these are covered bonds. *Pfandbriefe* are similar to MBSs, except that banks issuing *Pfandbriefe* generally keep the mortgages on their own books, whereas MBSs may be serviced by a third party.

33. Francis E. Warnock and Veronica Cardac Warnock, "International Capital Flows and U.S. Interest Rates," FRB International Finance Discussion Paper no. 840, Federal Reserve Bank, Washington, D.C., September 2006.

34. Technically speaking, the first pass-through MBS was issued in 1971 by Freddie Mac, and the first private version was issued by BankAmerica in 1977. But widespread use began in the early 1980s.

35. *Credit risk* is the risk that a bond will go into default, wiping out the lender's principal.

36. Federal Reserve Bank, table 13, available at: http://www.federalreserve.gov/pubs/oss/oss2/2004/bulletin.tables.int.xls.

37. Credit Suisse, "US Mortgage Strategy," June 2007, New York; Federal National Mortgage Agency, *Annual Report 2006*, FNMA, Washington, D.C.;, Federal Home Loan Mortgage Corporation, *Annual Report 2006*, FHLMC, Washington, D.C.

38. U.S. Treasury, *Report on Foreign Holdings, June 2006*, 11.

39. Ronald McKinnon, "The World Dollar Standard and Globalization: New Rules for the Game?" in *The Future of the Dollar*, edited by Eric Helleiner and Jonathan Kirshner (Ithaca: Cornell University Press, 2009); see also, Brad Setser, "A Bit More on the Agency Portfolios of the World's Central Banks," available at: http://blogs.cfr.org/setser/2008/07/14/a-bit-more-on-the-agency-portfolios-of-the-worlds-central-banks/.

40. Brad Setser, "Just Who in Europe Has Been Buying US bonds?" September 6, 2007, available at: http://www.rgemonitor.com/blog/setser/213750.

41. http://www.globalpropertyguide.com/investment-analysis/Housing-transaction-costs-in-the-OECD.

42. International Monetary Fund, *World Economic Outlook, April 2008* (Washington, D.C.: IMF, 2008). My index and the IMF index correlate at 0.84. But the IMF's index does not map well conceptually on to my argument because it incorporates measures of the use of covered bonds and loan-to-value ratios. Covered bonds do not encourage bank lending in the same the way that tradable MBSs do, and loan-to-value ceilings can diverge from actual practices.

43. Peter Neuteboom, "A Comparative Analysis of the Net Costs of a Mortgage for Homeowners in Europe," *Journal of Housing and the Built Environment* 19 (2004): 169–86, esp. 172.

44. MacLennan, Muellbauer, and Stephens, "Asymmetries in Housing," 64.

45. Kenworthy, "Corporatism and Unemployment."

46. U.S. Bureau of Labor Statistics, http://data.bls.gov/PDQ/outside.jsp?survey=ei.

47. See also Marcello deCecco, "International Currency Dynamics: Lessons from the pre-1914 Experience," in *The Future of the Dollar*, edited by Eric Helleiner and Jonathan Kirshner (Ithaca: Cornell University Press, 2009).

48. Roger Boyes, "Landesbanks at Risk as WestLB Becomes Latest to Show Strains," *London Times*, 30 August 2007, 46; David Gow, "Germany's Image of Probity Shattered

by US Mortgage Crisis: Banking Sector Is Given a Rude Awakening—and Faces a Huge Shakeup," *Guardian,* 6 September 2007, 33.

5. U.S. Industrial Decline?

1. Pierre-Olivier Gourinchas and Hélène Rey, "From World Banker to World Venture Capitalist: US External Adjustment and the Exorbitant Privilege," NBER Working Paper no. 11563, National Bureau of Economic Research, Cambridge, Mass., August 2005.

2. Barry Eichengreen, *Global Imbalances and the Lessons of Bretton Woods* (Cambridge, Mass.: MIT Press, 2007), 125–26.

3. Giovanni Arrighi, "Hegemony Unraveling—I," *New Left Review* no. 32 (March–April 2005), 64.

4. Robert Gilpin, *US Power and the Multinational Corporation: The Political Economy of Foreign Direct Investment* (New York: Basic Books, 1975), esp. chaps. 5 and 6.

5. See Marcello de Cecco, "International Currency Dynamics: Lessons from the pre-1914 Experience," in *The Future of the Dollar,* edited by Eric Helleiner and Jonathan Kirshner (Ithaca: Cornell University Press, 2009), for an explicit comparison; see Marcello de Cecco, *The International Gold Standard: Money and Empire* (New York: St. Martin's Press, 1984), for a thorough analysis.

6. James Foreman-Peck and Ronald Michie, "Performance of the Nineteenth Century International Gold Standard," in *The Emergence of a World Economy 1500–1913,* edited by Wolfram Fischer, R. Marvin McInnis, and Jürgen Schneider, Vol. 2, 399–405 (Wiesbaden: F. Steiner, 1986).

7. Susan Strange, *Sterling and British Policy* (New York: Oxford University Press, 1971).

8. See the contempory discussions in C. Fred Bergsten, "The World Economy after the Cold War," *Foreign Affairs* 69, no. 3 (summer 1990); Miles Kahler, "The International Political Economy," *Foreign Affairs* 69, no. 4 (fall 1990): 139–51. Hanns W. Maull, "Germany and Japan: The New Civilian Powers," *Foreign Affairs* 69, no. 5 (winter 1990–1991): 91–106, is more measured about dollar weakness. Daniel Burstein, *Yen!: Japan's New Financial Empire and Its Threat to America* (New York: Simon and Schuster, 1988), is much less so.

9. Federal Reserve Bank, "Nominal Major Currencies Dollar Index," and "Price-adjusted Major Currencies Dollar Index," both available at: http://www.federalreserve.gov/releases/H10/Summary/indexnc_m.txt.

10. David Lake, *Power, Protection and Free Trade* (Ithaca: Cornell University Press, 1988), 31.

11. de Cecco, *International Gold Standard,* 27; Angus Maddison, "The World Economy Historical Statistics," available at: http://www.ggdc.net/.

12. Jonathan Nitzan, "Differential Accumulation: Towards a New Political Economy of Capital," *Review of International Political Economy* 5, no. 2 (1998): 169–216.

13. William Lazonick and Frank Williamson, "Industrial Relations and Uneven Development: A Comparative Study of the American and British Steel Industries," *Cambridge Journal of Economics* 3, no. 3 (September 1979): 275–303; Katherine Stone, "Origins of Job Structures in the Steel Industry," *Review of Radical Political Economy* 6 (1974): 113–73.

14. Pepper Culpepper, *Creating Cooperation: How States Develop Human Capital in Europe* (Ithaca: Cornell University Press, 2003).

15. Fritz Stern, *Iron and Gold: Bismarck, Bleichroeder, and the Building of the German Empire* (New York: Knopf, 1977).

16. Alfred Chandler, "The Emergence of Managerial Capitalism," *Business History Review* 58 (winter 1984): 497.

17. Data in the next four paragraphs are drawn from http://www.SourceOECD.org.

18. Bark van Ark, Mary O'Mahoney, and Gerard Ypma, "The EU KLEMS Productivity Report," no. 1, EU KLEMS Project, Groningen University, March 2007; Bart van Ark, Mary O'Mahoney, and Marcel Timmer, "The Productivity Gap between Europe and the United States: Trends and Causes," *Journal of Economic Perspectives* 22, no. 1 (winter 2008): 25–44. The data in this paragraph are drawn from the latter source.

19. Josh Whitford, *The New Old Economy* (Madison: Wisconsin University Press, 2005).

20. On the central importance of education for growth, see Isaac Ehrlich, "The Mystery of Human Capital as Engine of Growth, or Why the US became the Economic Superpower in the Twentieth Century," NBER Working Paper no. 12868, National Bureau of Economic Research, Cambridge, Mass., January 2007.

21. National Science Foundation, *Asia's Rising Science and Technology Strength: Comparative Indicators for Asia, the European Union, and the United States* (Washington. D.C.: NSF, May 2007); Gary Gereffi and Viveek Wadhwa, "Framing the Engineering Outsourcing Debate," unpublished paper, Duke University, Durham, N.C., December 2005; Gary Gereffi and Ryan Ong, "Upgrading in the Global Knowledge Economy: Insights from China and India," paper presented at the Global Value Chains Workshop, Durham, N.C., November 2006.

22. Carsten Holz, "China's Economic Growth, 1978–2025: What We Know Today about China's Economic Growth Tomorrow," unpublished paper, Hong Kong University of Science and Technology, 2006, 19–22, 38.

23. Leo Panitch and Sam Gindin, "Finance and American Empire," *Socialist Register* (2005): 46–81; Leo Panitch and Sam Gindin, "Superintending Global Capital," *New Left Review* no. 35 (September–October 2005): 101–23.

24. Thus, for example, one of the biggest customers of GE Commercial is GE Commercial Aviation Services (GECAS), an aircraft-leasing firm that, among other things, buys GE aircraft engines for its 1,500 planes. The GECAS decision to buy product from the four main producers of regional jets perhaps explains why GE engines power 90% of those regional jets.

25. Rudolph Hilferding, *Finance Capital: A Study of the Latest Phase of Capitalist Development* (London: Routledge and Keegan Paul, 1981), 225.

26. Unfortunately, consistent data are unavailable for the entire 1991–2006 period as a result of the change from the Standard Industrial Classification (SIC) to the North American Industry Classification System (NAICS) of national income accounting; similarly, consistent FDIUS data run only from 1997 to 2005.

27. Raymond Mataloni, "An Examination of the Low Rates of Return of Foreign Owned U.S. Companies," *Survey of Current Business* (March 2000): 55–73.

28. Rebecca McCaughrin, "Global: Rising Risk of US Debt Costs," *Morgan Stanley Global Economic Forum,* 19 July 2004, 1.

29. Ricardo Hausmann and Federico Sturzenegger, "The Missing Dark Matter in the Wealth of Nations and Its Implications for Global Imbalances," *Economic Policy* (July 2007): 469–518; Daniel Gros, "Foreign Investment in the US, (I: Disappearing in a Black Hole?" Center for European Policy Studies Working Document no. 242, Brussels, April 2006; Daniel Gros, "Foreign Investment in the US, II: Being taken to the Cleaners?" Center for European Policy Studies Working Document no. 243, Brussels, April 2006. Note that Gros assumes that the management of European firms is a rational economic actor pursuing the best interests of the firm and its shareholders rather than a power-maximizing or "opportunistic with guile"–type actor.

30. "Overhauling the Old Jalopy," *Economist,* 4 August 2007, 58; Congressional Budget Office, *Corporate Tax Rates: International Comparisons* (Washington. D.C.:, Congressional Budget Office, November 2005).

31. Congressional Budget Office, *Corporate Tax Rates,* xl, 45.

32. Harry Grubert, "Another Look at the Low Taxable Income of Foreign Controlled Companies in the United States," OTA Paper no. 74, U.S. Treasury Department, October 1997.

33. Mataloni, "An Examination of the Low Rates of Return," 66.

34. Grubert, "Another Look at the Low Taxable Income," 1, 22.

35. Mataloni, "An Examination of the Low Rates of Return," 56.

36. Charles Kindleberger, "Theory of Direct Foreign Investment," in *Transnational Corporations & World Order,* edited by George Modelski (San Francisco: W. H. Freeman, 1979), 91–107; John H. Dunning, *Multinational Enterprise and the Global Economy* (Reading, Mass.: Addison Wesley, 1993). Nick Bloom and John Van Reenen, "Measuring and Explaining Management Practices across Firms and Countries," Center for Economic Performance Discussion Paper no. 0716, March 2006, 20, claim that U.S. MNCs are considerably better managed than native firms in the United Kingdom, France, and Germany.

37. My colleague Leonard Schoppa notes that a Japanese executive once confessed that the U.S. plant held by his company was an insurance policy against protectionist legislation, and the Toyota assembly plants appear to be located with an eye toward maximizing political protection.

38. McKinsey Global Institute, *US Productivity Growth, 1995–2000: Understanding the Contribution of Information Technology Relative to Other Factors* (Washington, D.C.: McKinsey Global Institute, 2001), 11–12.

39. United Nations Conference on Trade and Development, *World Investment Report, 2006* (New York: UN, 2006), 332–33; Bureau of Economic Analysis, "An Ownership Based Framework of the US Current Account, 1995–2005," *Survey of Current Business,* January 2007, 45; Organisation for Economic Cooperation and Development, *Measuring Globalization: Activities of Multinationals, II: 2008* (Paris: OECD, 2008), 378, 382.

40. This paragraph and the next draw on Richard Aboulafia, "Airbus Reinvests to Reinvent," *Aerospace America* (May 2007): 18–20; Richard Aboulafia, "Airbus Faces Tough Midmarket Choices," *Aerospace America* (June 2006): 14–16; "Commercial Aviation: Barrelling Along," *Economist,* 29 September 2007, 70–72; and, more generally, John Newhouse, *Boeing versus Airbus* (New York: Knopf, 2007).

41. Nick Bloom, Raffaella Sadun, and John van Reenen, "It Ain't What You Do It's the Way You Do I.T.: Testing Explanations of Productivity Growth Using U.S. Affiliates,"

argues that the creation of SWFs creates an additional complication in this collective action problem because these funds have an incentive to sell U.S. securities to their own central banks in order to shift the risk off their books. But this argument has less bite when we consider that, first, SWFs are as subject to political control as central banks and, second, concentrating holdings in central banks makes an analysis based on K groups even more powerful.

6. I do not consider the Corporate Shells here. Consistent with chapters 1 and 3, many of their claims on the United States are most probably dollar liabilities funded with dollar assets for tax purposes. These investments have credit risk but not currency risk.

7. Stephen Jen and Charles St.-Arnaud, "Global Official Reserves Just Breached US$6.0 Trillion," November 9, 2007, available at: http://www.morganstanley.com/views/gef/archive/2007/20071109-Fri.htm.

8. Carol Bertaut and William Griever, "Recent Developments in Cross Border Securities," *Federal Reserve Bulletin* (winter 2004): 19–31, esp. 22.

9. Fernand Braudel, *Civilization and Capitalism, Fifteenth–Eighteenth Century: The Perspective of the World,* vol. 3, trans. Sian Reynolds (New York: Harper and Row, 1984).

10. Funded public pensions in Europe include only the oil-funded Norwegian SWF and the various Swedish and Danish wage earner funds; see Ellen Immergut, Karen Anderson, and Isabelle Schulze, *The Handbook of West European Pension Politics* (New York: Oxford University Press, 2007); Organisation for Economic Cooperation and Development (OECD), *Pensions at a Glance: Public Policies across OECD Countries* (Paris: OECD, 2007).

11. Ronald McKinnon, *Exchange Rates under the East Asian Dollar Standard: Living with Conflicted Virtue* (Cambridge, Mass.: MIT Press, 2006).

12. Barry Eichengreen, "Global Imbalances and the Lessons of Bretton Woods," NBER Working Paper no. 10497, National Bureau of Economic Research, Cambridge, Mass., May 2004.

13. Russell Hardin, *Collective Action* (Baltimore: Johns Hopkins University Press, 1982), 40–48.

14. U.S. Treasury, *Report on Foreign Holdings of US Portfolio Securities as of June 30, 2007* (Washington, D.C.: U.S. Treasury Department, June 2008), 10. Brad Setser has repeatedly argued that the U.S. Treasury official tallies for both oil exporters and China understate their total holdings of U.S. securities; see his analyses at http://blogs.cfr.org/setser.

15. See, for example, the discussions in Judith Hardt, "European Integration: Prospects for the Mortgage Lending Industry," European Mortgage Federation, Brussels, 1998; Manuel Aalbers, "The Geography of Mortgage Markets," Amsterdam Institute for Metropolitan and International Development Studies Working Paper, Amsterdam, 2006.

16. Peter Hall and David Soskice, eds., *Varieties of Capitalism* (New York: Oxford University Press, 2001); see also the essays in Bob Hancké, Martin Rhodes, and Mark Thatcher, eds., *Beyond Varieties of Capitalism: Conflict, Contradictions and Complementarities in the European Economy* (New York: Oxford University Press, 2007).

17. There is, however, considerable variation. German firms reportedly self-finance 90% of investment via retained earnings versus only 60% for France and Italy. See Elga Bartsch, "Germany: Pulling a Slow Train," *Morgan Stanley Global Economic Forum,* 17 December 2007, available at: http://www.morganstanley.com/views/gef/index.html#anchor5916.

18. Peter Hall, "The Evolution of Varieties of Capitalism in Europe," in *Beyond Varieties of Capitalism: Conflict, Contradictions and Complementarities in the European Economy,* edited

Centre for Economic Performance, London, July 2005; Nick Bloom, Raffaella Sad John Van Reenen, "Americans Do I.T. Better: US Multinationals and the Prod Miracle," CEP Discussion Paper no. 788, London School of Economics, April 2007

42. The data in this paragraph are from National Science Foundation, *Asia's Risi ence and Technology Strength.*

43. Bureau of Economic Analysis, "Balance of Payments," table 1, available at h www.bea.gov.

44. Robert Inklaar, Marcel P. Timmer, and Bart van Ark, "The End of Converge Market Services Productivity in Europe," unpublished paper, University of Gronin, March 2007; see also Mary Amiti and Kevin Stiroh, "Is the US Losing Its Producti Edge?" *New York Federal Reserve Bank Current Issues in Economics and Finance* 13, no. 8 (Se tember 2007): 1–7.

45. Hendrik S. Houthakker and Stephen P. Magee, "Income and Price Elasticities World Trade," *Review of Economics and Statistics* 51, no. 2 (May 1969): 111–25.

46. Data from Organisation for Economic Cooperation and Development, *OEC Economic Outlook no. 83* (Paris: OECD, June 2008), 239, 247.

47. Quoted in Richard McCormack, "General Electric CEO Jeffrey Immelt: The US No Longer Drives Global Economic Growth and Must Decide If It Wants to Be a Competitive Nation," *Manufacturing and Technology News* 14, no. 21 (November 30, 2007), available at: http://www.manufacturingnews.com/news/07/1130/art1.html.

48. Barry Bosworth and Jack Trippett, "The Early 21st Century U.S. Productivity Growth Is *Still* in Services," *Brookings Institution International Productivity Monitor* no. 14 (spring 2007): 1–19.

6. The External Political Foundations of U.S. Arbitrage

1. Lloyd Gruber, *Ruling the World: Power Politics and the Rise of Supranational Institutions* (Princeton: Princeton University Press, 2001).

2. Barry Eichengreen and Yung Chul Park, "Global Imbalances and Emerging Markets," in *Global Imbalances and the US Debt Problem,* edited by Jan Joost Teunissen and Age Akerman, 14–44 (The Hague: Fondad, 2006).

3. Chetan Ahya, "The Decoupling Debate," *Morgan Stanley Global Economic Forum,* 4 September 2007, available at: http://www.morganstanley.com/views/gef/archive/2007/20070904-Tue.html#anchor5449. Citibank analysts come to a similar conclusion, noting a 0.7 correlation between U.S. GDP growth and Asian (excluding Japan) export growth and elasticities of GDP of 1.3–1.7 in Southeast Asia to U.S. GDP growth; Markus Rosgen, Elaine Chu, Chris W Leung, "Myth: Decoupling; Busted, for Now," Citibank, Hong Kong, October 24, 2007.

4. Brad Setser, "Too Big to Fail or Too Large to Save: Thinking about the US One Year into the Subprime Crisis," available at: http://blogs.cfr.org/setser/2008/07/24/too-big-to-fail-or-too-large-to-save-thinking-about-the-us-one-year-into-the-subprime-crisis/.

5. Brad Setser, "Two Coordination Problems Likely to Arise inside Bretton Woods 2," *RGE Monitor,* 30 October 2007, available at: http://www.rgemonitor.com/blog/setser/222634/,

by Bob Hancké, Martin Rhodes and Mark Thatcher (New York: Oxford University Press, 2007), 49, 77. See also, Richard Deeg, "Change from Within: German and Italian Finance in the 1990s," in *Beyond Continuity: Institutional Change in Advanced Political Economies,* edited by Wolfgang Streeck and Kathleen Thelen, 169–202 (New York: Oxford University Press, 2005).

19. John Zysman, *Governments, Markets and Growth* (Ithaca: Cornell University Press, 1983); Peter Hall, *Governing the Economy* (New York: Oxford University Press, 1986), 204.

20. See, Jonathan Nitzan, "Differential Accumulation: Towards a New Political Economy of Capital," *Review of International Political Economy* 5, no. 2 (1998): 169–216.

21. Paul Combes and Mark Watson, "Three Surveys on Corporate Governance," *McKinsey Quarterly* no. 4 (2000): 74–77.

22. Martin Höpner and Lothar Krempel, "The Politics of the German Company Network," *Competition and Change* 8, no. 4 (December 2004): 339–56.

23. Mark Roe, *Political Determinants of Corporate Governance* (New York: Oxford University Press, 2003).

24. David Soskice, "Macroeconomics and Varieties of Capitalism," in *Beyond Varieties of Capitalism: Conflict, Contradictions and Complementarities in the European Economy,* edited by Bob Hancké, Martin Rhodes and Mark Thatcher, 89–121 (New York: Oxford University Press, 2007), esp. 98–100.

25. Mark Roe, *Strong Managers, Weak Owners: The Political Roots of American Corporate Finance* (Princeton: Princeton University Press, 1994); Roe, *Political Determinants of Corporate Governance.*

26. Nick Bloom and John Van Reenen, "Measuring and Explaining Management Practices across Firms and Countries," Center for Economic Performance Discussion Paper no. 0716, London, March 2006.

27. Data from OECD, *National Accounts, Vol. 2,* available at: http://www.sourceOECD.org.

28. Bank for International Settlements, *77th Annual Report* (Basel: BIS, 2007), 120.

29. Bloom and Van Reenen, "Measuring and Explaining Management Practices," 7–8.

30. Barry Eichengreen, *The European Economy since 1945: Coordinated Capitalism and Beyond* (Princeton: Princeton University Press, 2007).

31. Data in this paragraph are from Watson Wyatt Worldwide, *The World's 300 Largest Pension Plans,* available at: http://www.watsonwyatt.com/europe/research/pdf/PI_300_Analysis_2007.pdf.

32. Although 42% of Germans have some form of private pension, the public pension provides 85% of total pension income, with private second-tier occupational pensions providing another 5% of total pension income and private third-tier pensions providing the final 10%; OECD, *Pensions at a Glance.*

33. Jonas Pontusson, *Limits to Social Democracy: Investment Politics in Sweden* (Ithaca: Cornell University Press, 1992).

34. The European Mortgage Federation/European Covered Bond Council and its associated lobby, Hypo (http://www.hypo.org) is an obvious and self-interested exception. They have promoted mortgage securitization.

35. International Monetary Fund, *Annual Report, 1992* (Washington, D.C.: IMF, 1992); in 1991, the yen accounted for 10.4% of official reserves versus 55% for the dollar and 20% for the deutchemark.

36. Consider the car industry, which in 1955 ranked seventy-second out of eighty-two Japanese industries in terms of revealed comparative advantage; Andrea Boltho, "China— Can Rapid Growth Continue?" *Singapore Economic Review* 49, no. 2 (2004): 267; Marcus Noland, "The Impact of Industrial Policy on Japan's Trade Specialization," *Review of Economics and Statistics* 75, no. 2 (May 1993): 241–48.

37. Bill Emmott, *The Sun Also Sets: The Limits to Japanese Power* (New York: Times Books, 1989); David Friedman, *Misunderstood Miracle: Industrial Development and Political Change in Japan* (Ithaca: Cornell University Press, 1988); Richard Katz, *Japan: The System That Soured* (Armonk, N.Y.: M. E. Sharpe, 1998); Karel van Wolferen, *Enigma of Japanese Power: People and Politics in a Stateless Nation* (New York: Knopf, 1989). Richard Katz apparently popularized the term *convoy capitalism* in *Japanese Phoenix: The Long Road to Economic Revival* (Armonk, N.Y.: M. E. Sharpe, 2003).

38. Dirk Pilat, "Competition, Productivity and Efficiency," *OECD Economic Studies* no. 27 (1996/II): 107–46, esp. 139–40.

39. The coefficient of variation for productivity of thirty-five Japanese manufacturing sectors was 41.4 versus only 16.9 for the United States, indicating considerable dispersion in the relative abilities of firms and suggesting that some form of protection precluded the usual leveling tendencies of the market. Ibid., 139–40.

40. Organisation for Economic Cooperation and Development, *OECD Economic Surveys: Japan 2003/2004* (Paris: OECD, 2004), 112, suggests that Japanese prices from 1990 to 2001 were approximately 30% higher than in the United States relative to real income.

41. Herman Schwartz, "Small States in Big Trouble: The Politics of State Reorganization in Australia, Denmark, New Zealand and Sweden in the 1980s," *World Politics* 46, no. 4 (July 1994): 527–55.

42. *Maekawa Report* (Report of the Advisory Group on Economic Structural Adjustment for International Harmony), Ministry for International Trade and Industry, Toyko, April 1986.

43. Leonard Schoppa, *Race for the Exits* (Ithaca: Cornell University Press, 2006).

44. Katz, *Japan;* Adam Posen, *Restoring Japan's Economic Growth* (Washington, D.C.: Institute for International Economics, 1998).

45. R. Taggart Murphy, "East Asia's Dollars," *New Left Review* no. 40 (July–August 2006): 39–64, quotation on 51; Mikuni Akio and R. Taggart Murphy, *Japan's Policy Trap* (Washington. D.C.: Brookings Institution, 2002).

46. U.S. Treasury, *Report on Foreign Holdings of US Portfolio Securities, 2006* (Washington, D.C.: U.S. Treasury Department, 2006); BEA, http://www.bea.gov.

47. Mikune and Murphy, *Japan's Policy Trap,* 34.

48. Michael P. Dooley, David Folkerts-Landau, and Peter Garber, "An Essay on the Revived Bretton Woods System," NBER Working Paper no. 9971, National Bureau of Economic Research, Cambridge, Mass., 2003; Michael P. Dooley, David Folkerts-Landau, and Peter Garber, "The Revived Bretton Woods System: The Effects of Periphery Intervention and Reserve Management on Interest Rates and Exchange Rates Center Countries," NBER Working Paper no. 10332, National Bureau of Economic Research, Cambridge, Mass., 2004; Michael P. Dooley, David Folkerts-Landau, and Peter Garber, "Direct Investment, Rising Real Wages and the Absorption of Excess Labor in the Periphery," NBER Working Paper no. 10626, National Bureau of Economic Research, Cambridge, Mass., 2004;

Michael P. Dooley, David Folkerts-Landau, and Peter Garber, "The US Current Account Deficit and Economic Development Collateral for a Total Return Swap," NBER Working Paper no. 10727, National Bureau of Economic Research, Cambridge, Mass., 2004.

49. Yongding Yu, "The Chinese Economy in 2008," *RGE Monitor*, 16 July 2008, available at: http://www.rgemonitor.com/asia-monitor/253019/the_chinese_economy_in_2008.

50. Boltho, "China," 255–72.

51. But see Morris Goldstein and Nicholas Lardy, "China's Role in the Revived Bretton Woods System: A Case of Mistaken Identity," Institute for International Economics Working Paper no. WP05-2, Washington, D.C., 2005, for a critique of the DFG argument that Chinese growth is export dependent. Goldstein and Lardy's critique is at times disingenuous and would benefit from attention to how Verdoorn effects from Chinese exports increase productivity. Nonetheless, they make a significant case that the major problem of China is not export promotion but, rather, the need for regulatory reform of the financial sector.

52. Keith Bradsher, "China's Central Bank Is Short of Capital," *New York Times*, 5 September 2008, D1.

53. McKinnon, *Exchange Rates*.

54. Net exports directly contribute between 2 and 3 percentage points of the annual Chinese GDP growth; assuming Chinese domestic content at 50% of the 35% of GDP total exports yields the 17% used here, based on Robert Koopman, Zhi Wang, and Shang-Jin Wei, "How Much of Chinese Exports Is Really Made in China?: Assessing Domestic Value-Added When Processing Trade Is Pervasive," NBER Working Paper no. 14109, National Bureau of Economic Research, Cambridge, Mass., 2008. See, however, Goldstein and Lardy, "China's Role in the Revived Bretton Woods System," for an argument that the contribution of exports to Chinese growth is overstated.

55. I am indebted to my colleague Brantly Womack for providing the data used in this paragraph, which are based on his elaboration of Chinese national statistics.

56. Data from the United Nations Conference on Trade and Development (UNCTAD)/ World Trade Organization (WTO) International Trade Center website, http://www. intracen.org.

57. Li Cui and Murtaza Syed, "The Shifting Structure of China's Trade and Production," IMF Working Paper no. WP/07/214, International Monetary Fund, Washington, D.C., 2007, 7.

58. *China Statistical Yearbook*, 2006. http://www.stats.gov.cn/eNgliSH/statisticaldata/yearlydata/.

59. Data from UNCTAD/WTO International Trade Center website, http://www. intracen.org. ADP equipment is SITC759.

60. This is a somewhat contested point. See Cui and Syed, "Shifting Structure"; Betina Dimaranan, Elena Ianchovichina, and Will Martin, "China, India and the Future of the World Economy: Fierce Competition or Shared Growth?" World Bank Policy Research Working Paper no. 4304, World Bank, Washington, D.C., 2007; Congressional Budget Office, "How Changes in the Value of the Chinese Currency Affect U.S. Imports" (Washington. D.C.: Congressional Budget Office, July 2008); Prema-chandra Athukorala, "The Rise of China and East Asian Export Performance: Is the Crowding-Out Fear Warranted?" unpublished paper, Australian National University, 2007, 7; Prema-chandra Athukorala, "Product Fragmentation and Trade Patterns in East Asia," *Asian Economic Papers* 4, no. 3 (fall

2005): 1–27; Koopman, Wang, and Wei, "How Much of Chinese Exports.". For a revealing illustration, see Greg Linden, Kenneth Kraemer, and Jason Dedrick, "Who Captures Value in a Global Innovation System: The Case of Apple's iPod," unpublished paper, University of California, Irvine, June 2007, which suggests that Chinese firms added at most only a few dollars to the total $150 cost of production.

61. Eswar Prasad, "Is the Chinese Growth Miracle Built to Last?" unpublished paper, Cornell University, Ithaca, July 2007.

62. Louis Kuijs, "China Quarterly Update," World Bank Office, Beijing, May 2006; Song-Yi Kim and Louis Kuijs, "Raw Material Prices, Wages, and Profitability in China's Industry—How Was Profitability Maintained When Input Prices and Wages Increased So Fast?" World Bank China Research Paper no. 8, Washington, D.C., October 2007, 12–14.

63. Eswar Prasad, "Is the Chinese Growth Miracle Built to Last?" unpublished paper, Cornell University, July 2007, 4.

64. Boltho, "China," 261.

65. See Kellee Tsai, *Back Alley Banking: Private Entrepreneurs in China* (Ithaca: Cornell University Press, 2002).

66. Carsten Holz, "Have China Scholars All Been Bought?" *Far Eastern Economic Review* 170, no. 3 (April 2007): 36–40.

67. Hongying Wang, *Weak State, Strong Networks* (New York: Oxford University Press, 2001).

68. "A Money Machine: The People's Bank of China Is the World's Most Profitable Bank," *Economist*, 25 January 2007, available at: http://www.economist.com/finance/display story.cfm?story_id=8597322.

69. Michael Pettis, "Minimum Bank Reserves Are Up (Again)," *RGE Monitor*, 11 November 2007, available at: http://rs.rgemonitor.com/blog/setser/226049; Keith Bradsher, "China's Central Bank Is Short of Capital," *New York Times*, 5 September 2008, D1.

70. On savings levels, see Louis Kuijs, "Investment and Saving in China," World Bank Policy Research Working Paper no. 3633, Washinton, D.C., June 2005.

71. Stephen S. Roach, The Heavy Lifting of Chinese Rebalancing," *Morgan Stanley Global Economic Forum*, 5 March 2007, available at: http://www.morganstanley.com/views/gef/archive/2007/20070305-Mon.html. As Tsai, *Back Alley Banking*, shows, small firms and the politically disconnected rely on informal credit channels rather than the formal banking system; see also the comments in Yun-Wing Sung, "Made in China: From World Sweatshop to Global Manufacturing Center?" *Asian Economic Papers* 6, no. 3 (2007): 43–72.

72. International Monetary Fund, *World Economic Outlook* (Washington, D.C.: IMF, September 2005).

73. Ronald McKinnon, *Exchange Rates under the East Asian Dollar Standard: Living with Conflicted Virtue* (Cambridge, Mass.: MIT, 2006).

74. Brad Setser, "The Worse the Dollar Does, the More Dollars Central Banks Want…" *RGE Monitor*, 13 November 2007, available at: http://www.rgemonitor.com/blog/setser/243109.

75. Brad Setser, "The Flight from Risky US Assets Continues," September 16, 2008, available at: http://blogs.cfr.org/setser/2008/09/16/the-flight-from-risky-us-assets-continues/.

76. Ibid.

7. Boom to Bust

1. Joseph Schumpeter, *Business Cycles* (New York: McGraw Hill, 1939).

2. Christian Broda and John Romalis, "Inequality and Prices: Does China Benefit the Poor in America?" unpublished paper, University of Chicago, March 2008; Christian Broda and David Weinstein, "Exporting Deflation?: Chinese Exports and Japanese Prices," unpublished paper, University of Chicago, 2008.

3. Stephen Jen and Luca Bindelli, "AXJ as a Source of Global Disinflation and Inflation," *Morgan Stanley Global Economic Forum,* 30 November 2007, available at: http://www. morganstanley.com/views/gef/archive/2007/20071130-Fri.html.

4. Matthew Chambers, Carlos Garriga, and Don E. Schlagenhauf, "Accounting for Changes in the Homeownership Rate," Federal Reserve Bank of Atlanta Working Paper no. 2007-21, Washington, D.C., September 2007, 2.

5. "Mortgage Delinquencies Accelerated during 2007," *Wall Street Journal,* 9 August 2008, available at: http://online.wsj.com/article/SB121805947661818327.html.

6. Herman Schwartz and Leonard Seabrooke, eds., *The Political Consequences of Property Bubbles,* Special Issue of *Comparative European Politics* 6, no. 2 (September 2008), provides a comparative look at the new politics of housing.

7. Credit Suisse, *Mortgage Liquidity du Jour,* 12 March 2007, New York, 28.

8. Jim Kemeny, "Home Ownership and Privatisation," *International Journal of Urban and Regional Research* 4, no. 3 (1980): 372–88; Jim Kemeny, "'The Really Big Trade-Off' between Home Ownership and Welfare: Castles' Evaluation of the 1980 Thesis, and a Reformulation 25 Years On," *Housing, Theory, and Society* 22, no. 2 (2005): 59–75; Francis G. Castles, "The Really Big Trade-off: Home Ownership and the Welfare State in the New World and the Old," *Acta Politica* 33 (1998): 5–19. A recent study of Australian public opinion suggests that homeowners with mortgages are 50% more likely to express tax resistance than free-and-clear homeowners or renters; Shaun Wilson, "Not My Taxes!: Explaining Tax Resistance and Its Implications for Australia's Welfare State," *Australian Journal of Political Science* 41, no. 4 (2006): 517–35.

9. Alan Greenspan and James Kennedy, "Sources and Uses of Equity Extracted from Homes," FEDS Research Paper no. 2007-20, Federal Reserve Bank, Washington, D.C., 2007, 26; Freddie Mac, *2005 Annual Report,* 2 (Washington, D.C.: FHLMC, 2005); Federal Reserve Bank, http://www.federalreserve.gov/pubs/oss/oss2/2004/bulletin.tables.int.xls. For comparison, home equity represented 40% of British household wealth; Kosuke Aoki, James Proudman, and Gertjan Vlieghe, "House Prices, Consumption, and Monetary Policy: A Financial Accelerator Approach," *Journal of Financial Intermediation* 13, no. 4 (2004): 414–35.

10. Data from Calculated Risk website, http://calculatedrisk.blogspot.com.

11. Bureau of Labor Statistics, *Consumer Expenditure Survey 2004* (Washington, D.C.: Bureau of Labor Statistics, 2004), 9; Matthew Chambers, Carlos Garriga, and Don E. Schlagenhauf, "Accounting for Changes in the Homeownership Rate," Federal Reserve Bank of Atlanta Working Paper no 2007-21, September 2007. More recent Bureau of Labor Statistics data are unfortunately not available yet. This introduces a conservative bias into the analysis because housing prices rose substantially faster than incomes from 2004 to 2007.

12. Credit Suisse, *Mortgage Liquidity du Jour,* 4–5, 19, 21, 26; see also Freddie Mac, *2005 Annual Report,* 12.

13. Bureau of Labor Statistics, *Consumer Expenditure Survey 2004*. A closed loan has a fixed term; a HELOC is permanently available to be drawn on.

14. Greenspan and Kennedy, "Sources and Uses of Equity," 11, 43.

15. Harvard University Joint Center for Housing Studies, *The State of the Nation's Housing* (Cambridge, Mass.: Harvard University Press, 2008); Credit Suisse, *Mortgage Liquidity du Jour*, 26.

16. Calculated Risk, "Homeowners with Negative Equity," September 30, 2008, available at: http://calculatedrisk.blogspot.com/2008/09/homeowners-with-negative-equity.html.

17. Calculated from Federal Reserve Bank, *Survey of Consumer Finance*, 2001 and 2004, available at: http://www.federalreserve.gov/pubs/oss/oss2/2004/bulletin.tables.int.xls;"Recent Changes in US Family Finances," *Federal Reserve Bulletin* (2006): A8.

18. Organisation for Economic Cooperation and Development revenue database, http://www.sourceOECD.org.

19. Tax Foundation, http://www.taxfoundation.org/taxdata/show/1775.html; http://www.taxfoundation.org/taxdata/show/1913.html.

20. Patrick Jonsson, "High Property Taxes Driving a New Revolt," *Christian Science Monitor*, 28 March 2006, 1; Ron Scherer, "States Try to Ease Property Tax Rise," *Christian Science Monitor*, 7 June 2005.

21. Peter Thal Larsen and Paul J. Davies, "Trouble off Balance Sheet Raises Concerns," *Financial Times*, 23 August 2007; Emma Moody, "Citigroup Bails Out Troubled SIV Funds," *Washington Post*, 14 December 2007, D3; Salomon, "What's a CDO?" available at: http://www.portfolio.com/interactive-features/2007/12/cdo. Of course, SIV asset levels have been a moving target because their value has fallen precipitously during the credit crunch crisis.

22. Kristopher Gerardi, Adam Hale Shapiro, and Paul S. Willen, "Subprime Outcomes: Risky Mortgages, Homeownership Experiences, and Foreclosures," Federal Reserve Bank of Boston Working Paper no. 07-15, December 2007.

23. The Countrywide Finance website listings for some of their foreclosed properties in Michigan (http://www.countrywide.com/purchase/f_reo.asp) had just over two hundred properties for sale for less than $10,000 on August 8, 2008.

24. Data from http://www.foreclosures.com/stats/.

25. Data from Calculated Risk, http://calculatedrisk.blogspot.com/2008/05/historical-housing-graphs-months-of.html; Stan Humphries, "Second Quarter Housing Performance—Ouch!" available at: http://www.zillowblog.com/second-quarter-housing-performance%e2%80%a6ouch/2008/08/.

26. Yalman Onaran, "Banks' Subprime Losses Top $500 billion on Writedowns," *Bloomberg*, 12 August 2008, available at: http://www.bloomberg.com/apps/news?pid=20601087&sid=a8sW0n1Cs1tY&.

27. The Office of Federal Housing Enterprise Oversight (OFHEO) traditionally set the upper limit for conforming mortgages at roughly 139% of the resale price of the average existing home, which was $417,000 in 2006. Congress then temporarily bumped the limit up to $729,750 for 2008. It remains to be seen whether the limit will be allowed to float down as average prices fall in the next few years or as the crisis abates.

28. Gillian Tett and Paul J Davies, "Out of the Shadows: How Banking's Secret System Broke Down," *Financial Times*, 16 December 2007, available at: http://www.ft.com/cms/s/0/42827c50-abfd-11dc-82f0-0000779fd2ac.html.

29. Charles W. Calomiris, "Not (Yet) a 'Minsky Moment,'" unpublished paper, Columbia University, October 5, 2007, 19.

30. See Dick Bryan and Michael Rafferty, *Capitalism with Derivatives: A Political Economy of Financial Derivatives, Capital and Class* (London: Palgrave Macmillan, 2005), for a general argument about how derivatives function in credit markets. See Donald MacKenzie, *An Engine Not a Camera: How Financial Models Shape Markets* (Cambridge, Mass.: MIT Press, 2006), for a sociological analysis of how belief in particular mathematical models changed behaviors in financial markets.

31. Finance industry wags call this "mark-to-make-believe" because of the obvious conflicts of interest.

32. Credit Suisse, *Mortgage Liquidity du Jour.*

33. Ibid.

34. The telling joke was that banks were afraid of becoming "SIV positive."

35. Tett and J Davies, "Out of the Shadows."

36. "Nightmare on Wall Street," *Economist,* 15 September 2008, available at: http://www.economist.com/finance/displaystory.cfm?story_id=12231236.

37. Countrywide and IndyMac each originated roughly 16% of Alt-A mortgages in 2006; Countrywide and Fremont each originated approximately 6% of 2006 vintage subprime mortgages. Credit Suisse, *Mortgage Liquidity du Jour,* 17, 22.

38. Data from Bloomberg Financial, http://www.bloomberg.com/apps/cbuilder?ticker1=.TEDSP:IND.

39. Richard Iley, "Going with the Flow, Again," *BNP Paribas,* 14 January 2008, 2–6, suggests that the unsustainable growth of Federal Home Loan Bank (FHLB) lending (discussed later in the chapter) was another major reason the Fed boosted liquidity.

40. http://www.frbdiscountwindow.org/discountmargins.pdf.

41. Federal Reserve Bank, press release, 2 May 2008, available at: http://www.federalreserve.gov/newsevents/press/monetary/20080502a.htm.

42. "Mission Creep at the Fed," *Economist,* 9 August 2008, 69.

43. ECB Open Market Operations, http://www.ecb.int/mopo/implement/omo/html/20070090_all.en.html.

44. Federal Reserve Bank, press release, 15 July 2008, available at: http://www.federalreserve.gov/newsevents/press/bcreg/20080714a.htm.

45. Federal Home Loan Bank Office of Finance, http://www.fhlb-of.com/issuance/statisticsframe.html; Iley, "Going with the Flow, Again," 3.

46. See Ben Bernanke's letter to Senator Charles Schumer, 29 August 2007, archived at http://blogs.wsj.com/economics/2007/08/29/text-of-bernankes-letter-to-schumer/.

47. James Hagerty, "Fannie Mae Loss of $2.3 Billion Exceeds Forecast," *Wall Street Journal,* 9 August 2008, available at: http://online.wsj.com/article/SB121818529773923803.html.

48. Brad Setser, "The Flight from Risky US Assets Continues," September 16, 2008, available at: http://blogs.cfr.org/setser/2008/09/16/the-flight-from-risky-us-assets-continues/.

49. Daniel Gros and Stefano Micossi, "The Beginning of the End Game..." September 20, 2008, available at: http://www.voxeu.org/index.php?q=node/1669.

50. High tide in the sense of last change made before the political tides changed because a few major Keynesian welfare state–era programs remained unprivatized or nonindividuated as of 2008: Social Security, unemployment insurance, and Medicare/Medicaid.

51. Leonard Seabrooke, *Social Foundations of Financial Power* (Ithaca: Cornell University Press, 2006).

52. Iley, "Going with the Flow, Again"; Damien Paletta, "Grip on Freddie, Fannie May Ease," *Wall Street Journal,* 17 January 2008, available at: http://online.wsj.com/article/SB120054069098196863.html.

53. See Brad Setser, "Brazil Backstops the Treasury Market, Russia Backstops the Housing Market, and China Backstops Flows through London," *RGE Monitor,* 17 January 2008, available at: http://www.rgemonitor.com/blog/setser/238328/.

8. Toward the Future

1. Brad Setser, "Sovereign Wealth and Sovereign Power," Council on Foreign Relations Special Report no. 37, September 2008, New York.

2. Saskia Scholtes and James Politi, "Bank of China Flees Fannie-Freddie," *Financial Times,* 28 August 2008, available at: http://www.ft.com/cms/s/0/74c5cf58-7535-11dd-ab30-0000779fd18c.html.

3. Max Weber, *Economy and Society,* edited by Gunther Roth and Claus Wittich (Berkeley: University of California Press, 1978), 164—66.

4. U.S. Treasury, "Remarks by Acting Under Secretary for International Affairs Clay Lowery on Sovereign Wealth Funds and the International Financial System," press release hp-471, June 21, 2007, available at: http://www.treas.gov/press/releases/hp471.htm; Simon Johnson, "The Rise of Sovereign Wealth Funds," *Finance and Development* 44, no. 3 (September 2007): 56—57.

5. "Sovereign-Wealth Funds: Asset Backed Insecurity," *Economist,* 19 January 2008, 78—80. See also the dismissals by Nouriel Roubini, "SWF Hype and the Rolling 'Masters of the Universe' Fads at Davos," *RGE Monitor,* 24 January 2008, available at: http://rs.rgemonitor.com/blog/roubini/239509; George Will, "Investors We Need Not Fear," *Washington Post,* 3 February 2008, B7.

6. Singapore, of course, has done both, upgrading both human capital and its physical infrastructure while creating two SWFs. But as a small city-state, the case for offshore diversification is compelling compared to, say, China.

7. Jonathan Nitzan, "Differential Accumulation: Towards a New Political Economy of Capital," *Review of International Political Economy* 5, no. 2 (1998): 169—216.

8. Bureau of Economic Analysis, National Income and Product Accounts, section 6, available at:http://www.bea.gov/bea/dn/nipaweb/GetCSV.asp?GetWhat=SS_Data/Section6All_xls.xls&Section=7. See also the analyses in Gérard Duménil and Dominique Lévy, "The Real and Financial Components of Profitability (United States, 1952–2000)," *Review of Radical Political Economics* 36, no. 1 (winter 2004): 82–110; "The Profit Rate in the US: Where and How Much Did It Fall? Did It Recover? (USA 1948–2000)," *Review of Radical Political Economics* 34 (2002): 437–46. Comparable profit data for the OECD are not available.

9. Brad Setser, "Shanghai, Mumbai, Dubai or Goodbye: The Year of Reverse Bailouts," *RGE Monitor,* 10 January 2008, available at: http://www.rgemonitor.com/blog/setser/234393.

10. Brad Setser and Rachel Ziemba, "Understanding the New Financial Superpower— The Management of GCC Official Foreign Assets," *RGE Monitor,* December 2007, 4.

11. Weber, *Economy and Society,* 164–66.

12. Gregory Nowell, "Hilferding's *Finance Capital* versus Wal-Mart World: Disaggregating the Dollar's Hegemony," unpublished paper presented at the International Studies Association Annual Meeting, San Francisco, March 2008.

13. Shelley Hurt, "Science, Power, and the State: U.S. Foreign Policy, Intellectual Property Law, and the Origins of Agricultural Biotechnology, 1969–1994," unpublished PhD dissertation, New School for Social Research, 2008.

14. Jeffrey Garten, *The Big Ten: The Big Emerging Markets and How They Will Change Our Lives* (New York: Basic Books, 1997). Garten was undersecretary of commerce for international trade in the Clinton administration, 1993–1995, before moving on to the Yale School of Management and the Blackstone Group.

15. See Nicos Poulantzas's perceptive article on this process in Europe of the 1960s, "Internationalisation of Capitalist Relations," *Economy & Society* 3 (1972): 145–79.

16. Lloyd Gruber, *Ruling the World: Power Politics and the Rise of Supra-national Institutions* (Princeton University Press, 2000).

17. Consider, for example, Thailand, where Thaksin Shinawatra's telecoms firm was sold to Singaporean SWF Temasek, or Carlos Slim's empire, which encompasses telecoms, cement, insurance, and banking and equals roughly 6 or 7% of the GDP of Mexico.

18. Paul Blustein, *The Chastening: Inside the Financial Crisis That Rocked the Global Financial System and Humbled the IMF* (New York: Public Affairs, 2003).

19. "Beyond the Border: Financial liberalization—Manna or Menace?" *Southwest Economy,* Dallas Federal Reserve Bank, January 2002, available at: http://www.dallasfed.org/research/swe/2002/swe0201d.html.

20. Korea Federation of Banks, *Annual Report* (2006), 24–25, Seoul: Korea Federation of Banks.

21. Brad Setser, "Understanding the World through Pictures: China, Japan, Europe and US Current Account Adjustment," *RGE Monitor,* 6 February 2008, available at: http://www.rgemonitor.com/blog/setser/238837.

22. Karl Kautsky, "Ultra-imperialism," *Die Neue Zeit,* September 1914, translation archived at http://www.marxists.org/archive/kautsky/1914/09/ultra-imp.htm.

23. Rudolf Hilferding, *Finance Capital: A Study of the Latest Phase of Capitalist Development* (London: Routledge and Keegan Paul, 1981); Nikolai Bukharin, *Imperialism and World Economy* (New York: International Publishers, 1929), presents a similar analysis.

24. Gregory Nowell, *Mercantile States and the World Oil Cartel, 1900–1939* (Ithaca: Cornell University Press, 1994), presents a careful analysis of this process for oil.

25. Vladimir I. Lenin, *Imperialism: The Highest Stage of Capitalism* (New York: International Publishers, 1939).

26. Organisation for Economic Cooperation and Development, *Economic Outlook No. 42* (Paris: OECD, December 1987), 70–71; World Trade Organization, http://www.wto.org.

27. See Mitchell Bernard and John Ravenhill, "Beyond Product Cycles and Flying Geese: Regionalization, Hierarchy, and the Industrialization of East Asia," *World Politics* 47, no. 2 (January 1995): 171–209.

28. Leila Heckman, "Insight: Refuge May Be Found via New Frontiers," *Financial Times,* 13 February 2008, available at: http://www.ft.com/cms/s/0/234aaafe-da4e-11dc-9bb9-0000779fd2ac.html.

29. Eric Chaney, "Euroland: Resilience and Risks," *Morgan Stanley Global Economic Forum,* 15 February 2008, available at: http://www.morganstanley.com/views/gef/; Takehiro Sato, "Japan: Forecast Change: ZIRP Looms Again," *Morgan Stanley Global Economic Forum,* 28 January 2008, available at: http://www.morganstanley.com/views/gef/archive/2008/20080128-Mon.html; Daniel Gros, "Decoupling: Can Europe Avoid a Recession?" *RGE Monitor,* 22 January 2008, available at: http://www.rgemonitor.com/euro-monitor/567/decoupling_can_europe_avoid_a_recession.

30. Robert Boyer, *The Regulation School: A Critical Introduction* (New York: Columbia University Press, 1990); Barry Eichengreen, *The European Economy since 1945: Coordinated Capitalism and Beyond* (Princeton: Princeton University Press, 2007).

31. Herman Schwartz, "Small States in Big Trouble," *World Politics* 46, no. 4 (July 1994): 527–55.

32. Maurice Obstfeld and Kenneth Rogoff, "Global Current Account Imbalances and Exchange Rate Adjustments," *Brookings Papers on Economic Activity* 1 (2005):. 67–123, esp. 73.

33. Federal Reserve Bank, *Survey of Consumer Finances* (Washington, D.C.: Federal Reserve Bank, 2006), A8.

34. Leonard Seabrooke, *Social Foundations of Financial Power* (Ithaca: Cornell University Press, 2006).

Index